In Search of the
Lost Heart

In Search of the Lost Heart

Explorations in Islamic Thought

WILLIAM C. CHITTICK

Edited by

Mohammed Rustom, Atif Khalil, and Kazuyo Murata

SUNY PRESS

Cover art by Haji Noor Deen.

Published by State University of New York Press, Albany

Printed in the United States of America

For information, contact State University of New York Press, Albany, NY
www.sunypress.edu

Production by Kelli W. LeRoux
Marketing by Anne M. Valentine

Library of Congress Cataloging-in-Publication Data

Chittick, William C.
In search of the lost heart : explorations in Islamic thought / William C. Chittick ; edited by Mohammed Rustom, Atif Khalil, and Kazuyo Murata.
p. cm.
Includes bibliographical references and index.
ISBN 978-1-4384-3935-8 (hardcover : alk. paper)
ISBN 978-1-4384-3936-5 (paperback : alk. paper)
1. Sufism. 2. Mysticism—Islam. 3. Islam—Doctrines. I. Rustom, Mohammed. II. Khalil, Atif. III. Murata, Kazuyo. IV. Title.

BP189.C53 2011
297.4'1—dc22 2011006365

10 9 8 7 6 5 4 3 2

Dedicated to the memory of Omer Fereig (1979–2008)

Contents

A Note on Transliteration and Style

Arabic and Persian terms have been transliterated in accordance with the system employed by the *International Journal of Middle Eastern Studies* (*IJMES*), with the following major exceptions: (1) no distinction is made in transliterating consonants shared between Arabic and Persian; (2) complete transliterations of book and article titles have been retained throughout; (3) in contexts where transliteration is not an absolute necessity (i.e., book/article titles and technical expressions), certain terms that appear on the *IJMES* word list, namely hajj, imam, *kalām, qibla,* Qurʾan, *shahāda,* shariʿa, Shiʿi, sunna, *ṭarīqah,* and ʿulamaʾ, appear here as Hajj, Imam, Kalam, kiblah, Koran, Shahadah, Shariah, Shiʿite, Sunnah, Tariqah, and ulama respectively; (4) in several special cases (e.g., when paired with the word Koran), the term hadith appears as Hadith.

Grammar and punctuation has been standardized in accordance with *Garner's Modern American Usage* (3rd ed.). The bibliographical format for references in this book closely follows the *Chicago Manual of Style* (15th ed.), with some minor adaptations. With the exception of the "Editors' Introduction," a shorthand citation method has been adopted in the volume's notes.

Editors' Introduction

William C. Chittick was born in Milford, Connecticut in 1943. As an undergraduate student majoring in history at the College of Wooster (Ohio), Chittick spent the 1964–1965 academic year abroad, studying Islamic history at the American University of Beirut. It was here that he first came into contact with Sufism, as he decided to write his junior year independent study on the topic. Having become familiar with the standard accounts of Sufism, Chittick attended a public lecture on the topic by Seyyed Hossein Nasr, who was the University's Agha Khan Visiting Professor that year. Nasr's lecture deepened Chittick's interest in Sufism to the point that he eventually resolved to pursue graduate studies in Tehran.

Chittick began his graduate work in the foreign students program at the University of Tehran's Faculty of Letters in 1966. In 1974, he obtained a doctoral degree in Persian language and literature under Nasr's supervision. Chittick then began teaching comparative religion at Aryamehr Technical University (now Sharif University of Technology) and, in 1978, joined the faculty of the Imperial Iranian Academy of Philosophy (now the Iranian Institute of Philosophy). Shortly before the revolution in 1979, he returned with his wife, Sachiko Murata, to the United States. In the early 1980s, Chittick served as an associate editor for *Encyclopaedia Iranica*. In 1983, he and Murata took up posts at the State University of New York (Stony Brook), where they are currently full professors in the Department of Asian and Asian American Studies.

During his long stay in Tehran, Chittick studied under and/or collaborated with some of the most distinguished scholars of Islamic thought: Jalāl al-Dīn Āshtiyānī, Henry Corbin, Toshihiko Izutsu, Badīʿ al-Zamān Furūzānfar, Jalāl al-Dīn Humāʾī, Mehdi Mohaghegh, and ʿAllāma Sayyid Muḥammad Ḥusayn Ṭabāṭabāʾī. Suffice it to say that Chittick's prolonged contact with these and other scholars has provided him with a unique appreciation and grasp of classical Arabic and Persian on the one hand, and a variety of medieval Islamic philosophical, theological, and mystical texts on the other.

In addition to his academic training, Chittick is a highly skilled translator who possesses a rigorous analytical mind and a rare ability to explain some of the most difficult ideas in remarkably lucid fashion. This helps explain why his works have had such wide appeal among students of Islamic civilization, comparative philosophy, and religious studies, and have been translated into

Albanian, Arabic, Bosnian, Chinese, French, German, Indonesian, Italian, Japanese, Persian, Russian, Spanish, Turkish, and Urdu.

Beyond North American and European academia, Chittick's books have also been well-received by Muslim communities in the West.[1] In the East, his works are taught and discussed in Indonesia, Malaysia, Turkey, Egypt, Pakistan, India, and, of course, Iran, where his *Me & Rumi* (2004) was awarded the World Prize for the Book of the Year in 2005, and was named the best work in the field of Iranian Studies. More recently, a Tehran-based cultural society paid tribute to Chittick's scholarly achievements by holding a ceremony and publishing a Festschrift in his honor.[2]

It would be an understatement to say that Chittick's scholarship has brought the ideas of a number of Islam's most significant intellectual and spiritual figures out of relative obscurity. In *The Heart of Islamic Philosophy* (2001), he highlights the central concerns of the Islamic philosophical tradition through his study of the writings of Afḍal al-Dīn Kāshānī (commonly known as Bābā Afḍal). The book also goes a long way toward demonstrating how Bābā Afḍal molded the Persian language in order to convey the practical concerns of philosophy to those who did not have specialized training in the discipline. Chittick's *The Sufi Path of Love* (1983) and award-winning *The Sufi Doctrine of Rumi* (1974; 2005) are arguably the best expositions of Rūmī's worldview to date. They also stand as correctives to the widespread misinformation about the teachings and even "religion" of this spiritual giant of Islam.

It may come as a surprise to many that, along with Sachiko Murata and Tu Weiming, Chittick has recently published a book on Chinese Sufism entitled *The Sage Learning of Liu Zhi* (2009). This important work investigates the cross-pollination that took place between Neo-Confucian thought and Sufism in the figure of Liu Zhi (or Liu Chih), one of the two important Chinese Muslim thinkers introduced by Murata in an earlier study.[3]

Chittick's works on Ibn al-ʿArabī, such as *The Sufi Path of Knowledge* (1989) and *The Self-Disclosure of God* (1998), have shed a great deal of light on some of the fundamental metaphysical and practical teachings that have influenced over seven hundred years of Islamic thought from North Africa to Malaysia. Indeed, Ibn al-ʿArabī's writings are just as if not more relevant today, which is why a number of prominent thinkers have drawn on his ideas in developing responses to a variety of pressing contemporary issues, such as the question of the religious "other."[4]

Students of Islamic thought are, in one way or another, indebted to Chittick's writings. Needless to say, the editors of this volume are no exception. His works have greatly assisted us in navigating our way about the often bumpy terrain of Islamic thought. Over the years we have found that, apart from Chittick's books, many of his most helpful studies can only be found in journals, Festschrifts, collective volumes, encyclopedias, and the like. Unlike his books, many of these works are not easily accessible to scholars and students, let alone the wider public.

The present volume, therefore, brings together a diverse selection of Professor Chittick's seminal studies (published between 1975 and 2011) on key themes and figures in Islamic thought. For the most part, materials readily available in Chittick's books or on the Internet have not been included.

After having selected material for this volume, we divided the essays into four categories, updated the notes where necessary, and thoroughly edited the essays such that each piece naturally flows into the other without any awkward breaks or repetitions. Thus, although this work is a collection of essays, it is also meant to be a book sufficient unto itself, which, when taken as a whole, can be said to explore the underlying worldview of Islam.

The volume's first category is entitled "Sufism and the Islamic Tradition." The essays in this section investigate the general theoretical and practical dimensions of Sufism, highlighting its relationship to Islamic law and theology, scriptural hermeneutics, and religious pluralism.

Since the details of Ibn al-ʿArabī's impact on later Islamic thought are only known to a handful of specialists, the second part of this book, "Ibn al-ʿArabī and His Influence," mainly seeks to demonstrate the extent of his legacy. Particularly noteworthy in this regard are the section's last three pieces, which introduce the ideas of several key eleventh/seventeenth-century Indian representatives of the school of Ibn al-ʿArabī.

The third section, "Islamic Philosophy," offers readers a glimpse into the worldview of the Islamic philosophical tradition by covering some of its main themes, such as ontology, psychology, cosmology, and eschatology. Several of the essays in this section bring the concerns of Islamic philosophy and theoretical Sufism into perspective, demonstrating how these two traditions agree on a number of crucial points.

The essays under the fourth heading, which we have labeled "Reflections on Contemporary Issues," present a coherent picture of the least-known aspect of Chittick's writings. Here are to be found his appraisals of such issues as the ecological crisis, religious exclusivism, and the universal concern for global peace.

If the first three sections of *In Search of the Lost Heart* give readers a good idea of the worldview of premodern Islamic thought, the fourth will demonstrate for them how the Islamic intellectual tradition can address our concerns today. Whether it is the treatment of issues in politics or theology, many contemporary Muslim thinkers fail to take Islam's rich intellectual resources—theoretical Sufism and Islamic philosophy in particular—into account in their formulations. They more often than not opt for paradigms outside of the tradition, or superficially attempt to integrate these paradigms into the tradition. Like these scholars, Chittick also has a lot to say about the current human "situation," but from the perspective of a civilization whose worldview is not constrained by the categories in vogue today. Because Chittick's worldview is, first and foremost, shaped by the traditions of Sufism and Islamic philosophy, when he attempts to offer a solution to a contemporary problem, he does so from the perspective of classical Islamic thought.[5]

Following the essays are three appendices. The first appendix is a chronological table of the historical figures cited in the volume, the second a list of the sources for the essays presented, and the third a catalogue of Chittick's published books to the beginning of 2012.

It remains for us to thank Professor Chittick for kindly accepting our offer to bring this collection of essays together, supplying us with electronic copies of his articles, providing us with many helpful suggestions, and reading over the manuscript. We are grateful to Seyyed Hossein Nasr for his encouragement with this project. Thanks also go to Alexander Knysh, Leonard Lewisohn, Sachiko Murata, Salman Naqvi, Haji Noor Deen, Shiraz Sheikh, and Shafique Virani for sharing their precious resources with us; Aasim Hasany, Arin McNamara, Nosheen Mian, and the State University of New York Press's anonymous reviewer for their insightful feedback on the book's contents and organization; Ali Lakhani, G. A. Lipton, Omid Safi, Muhammad Suheyl Umar, and Jeff Zaleski for providing us with important references along the way.

While we were working on *In Search of the Lost Heart*, we received the sad news of the tragic death of our dear friend Omer Fereig. Omer was the most ardent supporter of this book, and we are grateful to him for his sound advice and guidance during its preparation. This volume is dedicated to his memory.

I

Sufism and the Islamic Tradition

1

Islam in Three Dimensions

When we talk about "Islam" today, our understanding of the term is shaped by a host of historical and social factors. Not least of these is the way in which journalists, politicians, and television announcers understand the term. Contemporary opinions and ideologies—themselves based on presuppositions that are far from self-evident—instill in us certain views about what has significance in human life. Given our own assumptions about reality, it is not easy to grasp how premodern Muslim authors looked upon their religion. They often had an idea of Islam very different from that which is met with today—not only in the media but also in the works of specialists. In order to grasp the significance of the worldview of the authors encountered in this volume, we need a definition of Islam that is at once faithful to their perspective and comprehensible to the contemporary reader.

Works, Faith, and Perfection

It is self-evident, even in modern terms, that human affairs have different foci. Some are centered in bodily activity, some in the life of the mind, and some in the heart. One possible means of classifying these domains is to speak of three basic dimensions of human existence, such as acting, knowing, and willing, or activity, intellectuality, and spirituality. Such a tripartite division is commonly encountered in Islamic texts. One of its earliest formulations is found in a famous tradition called the "Hadith of Gabriel," in which the Prophet divides "the religion" (*al-dīn*)[1]—that is, Islam—into three dimensions that I call *works, faith,* and *perfection.*[2]

In naming these three dimensions, the Prophet employed words that have played important roles in Islamic intellectual history: *islām* (submission), *īmān* (faith), and *iḥsān* (virtue). In order to understand the religion of Islam as a reality possessing these three dimensions, one must grasp some of the implications of these words in the Koran, Hadith, and Islamic tradition.

Already in the Koran, the word *islām* or "submission" has at least four senses, all of which have to do with the relationship between God and His creatures. In the broadest sense, *islām* is used to indicate that every creature, by the fact of being God's handiwork, is controlled by Him: *To Him submits everything in the heavens and the earth* (3:83).

In a narrower sense, *islām* means voluntary submission to God's will by following His revealed messages. The Koran mentions among the "Muslims"—that is, those who have freely submitted to God—Abraham (2:131, 3:67), Joseph (12:101), Noah (10:72), Lot and his family (51:36), the apostles of Jesus (5:111), and other pre-Islamic figures. Even Pharaoh claims to be a Muslim when he realizes that he is going to be drowned (10:90), and a Sufi such as Ibn al-ʿArabī (d. 638/1240) could stir up a controversy by suggesting that Pharaoh's Islam was sufficient for salvation.[3]

In a third and still narrower meaning, *islām* designates the religion revealed to Muhammad through the Koran. The most obvious Koranic example of this usage is the following verse: *Today I have perfected your religion for you, and I have completed My blessing upon you, and I have approved Islam for you as a religion* (5:3). It is this meaning of the term that I want to clarify and for which I will be employing the term "Islam" without italics.

In the fourth and narrowest sense, *islām* refers to the outward works of the religion as distinguished from an inner something that makes the religion genuine and sincere. One verse is especially significant because it differentiates between *islām* and *īmān*, submission and faith: *The Bedouins say, "We have faith." Say [O Muhammad!]: "You do not have faith; rather, say: 'We have submitted;' for faith has not yet entered your hearts"* (49:14). In this fourth sense, *islām* corresponds to one of the three dimensions of Islam, and hence its meaning needs to be clarified if we are to understand the meaning of *islām* in the third sense.

The Hadith of Gabriel differentiates even more clearly than this Koranic verse between *islām* in this fourth sense and *īmān*. It is true that some Koranic verses and hadiths use the two terms as synonyms, but this does not prevent the texts from drawing distinctions in other contexts. According to this hadith, *islām* consists of the "Five Pillars": saying the double Shahadah or testimony (bearing witness that there is no god but God and that Muhammad is His messenger), performing the *ṣalāt* or ritual prayer, fasting during the month of Ramadan, paying the alms-tax, and making the Hajj if one has the means to do so.

Once the Islamic community moved beyond the earliest period and became differentiated into a variety of schools and approaches, *islām* in the fourth sense came to refer to the domain in which the science of jurisprudence (*fiqh*) exercises its authority. The jurists are those of the ulama who are experts in the five pillars and the other activities of the Shariah. If people want to know how to make an ablution or draw up a will or a marriage contract, they ask a jurist.

A jurist as jurist can have nothing to say about faith or perfection because these belong to other dimensions of the religion. As Abū Ḥāmid al-Ghazālī (d. 505/1111) puts it:

> The jurist speaks about what is correct and corrupt in *islām* and about its preconditions, but in this he pays no attention to anything but the tongue. As for the heart, that is outside the jurist's authority [*wilāyat al-faqīh*].[4]

If the jurist also happens to be a theologian, then, as theologian, he can speak about faith since faith is one of theology's concerns. One might object that the Shahadah—the gist of Islam's theology—is one of the five pillars and is therefore part of the first dimension. However, this is Shahadah as work, not as theory. Islam in the sense of submitting to the five pillars demands simply that a Muslim voice the Shahadah in order to bear witness to submission. Whether or not a person believes in or understands the Shahadah—and more importantly, *how* a person understands the Shahadah—are different issues, dealt with in theology and other parallel sciences, not in jurisprudence.

The second dimension of Islam is *īmān*. The Koran frequently employs the term and various derived words, especially the plural of the active participle, *muʾminūn* (believers, the faithful). Although translators normally render *īmān* as "faith" or "belief," such translations leave out an important connotation, because the word derives from a root that means to be secure, safe, and tranquil. Hence, the literal sense of *īmān* is to render secure, safe, calm, and free from fear. The implication is that, through faith in God, one becomes secure from error and rooted in the truth. Faith has a cognitive dimension that is a step in the direction of certainty.

In a number of verses the Koran provides a list of the objects of faith. For example, *True piety is this: to have faith in God, the Last Day, the angels, the Book, and the prophets* (2:177). In the Hadith of Gabriel, the Prophet gives a formulaic expression to these objects by defining *īmān* as "having faith in God, His angels, His scriptures, His messengers, the Last Day, and the measuring out [*qadar*] of good and evil."[5] Notice that the Prophet repeats the word faith in the definition itself, which indicates that here—in contrast to certain other hadiths—the *meaning* of faith is not at issue, but rather the *objects* of faith. These objects later become systematized into the three principles of the religion—declaring God's unity (*tawḥīd*), Prophecy (*nubuwwa*), and the Return to God (*maʿād*, commonly translated as "eschatology"). All the objects mentioned in this hadith are studied in the Islamic sciences. Muslim scholars did not approach them as articles of belief in the modern sense of this term. They did not suppose that these objects may or may not be true and real. On the contrary, they accepted them as objective realities to be found in the nature of things.

If the first dimension of Islam becomes the specialty of the jurists, the second dimension becomes the object of study of three main groups of scholars—specialists in Kalam or dogmatic theology, the proponents of philosophy, and those Sufis who were concerned with theoretical issues such as theology and cosmology. These three broad schools of thought—each having several branches—can be distinguished in many ways. Elsewhere, I have suggested that one way to understand their differing approaches is to notice the stress that they place on various forms of knowledge.[6] By and large, philosophers claim that reason (*ʿaql*) is a sufficient means to understand the nature of things. No prophetic intervention is necessary—at least not for philosophers. The proponents of Kalam stress the primacy of revelation, although they interpret it in rational terms and hence, on the question of reason's role, can be placed rather close to the philosophers. In contrast to both philosophers and Kalam authorities, the Sufis maintain that reason has clearly defined limits. They agree with the Kalam specialists that revelation has a primary role to play, but they hold that interpretation of the revealed texts by the sole means of reason prevents full understanding. Reason must be supplemented by direct knowledge given by God. This knowledge is called by many names, including "unveiling" (*kashf*), "tasting" (*dhawq*), and "insight" (*baṣīra*).

In the dimension of faith, divergence of opinion is much more pronounced than in the first dimension, and naturally so. The jurists are concerned with outward works, which can be seen with the eye and analyzed in concrete details. But the specialists in faith are concerned mainly with invisible realities that require the full application of human intelligence, if not direct divine aid, in order to be grasped to any extent. Differences of opinion abound, even though there is a surprising unanimity on certain fundamental issues.

The third dimension of Islam is perfection or virtue. The Prophet employed the word *iḥsān*, which is the most difficult of the three terms to translate. It is an active form from the root *ḥ.s.n.*, which connotes beauty and goodness. Hence, the word *iḥsān* means to accomplish what is beautiful and good, to do something well, to do something perfectly, to gain perfect and virtuous qualities. The standard by which the good, the beautiful, and the virtuous are judged cannot be an individual's opinion, because at issue here is what the religion teaches. In the Hadith of Gabriel, the Prophet defines *iḥsān* as serving or worshiping God "as if you see Him, because if you do not see Him, He nonetheless sees you." In other words, this third dimension of Islam is concerned with depth, or the inner attitudes that accompany activity and thought. One must be aware of God's presence in everything one does—which is to say that one must have a state of soul in conformity with works and faith.

If people fail to deepen the first two dimensions of the religion, they are left with meaningless activity and verbal definitions. But everyone knows that the worth of activity is intimately bound up with the intention that animates it, while verbal definitions are useless without understanding. All those who take religion seriously must ask how to go below the surface and enter into the depths. Naturally, there are degrees. Most Muslim thinkers hold that human beings will ultimately be differentiated in accordance with the extent to which they live up to the standard of perfection in works and faith.[7] This is one of the meanings of the traditional teaching that both paradise and hell embrace many levels.

Just as the first two dimensions of Islam have their specialists, so also does the third dimension have scholars and sages who dedicate their lives to explicating its nature. Most of these individuals have been called "Sufis," although many of the ulama known as philosophers or theologians also investigated this dimension of the religion. And just as the dimension of faith leads to more debate and disagreement than does the dimension of works, so also, for analogous reasons, is the dimension of perfection more controversial than that of faith.

In short, Islam, as defined by the Prophet in the Hadith of Gabriel, consists of works, faith, and perfection. One can classify many of the scholarly disciplines that become established in Islam on the basis of the respective emphasis placed on one or more of these dimensions. However, there is no need to make a clear differentiation. This tripartite division serves simply to provide an overview, not a hard and fast rule. Moreover, when Islam's dimensions are embodied in the actuality of being human, they become different aspects of a single whole. The more harmoniously the three dimensions are integrated, the closer the person approaches to a perfected human personality and to the nature of the Real Itself, which is utter harmony and pure oneness.

Faith and Knowledge

In Islamic texts, faith is discussed from two basic points of view: its subjective impact and its objective content. The first type of discussion deals with the definition of the word and its implications for the person who possesses it.[8] The second type addresses the objects of faith—God, the angels, and so on.

The locus of faith is the heart (*qalb*), which is the center or essence of the human being.[9] The heart is the place of intelligence, understanding, and every positive human quality. The heart's deviation and illness lead to ignorance, unbelief, and negative character traits. Its faith is inseparable from knowledge and noble character traits. Many Koranic verses and hadiths mention the good qualities of the faithful or the bad qualities that cannot dwell in the same heart with faith.

Specialists in Kalam were especially interested in the cognitive dimension of faith and its implications for putting the Shariah into practice. Sufi theoreticians were most interested in the moral and spiritual dimension of faith, and their explanations of the nature of faith in the heart coalesce with the explanations of *iḥsān* and its near-synonym, *ikhlāṣ* (sincerity).

If both the Koran and the Hadith make it clear that faith is intimately related to positive character traits, they also bring out the cognitive dimension implicit in the word itself. Some hadiths connect faith with knowledge in a way that fits into the concerns of the Kalam specialists. For example, the Prophet said "Faith is a knowledge [*maʿrifa*] in the heart, a voicing with the tongue, and an activity with the limbs."[10] Abū Ḥanīfa (d. 150/767) followed up on this approach by defining faith as "confessing with the tongue, recognizing the truth [of something, *taṣdīq*] with the mind, and knowing with the heart."[11] Ghazālī expresses the basic position of the Ashʿarite theologians when he defines faith as "recognizing the truth [of something] in the heart, voicing [that truth] with the tongue, and acting [on its basis] with the limbs."[12]

Notice that Ghazālī's definition—like the just-cited hadith—includes activity and works (i.e., *islām*) as part of *īmān*. For most authorities, faith includes works, but works do not necessarily imply faith. One cannot judge from a person's observance of the Shariah that faith is the motive. No suggestion is made that the domains of the Shariah and faith are equal, and a clear distinction is drawn between the two. Faith transcends works and includes them, whereas works without faith have no value.[13] One can have the first dimension of Islam without the second, works without faith, but one cannot have faith without works.

The cognitive and moral dimensions of faith are affirmed by its opposite, *kufr*, a word that is normally translated as "unbelief" or "infidelity." But as Muhammad Asad has pointed out, the term *kāfir* "cannot be simply equated, as many Muslim theologians of post-classical times and practically all Western translators of the Koran have done, with 'unbeliever' or 'infidel' in the specific, restricted sense of one who rejects the system of doctrine and law promulgated in the Koran and amplified by the teachings of the Prophet,"[14] since the term is already present in the earliest verses of the Koran to be revealed. The root meaning of the term *kufr* is "to cover over, to conceal." By extension, it means to cover over something that one knows. In the Koranic sense, it means to cover over the truth that God has revealed through the prophets and to conceal the blessings that God has given to His creatures. The Koran frequently uses the term *kufr* as the opposite of *shukr* (gratitude). Hence, the *kuffār* (plural of *kāfir*) are at once those who are ungrateful and those who cover over the truth that they know. The truth that people cover over is the self-evident reality of God. They conceal it while knowing in their hearts that it is true.[15] It is only from this perspective that *kufr* can justifiably be translated as "unbelief."

To come back to the word *īmān* itself, one of the most common terms employed in Kalam to define it, as we have already seen, is *taṣdīq*, which means to recognize or affirm the truth of something. The essence of faith is to know that something is true and to acknowledge its truth in word and deed. As Wilfred Cantwell Smith has remarked, to say that faith is *taṣdīq* means that "Faith is the ability to trust, and to act in terms of, what one knows to be true."[16] What one knows to be true are the objects of faith—God, the angels, the scriptures, and so on.

In English, "faith" is normally understood as volitional rather than cognitive. People think of faith as related to supposition and opinion rather than to knowledge and certainty. In contrast, faith in Islam pertains primarily to knowledge and the commitments that people make on the basis of knowledge. It stands above knowledge, not below it. It adds to knowledge a dimension of personal commitment, an engagement with the truth that one knows. As Smith puts it, "The object of faith being thought of as pellucid and incontrovertible, the issue is, what does one do about what one knows?"[17]

Most authors who discuss the objects of faith do not discuss the subjective side of faith any more than contemporary biologists or astronomers analyze the assumption that they are dealing with real things. Muslim scholars were interested in the objects of faith because they knew them to be components of the real configuration of existence. They often do not even bother reminding us, because it is self-evident, that discussion of God, the angels, or eschatology pertains to one of the three principles of faith—principles that, as suggested previously, simply classify the objects of faith into convenient categories.

As already mentioned, there are three basic approaches to understanding the objects of faith: Kalam, philosophy, and theoretical Sufism. Accepting the articles of faith on the basis of imitation or following authority (*taqlīd*) was the business of the common people or the beginners—those who have no real grasp of the creed. In contrast, the theological, philosophical, and Sufi sciences brought out what could be known—with various degrees of certainty—about faith's objects. In short, discussion of the three principles of faith and their ramifications fills up most texts on Kalam and philosophy, and many texts on Sufism.

That the discussion of the contents of faith occupies the philosophers may be less obvious than in the case of Kalam. Indeed, many contemporary scholars, having applauded the philosophers' open-mindedness, might object to the use of the word "faith." But this is to fall into the trap of understanding faith in our terms, in which it has little cognitive content. In Islamic terms, the contents of faith are objects of real knowledge, and the philosophers analyze the same objects as do the theologians and Sufis. After all, the object of philosophical study is *wujūd* (which we can translate here as "existence" or "being"), and *wujūd* is the underlying stuff of reality. For most philosophers, it is ultimately the Real Itself—God—while it is also present in some mode through the things of experience. In effect, by studying *wujūd*, the philosophers investigate the first of the three principles of faith: *tawḥīd*, or the relationship of the many (which they like to call "possible things," *mumkināt*) to the One (the "Necessary Being," *wājib al-wujūd*). Most philosophers also discuss prophecy and eschatology.

No one is claiming that the philosophers always come to the same conclusions as the Sufis and Kalam authorities. Far from it. But they study the same realities, and they have faith in them, which is to say that they know them to be objectively true and attempt to live their lives accordingly.

Sufis join the theoretical discussions of the three principles of faith at a relatively late date in Islamic history. There were detailed books on Kalam and philosophy long before the Sufis began systematic discussions of the theoretical—rather than the practical and applied—dimensions of their science. Almost all early Sufis deal primarily with the deepening of faith and works and the nature of the various human qualities that can be achieved through imitating the Prophet. To the extent that the early Sufis address the contents of faith, they prefer enigmatic or gnomic language.

In all sophisticated studies of faith's principles, epistemology is a central issue. How do we know what we know? What can we know for certain? In what sense can we know God? In what sense can we know anything other than God? Such questions—with tremendous variety and nuance amplified by the different perspectives of diverse schools of thought—fill up countless volumes.

The authorities in all these sciences differentiate between the common people (*ʿāmma*) and the elect (*khāṣṣa*). The first imitate the faith of others and follow authority (*taqlīd*), while the second verify the truth of what they know (*taḥqīq*). In the context of Sufism, these terms refer to the Sufis as opposed to the general run of Muslims who are not Sufis. The implication is that what Sufis understand is beyond the understanding of the common people. This "elitism" of Sufism has sometimes been criticized, but the perspective is far from being exclusive to Sufism or to the various schools that deal with faith. The Koran itself supplies the principle in the verse, *Above everyone who has knowledge is one who knows* (12:76). No one objects when Muslim grammarians or mathematicians talk about the elect and the common people, meaning thereby those who know their science and those who do not. Ghazālī points out that all scholars consider their own domain as God's chosen realm (and this seems to be no less true today). He says that each of more than twenty schools of thought claims that its own science is what the Prophet meant when he said that the search for knowledge is incumbent on every Muslim.[18]

The fact that Sufis—like other possessors of knowledge in Islam—consider themselves to be an elect helps explain the often-encountered description of Sufism as "Islamic esoterism." One cannot object to this expression, so long as it is kept within bounds. It does not mean that the Sufis jealously guarded certain teachings and practices from the majority. Rather, Sufi knowledge and practice remained relatively hidden because the majority were either uninterested or incapable of understanding. In this respect, grammar and mathematics are also esoteric. What stands out in Sufi esoterism is that it relates to the domain of Islam's faith and works, and it is contrasted with an exoterism that relates to the same domain. But here again, the first thing one should understand from this distinction is that the majority of people—the "common people" as opposed to the "elect"—had no interest in Sufism, or considered it to be suspect and dangerous if not heretical. Most people are satisfied to remain with works and faith as defined in simple terms. They do not want subtleties and complications, nor do they like to be told that they are not good people and that they should try to change themselves.

This is not to say that Sufism has no connection with esoterism in the sense of knowledge of the mysteries, the unseen things, the occult, the mysterious, the mystical. All this is implied in the attention that the Sufis pay to unveiling as a valid source of knowledge.

Iḥsān, *Ikhlāṣ*, and *Taqwā*

In the Hadith of Gabriel the Prophet defined *iḥsān*, Islam's third dimension, as worshipping God "as if you see Him, because if you do not see Him, He nonetheless sees you." The Koran employs the word *iḥsān* and its active participle, *muḥsin* (the person who has *iḥsān*), more than seventy times. Sometimes, the subject of the verb is God, and *al-muḥsin* is usually found in the lists of the divine names. As a human quality, *iḥsān* is always praiseworthy. Verses such as the following illustrate that human *iḥsān* is closely connected to divine *iḥsān*: *Who is better in religion than the one who submits his face to God, being a* muḥsin? (4:125); *Have* iḥsān. *God loves those who have* iḥsān (2:195); *God's mercy is near to the* muḥsins (7:56); *God is with the* muḥsins (29:69).

Literally, *iḥsān* means putting the good and the beautiful into practice. The Koranic usage makes it clear that this is not only an external and ethical good, but also an internal, moral, and spiritual good. Hence, "virtue" may suggest some of what it involves. The Prophet's definition stresses the internal dimensions of the quality, tying it to an attitude of soul. For the Sufi sages, the internal and spiritual dimensions of *iḥsān* are, in any case, obvious.

Among the Koranic evidence that Sufis cite to show the spiritual dimensions of *iḥsān* is that the Book describes God's own qualities with the superlative adjective from the same root. In four verses it speaks of God's "most beautiful names" (*al-asmāʾ al-ḥusnā*). As the first Shahadah makes clear, everything good belongs essentially to God, and accidentally—if at all—to the creatures. "There is no god but God" means that all the qualities denoted by the most beautiful names belong to God in a true sense, and to other things in some other sense. It follows logically that "There is no good but the divine good," "There is no mercy but the divine mercy," and ultimately, "There is nothing truly real but the Real." *Iḥsān*, putting the good and the beautiful into practice, implies bringing God's goodness and beauty—real goodness and beauty—into the soul and the world.

One of the many ways of describing the process of achieving human perfection is to say that it involves "assuming the character traits of God" (*al-takhalluq bi-akhlāq Allāh*), an expression based on a hadith that we will encounter in Chapter 20. God's character traits are identical with His most beautiful names. The prophetic saying (which has a biblical equivalent), "God created Adam in His own form (*ṣūra*)," was interpreted to mean that the innate disposition (*fiṭra*) of human beings embraces all the qualities designated by God's names.

To become perfect is to bring the latent divine qualities within oneself into full actuality. It is to act, know, and be as God would act, know, and be, were He to assume human form.

The acting is the easiest because it can be described and delineated in exact terms. Hence, everyone is told to act. This is the Shariah, incumbent upon all.

The knowing is much more difficult. Although "The search for knowledge is incumbent on every Muslim," the extent to which a person seeks and actualizes knowledge will depend on personal qualifications.

Finally, to be as God would be is by far the most difficult because it involves an utter transformation of the personality. This is Sufism's primary concern, and relatively few people attempt to achieve it.

On the level of seeking knowledge, a person might take any of several routes. The minimum knowledge that is incumbent on every Muslim, as Ghazālī points out, is what allows a person to know the creed and perform the required practices.[19] People who feel themselves drawn to a broader and deeper knowledge of the religion will not follow the same paths. Some will become experts in jurisprudence, others in Kalam or philosophy, and still others in various other fields of learning. Both philosophy and theoretical Sufism have described the possibilities of human knowledge and awareness in terms that make it clear that these are unlimited since the ultimate degree of knowing involves a lifting of many of the barriers that separate the finite from the Infinite.

It needs to be kept in mind that this seeking of knowledge—to the extent that it pertains to knowledge of the objects of faith—helps in the deepening and perfecting of faith. One cannot have faith in something about which one has no knowledge. In the same way, the more knowledge one gains of the nature of things—that is, the things dealt with under the heading of Islam's three principles—the firmer becomes one's commitment to what one knows.

The process of deepening one's knowledge is inseparable from that of knowing the most beautiful names of God, which are the archetypes of all that exists. To the extent that one knows these names and their implications, one becomes committed to and engaged in the human goodness and beauty that they demand. To "worship God as if you see Him" is to serve Him through becoming His vicegerent (*khalīfa*) and manifesting His qualities within oneself and the world.

A number of Koranic terms have semantic fields that overlap with *iḥsān* and are used in similar senses in the literature. Two are of particular interest: *ikhlāṣ* and *taqwā*.

Ikhlāṣ derives from a root having to do with purity, cleanliness, and freedom from the admixture of extraneous elements or factors. The Koran employs the verb in the sentence, *akhlaṣū dīnahum li'llāh, They freed their religion from admixture for God,* or *They purified their religion for God* (4:146). Koran translators have rendered this sentence in a variety of ways: *They are sincere in their religion to God* (Palmer); *They make their religion pure for Allah (only)* (Pickthall); *They make their religion sincerely God's* (Arberry); *They are sincere in their devotion to God* (Dawood); *They grow sincere in their faith in God alone* (Asad); *They dedicate their religion solely to God* (Irving). In eleven more verses, the Koran speaks approvingly of *"the* mukhliṣūn *[those who have* ikhlāṣ*] for God in their religion."*

The hadith literature employs the term *ikhlāṣ* in suggestive ways, such as "purifying works for God" and "purifying the heart for faith." Hadiths sometimes mention the "sentence of *ikhlāṣ*," meaning the first Shahadah, which turns the mind and heart away from everything other than God. *Ikhlāṣ* is often taken as the antonym for *shirk* (associating others with God), which is the only unforgivable sin, and as a synonym for *tawḥīd*, which is also defined by the first Shahadah. Sura 112 of the Koran, which begins, *Say: "He is God, One,"* is called both the "Sura of *Tawḥīd*" and the "Sura of *Ikhlāṣ*." In short, the hadith literature makes explicit what the Koran implies—sincerity is a deepening of works and faith such that one's only motive in acting and thinking is God. If *tawḥīd* can be understood to mean the voicing of the sentence, "There is no god but God," *ikhlāṣ* implies that *tawḥīd* is internalized so that it becomes the determining factor in thought and action.

The word *taqwā* and related terms from the same root are employed far more frequently in the Koran than either *iḥsān* or *ikhlāṣ* and their derivatives. The term is especially difficult to translate and, with some trepidation, I have chosen "God-wariness."

The root of the word *taqwā* has two interwoven senses: to fear and to protect oneself. The basic meaning in the Koranic context is to stand in awe of God, to fear the consequences of acting against His will, and to do everything in one's power to protect oneself from these consequences. The term implies observing the religion meticulously, sincerely, and with full presence of mind. In the verbal form of *ittaqā*, the word often takes God as object, and I translate it as "to be wary of God." That *taqwā* is a human quality established in relation to God is clear in any case, whether or not God is mentioned in the immediate context.

The Koran always mentions the God-wary in positive terms. They have taken God's message to heart, have put it into practice completely, and will go to paradise. In contrast, both those who have submitted (*muslimūn*) and those who have faith (*mu'minūn*) are sometimes criticized, whether explicitly or implicitly. Most of the Koran's commandments are addressed to those who have faith—that is, those who have recognized the truth of the message and are attempting to put it into practice. The Koran frequently tells the faithful that they must have *taqwā*, so it is a goal toward which they should be striving. Several verses say that the God-wary are the ones whom God loves and has guided. In effect, it is they who have perfected their works and faith.[20] The hadith literature employs the term *kalimat al-taqwā* (the sentence of God-wariness) as a synonym for the sentence of *ikhlāṣ* or *tawḥīd*—that is, the first Shahadah.

The Koran provides a great deal of evidence for suggesting that *taqwā* expresses in a single word the sum total of all good and beautiful human attributes, or the perfect human embodiment of Islam in its deepest sense. This is particularly clear in the verse, *The noblest of you in God's eyes is the one among you who has the most* taqwā (49:13). Translators have tried in various ways to bring out the fundamental importance of this term for Koranic religiosity. Each of the following translations reflects the translator's idea of the key virtue in Islam: *The most honourable of you in the sight of God is the most pious of you* (Palmer); *The noblest among you with Allah is the most dutiful of you* (Muhammad Ali); *The noblest of you, in the sight of Allah, is the best in conduct* (Pickthall); *The noblest among you in the sight of God is the most godfearing of you* (Arberry); *The noblest among you with Allah is the one among you most careful (of his duty)* (Habib); *The noblest of you in God's sight is he who is most righteous* (Dawood); *The noblest of you in the sight of God is the one who is most deeply conscious of Him* (Asad); *The noblest of you with God is that one of you who best performs his duty* (Irving).

Understanding *taqwā* as "God-wariness," on the other hand, makes *taqwā*'s orientation toward God explicit, brings out the implication of being aware and mindful, and avoids the negative and sentimental undertones of words such as "piety," "dutifulness," and "righteousness."

Felicity

The goal of observing Islam's three dimensions is to gain salvation. The term most commonly employed for salvation in Islamic texts is *sa'āda,* which means happiness. I translate it with the Latinate word "felicity" in order to remind the reader that this happiness pertains fundamentally to life after death. The opposite of felicity is "wretchedness" (*shaqā'*).

The tradition locates felicity in paradise and wretchedness in hell, even though both have foretastes in this world. But Sufis stress *tawḥīd* and *ikhlāṣ*. In their view, perfecting works and faith involves relating all things back to God as well as purifying activity, thought, and will from service to anything other than God. If a person worships God with the intention of avoiding hell and gaining paradise, an ulterior motive has crept in, a concern for oneself rather than God. Since a god is anything that one serves, some authorities maintain that this is a subtle form of associating other gods with God (*shirk khafī*), and hence it prevents complete *ikhlāṣ*.

In Sufi literature, one commonly meets the theme of desiring God alone and rejecting paradise. Many Muslim authors divide human beings into three major groups on the basis of Sura 56. The "Companions of the Left" will inhabit hell. The "Companions of the Right" will live in paradise, and "those brought near to God" (*al-muqarrabūn*) actualize full *tawḥīd* and *ikhlāṣ*. In the Sufi view, the members of this last group have erased both paradise and hell from their vision.

To reach felicity is to dwell in paradise or to live with God. But felicity has many levels. The Koran implies—and the tradition affirms—that the greatest felicity is the encounter (*liqā'*) with God, an encounter that entails a vision (*ru'ya*) of God. Theological debates about the nature of this vision—and whether it was attainable in this world—were common. If a distinction can be drawn here between the perspective of the Sufis and the theologians, it is that the Sufis held that one could encounter God already in this world, whereas the theologians maintained that the encounter will not occur until after death.

Although Sufis maintain that God can be encountered in this world, many—if not most—give an ambiguous answer to the question of actually seeing Him, whether here or in paradise. They usually maintain that God *in Himself* cannot be seen, although He can be seen in the form in which He chooses to disclose Himself. Moreover, He discloses Himself in keeping with the receptacle. From here it is only one step to the position that God discloses Himself to all things—in this world as well as the next—in keeping with their capacities or preparednesses (*isti'dād*). God is never absent from His creatures. God is nearer *than the jugular vein* (50:16) and *with you wherever you are* (57:4). However, people are absent from God. He is there to be seen, but seeing Him takes a special kind of eye. Gaining that eye depends on actualizing *tawḥīd* and *ikhlāṣ*.

To encounter God is to encounter the object of one's faith. Here again, the importance of faith's cognitive dimension comes to the forefront. If Islam's third dimension stresses the deepening of faith, this implies that the object of one's faith comes to coincide more and more exactly with the Real. Ibn al-ʿArabī among others insists that the "god of belief" is always distinct from God in Himself, since a finite receptacle can never grasp the Infinite.[21] But the knowledge achieved through deepened faith is far beyond that which depends on rational arguments and conclusions. Through God-wariness, faith can be transmuted into unveiling or the direct vision of the realities of things.

Unveiling allows people to "see God," since their faith and knowledge are transmuted into witnessing God's self-disclosures. The vision of God brings us back to *iḥsān*, which is "to worship God as if you see Him." As the Sufis like to point out, the highest degree of *iḥsān* is to worship God without the "as if"—that is, while actually seeing and recognizing Him through His self-disclosures. This is how many of them interpret the saying of the Prophet's cousin and son-in-law ʿAlī (d. 40/661), "I would not worship a God whom I do not see."

In sum, Islam's third dimension completes the first two. Its characteristics confirm the hierarchical relationship that was mentioned in connection with works and faith. There can be works without faith, but no faith without works. In the same way, there can be faith without perfection, but no perfection without faith and the works that are a part of faith.

Hence, Islam and being a Muslim have three basic degrees. The first and most superficial degree is defined as "voicing the Shahadah," the first of the five pillars. Within the first degree, there are, of course, many subdegrees that jurisprudence is able to differentiate. This explains the debates over issues such as whether simply voicing the Shahadah is sufficient to be a Muslim, or whether a person also has to observe the other pillars.

On the second level, people are Muslim if, being Muslim in the first sense, their beliefs are correct. This is the domain in which theologians set up their catechisms and creeds.

On the third and final level, the issues of sincerity, virtue, and human worth are discussed. On every level, there is a different understanding as to what "Islam" implies. Different schools of thought offer different interpretations. If anything differentiates the Sufis from other Muslims here, it is not only that they consider all three dimensions worthy of attention, but also that they view the third dimension as the proper fruition and completion of the first two.

Priorities

The Sufi authorities along with other ulama take the first Shahadah as the fundamental truth in terms of which all other things must be understood. Hence their primary concern is God. But Sufi texts have a way of bringing out God-centeredness more clearly than do, let us say, texts on jurisprudence, Kalam, or philosophy.

The jurists soon ignore God by devoting all their attention to the details of the Shariah. The proponents of Kalam are interested in God, but primarily as an object of rational thought and cold analysis. They keep Him at arm's length, stressing His inaccessibility and incomparability. God becomes largely an abstraction—an "It"—of interest only inasmuch as He reveals certain laws and principles through the prophets. The philosophers usually put the religious language of Islam into the background, and they often seem careful to avoid mentioning the Koranic names of God. They prefer an approach that today we would call "objective" and "academic." Hence, they like to refer to God with terms such as "Necessary Being" or "First Principle."

The Sufis agree with the Kalam authorities that God is inaccessible. But they add that, just as He is ever-absent, so also is He ever-present. Inasmuch as He is present, He is eminently desirable and lovable. The God that Sufis keep at the center of their concerns is the God whom people want to have around, not the God who instills terror in their hearts and plays a dominant role in jurisprudence and Kalam. Awareness of God's presence gives birth to joy and delight. This helps explain why Sufi texts are characterized by a stylistic lightness not found in writings from other branches of religious learning. It also suggests why most of the great poets of Islamic civilization are rooted in the Sufi tradition.

Scholars have often pointed out that "post-axial" religions are concerned mainly with salvation, and Islam is no exception. Although the religion is all about God, it is also totally anthropocentric, because knowledge of God is oriented toward the ultimate concern of every human being—one's personal destiny. The Koran and the Hadith focus all of their attention, directly or indirectly, on the question of what the reality of God implies for human beings.

In the Sufi reading, human felicity is inseparable from God Himself. This is implied in the aforementioned saying of the Prophet, "God created Adam in His own form." The human being is a form (*ṣūra*), and every form demands an inner reality, a "meaning" (*maʿnā*). In some mysterious fashion, this inner reality is God Himself. Understanding this, and fully experiencing and living all its consequences, is the ultimate goal of *tawḥīd*. Through *iḥsān*—the perfection of what is good and beautiful in human beings—people come to embody and manifest the most beautiful names of God, or the reality of God Himself. Then they become worthy of the honor that God accords to Adam in the Koran, that of being God's vicegerent on earth.

In general, the Muslim authorities—and this is especially true of the Sufis—put first things first (*al-ahamm fa'l-ahamm*). The Prophet said, "I seek refuge in God from a knowledge that has no benefit." Beneficial knowledge is knowledge that leads people to felicity. Any knowledge that does not pertain directly to the achievement of felicity must be placed in the background. Thus, if Sufis are concerned only with works, the contents of faith, and perfection, it is because they see these alone as immediately relevant to felicity.

The accent on achieving felicity demands a strict hierarchy of values. This hierarchy is defined in terms of God, the ultimate Value. Secondary values are those that come directly from God, such as the Koran and the Prophet. Third-level values—such as the Hadith and the Shariah—come from God through the intermediary of the second-level values. In this hierarchical way of looking at things, what is nearer to God is better. What brings about nearness to God (*qurb*, a term that is practically synonymous with felicity) is better than what brings about separation from Him. Any knowledge that helps bring about nearness is beneficial, and any knowledge that works against nearness is unbeneficial and should be avoided. That is why Ghazālī can write, alluding to the saying of the Prophet just cited:

> "Beneficial" knowledge is what increases your fear of God, your ability to see your own faults, and your knowledge of how to serve your Lord. It decreases your desire for this world and increases your desire for the next. It opens your eyes to the defects of your own works so that you guard against these defects.[22]

To the extent that the Islamic sciences are oriented toward goals other than human felicity, they do not deal with beneficial knowledge. Hence, they do not pertain to Islam but to what Marshall Hodgson calls "Islamdom." Of course, I am speaking in relatives, not absolutes. I would not remove from the category of Islamic knowledge any specific science cultivated by Muslims. But some sciences are closer to the salvific ideals of the religion, and some are further away. All of them can have their benefit. The criterion of "Islamicity" here is much more subjective than objective. For some people, knowledge of the natural world may be a barrier to faith in the unseen reality of God, for others it may be a necessity for the same faith. The differing perceptions of the soteriological relevance of the sciences helps explain the differing opinions of the Muslim intellectuals—such as jurists and philosophers—on what sort of knowledge needs to be acquired.

Unveiling and Practice

The ulama often divide religious knowledge into two types: the sciences of unveiling and those of practice. Ghazālī, for example, goes to great lengths in the first book of the *Iḥyāʾ ʿulūm al-dīn* ("The Revival of the Religious Sciences") to explain the nature of knowledge in general, and of these two types of knowledge in particular. His major point is that the knowledge incumbent on every Muslim is the science of practice.

Note the distinction between the word *ʿamal*, which I translate as "works," and *muʿāmala* (practice), which is the third-form *maṣdar* from the same root. *ʿAmal* means working, doing or making something, something done, an activity, a work. *Muʿāmala*, on the other hand, implies interaction. Hence, "practice" is a work that keeps God in view, whereas works do not necessarily involve God. However, they *should*—and this is precisely the point. One can perform works that do not follow the Shariah, or works that observe its rules but are contradicted by the intention or the attitude. Ghazālī repeatedly reminds his readers that the competence of the jurists extends only to activity—the works themselves—not to the intention behind the activity. Their jurisdiction is the Shariah alone. As he remarks about the *ṣalāt*:

> The jurist rules that a person's *ṣalāt* is correct if it exhibits the form of the acts along with the outward preconditions, even if the person is negligent throughout the whole *ṣalāt*, from its beginning to its end, thinking instead about the calculation of his transactions in the market.[23]

For Ghazālī, in short, the science of practice deals with the deepening of works. In contrast, the science of unveiling pertains to the deepening of faith. *Mukāshafa* (unveiling) is a third-form *maṣdar* from *kashf*. Most Sufi texts employ *kashf* and *mukāshafa* interchangeably. If there is a difference in nuance, it has to do with the interpersonality implied by the third-form *maṣdar*. Unveiling is not one-sided since it pertains to a relationship between the human being and God.

It should be kept in mind that although the knowledge gained through unveiling is different from that gained through reason, it is not irrational. Rather, unveiling is suprarational in the sense that it is inaccessible to reason without God's direct help.

One of the classic tales told to illustrate the difference between rational knowledge and unveiling concerns the famous Sufi Abū Saʿīd ibn Abī'l-Khayr (d. 440/1049) and the great philosopher Avicenna (428/1037). The story, of course, comes from Sufi sources since unveiling is pictured as superior to reason. It is noteworthy that no contradiction is seen between the two types of knowledge, because it is recognized that they have the same objects. I tell the story as I remember it, without reference to a source. In any case, the point of the story does not lie in its historical accuracy.

Avicenna went to Maymana with his train of students to visit Abū Saʿīd, who lived there surrounded by many disciples. The two immediately took a liking to each other, and Abū Saʿīd led Avicenna into his private chamber, where they sat together for three days and three nights. No one interrupted them, except to take in food and refreshments. After three days, Avicenna mounted his horse and rode off, his students following. After a respectful lapse of time, the eldest student asked Avicenna, "O great master, how did you find that man Abū Saʿīd? His disciples make extravagant claims about him." Avicenna replied, "Well, everything I know, he sees."

Back in Maymana, one of Abū Saʿīd's close disciples was delegated by the others to inquire about this philosopher, whose disciples were so cocksure about his knowledge of everything under the sun. Abū Saʿīd replied, "It's true. Everything I see, he knows."

Sufis and philosophers frequently distinguish between suprarational and rational knowledge by calling one of them *maʿrifa* (gnosis) and the other *ʿilm* (knowledge or learning). One of my favorite aphorisms is cited anonymously by Abū'l-Qāsim al-Qushayrī (d. 465/1072): "The gnostic [*ʿārif*] is above what he says, but the possessor of learning [*ʿālim*] is below what he says."[24]

The ulama are below what they say because they understand only the surface implications of the words that they quote from the Koran, the Sunnah, and the traditional authorities. If the Sufi shaykhs are above what they say, this is because their words express only dimly the realities that they have seen and verified.

The description of Sufism as Islamic "esoterism" relates directly to the type of knowledge gained through unveiling and gnosis since it cannot be expressed in terms completely accessible to the ulama and the common people. The Sufi shaykhs do not necessarily conceal their knowledge, but people who have not verified it are "below" it.

Ghazālī points out that all Muslims have the obligation to deepen their works through understanding the sciences of practice, but he stresses that the sciences of unveiling are of a different sort. Everyone must know a certain amount about practice in order to be able to establish a correct relationship with God. But Ghazālī makes clear that unveiling, by its very nature, pertains to an elect—those whose hearts have been opened up to knowledge by God. Hence Ghazālī makes no attempt to explain the sciences of unveiling in the *Iḥyāʾ*, a book that, he tells us, deals specifically with practice. He defines and describes unveiling as follows:

> Unveiling is knowledge of the nonmanifest domain [*al-bāṭin*] and the goal of all the sciences. One of the gnostics said, "I fear that if a person has no share in this knowledge, he will come to an evil end." The least share of it is that you acknowledge its truth and concede its existence in those who are worthy of it.
>
> Another gnostic said, "If a person has two traits—innovation [*bidʿa*] and pride [*kibr*]—nothing of this knowledge will be opened up to him."
>
> It has been said that whoever loves this world and insists on following caprice [*hawā*] will never reach the reality of this science, even though he may reach the reality of the other sciences. . . .
>
> The science of unveiling is the knowledge of the sincere devotees [*ṣiddiqūn*] and those brought near to God [*muqarrabūn*]. It consists of a light that becomes manifest within the heart when the heart is cleansed and purified of blameworthy attributes. Many things are unveiled by means of this light. Earlier the person had been hearing the names of these things and imagining vague and unclear meanings. Now they become clarified.
>
> The person gains true knowledge of God's Essence, His perfect and subsistent attributes, His acts, His wisdom in creating this world and the next world, and the manner in which He makes the

next world the consequence of this world; the true knowledge of the meaning of prophecy and the prophets, the meaning of revelation, the meaning of Satan, the meaning of the words "angels" and "satans," how the satans have enmity toward human beings, how the angel becomes manifest to the prophets, and how revelation reaches them; the true knowledge of the heart and how the hosts of the angels and the satans confront each other within it; the true knowledge of the difference between the suggestion of the angel and the suggestion of the satan; the true knowledge of the next world, the Garden, the Fire, the chastisement of the grave, the Path, the Scales, and the Accounting[25]; the meaning of God's words, *"Read your book! Your soul suffices you this day as an accounter against you"* [17:14]; the meaning of His words, *Surely the abode of the next world is life, did they but know* [29:64]; the meaning of the encounter with God and looking upon His generous face; the meaning of nearness to Him and alighting in His neighborhood; the meaning of achieving felicity through the companionship of the Higher Plenum and connection to the angels and the prophets; the meaning of the disparity of degrees of the people of the Gardens, such that some of them see others as if they were shining stars in the middle of heaven; and so on.[26]

Ghazālī pays much more attention to practice and the inner attitudes that should accompany it than he does to the actual contents of faith. In contrast, many Sufi authors from the seventh/thirteenth century onward stress the contents of faith far more than practice. Ibn al-ʿArabī, of course, is the major milestone here, since no one before him (or after him) discussed the contents of faith in such exhaustive detail.

Practically every scholar who has written in broad terms about the history of Sufism has remarked on this shift of emphasis in Sufi writings. Various theories have been proposed as to what took place.[27] Let me simply suggest here that one of the many reasons for this shift has to do with a principle expressed in a famous aphorism by the fourth/tenth-century Sufi Abū'l-Ḥasan al-Būshanjī (d. 348/960): "Today Sufism is a name without a reality, whereas before it was a reality without a name." In earlier periods, the reality of Sufism to which Būshanjī is alluding was the full actualization of Islam on all three dimensions of works, faith, and perfection. By Būshanjī's time, the transformative power present in the initial period was already being lost. What had been the living reality of sincerity and God-wariness was turning into a topic for academic discussion or a means to deceive the simple-minded. Given that the essentials of Islam were becoming more and more inaccessible with the passage of time, Sufi authors found it necessary to go into greater detail than before. They felt that people needed more detailed explanation in order to understand what was at issue in being human.

Ghazālī represents a widespread opinion when he says that it is incumbent on people to learn as much as the science of faith as is necessary to keep their faith firm.[28] When their faith starts to waver, they have need of greater explanation. Certainly the historical circumstances between the fifth/eleventh and seventh/thirteenth centuries—a period that witnessed among other things the serious decline of the caliphate—provided people with reasons to question their presuppositions about the meaning of life. It is perhaps a sign of our times that many people today recognize a greater need than ever before for the elucidation of the internal logic of religious worldviews.

2

The Bodily Gestures of the *Ṣalāt*

Muslim authors who explain the significance of the *ṣalāt* presuppose a thorough grounding in Islamic practice. They address people who perform the *ṣalāt* every day and for whom it has become second nature. They discuss the meaning of the gestures rather rarely, and only in the context of what is known as "the mysteries of the acts of worship" (*asrār al-ʿibādāt*).[1] Authors of such works are typically Sufis, which is to say that they belong to that body of Muslims who are not satisfied with superficial interpretations and who stress meaning over form. These works, however, devote far more attention to explaining the significance of the various formulae and Koranic verses that are recited than to the gestures themselves. Part of the reason for this relative reticence is no doubt that the body assimilates the wisdom of the gestures, thereby making verbalization unnecessary. After all, the resurrection is bodily, and the Koran tells us that each of the bodily parts will be questioned about its activities in the world.

The Prophet called *ṣalāt* the "centerpole" of the religion. As the centerpole of the religion, the *ṣalāt* holds up the rest of Islam and expresses the most essential act that God wants from human beings. If the Shahadah is the oral acknowledgment of surrender to God's love and mercy, the *ṣalāt* adds the bodily activity most recommended by God.

The meaning of the *ṣalāt* can be approached from many directions. Perhaps the best way to gain insight into its movements is to situate them within the context of Islamic teachings on the human microcosm. These teachings differentiate clearly between the lower, dark, dense, unconscious, and dispersed dimension of the human being, called the "body" (*jism*), and the higher, luminous, subtle, conscious, and unified dimension, called the "spirit" (*rūḥ*). The body is the corporeal image of God, while the spirit is God's breath, blown into the body when God "shaped the clay" of the human being. There is one fundamental spirit (God's breath) and a great number of human bodies, all made in God's image. In each individual, spirit and body intermingle on an intermediary level—an "isthmus" (*barzakh*)—called the "soul."[2]

The soul represents the encounter between the qualities of spirit and body. It is the locus of awareness and personality, but it is neither purely spiritual nor purely corporeal. Within the soul, light comes together with darkness, knowledge with ignorance, unity with multiplicity, remembrance with forgetfulness, life with death, power with weakness. Through the soul, spirit and body interact, and this interaction becomes manifest as changes are undergone, moment by moment, in thought, speech, and movement. The goal of human existence in this world is to integrate the lower into the higher, the corporeal into the spiritual, the human into the Divine. Hence, a Muslim strives to entrust his body to his soul and his soul to his spirit. But this depends on establishing a firm relationship with the divine center and tying all the dispersed activity of the body and soul back into God.

The *ṣalāt* engages people on every level of their existence. The gestures provide the model for bodily activity integrated into the Real. Like the human being, the *ṣalāt* has three fundamental dimensions. Its spirit is mindfulness or "presence of the heart" (*ḥuḍūr al-qalb*). In every prayer the Muslim strives to root the heart firmly in the remembrance (*dhikr*) of God. The fact that a person performs the prayer is proof of a minimal mindfulness, just as the fact of human life is proof of the presence of the spirit. But full presence of the heart in prayer is as rare as human self-awareness situated at the level of the Divine Spirit. Such awareness is the goal of human existence, and only the prophets and the greatest friends of God (*awliyāʾ*) experience it.

Each gesture is accompanied by certain Koranic verses or prophetic formulae that provide the key to its significance. The verses or sayings bridge the gap between the spirit and body of the prayer, between mindfulness and bodily activity. They are like an isthmus between the prayer's spirit and body. They are the "soul" of the prayer, bringing together the luminosity of the prayer's spirit with the corporeality of its form. Thus, the words have an articulated, bodily nature like the gestures, but their ultimate meaning transcends all forms.

Among the many texts that the authorities quote to bring out the significance of the *ṣalāt* is the prophetic saying, "The *ṣalāt* is the *miʿrāj* of the believer [*al-ṣalāt miʿrāj al-muʾmin*]." The *miʿrāj* is the Prophet's "ascension" whereby he was taken through the heavens into the Divine Presence. The word *miʿrāj* literally means "tool for climbing," or "ladder." One climbs up on a ladder, but one also comes back down on the ladder. The significance of the *miʿrāj* lies not only in the Prophet's ascent, but also in his return to the world. These two movements mark the two main stages of spiritual perfection and are reflected in the *ṣalāt*'s structure.

According to the generally accepted doctrine, the Prophet's *miʿrāj* was bodily. Human perfection, in other words, is not confined to the invisible, luminous, and spiritual dimension of being. It also pertains to the visible, dark, and corporeal dimension, since the divine image manifests certain attributes that demand corporeal form. The body is an essential component in the quest for God. Like the soul, it undergoes transformations appropriate to its own level.

The *ṣalāt* has four main positions: standing straight; bowing so that one's back and head are parallel with the ground; prostrating oneself by putting the knees, hands, and forehead on the ground; and sitting with knees forward and back straight. Each mandatory *ṣalāt* is made up of two, three, or four cycles. One cycle consists of standing, bowing, standing again, prostrating oneself, coming up to a sitting position, prostrating oneself once again, and then coming up to a standing or a sitting position, depending on which cycle is being performed.

In the first part of each cycle the person stands with the hands either at the side or folded across the stomach (depending on one's juridical school). God has commanded people to assume the responsibility of the human state, and they reply by standing before Him as servants. The meaning of the standing comes out clearly when it is contrasted with the next two positions: bowing and prostrating oneself. Bowing, Ibn al-ʿArabī remarks, is an isthmus between standing and prostrating.[3] It is highly significant that the Koran employs the verb "to prostrate oneself" most often in the story of the angels prostrating themselves before Adam at God's command, and the refusal of Satan to do the same. Prostration before God is an acknowledgement of His supreme authority. The person expresses in body and soul utter surrender (*islām*) to God's command. Satan incarnates the self-willed and obstinate refusal to accept God's guidance. His motto is *"I am better than he"* (38:76). Seeing Adam as less than himself, Satan did not consider him worthy of prostration. The servant who refuses to prostrate himself before God is saying, "I am better than He."

In the standing position, the servant shares in a divine attribute, since God is *the Living, the Ever-Standing* (2:255). But both the bowing and the prostrating are attributes of the servant, not of the Lord. These two positions share in signifying submissiveness, humbleness, lowliness, and reverential fear (*khuḍūʿ*). As Ibn al-ʿArabī points out, through the prostration, the servant seeks his own origin, which is clay, while through the standing he seeks to return to the root of his positive qualities, which is spirit. Clay is made from water and earth and possesses by right such qualities as lowliness, darkness, density, heaviness, dullness, passivity, ignorance, and death. The spirit is the divine breath, one in substance with the angels. Its inherent qualities include elevation, luminosity, subtlety, lightness, brightness, activity, knowledge, and life. The standing displays one's spiritual nature, the prostration one's bodily nature, and the bowing the intermediate domain of the soul. The three gestures taken together express the servanthood of the total human being.

Although the spirit is high and luminous in relation to the body, it is low and dark in relation to God. Having stood through the spirit, the servant then bows to acknowledge that everything positive in the spirit derives from God. Bowing shows that the servant rejects the thought, "I am better than He," because he knows that whatever he possesses was given to him by his Lord. He rejects the claim to independence that the soul is tempted to make when it finds itself irradiated by the spirit's light and imagines that the light belongs to itself. Among the words that are often recited during the bowing is the sentence, "My hearing, my sight, my brain, my bones, and my nerves have humbled themselves before You." Each of these organs and faculties possesses certain divine qualities that allow the human person to exist, and each will be questioned on the Day of Resurrection.[4] The bowing indicates that the servant gives up all claims to these qualities by recognizing their rootedness in God.

The prostration, then, marks the point where the servant returns to that which belongs to himself, which is clay. Hence, the Sufi authorities maintain that prostration is the outward sign of one of the highest stages of perfection. It is the servant's recognition and experience of his own nothingness. It is his annihilation (*fanāʾ*) in the light of God.

The *ṣalāt* ends in a seated position, which expresses stability in an intermediate stage. Here the servant asks God to bless Muhammad, "Your servant and Your messenger." The sitting position combines the elevation of spirit and messengerhood—acting as God's representative in the world—and the lowliness of body and servanthood. It is the return from the *miʿrāj*, signifying the full actualization of the divine image. It is to subsist in God's attributes after having given up all of one's own attributes. It illustrates the meaning of the Koranic verse, *All that dwells upon the earth is annihilated, and there subsists only the face of your Lord, the Possessor of Majesty and Generosity* (55:26–27).

3

Weeping in Islam and the Sufi Tradition

Weeping is mentioned in a positive light in the Koran, the Hadith, and much of Islamic literature. Anyone who has attended a session of Koran recitation can attest that it is not only an accepted but even an expected phenomenon in Muslim praxis. But what exactly is its significance? If we want answers provided by Muslims, the best place to look is in the writings of the Sufis, who have played the role of depth psychologists and spiritual therapists for most of Islamic history. Two other major schools of thought—jurisprudence and Kalam—have little to say about the inner workings of the soul. As for the philosophers, they aimed at transmuting the soul into pure intelligence and acquiring virtue, but they rarely discussed phenomena associated specifically with religious practice.

The Koran and Hadith

The Koran mentions "weeping" (*bukāʾ* and derivatives) in seven verses and "tears" (*damʿ*) in two more, and these verses become points of reference for much of the later discussion. It praises weeping in connection with the recitation of its own verses: *When it is recited to those who were given knowledge before it . . . they fall down on their faces weeping, and it increases them in humility* (17:107–109). A hadith instructs the believers to weep while they recite the Koran, or at least to try to weep (*tabākī*).[1] Many hadiths speak of the Prophet's own weeping. One tells us that he was reciting the prayers of Abraham (14:36–37) and Jesus (5:118) for their respective communities. Then he lifted up his hands in supplication and said, "O God, my community, my community,!" and he wept. God revealed to him that he would not be disappointed.[2] Another hadith tells us that he wept upon visiting the grave of his mother.[3] Still another says that when his infant son Ibrāhīm died, he wept, and one of his companions said to him, "You too, O Messenger of God?" He replied that he was moved by mercy (*raḥma*). Then he said, "The eye sheds tears and the heart grieves, and we only say what pleases our Lord. O Ibrāhīm, we are grieved at parting from you!"[4]

Once when the Prophet was passing through a village, he saw a woman cooking bread in an open fire while holding her child on her hip. When flames shot up, she quickly jumped back. She later came forward and said, "Is not God *'the Most Merciful of the merciful'* [7:151]?" The Prophet replied that He was. She said, "A mother would never throw her child into the fire." The Prophet bowed his head and wept. Then he said, "God does not chastise any of His servants but the defiant and recalcitrant, those who defy God and refuse to say, 'There is no god but God.' "[5]

Many hadith texts ascribe weeping to the close companion of the Prophet, the first caliph Abū Bakr (d. 13/634). His daughter ʿĀʾisha (d. 58/678), the wife of the Prophet, summed up these sayings as follows: "Abū Bakr was a man who wept much [*bakkāʾ*]—he had no control over his eyes when he would recite the Koran."[6] He seems to be the prototype for the occasional ascetic who is described by the attribute *bakkāʾ*. Despite the opinion of some of the Orientalists, however, there is no evidence that there was a group of people known by this label.[7]

Although weeping is generally praised, some authors view it as a sign of immaturity, and Abū Bakr is also cited as someone who passed beyond the stage of weeping. In his seminal work, *Kashf al-asrār wa-ʿuddat al-abrār* ("The Unveiling of the Secrets and the Provision of the Pious"), one of the longest and most popular commentaries on the Koran in the Persian language, Rashīd al-Dīn Maybudī (d. after 520/1126) explains the meaning of the Koranic verse, *Then your hearts became hardened after that, so they are like stones, or even harder* (2:74), by telling us that there are two sorts of hardening. In the case of the ignorant, hardening means unkindness, cruelty, and distance from God. In the case of those who are pure and knowledgeable, hardening is firmness in knowledge and purity. Then he mentions Abū Bakr: "When he would see people weeping as they listened to the Koran, he used to say, 'I was like that until *hearts became hardened*.' "[8]

Given the dialectical structure of Koranic rhetoric and Islamic thinking in general, one can hardly speak of weeping without mentioning laughter (*ḍiḥk*).[9] The Koran suggests that the two need to be understood as one of the many cosmic pairs: *Surely it is He who makes to laugh and makes to weep, it is He who makes to die and makes to live, it is He who created the two kinds, male and female* (53:43–45). That there is something archetypal about laughter and weeping is indicated in a hadith about the Prophet's *miʿrāj*. When he reached the first heaven, he saw Adam sitting with two large groups of people, one on each side. When Adam looked to his right, he would laugh, and when he looked to his left, he would weep.[10] The Koran places *the companions of the right hand* (56:38) in paradise and *the companions of the left hand* (56:41) in hell.

The Koran alerts the enemies of the believers—who often take the latter as objects of "mockery" (*istihzāʾ*) and "derision" (*sukhriyya*)—to the fact that they should actually be weeping: *Do you wonder at this talk? Do you laugh and not weep?* (53:59–60). A frequently cited hadith makes a similar point: "Were you to know what I know, you would laugh little and weep much."[11] The Prophet also said, "Avoid much laughter, for much laughter deadens the heart."[12] Although I have not seen it mentioned, the corollary seems obvious: "Weep much, for much weeping enlivens the heart." Despite the praise of tears throughout the literature, however, the hadiths attribute laughter to the Prophet far more often than weeping.

If the Koran makes it clear that weeping is an appropriate attribute of the believers in this world, it also says that laughter will be their attribute in the next world: *Today the believers will be laughing at the unbelievers* (83:34). The Koran also associates laughter with the experience of the beatific vision: *Some faces on that day shall shine, laughing, joyous; some faces on that day shall be dusty, overspread with grime* (80:38–41). Even more interesting, the hadith literature tells us that God laughs. According to one report, God laughs at the despondency of someone whose fortune is about to change. When asked if God really laughs, the Prophet replied that He does, and a companion remarked, "We will lack no good from a Lord who laughs."[13]

Another hadith tells us that after the resurrection, a certain person will keep on pleading with God not to throw him into hell, and God will agree on condition that he not ask for anything more. The man breaks his promise, and God moves him closer to paradise, again extracting the promise that he will not ask for more. This happens several times. Finally, God laughs and places him in paradise. In one of the several versions of this hadith, the famous companion of the Prophet, Ibn Masʿūd (d. 31/652), concludes it like this:

> The man will say, "Are You making fun of me, and You are the Lord of the worlds?" Then Ibn Masʿūd laughed. He said, "Will you not ask me why I laughed?" They said, "Why?" He said, "God's Messenger laughed like this, and they asked him, 'Why do you laugh, O Messenger of God?' He answered, 'Because of the laughter of the Lord of the worlds when he said, 'Are you making fun of me, and You are the Lord of the worlds?' ' "[14]

Another hadith tells us that the prophets and their communities will be waiting for God to appear on the Day of Resurrection. When God reaches Muhammad's community, He will ask them why they are standing there, and they will say that they are waiting for their Lord. He will tell them that He is their Lord, and they will ask Him to show Himself: "Then He will disclose Himself to them, laughing."[15]

Early Sufism

When the early Sufi teachers mention weeping, one of their first concerns is to classify its causes. The Koran speaks of people weeping as the result of the "recognition" (*maʿrifa*) of the truth (*ḥaqq*) of the recited Koran: *When they hear what has been sent down upon the Messenger, you see that their eyes overflow with tears because of the truth that they recognize* (5:83). In commenting on this verse, Ibn ʿAṭāʾ (d. 310/922) adds four other positive qualities of the soul that may cause weeping: joy, regret, fear, and burning (*ḥurqa*), the last of which is the agony of being separate from the Beloved.[16] The Sufi manuals mention weeping but rarely give it a separate discussion. One exception is provided in the *Kitāb al-lumaʿ* ("The Book of Flashes") by Abū Naṣr al-Sarrāj (d. 378/988). In a miscellany toward the end of the book, he cites weeping as a significant topic and quotes the words of Abū Saʿīd al-Kharrāz (d. 286/899), who divides weeping into eighteen types according to three categories: from God, toward God, and over God. Weeping from God is fear of God's chastisement and grief at being kept apart from Him. Weeping toward God is the yearning of lovers to meet their Beloved. Weeping over God results from separation "after arrival or from the joy of arrival, when the seeker is enveloped by God's embrace like a child being nursed by his mother."[17]

As the Sufi authors began to put together more systematic works, one of their favorite genres was the description of the stages of spiritual growth. They offered diverse schemes describing the "stations" (*maqāmāt, manāzil*) on the path to God, typically enumerating them in terms of archetypal numbers—seven, ten, twelve, forty, and one hundred. Rarely do they single out weeping as a specific stage, although it often comes up in passing. Only when we look at some of the more complex meditations on the stations does weeping enter into the title headings. In the *Mashrab al-arwāḥ* ("The Drinking Places of the Spirits") Rūzbihān Baqlī (d. 606/1209) describes 1,001 stations in twenty categories of fifty stations each, capped by the realization of full perfection. Five of the stations are named after weeping: weeping, the drying up of weeping, weeping from the Real for the Real, weeping in laughter, and weeping in ecstasy. "Weeping," Rūzbihān tells us, "takes place in over a thousand stations," and this may suggest why it is rarely singled out for a separate discussion.[18]

Ghazālī has no separate discussion on weeping in his *Iḥyāʾ*. He gives the topic some attention, however, in the third section of its fourth and last part, which is dedicated to fear (*khawf*) and hope (*rajāʾ*). These two are often mentioned in the Koran and are frequently discussed in the Sufi manuals. Although he cites one of the early Sufis to the effect that fear and hope are the two wings of the soul in its flight to God, he devotes most of the chapter to fear. In doing so, he mentions many examples of weeping by the Prophet, his companions, and the pious. He tells us that those who fear God's justice, severity, and wrath will find it easy to perform the ritual obligations and to obey the revealed law, for "Fear is that which encourages good deeds, dulls the appetites, and discourages the heart from depending on this world."[19] His explanation of why he does not stress hope throws light on the whole tradition:

> It is best to let fear dominate over hope—only, however, until the imminent approach of death. At the time of death, it is best to let hope and a good opinion of God predominate, for fear plays the

role of a whip encouraging activity, and now the time for activity has passed. The person near death is not able to act and he cannot endure the causes of fear, for they would break his heart and hurry his death. As for the spirit of hope, that will strengthen his heart and make him love his Lord, in whom he hopes. No one should depart this world without loving God and loving to encounter Him. For, [as the Prophet said,] "When someone loves to encounter God, God loves to encounter him." Love is linked to hope, for when someone hopes for something from someone, he considers him beloved. And the goal in all knowledge and all practice is to recognize God, so that recognition may give rise to love.[20]

Ibn al-ʿArabī has relatively little to say about weeping in his *al-Futūḥāt al-makkiyya* ("The Meccan Openings"). He devotes only one of its 560 chapters specifically to the topic, namely the short chapter 313, "On the knowledge of the station of weeping and wailing." This chapter focuses on the role of the prophets in their communities and touches only briefly on weeping itself. He tells us that the prophets have achieved the station of perfect servanthood (*ʿubūdiyya*), which demands being empty of self and full of the Divine Presence. God, however, has made them His representatives, so they must make manifest the attributes of lordship (*rubūbiyya*) and divine authority. Making God's attributes manifest introduces a certain duality into their relationship with Him, for in effect they are setting themselves up as minor gods. Outwardly they display lordship and remain far from God, but inwardly they remain His servants and stay near to Him. They weep because of God-wariness and caution (*ḥadhar*), for they fear not giving the station of religious obligation (*taklīf*) its rightful due. In support of this interpretation, Ibn al-ʿArabī cites Muhammad's saying, "I am more wary of God than any of you, and I have the most knowledge."[21] He rightly points out that the Prophet said this after his companions remarked on his extraordinary exertion in acts of worship, even though this Koranic verse had already come down: *Surely We have given you [O Muhammad] a clear victory, that God may forgive you your former and your latter sins* (48:1–2).[22]

Elsewhere in the *Futūḥāt*, Ibn al-ʿArabī comments on the verse, *These are they whom God has blessed among the prophets . . . . When the signs of the All-Merciful were recited to them, they fell down prostrate, weeping* (19:58). In this case, he says, the prophets wept in joy, for the signs of the "All-merciful" reached them. After all, "Mercy does not demand severity and magnificence, but gentleness and tenderness."[23]

Several times Ibn al-ʿArabī comments on a saying of Abū Yazīd Basṭāmī (d. ca. 260/874), "I laughed for a time, I wept for a time, and now I neither laugh nor weep." Generally, he understands this as a reference to Abū Yazīd's having reached "the station of no station" (*maqām lā maqām*), the level of spiritual perfection in which the divine image has been fully actualized and absolute servanthood has been achieved.[24] In one passage, he invokes the saying in a legal discussion: if someone laughs while performing the *ṣalāt*, does this invalidate the prayer? Most jurists hold that it does. Ibn al-ʿArabī says that it depends on the state of the person. If the person is heedless of God, then laughter will invalidate the prayer. But if the person is receptive to the self-disclosure (*tajallī*) of God within the Koranic verses that he is reciting, laughter will simply display the appropriate response. This is why Abū Yazīd, who had been completely overcome by the Koran, would sometimes laugh and sometimes weep:

> During the Koran recitation in the *ṣalāt*, the states of people with God are diverse—if they are among the folk of God, those who ponder the Koran. One verse makes them sad, so they weep; another verse makes them happy, so they laugh; still another verse astonishes them, so they neither laugh nor weep. One verse bestows a knowledge, another verse makes them ask for forgiveness and engage in supplication.[25]

In another passage, Ibn al-ʿArabī confirms that God's self-disclosure determines whether a saint will laugh or weep. He mentions as examples two men whom he has met, though he makes it clear, both here and elsewhere, that such people are rare:

> There is a self-disclosure that causes laughter. I have never seen anyone in this path who was among the folk of laughter except for one man, who was called ʿAlī al-Salāwī. I journeyed with him and was his companion in both travel and town in Andalusia. He never ceased laughing, like someone enraptured who comes to his senses only occasionally. I never saw him say anything sinful. As for the weepers, I have seen only one of them: Yūsuf al-Mughāwir al-Jallā in the year 586 [1190] in Seville. He accompanied us and was showing his states to us. He was in great anguish, and his weeping never lapsed. I was his companion when I was also the companion of the laugher.[26]

Theological Implications

If everything derives from the Real and returns to the Real, tears are no exception. Given that both laughter and weeping derive from God, we can ask if they pertain to the Divine Itself, or if God brings them into existence only in created things. We have seen that the hadith literature offers examples of God's laughter, but nowhere does Islamic literature, so far as I know, suggest that God weeps. There is a definite disproportion between laughter and weeping. The first is a divine attribute, the second is not; both are attributes of creatures. As creaturely attributes, neither of the two is good in itself, but, by and large, weeping is praised and laughter blamed.

Given that God laughs and is the cause of laughter and weeping, we might derive three divine names, though they are not mentioned in the standard lists:

He who Laughs, the Bestower of Laughter, and the Bestower of Weeping.[27] These partake of the same structural relationship as three names commonly mentioned by the theologians: the Living (*al-ḥayy*), the Life-Giver (*al-muḥyī*), and the Death-Giver (*al-mumīt*). God is the Living who never dies, but all things in the universe are constantly shifting mixtures of life and death.[28] So also, it would seem, God is the laugher who never weeps, but all things in the universe are mixtures of laughter and weeping. In the same way, *God is the light of the heavens and the earth* (24:35) and *He made the darknesses and the light* (6:1). The Koran is then *A Book We have sent down to bring the people forth from the darknesses to the light* (14:1), that is, from death to life, from ignorance to knowledge, from tears to laughter. Only in joining with God can death, sadness, and suffering be overcome.

If the tradition suggests that weeping is more appropriate for the soul than laughter, this is because human beings are by definition separate from God and immersed in death and darkness. According to Koran 2:31, God created Adam and taught him all the names. This is simply to say that God has a special regard for human beings, not that happiness is guaranteed. Weeping appears as the natural response to the human awareness of distance from the Creator, who is the Source of all being, good, consciousness, and joy.

Ibn al-ʿArabī explains that people are divided into two basic sorts, as suggested by Koran 11:105, which tells us that in the next world they will be either wretched (*shaqī*) or felicitous (*saʿīd*): "In this world, the attributes that the wretched will have in the next world appear in the felicitous—that is, grief, affliction, weeping, abasement, and submissiveness." As for the attributes that the felicitous will have in paradise, such as happiness and joy, they appear now in those who will end up as wretched.[29]

One might object that weeping may stem not only from grief and suffering, but also from mercy and compassion, as indicated in various hadiths. If God sent Muhammad as *a mercy to the worlds* (21:107) and is "the Most Merciful of the merciful" whose mercy *embraces all things* (7:156), surely He should weep in sympathy for the suffering of His creatures. But Islamic theology stresses the divine qualities of the human rather than the human qualities of the divine. As Muhammad is instructed to say in the Koran, *I am but a mortal like you* (18:110). It is true that Muhammad manifests the divine attribute of mercy, but God does not display the all too human weakness of tears.

Moreover, to suggest that God weeps would be to give too much credit to the human standpoint relative to the timeless, God's-eye view of things. God creates the universe out of mercy, love, and wisdom. A *ḥadīth qudsī* or "Sacred Tradition" tells us that the inscription on His Throne, upon which the All-Merciful is sitting (20:5), reads, "My mercy takes precedence over My wrath." The disproportion between mercy and wrath does not allow God to weep—not even in the anthropomorphic imagery employed by much of the hadith literature—for God sees that in fact all is well. Thus Ibn al-ʿArabī cites a hadith that tells us God will take "the two handfuls"—the blessed and the damned, the felicitous and the wretched—and cast one handful into paradise and the other into hell, each time saying, "I don't care" (*lā ubālī*). Why should God not care, given that He is throwing a vast group of people into pain and suffering? Because, Ibn al-ʿArabī tells us, His mercy embraces all things, even those who end up in the deepest pit of the Fire, for "The final issue of both [handfuls] will be at mercy, and that is why He does not care."[30]

Maybudī on Weeping

Any attempt at a serious review of the role of weeping in Islamic literature would demand a major monograph. Sufi poetry alone provides countless examples. Let me instead provide a few samples of typical discussions from Maybudī's aforementioned Koran commentary, *Kashf al-asrār*. Maybudī divides his explanation of verses into three stages: literal Persian translation, detailed exposition of the diverse opinions of the early authorities, and "allusions" (*ishārāt*) to the inner meanings of the text. The third stage, in contrast to the first two, offers some of the most beautiful prose passages in the Persian language. The book provides a foretaste of the imagery that will soon come to predominate in the poetical traditions of Persian, Turkish, and the Indic languages—traditions that became the major vehicles for the Koranic worldview in the vast majority of the Islamic world.

Maybudī well understands that weeping may have a variety of causes. He suggests some of them in his remarks on Koran 17:109:

> Weeping is the state of the beginners and the attribute of the travelers—each person according to his own state and every traveler in the measure of his own activity. The repenter looks upon his own sin and weeps in fear of punishment. The obedient person looks upon his own defective obedience and weeps in fear of falling short. The worshiper weeps in fear of the outcome: "What will be done with me tomorrow?" The knower looks at the beginningless precedent and weeps: "What was done to me and decreed for me in eternity without beginning?" All this happens in the path of the travelers and is a sign of the weakness of their state. As for those who have been stolen away from themselves and achieved stability, for them weeping is an imperfection and a defect in their path. Thus it is related that Junayd [d. 298/910] was sitting with his wife and Shiblī [d. 334/946] entered. His wife wanted to cover herself, but Junayd said to her, "Shiblī is not aware of you, so sit." Junayd kept speaking to her, and then Shiblī wept. When Shiblī began to weep, Junayd said to his wife, "Cover yourself, for Shiblī has come back from absence to awareness."[31]

Like others, Maybudī sees both laughter and weeping as appropriate signs of sanctity. He explains this in the context of Koran 2:180, which instructs believers to prepare last wills and testaments. The rich leave behind their property, but the poor in spirit leave behind their stations, among which are laughter and weeping:

> The disobedient person fears for himself because of his bad deeds, but the knower fears for himself ten times as much because of the sincerity of his deeds and the limpidness of his states. There is, however, a difference between the two: the disobedient person fears the outcome and is afraid of punishment, but the knower fears God's majesty and manifestation. The fear of the knower is called "awe," and the fear of the disobedient is called "fright." . . .
>
> Awe is a fear that puts no veil before supplication, no blindfold over perspicacity, and no wall before hope. It is a fear that melts and kills. As long as the awestruck person does not hear the call, *"Do not fear and do not grieve"* [41:30], he does not relax. . . .
>
> Bishr Ḥāfī [d. ca. 227/841] began weeping and wailing when he was near death. They said, "O Abū Naṣr, do you love life?," [in other words], "Is it that you love life and you dislike death?" He said, "No, but stepping forth to God is hard." . . .
>
> There is another group who come forward to the disclosure of God's beauty and gentleness at the time of going. The lightning of intimacy flashes and the fire of yearning flames up. . . . Makḥūl Shāmī was a manly man, unique in his era, and overcome by the pain and grief of this tale. He never laughed. During his dying illness a group came to see him and he was laughing. They said, "O shaykh! You were always full of grief. Right now, grief is even more fitting for you. Why are you laughing?"
>
> He said, "Why should I not laugh? The sun of separation has reached the top of the wall, and the day for which I have been waiting has arrived. The doors of heaven are open and the angels are clearing the way: 'Makḥūl is coming to the Presence!' "[32]

In commenting on Koran 2:238, which commands people to be watchful over their daily prayers, Maybudī provides a long mythic disquisition that ascribes the origin of each of the five prayers to one of the prophets. He tells us that Adam, the first human being and the first prophet, was also the first to perform the morning prayer, in gratitude for the passing of night:

> When he came from heaven to earth, it was the end of the day. As long as he saw the brightness of the day, he had a bit of ease, but when the sun was concealed, Adam's heart became a mine of grief. . . . He had never seen night, nor had he suffered darkness and grief. Suddenly he saw the darkness that reaches the whole world, and he was a stranger, ill, and separate from his wife. In that darkness he sometimes sighed,

sometimes turned his face toward the moon, sometimes whispered silently to the Threshold. . . .

The first of all strangers was Adam, the forerunner of all those who grieve was Adam, the father of all the weepers was Adam. It was Adam who laid the foundation of love in the world and Adam who set down the custom of night vigils. He established the tradition of moaning in the pain of separation and crying in the middle of the night. . . .

At last, when the breeze of dawn began to breathe like a lover and when the army of morning burst forth from its ambush and clamored against the darkness of night, Gabriel came with the good news, "O Adam! Morning has come, peace has come! Light has come, joy has come! Brightness has come, familiarity has come! Arise, O Adam, and recite two cycles of prayer in this state—one in gratitude for the passing of the night of separation and distance, one in gratitude for the morning breath of good fortune and union."[33]

Maybudī typically associates weeping with the fire of love and the burning of the heart. In commenting on Koran 2:257, *God is the friend of those who have faith,* he begins by explaining why God is kinder and gentler to the weak than to the strong, and he cites the saying of God, related by the Prophet, "I am with those whose hearts are broken for Me." Then he provides various tales to illustrate the point:

It has been reported that on the Day of Resurrection, one of the broken and burnt will be taken to the Presence. God will say, "My servant, what do you have?"

He will say, "Two empty hands, a heart full of pain, and a spirit troubled and bewildered by the waves of grief and woe."

He will say, "Go right ahead into the house of My friends, for I love the broken and grieving." . . .

David said, "O God, I take it that I must wash my limbs with water to purify them of defilement. With what shall I wash my heart so that it may be purified of other than You?"

The command came: "O David! Wash the heart with the water of regret and grief so that you may reach the greatest purification."

He said, "O God, where can I find this grief?"

He said, "We Ourselves will send the grief. The stipulation is that you stick to those who are grieving and broken."

He said, "O God, what is their mark?"

He said, "They wait all day for the sun to go down and for the curtain of night to descend. Then they begin to knock on the door of the cell of *We are nearer to him than the jugular vein* [50:16]. Burning, weeping, and sighing all night, full of neediness and melting, their heads placed on the ground, they call on Us with longing voice: 'O Lord, O Lord!' " . . .

From the All-Compeller the call comes: "O Gabriel and Michael! Leave aside the murmur of glorification, for I hear the sound of someone burning. Although he has the load of disobedience, in his heart he has the tree of faith. He was kneaded with the water and clay of love for Me."

"From the day they came into existence until the Day of Resurrection, the proximate angels have placed their hands on the belt of serving Me. They observe My every command and burn in hope for one glance. But then they put the fingers of longing in the mouth of bewilderment: 'What is this? We do the service, and the love goes there! We do the running and rushing, and they have the arrival and seeing!' "

The Exaltation of Unity answers them with the description of esteem: "This work is done by burning and grief, and they are the mine of burning and the quarry of grief":

> Without the perfection of pain and burning,
> don't mention the name "religion."
> Without the beauty of desire for union,
> never lean upon faith.
> On the day of arrival, sacrifice
> your wretched, bleeding heart
> only to the spirit-catching, curling tresses
> of the Beloved.[34]

4

A Shādhilī Presence in Shiʿite Islam

Just as in the hadith literature of Sunni Islam there are many prayers, supplications, and litanies of the Prophet that form the basis for Sunni prayer to this day, so also in the annals of Shiʿism are there numerous prayers recorded from the Prophet and the Shiʿite Imams which throughout history have formed the basis of Shiʿite prayer.

Among the best-known of these prayers, most of which are recorded in the standard Shiʿite prayer book, *Mafātīḥ al-jinān* ("The Keys to the Gardens of Paradise"), is the *Duʿāʾ al-ʿArafa* ("The Prayer of the Day of ʿArafa") by the third Imam, Ḥusayn b. ʿAlī (d. 61/680).[1] This prayer, famous for its great beauty and spiritual nature, is read and chanted by pious Shiʿites every year on the day of ʿArafa during the Hajj—when the prayer was initially recited by the Imam—as well as at other times throughout the year. It also plays a particularly important role in Shiʿite gnosis, and the great philosopher/mystics, such as Mullā Ṣadrā (d. 1050/1640), often refer to it in their works.

In the Arabic text Imam Ḥusayn's prayer covers about thirty pages. When one is reading it, there is a sudden and noticeable change of style in the last three or four pages. The language and concepts of the long first section are presented in a type of synthetic exposition very similar to that found in the sayings of the Prophet, whereas the last few pages present a more analytic exposition along with explicit references to gnostic and mystical themes. When I asked a well-known contemporary Shiʿite sage about this sudden change in style, I was told that undoubtedly the Imam recited the last part of the prayer only for some of his select disciples.

There is, in any case, no doubt that many outstanding theologians and philosophers of Shiʿism have considered this section of the prayer to be an integral part of it. For example, Mullā Muḥsin Fayḍ Kāshānī (d. ca. 1091/1680), the son-in-law of Mullā Ṣadrā and one of the great figures of the school of Isfahan, quotes from it a number of times in his *Kalimāt-i maknūna* ("The Hidden Words")[2]; and Mullā Hādī Sabziwārī (d. 1289/1872), the famous philosopher/mystic of the Qajar period, refers to it in many of his works.[3]

Nevertheless, it is interesting to note the comment of ʿĀllamā Majlisī (d. 1111/1699) on Imam Ḥusayn's prayer. This well-known theologian and jurisprudent of the Safavid period is the compiler of the monumental encyclopedia of Shiʿite Hadith known as the *Biḥār al-anwār* ("The Oceans of Lights"). In this collection, after quoting the text of the prayer from the *Iqbāl al-aʿmāl* ("On Religious Devotions") of Ibn Ṭāʾūs (d. 664/1266), Majlisī remarks as follows:

> Al-Kafʿamī [d. 905/1500] has included this prayer in his *al-Balad al-amīn* ["The Secure City"] and Ibn Ṭāʾūs in [his other work] *Miṣbāḥ al-zāʾir* ["The Visitor's Lamp"] . . . but in these works the last folio is not found, from the words, "My God . . ." to the end of the prayer. Likewise, this part of the prayer is not found in some of the old manuscripts of the *Iqbāl*, and the sentences of this folio are not completely in agreement with the style of the prayers belonging to the inerrant members of the Household of the Prophet; rather, they are in keeping with the taste of the Sufis. Therefore, certain of the ulama have believed that this folio was added to the text afterward, and was composed by one of the Sufi shaykhs.
>
> In short, this addition was either included by one of the sources used by Ibn Ṭāʾūs, or it was added later—this second possibility being more likely, as is indicated by the fact that it is not found in some old manuscripts and in the *Miṣbāḥ al-zāʾir*. And God knows best the realities of things.[4]

Despite this reservation by one of the foremost Shiʿite scholars of hadith, the whole of this prayer is included in the standard prayer books and recited on appropriate occasions, undoubtedly because the content of the whole prayer, including the last and doubtful portion, is so much in keeping with Shiʿite spirituality.

As to the source of this addition, the famous *Ḥikam* ("Wisdoms") of the Shādhilī Sufi master Ibn ʿAṭāʾ Allāh al-Iskandarī (d. 709/1309) provides the answer, for the "intimate conversations" (*munājāt*) appended to them are, in fact, the same as the last part of the Imam's prayer.[5] A comparison with the Arabic text of the *munājāt*[6] shows that the prayer follows this text almost word for word.

Ibn Ṭāʾūs died about fifty years before Ibn ʿAṭāʾ Allāh, which might tempt one to guess that the prayer does in fact belong to Imam Ḥusayn and that Ibn ʿAṭāʾ Allāh used to recite it, although his disciples thought that he had composed it himself. But the fact that some prominent Shiʿites themselves have doubts about its attribution to the Imam, that the style of the Imam's prayer changes abruptly in the last section, and that early manuscripts of the only work in which this part of the prayer is attributed to Imam Ḥusayn do not contain it,[7] all contribute to making it relatively certain that Ibn ʿAṭāʾ Allāh is in fact the author. Additionally, one can conclude from the earlier findings of both Victor Danner and Paul Nwyia that Ibn ʿAṭāʾ Allāh's authorship of the prayer has never been called into question.

It is thus interesting to note how Shiʿism has adopted as its own an expression of the spirituality of one of the great shaykhs of Sunni Islam. Certainly, any Shiʿite who has been touched by the grace of this prayer would reply that, in any case, it is in fact Imam Ḥusayn—himself a link in the Shādhilī initiatic chain (*silsila*)—who inspired Ibn ʿAṭāʾ Allāh.

5

The Pluralistic Vision of Persian Sufi Poetry

When asked to address the question of religious pluralism in Persia, many people familiar with Persian literature would immediately think of a well-known strophic poem by Hātif Iṣfahānī (d. 1198/1783), a minor poet who died at the beginning of the Qajar period. Like most of the later poets, Hātif has remained largely unknown and unread. However, his strophic poem has become rather famous. In five stanzas, for a total of about ninety verses, it celebrates the unity of God in the standard imagery of Sufism.

God's unity may not strike most people as something to sing about. But the Persian language has a long poetical tradition of doing just that. What separates such poetry from theology is the extraordinarily vivid, evocative, and beautiful language that is employed, a language that invariably focuses on love as the key to understanding.

Each of the five stanzas of Hātif's poem ends with a refrain that is half Persian and half Arabic:

> He is one and there is nothing but He,
> He alone, no god but He.[1]

Even though few Persian poets have been as outspoken as Hātif on the issue of religious pluralism, what he says fits perfectly into the tradition. I will come back to the poem, but I first need to address a few general issues that can help us understand why Hātif can be taken as a fair example of a general pluralistic vision in the poetical tradition.

Let me begin by saying something about the role of Sufism in Persian Islam. The term Sufism has a complex and controversial history, and I cannot begin to do justice to it here.[2] Scholars often try to simplify the task of defining the word by replacing it with another word, such as "mysticism," or "esoterism," or "spirituality." However, these words are just as much in need of definition as is Sufism itself, so I prefer to keep a word that has an Arabic pedigree.

I use the word Sufism in the way that it has been understood by a large body of Muslims over the past thousand years throughout the Islamic world, from Africa to China. In this understanding, the Islamic tradition is like a walnut. Sufism is like the walnut's kernel, and the ritual, legal, and social teachings of Islam are like its husk. The kernel is the living essence, and the husk functions to protect and preserve the kernel. Without the kernel, the husk is hollow and worthless, and without the husk, the kernel cannot develop and mature. In this simile, the Sufi kernel is understood as a body of teachings and practices designed to help seekers of God experience the transformation of their own souls. The goal is conformity with the divine qualities that God instilled into human beings when He created them in His own image.

As for the relationship between Sufism and Persian poetry, we should first recall that over the last thousand years, the Persian language has witnessed a host of major and minor poets, even though few of them have been translated into Western languages. Many if not most of these poets were either explicit representatives of the Sufi tradition, or implicit exponents of Sufi teachings. The simple reason for this is that the Sufi tradition was instrumental in molding the imagery, symbolism, metaphors, tropes, and indeed the worldview that informs all but the earliest Persian poetry. If we can grasp the Sufi worldview, we can quickly understand two things: first, why it is that poetry is especially appropriate for the expression of Sufism; and second, why a certain tendency toward religious pluralism is inherent in the Sufi perspective.

In the general Islamic view of things, the universe is understood as "everything other than God." This includes not only physical things, but also spiritual things. According to the common Sufi image that has already been employed, the universe can be pictured as kernel and husk. The kernel represents the invisible realm, which is the domain of souls, spirits, and angels; the husk represents the visible realm, which is the domain of sense perception and bodily things. The kernel is essentially light, life, knowledge, and awareness; the husk is essentially darkness, death, ignorance, and unconsciousness. The kernel is meaning, the husk is expression and form. The kernel is the domain of unity, sameness, coherence, peace, and harmony; the husk is the domain of multiplicity, difference, incoherence, strife, and disharmony.

If we look at the universe in relation to God, God is the kernel, and the universe is the husk. In other words, relative to God, both spirits and bodies are husks. But, if we look at the universe in relation to our own human embodiment, then the physical realm is the husk, the spiritual realm is the kernel, and God is the kernel of the kernel.

Human beings play a unique role in the economy of the cosmos because they alone were created in God's full image. Everything other than human beings is a partial image of God. In other words, other creatures are parts of the kernel or parts of the husk. Human beings alone were created as equivalent to the whole nut, embracing both kernel and husk. As a result, only human beings have full access to the kernel of the kernel, or as Rumi often calls this ultimate kernel, "the spirit of the spirit," or "the life of life" (*jān-i jān*).

In this way of looking at things, everything in the universe has a proper role to play, and human beings have the unique role of coordinating and harmonizing all of creation. But human beings cannot play their proper role by focusing their efforts on the domain of husks, because that would be a never-ending and impossible task. They can only live up to their human potential by devoting themselves here and now to the kernel. If they can find their own kernel and then move on to the kernel of the kernel, all things can be put in their proper places.

This bifurcation of religious attention has deep roots in God's creativity. After all, God created both kernel and husk, both spiritual and corporeal realms. Human beings have spirits and bodies. Both sides of the human person need to be nurtured and cultivated. God sent the prophets to act as guides in this bipolar development. The prophets brought practices, rituals, rules, and regulations to keep the bodily, social, and political domains healthy and whole, and they brought wisdom, insight, and transforming grace to bring about the growth of the spirit. The various schools of Islamic teaching and practice focus on different dimensions of this task. Both theological dogma and social and ritual practices are concerned with protecting and strengthening the husk. In contrast, Sufi teachings focus on encouraging the growth of the kernel.

Given the bipolar nature of the universe and the human self, much of Islamic theology depicts God Himself in bipolar terms.[3] As the Koran puts it, God has "two hands." He is both merciful and wrathful, gentle and severe, majestic and beautiful, or, in more abstract terms, both transcendent and immanent. In the view of the Persian poets, the drama of human life is played out in the tension between the bipolar qualities of the universe, which manifest the simultaneous transcendence and immanence of God. The poets constantly sing about God's mercy and wrath, but they use the imagery of roses and thorns, day and night, spring and autumn, drunkenness and sobriety, union and separation, laughter and tears, sugar and vinegar.

Beyond the polarities, the poets find the reality of love. Love alone is able to bring together all contradictory qualities and to reinstate them in God's unity. The use of the word *love* (*ʿishq*) in preference to any other shows that this reinstatement can only be achieved by the transformation of the soul, not simply by theorizing and theologizing. Only love, among all human experiences, has the universality and open-endedness to suggest something of the nature of the ultimate transfiguration that is the goal of human life.

In short, God is both merciful and wrathful, both immanent and transcendent. His mercy is associated with kernels, roses, angels, daytime, union, spring, laughter, and joy. His wrath is associated with husks, thorns, devils, night, separation, autumn, sobriety, tears, and heartache. As for love, it welcomes whatever comes from God, whether roses or thorns. This helps explain why a poet like

Rūmī can celebrate separation and pain almost as much as he celebrates union and joy. Take for example his verses:

> Pains are an alchemy that renews—
> who can be bored when pain appears?
> Beware, do not sigh coldly in boredom—
> seek pain, seek pain, pain, pain![4]

Although Sufi teachers acknowledge that God created the universe in terms of His own bipolar attributes, they also recognize that the two poles are not equal. The simple reason for this is that the pole of mercy manifests the unitary nature of God's reality, whereas wrath comes into play only in terms of the multiplicity of creation. The dominant theological perspective of Sufism is exemplified in the *hadīth qudsī* we encountered in Chapter 3, "My mercy takes precedence over My wrath." In other words, God's mercy, gentleness, and compassion are more real and basic to the divine nature than wrath, severity, and judgment. Mercy pertains to God's essential, unitary Self, but wrath comes into play only after distinctions are made among God's diverse names and attributes. Unity will triumph over multiplicity, and mercy will have the final say. Wrath can only be a passing phenomenon, contingent upon difference, separation, and ignorance.

If we look at God and the universe together, then God, who is the kernel of the kernel, is pure mercy, because mercy is the essential description of God's unitary Self. In contrast, the universe, which is multiple, is a domain of mercy mixed with wrath. Within the universe, the kernel is closely allied with mercy, and the husk is closely bound up with the manifestation of wrath. Of course, there is also plenty of mercy in the husk, but only in the husk does wrath play a significant role, because the husk is the realm of bipolarity, multiplicity, difference, differentiation, conflict, and strife.

No one can find the kernel, which is the realm of peace, harmony, wholeness, and mercy, without taking the husk into account. This means that God's wrath and severity have real manifestations in human lives. For the sake of prudence and caution, it is best to ignore the fact that God's mercy takes precedence over His wrath, because we cannot know how long it will take for mercy to show its full effects. What we do know is that we live in a world of strife and difference, and we are constantly being forced to make choices. It is important to make the right choices, and to do so we need clear instructions and explicit differentiations based upon divine guidance, which is embodied in the prophets and their messages.

Many of the Sufi authorities were extremely concerned with the husk—make no mistake about that. There are numerous prose treatises written by Sufis detailing the difference between right and wrong activity and explaining the necessity of distinguishing between true and false teachings. People can adhere to the divine image latent in their own souls only if they discern between truth and falsehood, observe ritual obligations, and follow ethical guidance. Nonetheless, when the Sufis wrote poetry, they employed it mainly to do what poetry does best, and that is to sing and to celebrate. What is being celebrated is God's unitary reality, which demands the precedence of mercy. Love is then understood as a unifying divine power that is the unique prerogative of human beings, who alone were created in the full image of God.

The poets frequently remind us that love cannot be explained, only experienced. We all know this—at least all of us who have been in love. Theologically, part of the reason for this is that love pertains to the kernel of the kernel. Love is the experience of the realm of unity, mercy, sameness, and union. The Sufis sometimes call this experience "drunkenness" and "intoxication," because it results in the perception of sameness and divine immanence dominating over difference and transcendence. Distinctions among things are effaced because God is seen to be present in everything. Nonetheless, intoxication is not appropriate for the realm of husks, because here sobriety is the norm, and sobriety demands explanation and rational articulation, for which prose is the ideal vehicle. Poetry, in contrast, does not "explain," it points. It expresses the precedence of mercy by evoking an experience and calling forth love, and it does this by the magic of beautiful language, enticing imagery, and intoxicating rhythm.

Sufi poetry, then, is a celebration of love, a hymn to unity and union, a song of rejoicing that invites the listener to taste the eternal wine. It is not the place for making divisions, but rather for reveling in the universal presence of God. Rational categories split hairs, but poetry celebrates the Beloved's flowing tresses in all their beauty and splendor. To the extent that the poets address issues of religious pluralism, they do so within the context of the comprehensive divine mercy that invites all creatures to return to the kernel of the kernel.

This does not mean that the Sufi poets were nice, liberal, tolerant pluralists in any modern sense. They celebrated the unity of the kernel without forgetting the differentiation and conflict that pertain to the husk. They were fully aware that no one can possess the kernel unless the husk is treated in the proper manner. They knew that this demanded following the divine guidance as embodied in the prophets. For them, there was no contradiction between pluralism and exclusivism. Pluralism pertains to the kernel and the realm of intoxication, and exclusivism pertains to the husk and sobriety. Sufi pluralism recognized the unity of all humanity in God's creative act, and it acknowledged the unanimity of all the prophets in God's guidance. But Sufi exclusivism meant that the teachers and poets recognized significant differences in the domain of husks. In practice, they were Muslims like other Muslims. They had the standard Koranic preconceptions about other religions. In no sense did they think the husk was indifferent, or that all husks were equal. They were certain of the superiority of their own husk because it had allowed them to find the kernel of the kernel.

At the same time, the Sufi poets were completely aware that divine mercy and forgiveness take precedence over wrath and punishment, that God knows and that we do not know, and that there is no possible way to make final judgments about anyone. Final judgment belongs only to God, and He judges in His own good time and according to His standards, not ours. The only thing we can be absolutely sure about is God's unity and the precedence of His mercy.

Let me come back to Hātif, the poet with whom I began. His five-stanza poem is a perfect exemplar of the Sufi worldview that I have just described. In the second stanza, he uses the example of Christianity, but he clearly has in mind the same principle that Rūmī expresses in his well-known line:

> It is from the viewpoint, O marrow of existence,
> that disagreements arise among Muslim, Zoroastrian, and Jew.[5]

The second stanza addresses the issue of religious pluralism rather explicitly:

> With You, O Friend, I will never break my bond,
> though they cut me with sword, limb from limb.
> In truth, a hundred lives would be cheap
> if You were to give me half a sugar-smile.
> Father, don't give me advice in love—
> this child will not be tamed.
> People should give advice instead
> to those who advise me about Your love.
> I know the way to the road of safety,
> but what can I do? I've been taken by the snare.
> In church, I said to that Christian heart-thief,
> "O you who have caught my heart in your trap,
> O you to the threads of whose sacred belt
> each hair of mine is singly tied,
> Until when will you fail to find the road of unity?
> Until when will you place the shame of Trinity on the One?
> How can you call the One God
> 'Father, Son, and Holy Ghost'?"
> She parted her sweet lips and said to me,
> while candy fell from her sugar-smile,
> "If you are aware of Unity's secret,
> do not accuse us of unbelief.
> In three mirrors the eternal Beloved
> threw the rays of His shining face.
> 'Silk' does not become three
> if you call it *parniyān*, *ḥarīr*, and *parand*."
> We were having this talk when from the side,
> the church bell rang out in song,
> "He is one, and there is nothing but He,
> He alone, no god but He."[6]

6

The Real Shams-i Tabrīzī

Few people who have heard of Rūmī are unfamiliar with the name Shams-i Tabrīzī (disappeared in 643/1246). Little is known about him for certain. The only thing that is completely clear is that his arrival in Konya marked a decisive turning point in Rūmī's life and led to his prodigious output of inspired poetry. Given the importance of Rūmī's poetry for Persianate Islam, one can easily conclude that Shams played a providential role in Islamic history. Seyyed Hossein Nasr made this point in a study of Rūmī published nearly forty years ago:

> There is no doubt that Shams al-Dīn Tabrīzī was not just a Sufi master for Rūmī. Jalāl al-Dīn had already practiced Sufism for many years before meeting Shams al-Dīn. It seems, rather, that Shams al-Dīn was a divinely sent spiritual influence which in a sense "exteriorized" Rūmī's inner contemplative states in the form of poetry.[1]

The accounts of Shams in the popular literature on Rūmī in the West have tended to emphasize the dramatic sides to the Shams legend. We are given the picture of a wild lover of God who was utterly unconcerned with societal and religious conventions. Only in the past few years have Western scholars begun to look closely at the most important source on his life and teachings, the *Maqālāt* ("Sayings"), a seven hundred-page book that became available in a good edition only in 1990.[2] The task of producing a critical text of the *Maqālāt* was accomplished by the Iranian scholar Muḥammad ʿAlī Muwaḥḥid. It was especially difficult because the original manuscripts represent scattered notes apparently taken down by different people listening to Shams as he spoke. No final version was ever prepared, and the texts are full of breaks, ellipses, and obscure references. Many of the sayings are anecdotal, much like Rūmī's *Fīhi mā fīhi* ("In it is what is in it"). A rather high percentage recounts Shams's personal history and tells of the various teachers and shaykhs whom he had met. Although the legend tells us that Rūmī spent most of his time only with Shams, the sayings were clearly not taken down by Rūmī himself, and in many cases the text suggests that many people were in attendance while Shams was speaking.

One of the most striking features of Shams's personality that comes out in the *Maqālāt* is his utter certainty concerning his own highly elevated spiritual rank. He had no doubt that he was, in Nasr's words, "a divinely sent spiritual influence." His remarks about himself led Annemarie Schimmel to speak of his "immense spiritual pride."[3] A less sympathetic observer might be tempted to call him "arrogant" or "outrageously pretentious." Shams was perfectly aware of how his words must appear to those unaware of his inner states. He says:

> These people have a right not to find my words congenial. My words all come by way of greatness [*kibriyā*ʾ]. They all appear as pretension [*da*ʿ*wā*]. The Koran and the words of Muhammad all came in the way of need [*niyāz*], so they all appear as need.
>
> They hear words that are not in the path of seeking or need. The words are so high that if you look up at them, your hat falls off. But, it's no fault for God to claim greatness. If they find fault, it's as if they're saying, "God claims to be great." They speak the truth. Where's the fault?[4]

The texts are full of statements in which Shams appears to be making outrageous claims. Here are just a few of them:

> When someone finds the way to be my companion, his mark is that companionship with others becomes cold and bitter for him—not such that it becomes cold and he continues to be a companion, but rather such that he can no longer be their companion.[5]
>
> My existence is an alchemy that does not need to be put on the copper. When it's placed in front of the cooper, it all turns into gold.[6]
>
> I have nothing to do with the common people of this world—I haven't come for them. I've put my finger on the pulse of those who guide the world to the Real.[7]

When the top shaykhs of the Tribe's classes reach me, they have to start practicing all over from the beginning.[8]

> I am not one of those who go out to meet someone. . . . If God were to greet me ten times, I wouldn't answer. After the tenth time, I'd say, "and to You too." I'd make myself deaf.[9]

Part of the legend of Shams, somewhat confirmed in the *Maqālāt*, was that he had little use for book-learning. However, this does not mean that he himself was unlearned. His frequent mention of his own teachers and his use of the traditional sources show that he knew the Islamic sciences well. It even comes out that for a time he was a teacher in a Koran school, and the school was large enough to have many instructors and a headmaster. Moreover, in many passages, Shams refers to his own knowledge of jurisprudence:

> Someone asked my friend about me, "Is he a jurist [*faqīh*] or a fakir [*faqīr*]?" He said, "Both jurist and fakir." He said, "Then how come he only talks about jurisprudence?" He answered, "Because his poverty [*faqr*] is not of the superficial kind that he could properly speak about it with this group. It would be a pity to speak of it with these people. He brings out words by way of knowledge, and he speaks the secrets by way of knowledge and in the curtain of knowledge, so that his own words may not be spoken."[10]

Shams's contempt for book learning was aimed not only at jurists and exoteric scholars, but also at the circles of dervishes. In one passage he even tells us that he prefers the company of jurists to that of the Sufis:

> At first I didn't sit with jurists, I sat with dervishes. I used to say, "They're strangers to being dervishes." Then I came to know what it is to be a dervish and where they are, and now I would rather sit with jurists than with these dervishes. At least the jurists have taken trouble. The others simply brag about being dervishes. I mean, where is a dervish?[11]

Shams's basic complaint about the dervishes that he met was that they did not live up to their high calling. In one typical passage he writes:

> The speech of the lovers has an awesomeness. . . . I'm talking about the love that is true, the seeking that is true. . . . I wouldn't give you the dirt off the old shoe of a true lover for the "lovers" and "shaykhs" of these days.[12]

In another passage, he refers to the proliferation of false masters as well as what one might well understand as his own function. He was a cat who had come to rid Islam of mice:

> Most of these shaykhs have been the highwaymen of Muhammad's religion. All these mice in the house of Muhammad's religion have worked ruin. But, God has cats among His dear servants, and they clear away the mice. If a hundred thousand mice were to gather together, they wouldn't have the gall to look at the cat, because the cat's awesomeness does not leave them any togetherness.[13]

What may surprise those who are familiar only with the Shams legends is that the key attribute that Shams encourages in his listeners is "following" (*mutāba'a*), that is, following the Sunnah of the Prophet Muhammad. He certainly had in mind the Koranic verse, *Say [O Muhammad]: "If you love God, follow me, and God will love you"* (3:31):

> The lover alone knows the states of the lover—especially these sorts of lovers who go forward in following. If I were to display my following, even the great ones would despair. "Following" is that one does not complain about commandments. And if he does complain, he must not abandon following.[14]

Needless to say, Shams's idea of following does not always conform to that espoused by jurists and preachers. Nonetheless, it certainly does demand following the Shariah with care. Take, for example, this passage:

> The Prophet, upon whom be peace, said, "There is no *ṣalāt* without recitation [of the *Fātiḥa*]." He also said, "There is no *ṣalāt* without presence of the heart."
>
> A group of people suppose that when they find the presence of the heart, they have no need of the prayer's form. They say, "Seeking the means after obtaining the goal is ugly." In their opinion, they have taken the right position, because the state [*ḥāl*] has shown itself completely, along with sanctity [*walāya*] and the presence of the heart. Nonetheless, for them to abandon the prayer is a defect for them.
>
> "Did the Messenger—God bless him—achieve this perfection that you have achieved, or not?" If he says that he did not, then they should cut off his head and kill him. And if he says, "Yes, he did achieve it," then I say to him, "Then why don't you follow—such a noble messenger, the unparalleled good-news-giver and warner, the *light-giving lamp* [33:46]?"
>
> If there happens to be one of the saints of God, whose sanctity has been established such that there is no doubt whatsoever, and there is also Rashīd al-Dīn, whose sanctity has not become manifest; and, if the saint abandons form, whereas Rashīd al-Dīn is assiduous in the outward form, I will take after Rashīd al-Dīn and not even greet the other one.[15]

Of course, "following" the Prophet demands much more than simply performing the daily prayer, even in the midst of performing the prayer. As Shams puts it, "Following Muhammad is that he went on the *mi'rāj*—you also should go in his tracks."[16] The key to true following, then, is presence with God. Shams explains this in reference to a hadith often cited in Sufi circles, "An hour's meditation is better than sixty years of worship." This hadith lends itself to the type of misunderstanding that Shams criticizes in those who neglect following. In interpreting it, he has an eye on the hadith, encountered in Chapter 2, that identifies the *ṣalāt* as the *mi'rāj* of the believer:

> What is meant by this "meditation" is the presence of the sincere dervish—an act of worship in which there is no false show whatsoever. Certainly that is better than outward worship without presence. The *ṣalāt* can be made up for, but there is no making up for [lack of] presence.
>
> Muhammadan fakirs strive in this: "There is no *ṣalāt* without presence." It is not that they abandon its form so that the soul may be happy. In the outward Law, "There is no *ṣalāt* without the Fātiḥa."
>
> If Gabriel comes during presence, he will be given a slap. The Prophet had not yet reached presence when he said to Gabriel, "Come on!" Gabriel replied, "No! If I approach another inch, I will be burnt to cinders."[17]

Shams's learning often shows up in his frequent commentaries on Koranic verses. Sometimes he quotes other commentators, but then he will go off on his own. On occasion, he makes fun of the shortcomings of the usual sort of literal-minded commentaries that people read. As he remarks in one passage, "A literal translation of the Koran's words? Any five-year-old can tell you that."[18]

In one passage, he even makes fun of his own commentaries, which clearly must have set the minds of many of his listeners reeling:

> They said, "Make an exegesis of the Koran for us." I said, "As you know, my exegesis is not from Muhammad, nor is it from God. My 'I' also denies it. I say to it, 'How can you deny it? Leave me alone, go away. Why do you give me headaches?' 'It says, 'No, I won't go. I'll just keep on denying.' And that's my own self—it doesn't understand my words. This is like the calligrapher who used to write three kinds of calligraphy. One, he read but no one else. Another, he read and others too. The third, neither he nor anyone else could read. That's me when I talk. I don't understand, nor does anyone else."[19]

When Shams criticizes outward learning, he does so because it has been undertaken for the wrong reasons, or because it acts as a barrier to a deeper understanding. As he says:

> The reason these people study in the madrasas is, they think, "We'll become tutors, we'll run madrasas." They say, "Good deeds—one must act beautifully!" They talk of such things in these assemblies so that they can get positions.
>
> Why do you study knowledge for the sake of worldly mouthfuls? This rope is for people to come out of the well, not for them to go from this well into that well.
>
> You must bind yourself to knowing this: "Who am I? What substance am I? Why have I come? Where am I going? Whence is my root? At this time what am I doing? Toward what have I turned my face?"[20]

Many passages quote Shams as pointing out the shortcomings of well-known exoteric scholars, such as the great theologian and Koran commentator Fakhr al-Dīn al-Rāzī (d. 606/1210):

> If it were fitting to perceive these meanings by study and debate, then it would be necessary for Abū Yazīd and Junayd to rub their heads in the dirt out of regret before Fākhr-i Razī. They would need to become his students for a hundred years.[21]

However, Shams extends his critique of scholarship even to some of the well-known Sufi authors, including Qushayrī. Notice that he does this in keeping with his stress on the necessity of "following":

> I would not trade the least report from Muhammad for a hundred thousand treatises by Qushayrī, Qurayshī, and the others. They have no flavor, no taste. They have not found the tasting of that.[22]

In one passage, he criticizes Rāzī precisely for not having been a true follower of Muhammad:

> What gall Fakhr-i Rāzī had! He said, "Muhammad Tāzī [the Arab] says this, and Muhammad Rāzī says that." Isn't he the apostate of the time?! Isn't he an unqualified unbeliever? Unless he repents.[23]

One needs to remember that when Shams highlights the weakness of exoteric learning, he is speaking to people who already have that learning. He does not mean to suggest that it is worthless. If he sometimes preferred the company of jurists to the company of dervishes, it was precisely because many of the dervishes were proud that they knew little of the Islamic sciences, and at the same time were ignorant of spiritual and divine things. One of these dervishes seems to have been called Sayf Zangānī. His name tells us that he was from Zanjān, a city near Tabrīz. Concerning him Shams says:

> Who is Sayf Zangānī that he should speak ill of Fakhr-i Rāzī? If Fakhr were to break wind, a hundred like Sayf would come into existence and disappear. I defile his grave and his mouth. My fellow townsman? What kind of fellow townsman? Dirt on his head![24]

Shams, in short, had little patience with stupidity. He targeted the pretensions of his listeners and told them to empty themselves for the sake of God:

> Whoever becomes a completely learned man is completely deprived of God and completely full of himself. An Anatolian who becomes a Muslim right now finds a scent of God. But when someone is full, a hundred thousand prophets can't empty him.[25]

Shams was particularly hard on hypocrisy, which is to be full of one's own intentions while claiming to worship:

> The "God is greater" of the prayer is for sacrificing the soul. When will He be greater? As long as pride and existence are within you, you must say "God is greater," and you must intend the sacrifice. Until when do you want to take the idol under your arm and come to the prayer? You say "God is greater," but, like the hypocrites, you firmly hold that idol under your arm.[26]

Part of hypocrisy is the attempt by many believers to put God into their service, rather than submitting themselves to His service:

> Someone says, "O God, do this! O God, do that!" This is exactly as if he were to say, "O king, lift up that pot and bring it here!" He's made the king into his own blessed butler! He commands Him, "Don't do that, do this!"[27]

The goal of the Sufis is to become a friend of God. But Shams did not think that many of the dervishes whom he knew did much more than talk about being friends with God:

> I wonder what these people think friendship with God is. That God who created the heavens, who created the earth, who made the universe appear—is His friendship gained so easily that you come in and sit before Him, you talk and you listen? Do you fancy this is a soup kitchen? You come in and you drink it down? Then you just leave?[28]

In one passage Shams sums up the spiritual path by saying that it comes down to two things: knowledge of *tawḥīd* and emptiness before God:

> *Know that there is no God but He* [47:19]. This is a commandment to knowledge. *And ask forgiveness for your sin* [47:19]. This is a commandment to negate this existence, because it is newly arrived. How can this existence, which is newly arrived, see the knower of eternity?[29]

Such knowledge of *tawḥīd* is clearly not theoretical knowledge alone. It demands the transformation of the soul. I leave you with one more saying that nicely sums up the message of both Shams and Rūmī:

> Someone said, "God is one." I replied, "So, what's it to you? You are in the world of dispersion—hundreds of thousands of dust motes, each of the dust motes scattered, withered, and frozen in the worlds. He indeed *is*. He is eternal Being. What's it to you? For you are *not*."[30]

7

The Koran as the Lover's Mirror

It is well-known that Sufism places a premium on love, but Western observers rarely associate love with Islam itself. This helps to explain the tendency to see Sufism as somehow tangential to the tradition. I would argue that love for God is every bit as central to the Islamic perspective as it is to a tradition like Christianity, although the rhetorical stress is by no means the same. In the present context, one piece of evidence will suffice: Islamic praxis is based on following the Sunnah of Muhammad—that is, imitating his conduct, his customs, and his character traits. The Koran is utterly basic to Islamic ways of seeing and doing things, but the Koran is known and interpreted first of all through the manner in which it was embodied and acted out by Muhammad. Following the Prophet provides the parameters for the Muslim understanding of the Koran and of all things. But what exactly is the rationale for following the Prophet? A most succinct expression is found in the verse, *Say [O Muhammad!]: "If you love God, follow me, and God will love you"* (3:31). If one does not love God, there is no reason to follow the Prophet. This has hardly been lost on practicing Muslims.

If it is not obvious to outsiders that Muslims have been motivated by love for God, this has something to do with the many directions in which Islamic civilization developed—literature, law, art, philosophy, theology, political institutions. Modern scholarship has been much more interested in these observable aspects of culture than in psychological or spiritual motives. Nonetheless, most scholars recognize that Islamic civilization has always been concerned with unpacking the teachings of the Koran and applying them to diverse realms of human endeavor. In other words, expressions of Islamic civilization and culture flesh out the ways in which people imitate the Prophet, who embodied the Koran. And Muslims in turn are motivated to imitate the Prophet by love for God and the desire to call down God's love upon themselves.

Although Muslims have followed Muhammad in order to attract God's love, they have also recognized that God loves human beings in any case. Sufi authors commonly highlight the notion that the divine motivation for creating the universe is love. What makes human beings special, among all God's creatures, is that they have the capacity to love God freely in response to His love for them. All other things simply serve God as they were created to serve Him, with no free choice on their part.[1] As Rūmī puts it:

> Choice is the salt of worship—
> the spheres turn, but not because they want to.
> Their turning is neither rewarded nor punished,
> for, at the time of reckoning, choice bestows excellence.[2]

To say that God created the universe out of love means that the divine love brings into existence the ugly along with the beautiful, the bad along with the good. Only within the context of such an apparently mixed-up universe can free choice have any meaning. And only those who choose freely to love can love God with worthy love. If love were to be coerced, it would not be love. This is one reason why the Koran says, *There is no compulsion in the religion* (2:256). "The religion"—the right path taught by the Koran and the Prophet—is precisely to live up to the requirements of love for God and to do so by putting the Sunnah into practice.

In short, although God loves human beings and created them to love Him, they are free *not* to love Him. Thus, a second sort of divine love responds to the choice to love God, which itself demands following the divine guidance as embodied in the prophets. And, as God says in the famous *ḥadīth qudsī,* "When I love My servant, I am the hearing with which he hears, the eyesight with which he sees, the hand with which he grasps, and the foot upon which he walks."[3] When love reaches its culmination, the Lover is none other than those He loves, and the human lovers are none other than the Beloved. This is one of the meanings that Sufis see in the verse, *He loves them, and they love Him* (5:54).

Love and Interpretation

I chose to write about the Koran as a "mirror" because I wanted to stress the role of the interpreter in understanding scripture. The fact that people see the Koran through their own specific lenses is especially clear when one surveys the vast number of Koranic commentaries written over the centuries—not to mention the critiques and studies written by non-Muslims. Jurists have found in the Koran a book of law, theologians see all sorts of God-talk, philosophers find the guidelines for wisdom and virtue, linguists uncover fascinating intricacies of Arabic grammar, biologists find theories of life. As for Western scholarship, nothing is more obvious than the fact that scholars reach diverse conclusions on the basis of diverse premises and prejudices.

Explaining the central importance of the Koran, Shams-i Tabrīzī says, "For the travelers and the wayfarers, each verse of the Koran is like a message and a love letter [*ʿishq-nāma*]. They know the Koran. He presents and discloses the beauty of the Koran to them."[4] I suppose that nowadays not too many people read the Koran as a love letter. But, is this because of the contents of the Koran? Or is it because of the contents of the readers' souls? Shams thinks the answer is obvious: "The flaw is that people don't look at God with the gaze of love."[5]

At issue is not only interpretation of scripture, since the same argument applies to our views on everything. Our understanding of the world and of our own role within it depends on where we are coming from. And with even more reason, how we understand "God" depends on who we are. This should be obvious—everyone has a different understanding of the word "God." Ibn al-ʿArabī makes the point by arguing that no one can worship God as such. All people without exception worship the god or gods of their beliefs (*al-ilāh al-muʿtaqad*). Given that the term *god* can designate the point of reference for one's attitudes and activities, even those who claim not to worship any gods are deceiving themselves. All of us have points of reference and orientations.

I do not want to claim that interpretation of scripture is totally subjective, but it does seem clear that scripture has the capacity to allow people to see into their own souls. When people read scripture, they find themselves. If they do not like what they are seeing, they should—in the traditional way of looking at things—try to dissolve the knots in their souls that prevent them from seeing the beauty of the Divine Word. Needless to say, contemporary responses are somewhat different.

One needs to remember that Muslims never considered the Koran a book among other books any more than the Bible was simply a classic for Christians. The Koran was the Word of God, God's own Self-expression with the purpose of guiding those whom He loves. People read and recited the Koran not to entertain themselves with old stories, nor for personal edification, but to bring themselves into conformity with the Divine Reality that is disclosed in the text. The purpose of engaging with the Koran was to transform the soul. Reciting the text and conforming oneself to its teachings was a way to express one's love for God and to make oneself worthy for God's love.

The idea that reciting the Koran and observing the Sunnah are transformative acts goes back to Islamic teachings about what it means to be human, teachings with which the Koran is saturated—that is, if one is looking for them. People can become transformed because they can come to know God and love Him, and this is possible because human beings are not fixed in their status. It may be true that the God whom people worship is always the God of belief, and it may also be true that God in Himself is always beyond the capacity of human understanding. But, this does not mean that the God of my belief today is the same as the God of my belief tomorrow. Quite the contrary. Understanding and worship of God change constantly in keeping with the growth and development of the human self.

Ibn al-ʿArabī points out that the uniqueness of human beings goes back to the fact that they cannot be pinned down. Just as God cannot be defined, so also the creatures whom He created in His own image cannot be put into a box. In other words, the "definition" of what it means to be human has everything to do with indefinability.

In the Koran, the angels say, *"Each of us has a known station"* (37:164). This suggests that the angels are all different and that each has a specific function. None of the angels can do the job of any other angel. Ibn al-ʿArabī argues that the rule expressed in this verse applies to all created things; each thing in the universe is exactly what it is meant to be and is doing precisely what it was created for—with the partial exception of human beings. In their case, human status depends on not having a fixed station in this life, because only nonfixity can allow for freedom. People can develop and grow as they attempt to make themselves worthy of God's love.

Humans, in short, cannot be defined in any more than a general way. No one can know what he or she really is, because each of us is a work in progress. What we do in our daily activities constantly brings about changes in our psychic and spiritual make-up. We remain indefinable until death, at which point we enter into our own fixed stations, like the angels and other creatures.

When we apply the rule of nonfixity and indefinability to our own beliefs and practices—whether these be religious or nonreligious—we see that our understandings, words, and deeds are always in the process of changing, for better or worse. Moreover, we reap the fruits of these changes—the law of karma is ineluctable. Reality itself holds us responsible for what we think and do. Death is simply the point at which all this becomes obvious.

Given that people are constantly developing and changing, they should be concerned with making sure that they develop in a worthy and congenial way. Love for God provides the necessary focus. Following the Prophet, one needs to remember, does not simply mean performing certain acts. More than anything else it means assuming certain attitudes toward God and the world.

Islam provides the basic guidelines for the proper attitudes in the Shahadah. I have already indicated something of the importance of God's Messenger for actualizing love. The role played by the first Shahadah is less obvious, but, in fact, the declaration of *tawḥīd* is in some ways even more basic.

For Muslims, "There is no god but God" is a statement of fact, or a self-evident truth. Even more than that, it is a methodology. Specifically, it responds to the human limitation of always seeing God and scripture in our own measures, and it provides the means to bring our measures into conformity with God's measure. Given that our beliefs and attitudes alter and change day by day and even moment by moment, we need a method of focusing, training, and guiding them and allowing them to develop in a direction that will lead to long-term happiness.

The first Shahadah provides a way of thinking about God. What it basically says is that every thought about God needs to be negated. Whatever god we conceive of is not God in Himself, who alone truly is. Whatever interpretation we make of the Koran does not live up to the reality of God. There can be no definitive and final answers in our minds and souls. To say definitive and final is to say "absolute," and God alone is absolute, so God alone is definitive and final. As Shams puts it, "It is God who is God. Whatever is created is not God—whether it's Muhammad or other than Muhammad."[6] The definitive and final God is not the God that we can understand. Our God is always tentative.

In other words, the Shahadah provides a method to help people avoid trying to size up God. The great lovers of Islamic civilization say that if people want to understand God in God's measure, they need to look upon Him with the eye of love and strive to conform to His wishes. As a methodology for lovers, the Shahadah tells them that there is nothing worthy of love but God, because God alone is adequate to the ever-changing and unlimited substance of the human soul. God alone can fill up the divine image that is the human self. As for what is less than God, love for it is legitimate and desirable only to the degree in which the object of love is recognized as God's good and beautiful face (*wajh*) shining in the created realm. The principle of unity demands that all things be seen as signs and marks of God's goodness.

There is a hadith that can help us understand the role of love in interpreting the Koran: "Your love for a thing makes you blind and deaf." A typical way of reading this is to say that loving what is less than God makes people blind and deaf to the guidance provided by the Koran and the Sunnah. This will have ill consequences for the soul because, if people love something other than God, they will not follow Muhammad, and then God will not love them and will not bring them into His proximity after death.

This saying, however, can be read in other ways as well. We can take it not as a criticism of misguided love, but as a statement of fact concerning all love, guided or misguided. Love for the ugly and vicious makes people blind and deaf to the beautiful and virtuous, and love for the beautiful and virtuous turns them away from the ugly and vicious.

If we acknowledge that love makes us blind, it becomes obvious that all scriptural interpretation is inadequate. Why? Because every interpreter loves something, some god, some principle, some goal. And the love that drives us—the love for whatever it is that we worship—makes us blind and deaf to other gods and other loves. If our god is history, or psychology, or physics, for example, this would make us blind and deaf to metaphysics, not to mention "mysticism." This is obvious; we meet it in every facet of life, especially life in the academy. People not only do not see things the same way, they *cannot* see things in the same way, because they are blinded by their loves.

Every interpreter of scripture, therefore, is a lover—of something or other—and every lover sees scripture as his own mirror. For those who love the God of *tawḥīd*, the God described in the first Shahadah, their love makes them blind and deaf to every negative attribute that might be applied to God, for they can only see that He is adorned with every positive attribute. Love makes them give all credit for good to God, and all credit for evil to themselves.

If human beings were fixed in status like other creatures, it would be a waste of breath even to mention the fact that they are blinded by their loves and obsessed by their own interpretative stances. It is precisely because we are not fixed in status and are constantly changing that we need to remember our own limitations. We can always strive to lift our gazes higher and see through better lenses.

I am not arguing that "love for God" is necessarily a good thing. That all depends on the god of belief. If the god of belief does not conform with God as He truly is, what people call "love for God" can easily be hatred for the Beautiful, the Good, and the True. This is one reason that Islamic texts never divorce love for God from knowledge of God. Real faith cannot be a leap into the unknown, because it is impossible to love something that you do not know. This is precisely the problem: We cannot know God in Himself, so we can only love Him in the degree that we know Him. It becomes all important to expand our own measure in knowledge and understanding so as to achieve as close an approximation as possible to the divine measure.

In texts that discuss love for God, the expression "lover" and "knower" are often synonyms. Or, if love is taken as higher—as is done typically in Sufi poetry—knowledge becomes the means for achieving true love. Ghazālī often makes the connection between love and knowledge in his *Iḥyāʾ*, as in the following passage:

> Every part of the body was created for its own specific act. The illness of each part is for it not to be able to perform the act for which it was created, or to perform the act but in a disrupted manner. The illness of the hand is for it not to be able to grasp. The illness of the eye is for it not to be able to see.
>
> In the same way, the illness of the heart is for it not to be able to perform the specific act for which it was created. This act is knowledge, wisdom, recognition, love for God, worshiping Him, and taking joy in remembering Him. The heart should prefer these over every other desired thing and utilize all desires and all bodily parts in this path. . . .
>
> Thus, in each bodily part there is a benefit, and the benefit of the heart is wisdom and knowledge. This is the specific characteristic of the human soul through which human beings are distinguished from beasts. For, they are not distinguished from them by the power of eating, sexual intercourse, eyesight, and so on—only through knowing things as they are. And the Root of things, the one who brings them into existence and devises them, is God. It is He who made them things. So, if a man were to know all things but not to know God, it would be as if he knew nothing.
>
> The mark of knowledge is love. He who knows God loves Him. The mark of love is that he does not prefer this world or any other loved thing over Him. . . . Whenever anyone loves something more than he loves God, his heart is ill. It is as if his stomach loved clay more than it loved bread and water, or as if it ceased to have any

> desire for bread and water. Hence, the stomach is ill, and this is the mark of its illness.
>
> Thus it is known that all hearts are ill, except as God wills.[7]

I can sum up in these terms: Love for God pushes the lover to follow the Prophet, who embodies the message of the Koran. One cannot love God properly, however, without knowing Him, and to know God one needs to have a sound knowledge of God's Self-expression, which is precisely the Koran and its embodiment in Muhammad. In order to know and understand the Koran correctly, one needs to read it with the eye of love. As an interpretive method, love demands that the reader look at God in terms of the Shahadah, which negates every blameworthy attribute from God and ascribes every praiseworthy attribute to Him. This demands that interpreters understand every verse in the best light—in view of the real nature of God's wisdom, compassion, mercy, and guidance.

A Lover's Approach to Scripture

For the remainder of this chapter, I demonstrate how Rashīd al-Dīn Maybudī, whose Koran commentary was discussed in Chapter 3, treats the Koran as a love letter. I do so by looking at his comments on several Koranic verses. The first passage pertains to Koran 2:2. In stage three of his commentary on this verse, he takes the word *kitāb*, which is usually translated as "book," in its literal sense, which is "writing." He understands the verse to say, *This is the writing wherein is no doubt*. He then explains the meaning in terms of two other Koranic verses where writing is mentioned. Then he offers a brief meditation on the verse:

> It is said that *This is the writing* [2:2] is an allusion to what God has written against Himself for Muhammad's community: "My mercy takes precedence over My wrath." God does that in His words, *Your Lord has written mercy against Himself* [6:54]. It is also said that the verse is an allusion to the faith and knowledge that God has written upon the hearts of the believers. Thus He says, *He wrote faith in their hearts* [58:22].
>
> In this verse, it is as if God is saying, "My servant, I have written the outline of faith in your heart, I have mixed in the perfume of love, I have decorated paradise for you, I have adorned your heart with the light of knowledge, I have lit up the candle of union with Me, I have stamped the seal of kindness on your heart, and I have written the characters of love in your awareness.
>
> "*He wrote faith in their hearts*, I wrote in the Tablet,[8] but what I wrote there was only your description. I wrote in your hearts, and what I wrote there was only My description. I wrote your description

> in the Tablet, and I showed it to Gabriel. I wrote My description in your heart. Would I have shown it to an enemy?
>
> "In the Tablet I wrote your cruelty [*jafā'*] and faithfulness [*wafā'*]; in your heart I wrote laudation and knowledge. What I wrote about you has not changed. How could what I wrote about Myself change?
>
> "Moses carved out a stone from the mountain, and, when I wrote the Torah therein, the stone turned into emerald. The knower's heart was made of harsh stone—when I wrote My name therein, it turned into an exalted book."[9]

The next verse is the first half of Koran 2:148, which reads, *Everyone has a direction to which he turns.* This is often understood as explaining the diversity of creation. In stage two of his commentary, Maybudī reads the verse as referring to the "kiblah" of people, their orientation in their worship. Each of us has a god on which our aspirations are focused, and that god is determined by our created nature, which was given to us by our Creator. This idea is commonplace in Islamic thought, and is alluded to in Koranic verses like 25:43, *Have you seen the one who has taken his own caprice as his god?* I have already explained how Ibn al-ʿArabī develops some of its implications in terms of "the god of belief." Here are Maybudī's words in stage two:

> Everyone has a kiblah toward which he turns. The folk of falsehood have turned their faces toward a crooked kiblah—by [God's] decree and abandonment. The folk of truth have turned their faces toward a straight kiblah—by [God's] decree and giving success. And the whole affair is in God's hand.[10]

In this straightforward interpretation, Maybudī takes the verse as a statement of the actual situation, of the static relationship between creatures and the Creator. But our situations are not in fact fixed, so we can always do something to change them. The fact that we are abandoned today does not demand that we will be abandoned tomorrow, nor does the fact that we receive success today mean that we have a lock on success. If we look with the eye of love, we can see that the verse is urging us to recognize our true Beloved and to turn away from all the false objects of love that attract us. This is the way Maybudī interprets the verse in stage three of the commentary:

> He says by way of allusion, "All people have turned away from Me. They have become familiar with others instead of Me. They have made the ease of their hearts to lie in something less than Me and accepted it as their beloved.
>
> "You, who are the nobles on the path, you, who claim to love Me—lift up your eyes from anything less than Me, even if it be the highest paradise." Then you will walk straight, following the Sunnah

and the conduct of Muhammad, and you will fulfill completely the duty of emulating that greatest man of the world. For, his conduct, as the greatest of the prophets, was to turn his eyes away from all beings and not to see any refuge or to accept any resting place other than the shelter of unity [*aḥadiyya*]:

When a man wears down his soul in the path of love
he'd better not incline to anyone less than the Friend.
In the path of love the lover must never
give a thought to paradise or hell.

When someone puts himself right in following [Muhammad], the candle of love for God will be lit in his path such that he will never fall away from the road of love. To this is the allusion in the verse, *"Follow me, and God will love you"* [3:31]. Whenever someone goes straight on the avenue of love, he will be secure from the varied directions that are the kiblahs of the shallow-minded. One fervent lover has said in his state:

No matter that I don't have the world's kiblah—
my kiblah is the Beloved's lane, nothing else.
This world, that world, all that exists—
lovers see the Beloved's face, nothing else.

Al-Ḥallāj [d. 309/922] alluded to the kiblahs of the shallow-minded when he said, "The desirers have been turned over to what they desire." In other words, everyone has been placed with his own beloved.

The reality of this work is that all creatures have claimed love for the Real, but there was no one who did not want to be *somebody* in His court:

Whoever found himself a name found it from that Court.
Belong to Him, brother, don't think about anyone else!

Since everyone claimed to love the Real, He struck them against the touchstone of trial to show them to themselves. He threw something into them and made it their kiblah, so they turned their face to it, rather than to Him. In one it was possessions, in another position, in another a spouse, in another a beautiful face, in another vainglory, in another knowledge, in another asceticism, in another worship, in another fancy. He threw all of these into the creatures, so they busied themselves with them. No one spoke of Him, and the path of seeking Him stayed empty.

> This is why Abū Yazīd said, "I walked up to His gate, but I didn't see any crowding there, because the folk of this world were veiled by this world, the folk of the next world were veiled by the next world, and the claimants among the Sufis were veiled by eating, drinking, and begging. There were others among the Sufis of a higher level—but they were veiled by music and beautiful faces. The leaders of the Sufis, however, were not veiled by any of these. I saw that they were bewildered and intoxicated."
>
> It was in accordance with this sort of tasting that the Guide on the Path [Anṣārī] said, "I know the drinking place, but I'm not able to drink. My heart is thirsty and I wail in the hope of a drop. No fountain can fill me up, because I'm seeking the ocean. I passed by a thousand springs and rivers in hope of finding the sea.
>
> "Have you seen someone drowning in fire? I'm like that. Have you seen someone thirsty in a lake? That's what I am. I'm exactly like a man lost in the desert. I keep on saying, 'Someone help me!' I'm screaming at the loss of my heart.'"[11]

I conclude by citing one more passage, this time from the commentary on Koran 2:5. After saying that the Koran is the book or "writing" within which there is no doubt, the text goes on to say that it is a guidance for the God-wary, and then it describes the God-wary—those who have faith in the unseen and perform the commanded practices. Verse five then reads, *Those are upon guidance from their Lord; those are the ones who prosper*. The next verse turns to a description of those who do not prosper—those who reject God's guidance.

In the third stage of his commentary, Maybudī goes into quite a bit of detail to suggest what sort of "prosperity" is at issue:

> Here you have endless good fortune and unlimited generosity. God has opened up the door of their insight and has looked upon their hearts with the gaze of solicitude [*ʿināya]*. He has lit up the lamp of guidance in their hearts so that, what for others is unseen, for them is manifest, what for others is reports, for them is seeing eye-to-eye [*ʿiyān*].[12]

Next, Maybudī turns to accounts of the Prophet's companions and some of the early Sufis to suggest the difference between knowing something by means of transmitted reports and knowing it by means of direct vision and immediate experience. Then he turns to the sayings of Anṣārī—as he does so often—and cites a highly poetical dialogue between the spirit (*jān*) and the heart (*dil*), which concludes by reminding us that all this talk of love and transformation represents *tawḥīd* in practice, and it leads to the union in which God becomes the hearing with which the lovers hear and the eyesight with which they see:

The human substance is like a rusted mirror. As long as it has rust on its face, no forms appear within it. When you polish it, all forms will appear. As long as the opaqueness of disobedience is on the believing servant's heart, none of the mysteries of the spiritual realm [*malakūt*] will appear within it. But, when the rust of disobedience is removed from it, the mysteries of the spiritual realm and the states of the unseen begin to show themselves. This is precisely the unveiling of the heart.

Just as the heart has unveiling, the spirit has looking eye-to-eye [*muʿāyana*]. Unveiling is the lifting of the barriers between the heart and the Real, and looking eye-to-eye is seeing together [*ham-dīdārī*]. As long as you are with the heart, you are receiving reports. When you reach the spirit, you arrive at looking eye-to-eye.

Shaykh al-Islām Anṣārī let out the secret here in the tongue of unveiling, lifting from it the seal of jealousy. He said:

"On the first day of the beginningless covenant a tale unfolded between heart and spirit. No one was there—not Adam and Eve, not water and clay. The Real was present, the Reality was there.

"No one has heard such a marvelous tale. The heart was the questioner, and the spirit was the mufti. The heart had an intermediary, but the spirit received the report by seeing eye-to-eye. The heart asked a thousand questions from the spirit, and they all came to nothing. With one word the spirit answered them all.

"The heart did not have its fill of asking, nor did the spirit of answering. The questions were not about deeds, nor were the answers about rewards. Whenever the heart asked about reports, the spirit answered from looking eye-to-eye. Finally, the heart came to looking eye-to-eye, and it brought back the report to water [and clay]:

"'If you have the capacity to hear, listen. If not, don't hurry to deny, just stay silent.'

"The heart asked the spirit, 'What is faithfulness [*wafāʾ*]? What is annihilation [*fanāʾ*]? What is subsistence [*baqāʾ*]?'

"The spirit answered, 'Faithfulness is to bind the belt of love, annihilation is to be delivered from your own selfhood, subsistence is to reach the reality of the Real.'

"The heart asked, 'Who is the stranger, who the mercenary, who the familiar?'

"The spirit replied, 'The stranger has been driven away, the mercenary remains on the road, the familiar is called.'

"The heart asked the spirit, 'What is seeing eye-to-eye? What is love [*mihr*]? What is unneedingness [*nāz*]?'

"The spirit replied, 'Seeing eye-to-eye is the resurrection, love is fire mixed with blood, unneedingness is the handhold of need [*niyāz*].'

"The heart said, 'Add to that.'

"The spirit answered, 'Seeing eye-to-eye does not get along with explanation, love is paired with jealousy [*ghayra*], and wherever there is unneedingness, the story is long.'

"The heart said, 'Add to that.'

"The spirit replied, 'Seeing eye-to-eye cannot be analyzed, love takes the sleeper in secret, and he who reaches unneedingness in the Beloved will never die.'

"The heart asked, 'Has anyone ever reached that day by himself?'

"The spirit replied, 'I asked that from the Real. The Real said, 'Finding Me is by My solicitude. Thinking that you can reach Me by yourself is your sin.' "

"The heart asked, 'Is there permission for one glance? I'm tired of interpretation and reports.'

"The spirit replied, 'Here we have water running by someone sleeping with his fingers in his ears. Will he hear the sound of the Pond?'[13]

"The discussion of heart and spirit was cut off. The Real began to speak, and the spirit and heart listened. The tale unfolded until the words rose high and the place was emptied of listeners.

"Now the heart finds no end to unneedingness, and the spirit none to gentleness. The heart is in the grasp of Generosity, the spirit in the shelter of the Holy. No mark of the heart appears, no trace of the spirit. Nonexistence is lost in existence, reports in seeing eye-to-eye. From beginning to end this is precisely the tale of *tawḥīd*. To this, 'I am his hearing with which he hears' gives witness."[14]

II

Ibn al-ʿArabī and His Influence

8

A History of the Term *Waḥdat al-Wujūd*

Few technical terms of Sufism are as well-known as *waḥdat al-wujūd* or the "Oneness of Being."[1] Though this expression has historical connections with the school of Ibn al-ʿArabī, it is sometimes employed to refer to the views of other Sufis, including figures who lived long before Ibn al-ʿArabī.[2] Use of the term *waḥdat al-wujūd* therefore raises important historical and intellectual questions. In order to understand these questions, one needs to have a clear idea of the meaning of the term.

Tawḥīd

The expression *waḥdat al-wujūd* is built from two words—*waḥda* and *wujūd*—both of which were important for Islamic thought from early times. The word *tawḥīd* comes from the same root as *waḥda*, as do other related and often discussed terms such as *aḥad* and *wāḥid* ("one"), and *aḥadiyya* ("unity") and *waḥdāniyya* ("oneness"). Already in the sayings of ʿAlī we come across a reference to four different meanings for the apparently simple statement, "God is One."[3]

The discussion of *wujūd* enters Islamic thought somewhat later than the discussion of *waḥda* and plays an important role, especially in the development of philosophy, which is often defined as the study of *wujūd*. If the term *waḥdat al-wujūd* is not found in any texts before the works of Ibn al-ʿArabī's school, many statements of the Sufis approximate it.[4] Maʿrūf al-Karkhī (d. 200/815–816) is said to have been the first to re-express the Shahadah in the form often heard in later centuries: "There is nothing in *wujūd* but God."[5] Abū'l-ʿAbbās Qaṣṣāb (fl. fourth/tenth century) used similar terms: "There is nothing in the two worlds except my Lord. The existent things [*mawjūdāt*]—all things except His *wujūd*—are nonexistent [*maʿdūm*]."[6]

Anṣārī provides several formulations of *tawḥīd* in Persian and Arabic that surely inspired later authors. In defining five levels of *tawḥīd,* he speaks about the third level as *wujūd al-tawḥīd* or "the existence of *tawḥīd,*" which is "to leave all witnesses and enter into the Eternal Witness." The final stage, the "enfolding of *tawḥīd* within *tawḥīd,*" is "the absorption of that which never was into That which ever is." In another passage, Anṣārī refers to the "*tawḥīd* of the elect" as the fact that "No one is other than He" (*laysa ghayrahu aḥad*). "What is *tawḥīd*?," Anṣārī asks. "God, and nothing else. The rest is folly [*hawas*]."[7]

By the time of Ghazālī, the term *wujūd* is often employed in explanations of *tawḥīd*'s meaning. In his *Mishkāt al-anwār* ("The Niche of Lights"), Ghazālī describes the fruit of the spiritual ascent of the gnostics as follows: "They see through direct witnessing that there is nothing in *wujūd* but God and that *All things are perishing except His face* [28:88]."[8] Ghazālī did not consider this understanding of *tawḥīd* a specifically Sufi teaching, appropriate only for his more esoteric works, because he makes the same point in his *Iḥyāʾ*: "There is nothing in *wujūd* but God. . . . *Wujūd* belongs only to the Real One."[9] Passages such as these, which were later looked upon as statements of the doctrine of *waḥdat al-wujūd,* are numerous. But let us turn to the expression itself with respect to Ibn al-ʿArabī, to whom its first clear and detailed formulation is usually ascribed.

Ibn al-ʿArabī

All of Ibn al-ʿArabī's works exhibit an extremely high level of sophistication, definitely not for popular consumption. When he refers disparagingly to the "common people," he usually has in mind the exoteric scholars, the jurists or "knowers of formalities" (*ʿulamāʾ al-rusūm*) as he calls them—in other words, the learned class of Muslims in the ordinary sense of the term. But he also uses the term for Sufis who have not yet advanced to the stage of "verification" (*taḥqīq*) and who continue to follow authority (*taqlīd*). Ibn al-ʿArabī expected his readers not only to be practitioners of Sufism but also to be familiar with most fields of learning, especially Koran commentary, Hadith, jurisprudence, Kalam, and philosophy, and he made few allowances for those who did not know these sciences well. His writings are clear, consistent, and logically structured, even though they may appear opaque to those not familiar with them. As James Morris remarks:

> The bizarre epithets one sometimes finds applied to Ibn ʿArabī, whether in Islamic or modern Western sources—e.g., "incoherent," "pantheist," "heretic," "monist," "madman," etc.—are understandable less as reasoned judgments about the whole of his work than as reactions to the difficult challenge of unifying and integrating such diverse and challenging materials.[10]

Despite the fact that relatively little research has been carried out on Ibn al-ʿArabī's teachings, his fame along with that of *waḥdat al-wujūd* has spread far outside academic circles. But Ibn al-ʿArabī himself, so far as is known, never employed the term *waḥdat al-wujūd* in his enormous corpus of writings,[11] even though he frequently discussed *wujūd* and the fact that it can be described as possessing the attribute of oneness or unity (employing such terms as *waḥda, waḥdāniyya,* and *aḥadiyya*). For example, "Nothing has become manifest in *wujūd* through *wujūd* except the Real (*al-ḥaqq*), because *wujūd* is the Real, and He is one"[12]; "The entity (*ʿayn*) of *wujūd* is one, but its properties (*aḥkām*) are diverse"[13]; "Number (*ʿadad*) derives from the one that accepts a second, not the one of *wujūd* (*al-wāḥid al-wujūd*)"[14]; "All of *wujūd* is one in reality; there is nothing along with it."[15]

But what did Ibn al-ʿArabī mean when he said that *wujūd* is one? If ʿAlī provided four different meanings for the statement "God is one," the statement "*Wujūd* is one" cannot be as simple as it might appear, especially because the later use of the term *waḥdat al-wujūd*, by its supporters as well as its detractors, hinges on divergent understandings of what this oneness implies.

At the outset, we need to know that any attempt to explain the meaning of *waḥdat al-wujūd* as understood by Ibn al-ʿArabī will be deficient and misleading, all the more so if one tries to classify his teachings as pantheism, panentheism, existential monism, pantheistic monism, or the like. Ibn al-ʿArabī explains *waḥdat al-wujūd* in hundreds of different contexts, each time adding nuances that are lost when any attempt is made, as it soon is in most Western studies, to "come to the point." His "point" does not, in fact, lie in any simple formulation of *waḥdat al-wujūd*. If people want a simple statement, they should be satisfied with "There is no god but God." Ibn al-ʿArabī's point lies more in the very act of constantly reformulating *waḥdat al-wujūd* in order to reshape the reader's imagination. In each new context in which he expresses *waḥdat al-wujūd*, he demonstrates the intimate inward interrelationships among phenomena, basing himself on a great variety of texts drawn from the Koran, Hadith, Kalam, philosophy, cosmology, Arabic grammar, and other sources.

Ibn al-ʿArabī is a visionary, not a philosopher, which means among other things that he is not trying to reach a conclusion or build a system. He had no intention of systematizing Islamic thought, even though various passages in his writings take systematic form (and sometimes contradict the systematic formulations he has provided elsewhere). He is a sage who has a vision of reality that he is trying to communicate through all the means at his disposal, including logical discourse in the philosophical and theological style, exegesis of the Koran and Hadith, and poetry (we should not forget that Ibn al-ʿArabī was one of the great poets of the Arabic language). *Waḥdat al-wujūd* is one of the many dimensions of the overall vision Ibn al-ʿArabī wants to convey. He did not consider it the highest expression of his teachings, which helps explain why he himself has no single word for it.[16] The fact that *waḥdat al-wujūd* came to be chosen as the term that typifies his point of view has less to do with Ibn al-ʿArabī himself than with certain figures who followed him.

The statement that Ibn al-ʿArabī was a visionary and not a philosopher needs some clarification. Ibn al-ʿArabī frequently tells us that reason or intellect is inadequate as a source of knowledge of God, the world, and the self. His own teachings are based primarily on unveiling, tasting, and direct witnessing (*mushāhada*), all of which transcend the limitations of reason. He repeatedly quotes Koranic verses such as *Be wary of God, and God will teach you* (2:282). Only this teaching by God Himself, founded on observing the rules and regulations of the Shariah and the discipline of the Tariqah or spiritual path, can lead to true knowledge. Ibn al-ʿArabī does not think up or produce ideas. He simply records God's self-disclosures, which he perceives objectively and subjectively; nor would he draw a distinction between objective and subjective because this is our terminology, not his. Often, his unveilings take the shape of incredible formal visions of the unseen world. He would feel completely at home with Rūmī's verses:

> First there were intoxication, loverhood, youth and the like;
> then came luxuriant spring, and they all sat together.
> They had no forms and then became manifested
> beautifully within forms—
> behold things of the imagination assuming form!
> The heart is the antechamber of the eye: for certain,
> everything that reaches the heart will enter into
> the eye and become a form.[17]

Once we grasp the fact that we are not dealing here with a philosophical or theological system, we can begin to appreciate the difficulty of providing even an elementary understanding of *waḥdat al-wujūd*. As Toshihiko Izutsu has justly remarked:

> No philosophical explanation can do justice to [Ibn al-ʿArabī's] thought unless it is backed by a personal experience of the Unity of Being (*waḥdah al-wujūd*). . . . Philosophical interpretation is after all an afterthought applied to the naked content of mystical intuition.[18]

A major problem in understanding *waḥdat al-wujūd* is the term *wujūd*, which for the most part I have avoided translating in this chapter because there is no satisfactory equivalent in English. To render it either as "being" or "existence" raises difficulties, a thorough investigation of which could easily fill the remainder of this chapter. Here I want to point out another well-known problem connected with the term. Because *wujūd* derives from the root *w.j.d.*, "to find," it means not only to be found in an objective sense (in other words, to exist out there), but also the act of finding as a subjective experience. More specifically, *wujūd* refers both to God as the Absolute Reality and to the finding of God as experienced by God Himself and by the spiritual seeker. Hence, Ibn al-ʿArabī often refers to the "people of unveiling and finding" (*ahl al-kashf wa-l-wujūd*),[19] meaning those who have experienced the lifting of the veils that separate them from God, thus finding God in the cosmos and in themselves. In this sense, *wujūd* is practically synonymous with *shuhūd* ("witnessing" or "contemplation").[20] *Wujūd*, like *shuhūd*, refers to the divine self-disclosure, and both words have objective and subjective senses. For this and other reasons, the later debate between the supporters of *waḥdat al-wujūd* and those of *waḥdat al-shuhūd*, the "Oneness of Witnessing," obscures the fact that Ibn al-ʿArabī cannot be placed in one category or the other without distorting his overall teachings.[21]

If the question of *wujūd* as subjective experience is ignored, it can be seen that Ibn al-ʿArabī employs the term *wujūd* in two basic senses. First, the term refers to God, who is the "Real Being" (*al-wujūd al-ḥaqq*) or the "Necessary Being" (*wājib al-wujūd*) who cannot not be. Second, the term may also refer to the universe or the things within it. However, when Ibn al-ʿArabī speaks of the *wujūd* of "that which is other than God" (*mā siwā Allāh*), he is using the term in a metaphorical sense (*majāz*). Like Ghazālī and many others, he maintains that in reality (*ḥaqīqa*), *wujūd* belongs only to God. If things other than God appear to exist, this is because God has lent them *wujūd*, much in the same way that the sun lends light to the inhabitants of the earth.[22] In the last analysis, there is nothing in existence but the Real. There is only one Being, one *wujūd*, even though we are justified in speaking of many "existent things" in order to address ourselves to the plurality that we perceive in the phenomenal world.

If *wujūd* belongs only to God, then everything other than God is nonexistent in itself, although it is existent to the extent that it manifests the Real. In themselves the creatures are entities (*aʿyān*) or things (*ashyāʾ*), but they possess no existence of their own. The so-called fixed entities (*al-aʿyān al-thābita*), often misleadingly called archetypes,[23] are the things as they are known by God for all eternity; in other words, the fixed entities are the things without reference to their existence in the created world. Hence, they are more or less synonymous with what the philosophers call quiddities (*māhiyyāt*).

When God bestows existence on the entities, they appear in the universe, just as colors appear when light shines. But since the entities have no existence of their own, nothing is perceived but the *wujūd* of God imbued with the properties (*aḥkām*) of the entities. In trying to explain this point, one can do no better in a brief discussion than refer to the analogy of the rainbow, where the multiplicity of colors does not negate the oneness of light. Red and blue have no existence of their own because only light is manifest. We can speak of the reality, entity, or thingness (*shayʾiyya*) of red and blue, but not of their own, independent existence; their existence is only a mode of light's existence.

Although Ibn al-ʿArabī often discourses on the nature of *wujūd*'s oneness, he devotes far more attention to affirming the reality of multiplicity. His basic teaching goes back to the divine names mentioned so frequently in the Koran. The names are the archetypes of manyness, a divinely revealed affirmation of the reality of multiplicity. But again, to uphold the reality of multiplicity does not, in Ibn al-ʿArabī's view, necessitate upholding the independent *wujūd* of the multiple things.

Ibn al-ʿArabī commonly expresses his most fundamental view of *wujūd* through the theological concepts of *tanzīh* and *tashbīh*. The first term is often translated as "transcendence," the second as "anthropomorphism" or "immanence." Here I translate the words more literally as "incomparability" and "similarity." Ibn al-ʿArabī declares that God in Himself is incomparable with every created thing. In other words, *wujūd* is totally beyond the reach of everything in the cosmos; it is the Nonmanifest (*al-bāṭin*). But the Koran teaches that God is not only the Nonmanifest, but also the Manifest (*al-ẓāhir*). As such, God is similar to all things, because, by means of His names, He displays the properties of His own attributes in the cosmos. The universe is nothing but the outward manifestation of the innate properties of *wujūd*, just as colors, forms, and shapes are nothing but the outward manifestation of light. God is at once incomparable, because He is absolutely nonmanifest, and similar, because He displays His names and attributes by means of the existent things.

Wujūd, therefore, is not only one. The term *waḥdat al-wujūd* in its literal sense does not afford a sufficient description of the nature of reality. *Wujūd* is one in itself at the level of its nonmanifestation or its incomparability, and many through its manifestation or its similarity; God is one in His Essence (*dhāt*) and many through His names. Hence Ibn al-ʿArabī sometimes refers to God as the "One/Many" (*al-wāḥid al-kathīr*).[24]

The most succinct expression of Ibn al-ʿArabī's teachings about the nature of the one *wujūd* and its relationship to the multiplicity of the cosmos is probably the phrase "He/not He" (*huwa lā huwa*). What is a creature, a thing, an existent reality, a world? It is He/not He. A thing is identical with *wujūd* inasmuch as it exists, but other than *wujūd* inasmuch as it is itself. Ibn al-ʿArabī's opponents, in criticizing his teachings, look only at the first half of this phrase, "The cosmos is He." This sentence recalls the refrain employed by Persian poets long before Ibn al-ʿArabī, "All is He" (*hama ūst*).[25] For his part, Ibn al-ʿArabī constantly affirms that the cosmos is also *not He*. One must combine affirmation and negation, just as one must combine incomparability and similarity. To affirm that "All is He" and to forget that "All is not He" would be unacceptable. But it would be equally unacceptable to claim that "All is not He" in every respect, for that would make the cosmos into an independent reality, another divinity.

Ibn al-ʿArabī sometimes calls those who witness the cosmos as He/not He "the possessors of two eyes" (*dhū'l-ʿaynayn*). With one eye they look at God's absolute incomparability and with the other His similarity:

> The Perfect Man has two visions [*naẓar*] of the Real, which is why God appointed for him two eyes. With one eye he looks upon Him in respect of the fact that He is *Independent of the worlds* [3:97]. So he sees Him neither in any thing nor in himself. With the other eye he looks upon Him in respect of His name All-Merciful [*al-raḥmān*],

which seeks the cosmos and is sought by the cosmos. He sees His *wujūd* permeating all things.[26]

Ṣadr al-Dīn Qūnawī

Probably the most influential of Ibn al-ʿArabī's disciples was Ṣadr al-Dīn Qūnawī (d. 673/1274). Qūnawī's father, Majd al-Dīn Isḥāq, was a scholar and Sufi from Malatya in present-day Turkey who met Ibn al-ʿArabī on a pilgrimage to Mecca in the year 600/1204. In 602/1205–1206 the two traveled to Malatya together, and Ibn al-ʿArabī may have been present at the birth of Majd al-Dīn's son in 606/1210. After Majd al-Dīn's death, Ibn al-ʿArabī likely married his widow and undertook the training of Qūnawī, who became one of his closest disciples. When Ibn al-ʿArabī died in 638/1240, Qūnawī returned to Anatolia and settled in Konya, where he eventually became a friend of Rūmī. Shams al-Dīn Aflākī (d. 761/1360) provides many accounts of the high regard in which the two held each other, and he tells of Rūmī's request that Qūnawī lead the prayer at his funeral.[27] Qūnawī died seven months after Rūmī.

Of all Ibn al-ʿArabī's immediate disciples, Qūnawī was the most thoroughly acquainted with philosophy. Having studied the commentary of Naṣīr al-Dīn Ṭūsī (d. 672/1274) on Avicenna's *al-Ishārāt wa-l-tanbīhāt* ("Remarks and Admonitions"), Qūnawī initiated a correspondence, asking Ṭūsī many technical questions about the Peripatetic position. He felt he had enough mastery of Avicenna's writings to object to Ṭūsī's answers and to suggest that he reread a particular passage in Avicenna's *Taʿlīqāt* ("Glosses"). In explaining his motive for writing, Qūnawī said that he hoped to combine the conclusions derived from logical proofs (*burhān*) with the fruits of verified unveiling (*mukāshafa-yi muḥaqqaq*) and face-to-face vision of the unseen world (*ʿiyān*).[28]

Qūnawī's philosophical bent appears mainly in the logical and systematic structure of his writings. In contrast, Ibn al-ʿArabī's *Futūḥāt* is essentially a commentary on selected passages from the Koran and Hadith. In reading the *Futūḥāt,* one always feels close to the sources of the Islamic tradition and never senses a predominance of the systematic style of the philosophers. But Qūnawī's works are dominated by a rational and coherent style, even if the emphasis on mystical unveiling as a source of knowledge would not convince a logician.[29] At least partly because of his grounding in the philosophical tradition, Qūnawī stresses the centrality of *wujūd* to all discussion, whereas this point is not nearly so apparent in the works of Ibn al-ʿArabī, who is more likely to use Koranic terminology. Qūnawī's connections with philosophy provided Ibn Taymiyya (d. 728/1328) with a reason to attack him even more violently than he attacked Ibn al-ʿArabī. Ibn Taymiyya summarizes the difference of approach that appears in the writings of Ibn al-ʿArabī and Qūnawī by quoting their disciple ʿAfīf al-Dīn Tilimsānī (d. 690/1291):

> As for Ibn al-ʿArabī's companion Ṣadr al-Dīn of Rūm, he had pretensions to philosophy [*mutafalsif*], so he was further from the Shariah and Islam. That is why . . . Tilimsānī used to say, "My first shaykh was a philosophizing spiritual [*mutarawḥin mutafalsif*], while my second was a spiritual philosopher [*faylasūf mutarawḥin*]."[30]

Although Qūnawī employs the expression *waḥdat al-wujūd* (or *waḥdat wujūdihi*, the "Oneness of His Being") in at least two passages in his writings, he does not use it as an independent technical term. Rather, it comes up naturally in discussions of the relationship between God's *wujūd* and oneness. In the following passage he employs the philosophical language of *waḥda* and *wujūd* to explain the two modes of the Real—His oneness in Himself and His plurality in His manifestation:

> Know that the Real is sheer *wujūd* within which is no diversity, and that He is one with a true oneness in contrast to which no manyness can be conceptualized. . . . All things perceived in the entities and witnessed in the engendered things . . . are the properties of *wujūd*; or, call them the forms of the relationships within His knowledge. . . . Call them what you like: They are not *wujūd*, since *wujūd* is one. . . . *Wujūd* cannot be perceived by a human being inasmuch as it is one with a true oneness, like *waḥdat al-wujūd*. . . . Nothing issues from God, in respect of the *waḥda* of His *wujūd*, except one.[31]

In another passage, Qūnawī employs the expression "the oneness of His *wujūd*" in the midst of explaining that multiplicity does not contradict *wujūd*'s oneness since the multiple things are merely the "tasks" (*shuʾūn*) of the Divine Essence (these tasks, Qūnawī explains elsewhere,[32] are identical with the fixed entities):

> As for the interrelationship [*munāsaba*] between the One Real and everything else, that is established on the part of the "other" [*siwā*] in respect of the fact that God's tasks are not other than God, since they are the realities of the things which introduce plurality into the *waḥda* of His *wujūd* and are named the "others" [*aghyār*].[33]

As these two passages show, Qūnawī, like Ibn al-ʿArabī, held that the oneness of *wujūd* does not prevent the multiplicity of its self-disclosures. Although one in its essence or in respect of its incomparability, *wujūd* is many in its appearances or in respect of its similarity. In Qūnawī's own words:

> Though there is nothing but one *wujūd*, it manifests itself as diverse, multiple, and plural because of the diversity of the realities of the receptacles. Nevertheless, in itself and in respect of its disengagement

from the loci of manifestation [*maẓāhir*], *wujūd* does not become plural or multiple.[34]

Muʾayyid al-Dīn Jandī and Saʿīd al-Dīn Farghānī

Among Qūnawī's many disciples and students, two were especially important for the spread of Ibn al-ʿArabī's school. The first was Muʾayyid al-Dīn Jandī (d. ca. 700/1300), whose commentary on Ibn al-ʿArabī's *Fuṣūṣ al-ḥikam* ("The Ringstones of Wisdom") formed the basis for most of the numerous commentaries that were written later. Although he was deeply concerned with explaining the nature of *wujūd* and *waḥda*, he does not appear to have employed the term *waḥdat al-wujūd* even in passing.[35] Phrases approximating it, however, are not difficult to find. For example, "*Wujūd* is one reality that becomes intelligibly differentiated within distinct levels"; "None has *wujūd* except one entity, which is the Real."[36] Jandī wrote poetry in both Arabic and Persian, including this line:

> He is one, the existent in all,
> He alone, but imagination calls Him "other."[37]

The second major follower of Qūnawī is Saʿīd al-Dīn Farghānī (d. 699/1300), author of the first commentary on the famous *Naẓm al-sulūk* ("The Poem of the Way") of Ibn al-Fāriḍ (d. 632/1235).[38] Farghānī wrote this work first in Persian with the title *Mashāriq al-darārī* ("The Orients of Radiant Stars"), and then he wrote a much more detailed version in Arabic, renaming it *Muntahā'l-madārik* ("The Utmost Limit of Perception"). In a short preface to the Persian text, Qūnawī says that in the year 643/1245–1246 he traveled from Syria to Egypt with a group of learned and spiritually advanced Sufis. During this journey and on his return to Anatolia, he read and explained the *Naẓm al-sulūk* to his companions, who took notes with the aim of compiling commentaries on difficult passages; only Farghānī succeeded in this goal.[39] Hence, we have Qūnawī's testimony that Farghānī's works are based directly on his teachings, although in any case this is obvious from the style and content.

In the Persian environment, Farghānī's two commentaries seem to have been as influential as any other work of Ibn al-ʿArabī's school with the exception of the *Fuṣūṣ* itself. But while the *Fuṣūṣ* was considered difficult if not enigmatic, and was seldom quoted except to provide brief statements of ideas, Farghānī's works were frequently cited to explain Ibn al-ʿArabī's teachings. Farghānī found many devotees among the later students of *waḥdat al-wujūd* because, in contrast to Ibn al-ʿArabī in the *Fuṣūṣ*, he dealt with each point of doctrine in a systematic manner, and in contrast to Qūnawī, he explained each point in detail.

Farghānī employs the term *waḥdat al-wujūd* about thirty times in his *Mashāriq* and probably at least as many times in his *Muntahā*.[40] As remarked earlier, Ibn al-ʿArabī expresses the doctrine of *tawḥīd* by declaring that God is both incomparable and similar, or one in Himself and many through the loci of His self-disclosure. Farghānī sometimes expresses this same idea by contrasting *waḥdat al-wujūd* with *kathrat al-ʿilm*, the "Manyness of Knowledge."[41] God knows all things in Himself as fixed entities; then, on the basis of this knowledge, He creates the universe. An ultimate oneness underlies creation because God is one, but the creatures are many in a true sense because all multiplicity goes back to God's knowledge of the many things.[42] Oneness and manyness are both attributes of the Divine Reality, although from different points of view. In Farghānī's words, "Both *waḥdat al-wujūd* and *kathrat al-ʿilm* . . . are attributes of the Essence."[43]

When Farghānī employs the expression *waḥdat al-wujūd*, he usually considers it one of the three main stages of spiritual growth undergone by travelers on the path to God. From this point of view, the contemplation of *waḥdat al-wujūd* is the first and lowest stage, whereas the contemplation of *kathrat al-ʿilm* is the second stage. The third and final stage combines oneness and manyness in a harmonious balance. At this stage, the prophet or the friend of God sees with "two eyes," as Ibn al-ʿArabī puts it. There is also a fourth stage, but it pertains exclusively to the Prophet Muhammad.[44]

In Farghānī's writings, *waḥdat al-wujūd* has still not been established as an independent technical term, and certainly not as a designation for a specific school of thought. Moreover, the context of Farghānī's use of the term demonstrates that he does not consider it especially fundamental to Ibn al-ʿArabī's point of view. Although he makes the same basic points in the Persian and Arabic versions of his commentary on the *Naẓm al-sulūk*, he often does not carry the term *waḥdat al-wujūd* over from Persian into Arabic. If it were a technical term of any significance, he would certainly have kept it in the Arabic version. It is only the elements that make up the expression—*waḥda* and *wujūd*—that are important for the discussion, not the expression itself.

It is easy to see that Ibn al-ʿArabī and his immediate followers accepted that there is only one true *wujūd* and held that the multiplicity of the cosmos manifests the one *wujūd* without making it plural. But Ibn al-ʿArabī never employs the term *waḥdat al-wujūd*, whereas Qūnawī only mentions it in passing. Once Farghānī begins to employ the term repeatedly, it refers to a relatively low station of spiritual realization since the adept who witnesses *waḥdat al-wujūd* still has to ascend to *kathrat al-ʿilm* and beyond. Only the greatest of the prophets and friends of God attain to the station of combining the two perspectives, and at this point the term *waḥdat al-wujūd* plays no significant role. It is only in describing the first stage of the spiritual path that Farghānī sometimes uses it.

The question that naturally arises here is the following: How did the term *waḥdat al-wujūd* come to be singled out as the outstanding doctrine of Ibn al-ʿArabī and his school? Not enough is known about the works of the various figures writing immediately after Ibn al-ʿArabī to answer this question with certainty, but tentative conclusions can be suggested.

Ibn Sabʿīn

Among the authors who may have used the term *waḥdat al-wujūd* in a technical sense are such disciples of Ibn al-ʿArabī as Ibn Sawdakīn (d. 646/1248) and ʿAfīf al-Dīn Tilimsānī.[45] However, the most likely source of the term is Qūnawī's contemporary Ibn Sabʿīn (d. 669/1270), the author of the well-known treatise, *al-Masāʾil al-ṣiqiliyya* ("The Sicilian Questions"), which is a set of answers to questions posed by Emperor Frederick II Hohenstaufen.[46] Although Ibn Sabʿīn was certainly familiar with the Greek philosophers and their followers in Islam, his published writings display him primarily as a Sufi. One has to agree with Michel Chodkiewicz that Ibn Sabʿīn was thoroughly influenced by the perspective of Ibn al-ʿArabī, even if he does not acknowledge this fact in his works.[47]

When Ibn Sabʿīn expresses his own teachings, he often employs aphoristic, elliptical, and mysterious expressions more reminiscent of the sayings of the early Sufis than of philosophical treatises. His works stand in stark contrast to those of Qūnawī, whose philosophical training shows even when he recounts his most exalted visionary experiences, as in his *al-Nafaḥāt al-ilāhiyya* ("The Divine Breaths"). It seems that much of what Ibn Sabʿīn wrote was aimed at his own disciples and had practical applications to the spiritual life; hence he tends toward ellipses and paradoxes, throwing the disciples back on their own spiritual resources to understand the point.

In the context of Sufism, Ibn Sabʿīn appears primarily as a spiritual teacher who often employs the language of philosophy to make his point and who sometimes had to write philosophically for a public audience. All his works need to be read in the light of treatises such as his *Risālat al-naṣīḥa* ("The Treatise of Good Council"), which deals mainly with *dhikr*. In this work Ibn Sabʿīn makes the practical application of his teachings explicit. He aims to take away the assurances of logical discourse and throw the disciple back on the invocation of the divine name "Allah." Chodkiewicz points out that Ibn Sabʿīn frequently injects the phrase "Allah alone" (*Allāh faqaṭ*) into the midst of his writings as a sort of leitmotiv. This is not a statement of a philosophical position, but an incitement to his readers to follow the Koranic injunction, *Say: "Allah," then leave them to themselves, playing their game of plunging* (6:91).

What is of particular interest here is that in several passages Ibn Sabʿīn employs the term *waḥdat al-wujūd*, not in passing, but as a specific designation for the fundamental nature of things. In him we find what we did not find in Qūnawī and his followers, namely, instances in which the term appears to have become a technical expression referring to the worldview of the sages and the friends of God. For example, he writes:

> The common people and the ignorant are dominated by the accidental, which is manyness and plurality, while the elect—the men of knowledge—are dominated by the root, which is *waḥdat al-wujūd*. He

> who remains with the root does not undergo transferal or transformation; he remains fixed in his knowledge and his realization. But he who stays with the branch undergoes transformation and transferal; things become many in his eyes, so he forgets and becomes negligent and ignorant.[48]

Awḥad al-Dīn Balyānī

Among the important figures who followed in the line of Ibn Sabʿīn is Awḥad al-Dīn Balyānī (d. 686/1288), who was probably connected to him through Shushtarī. Balyānī is the author of *Risālat al-aḥadiyya* ("The Treatise on Unity"), which often is quoted to illustrate Ibn al-ʿArabī's understanding of the doctrine of *waḥdat al-wujūd*. This work was usually attributed to Ibn al-ʿArabī himself, but Chodkiewicz has shown that it is by Balyānī and that it does not present a balanced statement of Ibn al-ʿArabī's teachings.[49] The tone is familiar:

> By Himself He sees Himself, and by Himself He knows Himself. None sees Him other than He, and none perceives Him other than He. His Veil is His oneness; nothing veils other than He. His veil is the concealment of His existence in His oneness, without any quality. . . . His Prophet is He, and His sending is He, and His word is He. He sent Himself with Himself to Himself.[50]

In sum, the work is an ecstatic hymn set to the tune of the aforementioned Persian poetical exclamation, *hama ūst*. Hence, it should not be surprising to hear that its author lived in Shiraz and wrote Persian poems in a style full of precedents in his own language.[51]

Balyānī's exposition of *waḥdat al-wujūd* cannot be put into the same category as that of Ibn al-ʿArabī and his immediate disciples, who always took care to offset expressions of God's similarity with descriptions of His incomparability. Where Balyānī and others like him say "He," Ibn al-ʿArabī and his followers say "He/not He," although this does not mean that Balyānī had nothing more to say on the matter. His *Risāla* is no more an attempt to provide a full explanation of the nature of existence than was the oft-repeated "I am the Real" (*anā'l-ḥaqq*) of Ḥallāj.

Saʿd al-Dīn Ḥammūya and ʿAzīz al-Dīn Nasafī

One of the many important figures who may have played a role in establishing *waḥdat al-wujūd* as a technical term is Saʿd al-Dīn Ḥammūya (d. 649/1252), a Persian disciple of the great Najm al-Dīn Kubrā (d. 618/1221). Ḥammūya spent several years in Damascus, where he met both Ibn al-ʿArabī and Ṣadr al-Dīn

Qūnawī. He wrote a letter to Ibn al-ʿArabī in which he asked him to clarify certain points in some of his writings.[52] Although Ḥammūya is the author of more than fifty works, only one of these has been edited, probably because most of his writings offer little encouragement to scholars. Concerning him, Jāmī remarks, "He has many works . . . , full of mysterious sayings, difficult words, numbers, diagrams, and circles, which the eye of reason and thought is incapable of deciphering."[53] Some passages quoted from Ḥammūya by his disciple ʿAzīz al-Dīn Nasafī (d. before 699/1300) suggest that he expressed himself in an aphoristic and elliptical style similar to that of Ibn Sabʿīn. For example, Nasafī writes:

> The shaykh of shaykhs Saʿd al-Dīn Ḥammūya was asked, "What is God?" He replied, "The existent [*al-mawjūd*] is God." Then he was asked, "What is the cosmos?" He replied, "There is no existent but God."[54]

Nasafī probably played a much more important role than Ḥammūya in popularizing Ibn al-ʿArabī's teachings through such well-known Persian works as his *Insān-i kāmil* ("The Perfect Man"). Like Ibn Sabʿīn, to whom he sometimes refers in his works, Nasafī employs the expression *waḥdat al-wujūd* in a few instances as a technical term to refer to a whole doctrine, not part of a doctrine.[55] And like others after him, he frequently employs the expression *ahl-i waḥdat*, the "people of oneness," to refer to those who supported *waḥdat al-wujūd*.[56] He was probably the first to divide the people of oneness into different groups according to their differing formulations of *waḥdat al-wujūd*.[57]

In several instances, Nasafī includes his own master Ḥammūya among the people of oneness, and in one passage he says that some of them consider God's creation as "imagination and display" (*khayāl wa-namāyish*).[58] He probably has Ḥammūya in mind as a member of this group, since we read in one of Ḥammūya's works, "Whatever you see other than oneness is imagination."[59]

Ibn Taymiyya

The violent attacks mounted by Ibn Taymiyya against Ibn al-ʿArabī and those who followed him are well-known.[60] Ibn Taymiyya often refers to the term *waḥdat al-wujūd*, even employing it in the titles of two of his treatises: *Ibṭāl waḥdat al-wujūd* ("Showing the falsity of *waḥdat al-wujūd*") and *Risāla ilā man saʾalahu ʿan ḥaqīqat madhhab al-ittiḥādiyyīn, ay al-qāʾilīn bi-waḥdat al-wujūd* ("A treatise written to the one who asked about the reality of the position of the unificationists, that is, those who support *waḥdat al-wujūd*").[61] It is particularly significant that in the second of these titles Ibn Taymiyya identifies *waḥdat al-wujūd* with "unificationism" (*ittiḥād*). He repeats this identification in many passages of his works, often adding the term "incarnationism" (*ḥulūl*) as a second near synonym.[62] Both terms had long been attacked as the heresies of certain sects or figures, and both are specifically rejected by Ibn al-ʿArabī and his followers, at least in the meaning that is given to the terms by those who criticize them.[63]

Ibn Taymiyya sums up his objections to the proponents of *waḥdat al-wujūd* by claiming that they deny the three basic principles of the religion: They have no faith in God, His prophets, or the Last Day. I quote part of his explanation:

> As for faith in God, they think that His *wujūd* is identical with the *wujūd* of the cosmos and that the cosmos has no other maker than the cosmos itself. As for the prophets, these people think that they have more knowledge of God than God's Messenger and all the other prophets. Some claim to take knowledge of God—that is, *waḥdat al-wujūd* and *taʿṭīl*—from the Prophet's lamp.[64]

Note that in this passage, by citing *waḥdat al-wujūd* and *taʿṭīl* as parallel terms, Ibn Taymiyya is identifying the two. *Taʿṭīl* is variously defined in theological texts and always condemned. Its basic meaning is to consider God divested of His attributes.

Ibn Taymiyya claims that the supporters of *waḥdat al-wujūd* believe that the *wujūd* of the cosmos is identical with the *wujūd* of God: "Those who uphold *waḥdat al-wujūd* say that *wujūd* is one and that the necessary *wujūd* that belongs to the Creator is the same as the possible *wujūd* that belongs to the creature."[65] Elsewhere he writes, "The reality of the words" of those who speak of *waḥdat al-wujūd* "is that the *wujūd* of the engendered things is identical with the *wujūd* of God; it is nothing else and nothing different."[66]

In other words, Ibn Taymiyya holds that according to Ibn al-ʿArabī, God and the cosmos are identical. Thus he takes a simplistic view of one side of Ibn al-ʿArabī's teaching, that of similarity or immanence, and completely ignores the other side, that of incomparability or transcendence. Ibn al-ʿArabī's often restated position is "He/not He." The *wujūd* of the cosmos can be said to be identical with the *wujūd* of God in one respect, but strictly speaking, the cosmos has no *wujūd*. The whole problem is to define the subtle relationship that exists between the real *wujūd* of God and the unreal *wujūd* of the creatures. Ibn Taymiyya and most of those who followed in his footsteps seemed to have believed that there must be a simple, straightforward explanation for the relationship between God and the cosmos. In contrast, Ibn al-ʿArabī and most of his followers held that the highest understanding is utter bewilderment (*ḥayra*) in the face of a reality that defies the categories of yes and no, either/or.

In any case, it is not my purpose to defend Ibn al-ʿArabī against the charges of Ibn Taymiyya and others. I merely want to point out that Ibn Taymiyya considered *waḥdat al-wujūd* synonymous with atheism and unbelief because he saw it as a denial of the distinction between God and the cosmos. And because of his frequent explicit attacks on the term *waḥdat al-wujūd*, he probably deserves more credit than anyone else for making it a center of contention in Islamic history, since, as we have seen, it played no important role in the technical vocabulary of Ibn al-ʿArabī and his direct followers. Even third and fourth generation commentators on the *Fuṣūṣ*, like Jandī's student ʿAbd al-Razzāq Kāshānī (d. 730/1330) and Kāshānī's student Dāwūd Qayṣarī (d. 751/1350), both of whom were Ibn Taymiyya's contemporaries, rarely if ever mention the term.[67] In a treatise called *Asās al-waḥdāniyya*, in which he discusses the terms *waḥda* and *wujūd* in detail, Qayṣarī can get no closer to the expression *waḥdat al-wujūd* than one instance of *waḥdat wājib al-wujūd*, the "Oneness of the Necessary Being."[68] Hence, when Ibn Taymiyya singled out the term *waḥdat al-wujūd* as exemplifying the position of the unificationists, he probably derived it from the works of Ibn Sabʿīn, to which he often refers, or from one of Ibn Sabʿīn's disciples.

Although Ibn Taymiyya and others like him employed the term *waḥdat al-wujūd* to denote the heresies they perceived in the writings of Ibn al-ʿArabī's school, Ibn al-ʿArabī's later followers seemed to have had no qualms about accepting the term as a convenient denotation for their overall worldview. They were happy to consider it a term of praise, even if their critics considered it a term of blame. Thus, by the middle of the ninth/fifteenth century Jāmī commonly speaks of the "supporters of the Oneness of Being" (*al-qāʾilūn bi-waḥdat al-wujūd*), meaning thereby Ibn al-ʿArabī, Qūnawī, Farghānī, and the main line of *Fuṣūṣ* commentators.[69]

The history of the term *waḥdat al-wujūd* can be summarized as follows: The term is not found in the writings of Ibn al-ʿArabī. For Qūnawī, it has no specific technical sense; where it does occur, it means simply that there is only one true *wujūd*, the *wujūd* of God. The relationship of this *wujūd* to the things of the world needs to be explained; it is not implied in the term *waḥdat al-wujūd* itself. In Farghānī's writings *waḥdat al-wujūd* is well on its way to becoming a technical term, but it does not stand on its own since it needs to be complemented by the Manyness of Knowledge. Off to the side of this main line of Ibn al-ʿArabī's followers, other figures like Ibn Sabʿīn and Nasafī were employing the term as a kind of shorthand to allude to the fundamental nature of things. Ibn Taymiyya seized on the expression as a synonym for the great heresies of unificationism and incarnationism. By the time of Jāmī, and perhaps much before, *waḥdat al-wujūd* became the designation for an expression of *tawḥīd* that was typified by the writings of Ibn al-ʿArabī and his followers.

Orientalists

Western studies of Ibn al-ʿArabī have greatly complicated the task of discerning what is meant by *waḥdat al-wujūd*. Many of the earlier Orientalists, like historians of thought in general, felt that by putting a label on an idea, they had understood it and had no more need to think about it. Ibn al-ʿArabī in particular attracted labels, which is not surprising. One look at the difficulty and sheer volume of his writings convinced most people that it would be futile to spend a lifetime trying to decipher them. The easiest solution was to call Ibn al-ʿArabī a pantheist or to claim that he stood outside of "orthodox" Islam and to move on to greener pastures. This was far preferable to admitting that he was a spiritual teacher, sage, philosopher, theologian, Koran commentator, and jurist of the first order, a figure whose elaborate synthesis of Islamic thought cannot be approached without long years of training. After all, what would be gained by admitting that the Orient had produced forms of knowledge that cannot be filed into neat cubbyholes?

More recently, a number of serious scholars have taken the trouble to study some of Ibn al-ʿArabī's works and to meditate on his teachings in depth. The facile assumptions of an earlier generation have been largely discarded, but the old labels are still to be found in the secondary literature. Among specialists, it is now generally recognized that "the repeated use of alien and inappropriate interpretive categories . . . cannot but mislead those lacking a firsthand acquaintance with Ibn al-ʿArabī's works."[70]

To try to sort out the views of Ibn al-ʿArabī offered by various Orientalists over the past one hundred years would entail a major study. Here I can only suggest that Western scholars have reflected the split concerning Ibn al-ʿArabī found in Islam itself. Hence, they have been divided into two camps: those for and those against, even though the language of "objective" scholarship often conceals personal predilections. In the eyes of those who take a negative approach, *waḥdat al-wujūd* becomes an easily dismissed "ism," or perhaps a distortion of "authentic" and "orthodox" Islam brought about by a morbid preoccupation with imaginative speculation that was but a prelude to the decline of a civilization. Scholars who offer a positive evaluation have realized that the worldview of this figure who has dominated much of Islamic thought for the past seven hundred years cannot be dismissed so easily. Some even maintain that *waḥdat al-wujūd* represents a providential reformulation of *tawḥīd* in a philosophical language that can provide practical solutions for the spiritual malaise of contemporary man.

The Meanings of the Term *Waḥdat al-Wujūd*

This brief review of the history of the term *waḥdat al-wujūd* allows me to propose seven different ways in which the term has been understood, without intending to be exhaustive. First, *waḥdat al-wujūd* denotes a school of thought that goes back to Ibn al-ʿArabī and makes certain statements about the nature of the relationship between God and the world. This meaning of the term came to be accepted by supporters and opponents of Ibn al-ʿArabī and was established by the time of Jāmī.

The remaining six definitions depend on whether the person who employs the term has evaluated this school of thought positively or negatively.

Supporters

1. When Qūnawī and Farghānī employ the term *waḥdat al-wujūd,* it represents a statement about *wujūd* or reality itself, without any implication that a whole system of thought lies behind it; in their works the term is invariably complemented by an affirmation of the manyness and plurality of the Real's self-disclosure in the cosmos.

2. For Ibn Sabʿīn, Nasafī, and the whole later tradition of Ibn al-ʿArabī's followers, the expression *waḥdat al-wujūd* itself represents a sufficient statement about the nature of things. Those who employed the term in this sense felt no need to point out, at least not in the immediate context, that multiplicity also possesses a certain reality, although most of them do not deny this fact, except perhaps in moments of rhetorical excess.

3. In the later tradition of Sufism and Islamic philosophy, *waḥdat al-wujūd* is often employed as a virtual synonym for *tawḥīd,* with the understanding that it primarily refers to the Sufi approach to expressing *tawḥīd*. In this most general sense, the term can be used to refer to the ideas of Sufis who flourished long before Ibn al-ʿArabī.

Opponents

1. For Ibn Taymiyya, *waḥdat al-wujūd* is practically synonymous with incarnationism and unificationism, that is, the thesis that God and the world, or God and man, are identical. By a slight extension of this meaning, *waḥdat al-wujūd* becomes identical with broader negative categories, such as apostasy (*zandaqa*), atheism (*ilḥād*), and unbelief (*kufr*). I would also put in this category those Western interpretations of *waḥdat al-wujūd* that give it labels such as "pantheism," usually with the obvious intent of denigrating its supporters and convincing us that we need not take it seriously.

2. Certain later Indian Sufis, especially Aḥmad Sirhindī (d. 1034/1624), employ the term *waḥdat al-wujūd* in a less negative sense. In general, they acknowledge that it possesses a certain validity, but they maintain that *waḥdat al-shuhūd* represents a higher degree of spiritual attainment.[71] Although much research needs to be carried out before the sources and aims of this debate become completely clear, it seems that *waḥdat al-shuhūd* was proposed as a preferable position to *waḥdat al-wujūd* at least partly in order to foil the kinds of criticisms made by Ibn Taymiyya and his followers. As Marijan Molé pointed out, Sirhindī's way of expressing himself concerning *waḥdat al-shuhūd* "safeguarded the transcendence and absolute otherness of God."[72] If many Sufis continued to support *waḥdat al-wujūd* in opposition to *waḥdat al-shuhūd,* it was no doubt because, in their eyes, *waḥdat al-wujūd* never posed any threat to God's transcendence and absolute otherness in the first place.

3. The distinction between *waḥdat al-wujūd* and *waḥdat al-shuhūd* was taken up by several orientalists, including Louis Massignon, George Anawati, and

Louis Gardet, who then read this distinction back into Islamic history on highly questionable grounds. Massignon had a well-known personal preference for the love mysticism of Ḥallāj and a deep aversion to Ibn al-ʿArabī's approach. For him and those who followed him, *waḥdat al-wujūd* became "static existential monism," while *waḥdat al-shuhūd* was "dynamic testimonial monism," the latter far more preferable than the former, not least because it accorded with "orthodoxy." Massignon's attribution of a "static" mysticism to those who supported *waḥdat al-wujūd* illustrates the typical sort of oversimplification indulged in by those who place labels on Ibn al-ʿArabī, thus mutilating a highly complex doctrinal synthesis.[73] It is not my purpose to suggest all of the misunderstandings caused by reading such simplistically interpreted dichotomies back into Islamic history. I only add that later Sufism came to distinguish between *waḥdat al-wujūd* and *waḥdat al-shuhūd* for internal reasons, to some of which I have already alluded. But to make this distinction normative for the whole history of Sufism is nearly as misleading as employing categories such as pantheism. Although one cannot deny that Sufis illustrate deep differences of perspective, one can be certain that scholars who attempt to redefine terms such as *waḥdat al-wujūd* and *waḥdat al-shuhūd* in terms of Western philosophical and psychological categories only add to the confusion already present in our perception of Sufism's history.

These few remarks on the problems of understanding what is meant by the term *waḥdat al-wujūd* should at least warn us that we need to look carefully at how people who employ the term evaluate Ibn al-ʿArabī's teachings. In general, sympathizers see *waḥdat al-wujūd* as a restatement of *tawḥīd* in the language of the advanced and refined intellectuality of later Islamic history, whereas detractors consider it a deviation from the supposedly clear distinctions drawn between God and the cosmos by the early and relatively unsophisticated schools of theology. Nevertheless, the term *waḥdat al-wujūd* carries a good deal of baggage because of the long debate over its use. Thus all sorts of complications can arise that obscure what is at issue.

An interesting example of these complications is provided by the Festschrift prepared for the eight-hundreth anniversary of Ibn al-ʿArabī's birth, in which an Egyptian scholar, who is a fervent supporter of Ibn al-ʿArabī, writes that those who attribute *waḥdat al-wujūd* to Ibn al-ʿArabī commit a grievous error. Although this scholar never defines what he understands by *waḥdat al-wujūd*, it is clear that he has accepted the negative evaluation of the term offered by Ibn al-ʿArabī's opponents. In answer to this article, an Iranian scholar has written a strong rebuttal in which he demonstrates, in the light of the Iranian intellectual tradition, that *waḥdat al-wujūd* forms the backbone of Islamic thought.[74] It does not even occur to this critic to ask whether the Egyptian scholar understands the term in the same way as he does. Careful reading of the two authors shows that they do not disagree as to what Ibn al-ʿArabī believed and wrote about; both accept him as one of the greatest intellectual and spiritual authorities of Islam. They have merely stumbled over divergent understandings of the term *waḥdat al-wujūd*.

9

The Question of Ibn al-ʿArabī's "Influence" on Rūmī

Over the past century, many people have suggested that Rūmī was a follower or disciple of Ibn al-ʿArabī. This is largely due to the observations of the greatest Western authority on the *Mathnawī*, R. A. Nicholson, who maintained that Rūmī was influenced by him.[1] Before clarifying my position on the issue, I want to engage in a bit of introspection and ask why we are interested in such problems in the first place.

Scholars of an earlier generation seem to have felt that by saying "x influenced y," they had explained something of profound importance. Today, many people have come to understand that this sort of approach is deftly designed to turn their attention away from all that was considered important within the historical and cultural context in question. For Rūmī and Ibn al-ʿArabī, historical influence was simply irrelevant to what they were saying. Like other Muslim sages, they considered the divine as primary and the human and historical as lesser. The spirit or meaning (*maʿnā*) is the root and the source, while the body or form (*ṣūra*) is the branch and the shadow. Whether metaphysically, cosmologically, or intellectually, the meaning of a doctrine takes precedence, while the forms it assumes are of secondary interest. Both Rūmī and Ibn al-ʿArabī repeatedly affirm that they have not taken the content of their teachings from any human being. Their "vision" is of central importance, not the sources from which they derived the various formal elements used to express it. For them, the vision was all. Divine self-disclosures are central, not peripheral. The transformative power of a Rūmī or an Ibn al-ʿArabī derives from an intimate experience of God, and this power is not to be taken lightly, since it instilled a vibrant love and life into much of Islamic culture from the seventh/thirteenth century down to recent times, and it still possesses enough strength to attract "modern" and even "postmodern" men and women to esoteric conferences. One cannot read these authors without standing in awe of their incredibly deep and profound mastery not only of the "roots of the roots of the roots of religion," as Rūmī puts it in his introduction to the *Mathnawī*, but the roots of everything that allows for a full flowering of the human condition.

Rūmī speaks also for Ibn al-ʿArabī when he addresses his readers with the words:

> Having seen the form, you are unaware of the meaning.
> If you are wise, pick out the pearl from the shell![2]

But our business as scholars is to trade in shells, not pearls. By definition, we miss the point. Once we understand that our research, from the perspective of the teachings of those we are studying, is off the mark, we can turn to the shells with perhaps a small amount of humility, knowing that the pearls will never be found through our trade.

This does not mean that the shells should be denigrated. No matter how great the spiritual vision of a Rūmī or an Ibn al-ʿArabī, it was expressed in shells, and on this level it is possible to speak about elements deriving from earlier sources and to draw certain conclusions about Rūmī's predecessors. Those who claim that Rūmī was influenced by Ibn al-ʿArabī or his immediate followers will have to prove their contentions through these formal elements.

Henry Corbin remarks that "it would be quite superficial to dwell on the contrast between the two forms of spirituality cultivated by Mawlānā and Ibn ʿArabī."[3] One agrees with Corbin that at the level of meaning, Rūmī and Ibn al-ʿArabī converge profoundly, since they both spoke on behalf of the Supreme Meaning. But one also agrees that Ibn al-ʿArabī and Rūmī represent "two forms of spirituality" which, as forms, are different. If one wants to talk about influence, this can be perceived only on the superficial level where forms influence forms, the same level where similarities and differences are perceived. No one can reach inside the hearts of Rūmī and Ibn al-ʿArabī except through the forms and imagery that they use to express their inward states. At the inward level, there may indeed be deep and profound connections between Rūmī and Ibn al-ʿArabī, since both lived and breathed *tawḥīd*. But to speak of influence on the level of "meaning" or "spirit" is simply to indulge in speculation because knowledge of influence can only be gained by means of the formal level.[4] Once formal influence is found, there may be justification for concluding that there was a deeper, spiritual influence. Hence, one first has to look for borrowings of technical terms and poetical images.

In fact, at the level of linguistic forms, there is no concrete evidence that Ibn al-ʿArabī's doctrines influenced Rūmī's mode of expression. Rūmī employs few if any technical terms, poetical images, and concepts also employed by Ibn al-ʿArabī that are not found in earlier authors. Both Rūmī and Ibn al-ʿArabī were thoroughly familiar with all branches of religious knowledge, including Sufi classics such as Qushayrī's *Risāla* and Ghazālī's *Iḥyāʾ*, so it is only natural that they share certain common terms and themes. But Ibn al-ʿArabī also employs many terms in a specific manner that is not to be found in earlier writers; it is these specific terms and ideas that cannot be found in Rūmī's works, although they can be found in the poetry of his contemporary, namely ʿIrāqī, and in the verses of many poets of the next century, such as Maḥmūd Shabistarī (d. 740/1339) and Shams al-Dīn Maghribī (d. 809/1406–1407).

One might object that Rūmī was a greater poet than ʿIrāqī and therefore had no need to employ the terminology of Ibn al-ʿArabī, but that he was nevertheless influenced by him. This comes down to pure conjecture because, once again, it makes sense to speak of influence only on the level of the formal elements involved. Moreover, there are many obvious influences on Rūmī's poetry by such figures as the Sufi poets Ḥakīm Sanāʾī (d. 525/1131) and Farīd al-Dīn ʿAṭṭār (d. ca. 617/1220), or Rūmī's father Bahāʾ al-Dīn Walad (d. 628/1230) and Shams al-Dīn Tabrīzī.[5] One cannot claim that Rūmī was too great to show influence from Ibn al-ʿArabī, but not great enough to discard the influence of Sanāʾī and ʿAṭṭār. Nor can one object that it was a question of the difference between Arabic and Persian, since much of Rūmī's technical terminology is derived from Arabic and he himself was the author of several hundred Arabic verses. And rather than seeing in his Arabic poetry the influence of Ibn al-ʿArabī, one sees the imagery of an ʿAṭṭār or a Sanāʾī carried over from Persian.

In a broad historical context, it is not difficult to discern two relatively independent currents within Sufism, without denying cross-fertilization. Ibn al-ʿArabī brings to fruition several centuries of spiritual ferment in Andalusia, North Africa, and Egypt. Rūmī brings to a climax a tradition of Persian Sufism going back to such figures as Anṣārī, Sanāʾī, and Aḥmad Ghazālī (d. 520/1126), author of the *Sawāniḥ al-ʿushshāq* ("The Incidents of the Lovers"), which is surely the most seminal work on love in the Persian language.[6] The influence of Anṣārī was especially widespread because of Maybudī's *Kashf*. Rūmī may also have been familiar with the *Rawḥ al-arwāḥ* ("The Refreshment of Spirits"), a long Persian commentary on the divine names by Aḥmad Samʿānī (d. 534/1140). This work constantly reminds one of Rūmī's concerns and style. Its audacious approach to Islamic teachings,[7] constant stress on the importance of love, and highly poetical use of language, may well have been one of Rūmī's formal inspirations.[8] Moreover, no one was as close to Rūmī as Bahāʾ Walad and Shams, both of whose teachings have influenced his poetry profoundly.[9] Rūmī's father, who initiated him into Sufism, is said to have been a member of a Sufi order that went back to Aḥmad Ghazālī, one of whose disciples was ʿAyn al-Quḍāt Hamadānī (d. 525/1131), the author of an important work on love[10] and a major precursor of the type of theoretical Sufism characteristic of the followers of Ibn al-ʿArabī. The works of these authors provide more than enough material to account for any formal resemblances that might exist between Rūmī and earlier Sufism.

No one denies that earlier figures influenced Rūmī by providing him with imagery, symbols, technical terms, and doctrines. With this raw material Rūmī constructed a bodily form into which he breathed the spirit of his own vision of *tawḥīd*. But if the claim is to be made that a specific figure exercised influence on him, there must be concrete reasons for making such a claim. Since the influence from certain directions is indeed obvious, there is no need to posit other sources without solid evidence. If certain images or technical terms are found in the writings of Rūmī's father or ʿAṭṭār, no one has to look any further, even if the image or term in question was also employed by Ibn al-ʿArabī.

It is not only the lack of any specific evidence that convinces one that Rūmī was free of Ibn al-ʿArabī's influence, it is also the deep difference between their perspectives, even if this lies only at what Corbin calls the "superficial" level of form. For example, Rūmī places love at the center of all things, much in the tradition of Aḥmad Ghazālī and Samʿānī. He expresses the ultimate value of love through verses that constantly manifest the spiritual state of intoxication (*sukr*), although many lines of the *Mathnawī* in particular demonstrate an eminent sobriety (*ṣaḥw*). Ibn al-ʿArabī and his followers also place an extremely high value on love.[11] Nevertheless, love does not permeate every line of their writings, as it does with Rūmī. One can imagine Ibn al-ʿArabī without love—despite Corbin—but one cannot imagine Rūmī without love.

Another point: Rūmī and Ibn al-ʿArabī directed their works at two completely different audiences. Ibn al-ʿArabī and his followers wrote for the ulama, those with thorough training not only in the Koran, Hadith, and jurisprudence, but also in Kalam and philosophy. None but the highly learned were capable of studying their works. In contrast, Rūmī composed poetry in order to stir up the fire of love in the hearts of his listeners, whoever they might be, whether learned scholars, practitioners of Sufism, or simply the common people. He aimed his poetry at anyone with an understanding of the Persian language and a modicum of spiritual taste or a sense of love and beauty. No one meeting these minimal requirements could help but be swept away by the intoxicating power of his lyrics. Rūmī spoke the language of the masses, and much of his "technical" terminology was derived from everyday discourse. No one needed any special educational or intellectual qualifications to appreciate his message.[12] As a result, Rūmī's language and teachings are far more universal than Ibn al-ʿArabī's, in the sense that only a small number of scholars with Sufi training could hope to understand the latter.

To sum up the difference of approach between Rūmī and Ibn al-ʿArabī, I can do no better than relate an anecdote told to me by the late S. J. Āshtiyānī, himself a devotee of both Ibn al-ʿArabī and Rūmī. One day Qūnawī went to see Rūmī and sat with him at the head of his audience chamber. One of Rūmī's disciples came forward and asked a question that Qūnawī considered to be very difficult, but that Rūmī was able to answer instantaneously, employing his usual colloquial style. Qūnawī turned to Rūmī and asked, "How are you able to express such difficult and abstruse metaphysics in such simple language?" Rūmī replied, "How are you able to make such simple ideas sound so complicated?"

Like Rūmī, Ibn al-ʿArabī spent much of his time in the Divine Presence, but his mode of experiencing the Divine took a relatively sober and intellectual form, while Rūmī expressed his relationship with his Beloved in the intoxicating imagery of love and rapture. In short, these two towering spiritual masters personify deeply divergent modes of spirituality that were providentially aimed at different human types, for, as the well-known Sufi saying has it, "There are as many ways to God as there are human souls." If someone insists that Ibn al-ʿArabī and Rūmī were inspired by the same vision of reality, I cannot protest, so long as it is kept in mind that Rūmī experienced that vision directly, without historical intermediaries.

Ibn al-ʿArabī's "Influence" on the *Mathnawī*

In translating and explaining the *Mathnawī*, Nicholson seems to have paid a good deal of attention to Turkish commentaries that explain the text in terms of the worldview of Ibn al-ʿArabī's school, a worldview that has dominated the intellectual expression of Sufism until recent times. Nicholson frequently quotes parallels to Rūmī's verses in Ibn al-ʿArabī's writings or explains Rūmī's concepts in terms of Ibn al-ʿArabī's teachings.

Although Nicholson was familiar with Ibn al-ʿArabī, he paid little or no attention to the great Sufis who wrote in the Persian language before Rūmī, such as Sanāʾī, ʿAṭṭār, Maybudī, and Samʿānī. Nor did he have at his disposal two of the most important sources for Rūmī's technical terms and imagery: Bahāʾ Walad's *Maʿārif* ("Gnostic Sciences") and Shams's *Maqālāt*. The editors of these two works have indicated a few of the numerous instances where Rūmī was directly inspired by them, while pointing out that the influence is so pervasive that it would be impossible to describe it fully. Samʿānī's *Rawḥ* is a great treasury of Sufi teachings on love, and its contents suggest that many of Rūmī's ideas were already current among Persian Sufis a hundred years earlier. Thus, it is the high quality of Rūmī's poetry rather than what he has to say that has made him the center of attention. No doubt other Persian works that demonstrate the intellectual content of Persian Sufism prior to Rūmī are still lying in libraries unread, or have simply disappeared.

In what follows, I list the most important instances in which Nicholson asserts or suggests that Rūmī was influenced by Ibn al-ʿArabī. For each case, I first cite Nicholson's translation and commentary, and then go on to propose other far more likely sources for Rūmī's formulations.

1:606–610: "Thou didst show the delightfulness of Being unto not-being, (after) thou hadst caused not-being to fall in love with thee . . . ."

Commentary: "The leading ideas in this passage come from Ibnu 'l-'Arabí, though their provenance is disguised (as usual) by the poetical form in which they are presented. . . . Ibnu 'l-'Arabí, and Rúmí after him, frequently make use of . . . [the term 'not-being' (*'adam, nístí, níst*)] to denote things which, though non-existent in one sense, are existent in another . . . ."

Note Nicholson's attempt to show that Rūmī is full of borrowings from Ibn al-ʿArabī by employing the expression "as usual." One wants to know first of all why Rūmī should have felt it necessary to disguise the provenance of his ideas. Did he fear someone? He certainly could have employed Ibn al-ʿArabī's specific technical terms if he had wanted, just as ʿIrāqī did. The editors of Bahāʾ Walad's *Maʿārif* and Shams's *Maqālāt* list many instances where Rūmī employs expressions from the works of his predecessors without attempting to hide their provenance. Some of Shams's utterances are far more scandalous than anything Ibn al-ʿArabī ever said, but Rūmī does not conceal them; on the contrary, he sometimes tries to top them.

Rūmī constantly meditates upon the relationship between existence and nonexistence. How could it be otherwise, given the profundity of his thought? The basic idea of this whole passage can easily be taken back to the repeated Koranic assertion that when God wants to bring a thing into existence, He says to it *Be!* (2:117). Where is the thing before God tells it to "be" if not "nonexistent in one sense, . . . existent in another"? It is true that Ibn al-ʿArabī often employs the terms *being* and *not-being*, but so do numerous other figures with whom Rūmī was familiar, such as Bahāʾ Walad, Shams, ʿAṭṭār, and Ghazālī, as well as others whose works he probably read, like Aḥmad Ghazālī and ʿAyn al-Quḍāt.[13] Or take these typical passages from Samʿānī: "Your existence is like nonexistence, and your nonexistence like existence"[14]; "Consider all existent things nonexistent in themselves and count all nonexistent things existent through His power."[15]

1:1112: "Reason is hidden, and (only) a world (of phenomena) is visible: our forms are the waves or a spray of it (of that hidden ocean)."

Commentary: "Underlying all individualized forms of being is the Unconditioned Divine Essence. This verse states concisely the doctrine of pantheistic monism (*waḥdat u 'l-wujúd*) in the form in which Rúmí may have heard it enunciated by Ṣadru'ddín of Qóniyah, a pupil of Ibnu 'l-'Arabí."

The verse expresses the relationship between the inward (*bāṭin*) and outward (*ẓāhir*), or the meaning and the form, a doctrine that is fundamental to all of Rūmī's teachings. It is prefigured in the Koran and was perceived therein by spiritual teachers, Sufis, and philosophers from the earliest times. Neither Ibn al-ʿArabī nor Qūnawī—nor Rūmī, for that matter—ever identify the Intellect (*ʿaql*, "reason" in Nicholson's translation) with the Divine Essence. Rūmī often refers to the Intellect in the sense employed in this verse as "Universal Intellect" (*ʿaql-i kull*), whereas Ibn al-ʿArabī is far more likely to employ the term "First Intellect" (*al-ʿaql al-awwal*). Ibn al-ʿArabī sometimes considers the First Intellect as the source of the forms in this world, but the idea is not central to his teachings, since he most often identifies the forms of the universe with the self-disclosures or loci of manifestation of *wujūd*.

A century before Ibn al-ʿArabī, Sanāʾī discussed *ʿaql* (often employing the synonymous Persian term *khirad*) in sections of his works. In his *Ḥadīqat al-ḥaqāʾiq* ("The Garden of Realities"), he speaks of the Intellect's cosmological function and employs the term *ʿaql-i kull* in the process: "Every good and evil under the heavens picks fruit from the stock of the Intellect. . . . The bench of the Universal Intellect stands beneath the All."[16]

The imagery of the ocean and the spray is common. Bahāʾ Walad writes, "The waves rose up from the ocean of nonexistence, throwing the foam, the debris, and the shells (the forms) and the pearls (the meanings) upon the shore."[17]

1:1133: "Therefore thou knewest light by its opposite: opposite reveals opposite in (the process of) coming forth."

Commentary: "Characteristically the poet throughout this passage combines ideas derived from Plotinus with Ibnu 'l-'Arabí's view that God and the world are related to each other as the inward aspect (*bátin*) and the outward aspect (*záhir*) of Being."

As I have noted elsewhere, the word Nicholson renders as "in (the process of) coming forth" (*ṣudūr*) should probably be understood not as a *maṣdar* but as the plural of *ṣadr*, "breast," which accords more with the colloquial language and Rūmī's point.[18] Nicholson read *ṣudūr*, a technical term in philosophy, so that he could point to an "influence" and bring in Neoplatonism. Even if we accept Nicholson's unlikely reading, it shows only that Rūmī was familiar with philosophical language, which no one doubts in any case.

The word "characteristically" in Nicholson's commentary plays the same role as the expression "as usual" in the first passage quoted above. Despite the claim that this borrowing is "characteristic" and "usual," Nicholson provides no concrete evidence whatsoever that Ibn al-ʿArabī is the direct or indirect source of any of Rūmī's ideas. The relationship between the terms *bāṭin* and *ẓāhir* and their centrality for Sufi thought was mentioned earlier.

1:1736: "All kings are enslaved to their slaves, all people are dead (ready to die) for one who dies for them."

Commentary: "These verses give a poetical form to the doctrine, with which students of Ibnu 'l-'Arabí are familiar, that correlative terms . . . are merely names for different aspects of the same reality."

Here at least Nicholson does not claim explicitly that Rūmī has derived these ideas from Ibn al-ʿArabī. The importance of correlation and opposites for Islamic thought in general is obvious to anyone who has read the Koran with care, and it reappears in all sorts of connections throughout Islamic intellectual history. Nicholson sees in these verses a kind of ontological statement, as is usually the case with similar statements in Ibn al-ʿArabī. However, as Nicholson implies in the remainder of his commentary on this verse, Rūmī makes such statements in the light of his own experiences of love—and no one could claim that he did not know love in all its intricacies. Compare the underlying idea of this passage with Rūmī's statement: "One cannot conceive of the sound of one hand clapping. . . . *He loves them* is never separate from *they love Him* [5:54], nor is *God is well-pleased with them* ever without *they are well-pleased with Him* [5:119]."[19]

In two more passages, Nicholson suggests that Rūmī was influenced by Qūnawī. In commenting on the verse, "'The Reality is Allah,' said the Shaykh of the Religion. . . ." (1:3338), Nicholson provides reasons for why this shaykh may be Qūnawī, although he rejects his own reasoning in the appendix to his commentary, suggesting instead that it is Abū'l-Ḥasan Kharaqānī

(d. 425/1033). In fact, it is Shams, as his *Maqālāt* clearly demonstrates.[20] In commenting on 3:41, Nicholson quotes a long passage from Qūnawī's commentary on the opening chapter of the Koran, "which Rúmí may have had in mind." But Rūmī had no need of Qūnawī's elaborate commentary to come up with his simple meditation on the divine name the Provider (*al-rāziq*), mentioned in the previous verse.

These few passages are the significant instances where Nicholson states or implies an influence from Ibn al-ʿArabī on Rūmī. They are scant evidence indeed for the often repeated statement that Rūmī was Ibn al-ʿArabī's student or follower.

Ibn al-ʿArabī's "Influence" on ʿAṭṭār (!)

In order to demonstrate the weakness of Nicholson's argument that Ibn al-ʿArabī influenced Rūmī, I show how easy it is to draw the type of parallels that Nicholson provides as evidence. I hope thereby to "prove" that ʿAṭṭār was influenced by Ibn al-ʿArabī, even though no one has ever suggested this, especially since ʿAṭṭār had died long before Ibn al-ʿArabī wrote his influential works, the *Fuṣūṣ* (composed in 627/1230) and the *Futūḥāt* (final version completed 636/1238).

I will base my comments on a few verses from one of ʿAṭṭār's *qaṣīdas*[21]; similar verses are plentiful in his writings. In order to think that ʿAṭṭār was deeply influenced by Ibn al-ʿArabī, we only have to accept, as Nicholson does concerning Rūmī, that in each passage "The leading ideas . . . come from Ibnu 'l-'Arabí, though their provenance is disguised (as usual) by the poetical form in which they are presented."

O You who have veiled Your face
  and come into the bazaar,
A whole creation has been seized
  by this talisman!

Although nonmanifest and incomparable in Himself, God has become manifest and similar through creation. However, He is manifest as "other," so we do not perceive Him and remain ignorant of His presence: "People are veiled from the Real through the Real, because the Real is so clearly visible"[22]; "This present world is the locus of the Veil, except in the case of the gnostics"[23]; "Nothing exists but veils let down; the objects of perception are the veils."[24]

Everything other than You
  is a mirage and a display,
for neither little
  nor much has come [into the "other"].

Everything other than the Essence is what Ibn al-ʿArabī calls "imagination" (note that, in the previous chapter, we saw how some Sufis consider "imagination" to be synonymous with "display"). Nothing has "gone out" of God to enter into *wujūd,* since *wujūd* is God Himself and does not change. The appearances we perceive in *wujūd* are simply the properties of the entities, which remain forever nonexistent: "Everything other than the Essence of the Real is intervening imagination and vanishing shadow."[25]

> Here unificationism is unbelief,
>   and so also incarnationism,
> for this is oneness,
>   but it has come in repetition [*takrār*]!

ʿAṭṭār first points out, as Ibn al-ʿArabī's followers often do, that *waḥdat al-wujūd* is totally different from unificationism and incarnationism. The verse as a whole provides a concise statement of Ibn al-ʿArabī's doctrine of continuous creation, the fact that "self-disclosure never repeats itself": "There is no repetition whatsoever in *wujūd,* because of the divine vastness."[26] The idea that the "One" produces manyness through repeating itself is a common theme in Ibn al-ʿArabī's writings. The cosmos is nothing but a collection of "ones," since $1 \times 1 = 1$:

> There is nothing in *wujūd* except God. Though the Entity is many in witnessing [*shuhūd*], it is one in *wujūd*. To multiply one by one is to multiply a thing by itself, so it yields nothing but its own kind.[27]

> There is one Maker, while His handiworks
>   are thousands of thousands!
> Everything has come into manifestation
>   from the ready cash of knowledge.

The objects of God's knowledge—the fixed entities—are like God's ready cash because they are ever-present with Him: "God knows the cosmos in the state of its nonexistence, and He gives it existence according to its form in His knowledge."[28]

> The Ocean produced the "other"
>   with its own waves—
> a cloud identical with the drop
>   has come into the bazaar.

Things are "other than God" only in respect of their appearance of independence, not in respect of *wujūd*: "In reality, there is no 'other' except the entities of the possible things in respect of their fixity, not in respect of their *wujūd*"[29]; "In reality the 'other' is fixed/not fixed, He/not He."[30]

This has an exact analogy
in the sun: its reflection
fills the two worlds
with light.

Like others, Ibn al-ʿArabī identifies *wujūd* and light since each can be defined as that which is manifest in itself and makes others manifest:

> There is nothing stronger than light because it possesses manifestation and through it manifestation takes place, while all things are in utter need of manifestation, and without light no manifestation takes place.[31]

The One harmonious Entity,
other than whom not an atom exists,
became manifest; only then
did all these "others" come to be.
A reflection showed itself
from beneath the veil of oneness,
entering into a hundred thousand
veils of imagination.

These lines repeat what was said earlier, employing different imagery. In short, the things of the universe are but the manifestation of real *wujūd* in a multiplicity of forms.

He manifested to Himself
the mystery of self-breathing—
eighteen thousand worlds of mystery
came into being.

Ibn al-ʿArabī also speaks of the "eighteen thousand" worlds created by God. The expression "self-breathing" (*khwud-damī*) alludes to what Ibn al-ʿArabī calls the "Breath of the All-Merciful." The Breath is both identical to God ("manifested to Himself") and the locus within which the cosmos becomes manifest (the "eighteen thousand worlds"). The "mystery" has to do with the fact that the worlds are neither God nor other than God; they are "He/not He." Through God's saying *Be!* (2:117), "The entities become manifest within the Breath of the All-Merciful, just as words become manifest within the breath."[32]

He shone one ray of His light,
and the world was filled with lamps;
He planted one seed,
and all these fruits grew up!

In the garden of love
the One Unity flashed forth:
Branches, trees, petals, thorns—
all began to bloom!

Both these lines provide images to illustrate the oneness of *wujūd* in itself and the manyness of its manifestations.

Disclosing Yourself to Yourself
is Your work,
in order that a hundred thousand works
may spring forth from one work!

By the word "disclosing" (*jilwa*) ʿAṭṭār alludes to the oft-quoted statement in Ibn al-ʿArabī's school, "He disclosed Himself to Himself in Himself" (*tajallā li-dhātihi fī dhātihi*).

O You whose manifest side is Lover
and whose nonmanifest side is Beloved!
Who has ever seen the Sought
become the Seeker?

Those who love God are themselves nothing but loci of manifestation for His properties, so in effect God loves Himself: "There is no lover and no beloved except God, since there is nothing in *wujūd* except the Divine Presence, that is, His Essence, His attributes, and His acts"[33]; "He is the lover and the beloved, the seeker and the sought."[34]

Who is that, and from whence
has He displayed Himself?
What is that, and what is this,
that has come into manifestation?

At the highest stage of knowledge the gnostic is bewildered by both God and the cosmos. Is the cosmos God, or is it other than God?

> You say, it is creation, but in itself it is neither the Real, nor other than the Real. . . . The elect . . . sometimes say, "We are we and He is He," sometimes, "He is we and we are He," and sometimes, "We are not purely we and He is not purely He." . . . So knowledge of the Real is bewilderment, and knowledge of creation is bewilderment.[35]

10

Ibn al-ʿArabī on the Benefit of Knowledge

At the heart of Ibn al-ʿArabī's teachings lies the problem of the nature and significance of knowledge, a question to which he constantly returns.[1] In these discussions, he typically uses the term *ʿilm,* not its near synonym *maʿrifa.* In general, he considers *ʿilm* the broader and higher term, not least because the Koran attributes *ʿilm,* but not *maʿrifa,* to God. Nonetheless, he usually follows the general usage of the Sufis in employing the term *ʿārif* or "gnostic" to designate the highest ranking knowers. The gnostics are those who have achieved the knowledge designated by the hadith, "He who knows [*ʿarafa*] himself knows [*ʿarafa*] his Lord."[2]

According to Ibn al-ʿArabī, there is no goal beyond knowledge:

> There is no level more eminent [*ashraf*] than the level of knowledge.[3]
>
> There is no eminence higher than the eminence of knowledge, and there is no state above the state of understanding [*fahm*] from God.[4]
>
> There is no blessing [*niʿma*] greater than the blessing of knowledge, even though God's blessings cannot be counted.[5]
>
> The most excellent [*afḍal*] thing through which God has shown munificence to His servants is knowledge. When God bestows knowledge on someone, He has granted him the most eminent of attributes and the greatest of gifts.[6]
>
> God said, commanding His Prophet—upon him be blessings and peace—*Say: "My Lord, increase me in knowledge"* [20:114], for it is the most eminent attribute and the most surpassing [*anzah*] quality.[7]
>
> Knowledge is the cause of deliverance. . . . How eminent is the rank of knowledge! This is why God did not command His Prophet to seek increase in anything except knowledge.[8]

Given the extraordinary importance that Ibn al-ʿArabī accords to knowledge and the vast extent of his literary corpus, it is beyond the scope of this essay to even begin a survey of his views on its nature and significance. Instead, I try to suggest his understanding of knowledge's "benefit." I have in mind the famous hadith, "I seek refuge in God from a knowledge that has no benefit." According to another well-known hadith, "Seeking knowledge is incumbent on every Muslim." What is the benefit to be gained by seeking it, and what sorts of knowledge have no benefit and should be avoided?

Ibn al-ʿArabī agrees with the standard view that there is nothing clearer or more self-evident than knowledge, so it cannot be defined in the technical sense of the term "definition" (*ḥadd*). Nonetheless, he sometimes offers brief, descriptive definitions, often with a view to those offered by other scholars. Thus, he says:

> Knowledge is simply the perception [*dark*] of the essence [*dhāt*] of the sought object [*maṭlūb*] as it is in itself, whether it be existent or nonexistent; a negation or an affirmation; an impossibility, a permissibility, or a necessity.[9]

In a similar way, he says, "Knowledge is not knowledge until it is attached to what the object of knowledge [*maʿlūm*] is in itself."[10]

It would not be unfair to say that Ibn al-ʿArabī's writings are an attempt to expose the full range of the "objects of knowledge" available to human beings—not exhaustively, of course, but inasmuch as these may be "beneficial." After all, as Ibn al-ʿArabī says, "The sciences are not sought for themselves; they are sought only for the sake of that to which they attach,"[11] that is, for the sake of their object. Thus we must ask which object or objects of knowledge, once known, are useful and profitable for human beings. In Islamic terms, benefit must be defined by ultimate issues, not the passing phenomena of this world. Beneficial knowledge can only be that which profits man at his final homecoming, which is the return to God. Any knowledge that does not yield benefit in these terms—whether directly or indirectly—is not Koranic knowledge, so it is not Islamic knowledge, and, one might argue, it is beneath human dignity to devote oneself to it. Although acquiring various sorts of knowledge may be unavoidable on the social and individual levels, one should actively strive to avoid searching after any knowledge that does not prepare oneself for the greater knowledge. As the well-known formula puts it, secondary knowledge should only be sought *bi-qadr al-ḥāja*, "in the measure of need." To devote oneself exclusively or even mainly to secondary knowledge would be blatant ingratitude toward God (*kufr*), because it would be to ignore the eminence of human nature and God's explicit instructions through the prophets. As Ibn al-ʿArabī expresses it:

> Human beings have no eminence save in their knowledge of God. As for their knowledge of other than God, this is a diversion [*ʿulāla*] through which veiled human beings divert themselves. The right-thinking man [*al-munṣif*] has no aspiration save toward knowledge of Him.[12]

In a letter addressed to Fakhr al-Dīn Rāzī, Ibn al-ʿArabī suggests in somewhat more detail the benefit of knowledge, and he distinguishes knowledge that is truly important and imperative from the various types of knowledge with which the ignorant and the veiled (and most theologians) divert themselves. By asserting that genuinely worthwhile knowledge comes only by way of "bestowal" (*wahb*) and "witnessing" (*mushāhada*), he wants to say that genuine knowledge is not of the sort that can be gained by reading books. It cannot be acquired merely by human effort (*iktisābī*). Rather, it must be bestowed by divine specification (*ikhtiṣāṣī*). Or, to use a pair of terms that becomes common in later texts, true knowledge of things is not *ḥuṣūlī* ("acquired," or gained by learning), but rather *ḥuḍūrī* ("presential," or gained by presence with God). Ibn al-ʿArabī often cites Koranic verses that encourage people to prepare themselves to receive the God-given knowledge, such as Koran 2:282, which stresses the importance of *taqwā*: *Be wary of God, and God will teach you.* He writes to Rāzī:

> The intelligent person should not seek any knowledge save that through which his essence is perfected and which is carried along with him wherever he may be taken. This is nothing but knowledge of God in respect of bestowal and witnessing. After all, you need your knowledge of medicine, for example, only in the world of diseases and illnesses. When you are taken to a world in which there is no illness or sickness, whom will you treat with this knowledge? . . . Likewise is it with knowledge of geometry. You need it in the world of spatial area. When you are taken elsewhere, you will leave it behind in its world, for the soul goes forward untrammeled, without taking anything along with it.
>
> Such is occupation with every knowledge that the soul leaves behind when it is taken to the next world. Hence, the intelligent person should not partake of knowledge except that of it which is touched by imperative need [*al-ḥāja al-ḍarūriyya*]. He should struggle to acquire what is taken along with him when he is taken. This is none other than two types of knowledge specifically—knowledge of God, and knowledge of the homesteads of the next world [*mawāṭin al-ākhira*] and what is required by its stations, so that he may walk there as he walks in his own home and not deny anything whatsoever.[13]

One may ask here about knowledge of the rulings of the Shariah. Is such knowledge imperative? The answer is, "In the measure of need." Like most other forms of knowledge, knowledge of the Shariah has no benefit once a person reaches the next world. Ibn al-ʿArabī often reminds us that *taklīf*—God's "burdening" the soul by prescribing the Shariah for it—is cut off at death. In the posthumous realms, everyone will worship God with an essential worship, not with the secondary and accidental worship that is characteristic of believers in this world and depends on knowledge of the Shariah. Hence, knowledge of the Shariah is important to the extent that it is useful in guiding the individual in his worship and service of God in this world, but it has no use in the next world. One should learn it here only to the degree of imperative need. Ibn al-ʿArabī explains this point as follows, concluding once again by insisting on the priority that must be given to knowledge of God and the next world:

> The need of the soul for knowledge is greater than the constitution's need for the food that keeps it wholesome.
>
> Knowledge is of two sorts: The first knowledge is needed in the same way that food is needed. Hence it is necessary to exercise moderation, to limit oneself to the measure of need. This is knowledge of the Shariah's rulings. One should not consider these rulings except in the measure that one's need touches on them at the moment, for their ruling property pertains only to acts that occur in this world. So take from this knowledge only in the measure of your activity!
>
> The second knowledge, which has no limit at which one can come to a halt, is knowledge that pertains to God and the homesteads of the resurrection. Knowledge of the resurrection's homesteads will lead its knower to a preparedness for what is proper to each homestead. This is because on that day the Real Himself will make demands through lifting the veils. That is *"the day of differentiation"* [37:21]. It is necessary for intelligent human beings to be *"upon insight"* [12:108] in their affairs and to be prepared to answer for themselves and for others in the homesteads within which they know that answers will be demanded from them.[14]

Ibn al-ʿArabī offers many arguments to support his position on the priority that must be given to knowledge of God and the next world. These arguments are rooted in ontology, theology, anthropology, and psychology—taking all of these in the senses demanded by the traditional Islamic sciences.

Ibn al-ʿArabī's most basic argument can perhaps be called "anthropological," in that it is rooted in an understanding of what it means to be human. The axiom here is the hadith, "God created Adam in His own form," or, to cite the Koran, that *He taught Adam the names, all of them* (2:31). Given that human beings represent the form of a meaning that is God, or that they have been given knowledge of *all* things, the human soul is in principle infinite, which is to say that, although it has a beginning, it has no end. Only this can explain its everlastingness in the world to come.

God—who is the meaning made manifest by the human form—creates a cosmos. Understood in this sense, the cosmos can have no final boundaries, for God is eternally the Creator. It follows that man's knowledge of the cosmos, like his knowledge of its Creator, can have no final limit. Moreover, knowledge of the universe is itself knowledge of God, a point that Ibn al-ʿArabī sees already implicit in the Arabic language. Thus he writes, "We refer to the 'cosmos' [*ʿālam*] with this word to give 'knowledge' [*ʿilm*] that by it we mean that He has made it a 'mark' [*ʿalāma*]."[15]

Knowledge of the cosmos, however, can also be the greatest veil on the path to God, because the more man focuses on signs and marks without recognizing what they signify, the more he is overcome by the darkness that prevents him from seeing things as they are. From this point of view, any knowledge of the universe that does not recognize the divine workings and acknowledge the signs of God for what they are does not deserve the name "knowledge." Rather, it is a diversion, a veil, and a form of ignorance dressed up as knowledge.

The universe is the domain of possibility. As such, it is contrasted with the domain of Necessity, which is God Himself; and with impossibility, which is sheer nonexistence. With God, all things are possible. Because He has power over everything, the realm of possibility has no end. Hence, as Ibn al-ʿArabī puts it, "Knowledge of the possible realm is an all-embracing ocean of knowledge that has magnificent waves within which ships founder. It is an ocean that has no shore save its two sides,"[16] which are Necessity and impossibility, or the Essence of God and absolute nothingness.

Trying to know things in terms of other things is like trying to pinpoint a wave in the ocean. Nor can Necessity be known in Itself, for none knows God as God knows Himself. And absolute nothingness is also unknowable, for there is nothing there to be known. This helps explain Ibn al-ʿArabī's radically agnostic attitude toward true and final knowledge of anything: "It is impossible for anything other than God to gain knowledge of the cosmos, of the human being in himself, or of the self of anything in itself."[17] We know things not in themselves, but in relation to other things or in relation to God, and we come to know God only relationally (which is why Ibn al-ʿArabī calls the divine names and attributes "relations," *nisab*). Only God has direct, unmediated knowledge of Himself and of things in themselves.

Given the impossibility of true knowledge without God's help and without recognizing how the objects of knowledge relate to God, it should come as no surprise that one of Ibn al-ʿArabī's frequent themes is the inadequacy of human reason in grasping the realities of things. Every knowledge gained through reason or any other created mode of knowing is defined and constricted by the limitations of everything other than God. Man can understand things only inasmuch as his native ability, circumstances, upbringing, and training allow him. The theories and thoughts of those who try to know things without recognizing the manner in which things act as signs and marks of God illustrate little but human incapacity.

In effect, as Ibn al-ʿArabī tells us repeatedly, man can know things only in the measure of himself, and this is especially true concerning knowledge of God, who lies infinitely beyond the range of created things. In the last analysis, we can only know ourselves:

> The thing knows nothing but itself, and nothing knows anything except from itself.[18]

> God knows the created thing and He knows that to which it goes back. But the created thing knows nothing of its own states save what it has at the moment.[19]

One of Ibn al-ʿArabī's many arguments to show the futility of independent human efforts to achieve real knowledge is based on the concept of *taqlīd*, "imitation" or "following authority," a term well-known in jurisprudence. All knowledge comes from outside the soul's essence. We acquire knowledge from teachers, books, the media, scientists, and our own senses and faculties. All knowledge derives from other than our own intellective essence, and we have no choice but to follow the other's authority. The only rational course is to follow God, who alone knows, given that we can know nothing for certain without God's help. Ibn al-ʿArabī writes, for example:

> Knowledge is not correct for anyone who does not know things through his own essence. Anyone who knows something through something added to his own essence is following the authority of that added thing in what it gives to him. But nothing in existence knows things through its own essence other than the One. As for anything other than the One, its knowledge of things and non-things is a following of authority. Since it has been affirmed that other than God cannot have knowledge of a thing without following authority, let us follow God's authority, especially in knowledge of Him.[20]

God-given, reliable knowledge is provided by the prophets, but here we run up against the same difficulty, given that prophetic knowledge can only be understood in the measure of our own capacity. Of course, faith is a gift that can remove doubts, but faith is not the furthest limit of human possibility. Beyond faith is found the direct knowledge of "bestowal and witnessing." Ibn al-ʿArabī points to a Koranic verse that mentions God's questioning His messengers on the Day of Resurrection. They respond by saying that they have no knowledge. For Ibn al-ʿArabī, this is a general rule that applies to all human beings:

> *The day God will gather the messengers and say, "What response did you receive?" They will say, "We have no knowledge; You are the All-Knowing of the unseen things"* [5:109]. No one has any knowledge save those whom God has taught. Other than this divine path in teaching, there is nothing but the predominance of conjecture, coincidence with knowledge, or being convinced by fantasy. As for knowledge, all the paths that convey to knowledge are assailed by doubts. The pure soul that God acquaints with these doubts will never be confident of having certitude by gaining knowledge, save through the divine path, and that is His words, *If you are wary of God, He will assign you a discrimination* [8:29], and His words, *He created man, He taught him the clarification* [55:3–4]—He clarifies what is in Himself.[21]

In short, only *real* knowledge, which is true knowledge of the Real, is beneficial. It alone is worthy of human aspiration. Every other sort of knowledge must be subservient to it. And this real knowledge cannot be acquired without following God's authority. What then is Ibn al-ʿArabī's goal in his writings? In brief, it is to explain the truth and reality of each created thing as it stands in relation to its Creator on the basis of real knowledge, and to explain the benefit of knowing this. He is not concerned with explaining the way in which things are interrelated outside the divine context. That is the goal of other forms of knowledge, none of which has any real benefit apart from the service it can render to the primary knowledge, and each of which necessarily reads the book of the cosmos in terms of its own limited perspective.

In Ibn al-ʿArabī's view, no modality of knowing and no standpoint allows for transcending its own limitations except the one standpoint that recognizes the relative validity of each but does not become bound and restricted by any. He sometimes calls this standpoint "the standpoint of no standpoint" (*maqām lā maqām*). He also calls it *taḥqīq* or "realization."

If we want to use Ibn al-ʿArabī's terminology to represent his theoretical position, we can do no better than *taḥqīq*. He often calls the greatest of the Muslim sages *muḥaqqiqūn*, those who practice *taḥqīq*. For his followers, *taḥqīq* is a methodology that is rooted in knowledge of things as they are, that is, knowledge of their very essences, which is knowledge of the things as they are known to God, a knowledge that can only be attained through God's guidance and bestowal.

The word *taḥqīq* is a verbal form derived from the root *ḥ.q.q*, from which we have two words of great importance for the Islamic sciences—*ḥaqīqa* and *ḥaqq*. *Ḥaqīqa* means "reality" and "truth." Although not employed in the Koran, it is used in the hadith literature and comes to play a major role in the Islamic sciences in general, as well as in Ibn al-ʿArabī's writings. The metaphysical, philosophical, and theological significance of the word is suggested by the English translation. As soon as we pose questions like "what is reality?," "what is truth?," and "what is the reality of a thing?," we fall into the most difficult of theoretical issues.

If we take the meaning of the word *ḥaqīqa* into account in trying to understand the meaning of *taḥqīq*, we can say that the word means "to search out reality," or "to discover the truth." This helps explain why in contemporary Persian, *taḥqīq* is used to mean "scientific research," whereas in Egyptian Arabic, it commonly means "interrogation."

In order to grasp the sense of the word *taḥqīq* as Ibn al-ʿArabī and others use the term, it may be more useful to look at the word *ḥaqq*, which is employed 250 times in the Koran. *Ḥaqq* is a noun and an adjective that means truth and true, reality and real, propriety and proper, appropriateness and appropriate, rightness and right. When used as a name of God, it means the Real, the Truth, the Right. It is commonly employed as a virtual synonym for the name Allah.

In a common usage of the term, *ḥaqq* or the "Real" is juxtaposed with *khalq* or "creation." These are the two basic realities (*ḥaqīqa*). The status of *ḥaqq*, the

Real, is perfectly clear, because "There is no god but God," which is to say that there is nothing real, true, right, proper, and appropriate in the full senses of these terms except God. The Necessary Being of God, which makes Itself known through everything that exists, is not simply "that which truly is," but also that which is truly right, worthy, fitting, and appropriate.

This leaves us with the question of how to deal with *khalq*. If God alone is *ḥaqq* in a strict sense, where exactly do creation and created things stand? The question is especially significant because of the manner in which the Koran, in a dozen verses, juxtaposes a second term with *ḥaqq*. This is *bāṭil*, which means unreal, wrong, inappropriate, null, void, and absurd. Although the later literature pairs both *khalq* and *bāṭil* with *ḥaqq*, the distinction between these two terms is fundamental. *Bāṭil* is totally other than *ḥaqq*—it is the negation of *ḥaqq*. In contrast, although *khalq* is not the same as *ḥaqq*, it is also not completely different, for it is certainly not unreal, wrong, vain, and null: *We did not create the heavens, the earth, and what is between the two as* bāṭil (38:27).

The exact status of *khalq* is the first question of Islamic philosophy and much of Islamic theology and Sufism. It is precisely the question of reality (*ḥaqīqa*) or quiddity (*māhiyya*): "what is it?"[22] In Ibn al-ʿArabī's view, no clear and categorical answer to this question can be given. Creation's status is always ambiguous, because it always hangs between *ḥaqq* and *bāṭil*, God and nothingness, real and unreal, right and wrong, proper and improper, appropriate and inappropriate. Nonetheless, creation needs to be investigated. We cannot avoid asking "what are we?" As creatures, we need to know our status in relation to our Creator. To the extent that we can answer the question of what we are, or where we stand in relation to God, we come to understand our purpose in being here.

The basic questions that face us in our humanity can be reduced to two: "what (*mā*)?" and "why (*limā*)?" What are we, and why are we here? What is our actual situation, and what do we need to do with it to achieve our purpose? The process of asking these questions, answering them, and then putting the answers into practice is called "realization."

As with most of Ibn al-ʿArabī's technical terminology, the meaning that he gives to *taḥqīq* is rooted in the Koran and the Hadith. One Koranic verse plays an especially important role: *"He has given each thing its creation, then guided"* (20:50). Here we have the beginnings of an answer to the questions, "what?" and "why?"

What are we? Are we *ḥaqq* or *bāṭil*, real or unreal, appropriate or inappropriate? The answer is given by the first clause of the verse, *He has given each thing its creation*, which is to say that the *ḥaqq* has determined and bestowed the *khalq*, so the divine determination erases the unreality and falseness that dominate over created things when they are isolated from the Real. As the Koran puts it, *The* ḥaqq *has come and the* bāṭil *has vanished* (17:81). The Absolute *ḥaqq* has defined, determined, and given existence to the creature.

Why are we here? The answer is provided by the second part of the verse, *"then guided."* We are here to follow guidance and engage in right thought and appropriate activity. Right and worthy thought and activity is called "worship"

(*ʿibāda*), that is, being a "servant" (*ʿabd*) of the Lord who created us. As God says in the Koran, *I created jinn and mankind only to worship Me* (51:56). Worshiping and serving God—that is, putting oneself in harmony with the Absolute *ḥaqq* by observing the *ḥaqq* that is present in all things—is the means whereby human beings achieve their purpose in creation.

In view of the engendering command (*al-amr al-takwīnī*), every creature is *ḥaqq*, which is to say that it is real, right, true, and appropriate: *We created the heavens and the earth and what is between them only through the* ḥaqq (15:85). In view of the prescriptive command (*al-amr al-taklīfī*), which is addressed specifically to human beings, everyone must act in keeping with the *ḥaqq* of things and strive to avoid the *bāṭil* in things. The engendering command tells us what we are, and the prescriptive command tells us why we are here.

The relation of God's guidance with the term *ḥaqq* is suggested by a hadith that also plays a basic role in Ibn al-ʿArabī's understanding of *taḥqīq*. The hadith has several versions, probably because the Prophet repeated the words in slightly different forms on a variety of occasions. Certainly it sets down an everyday guiding principle for people concerned with the truth and the right. In a typical version, it reads, "Your soul has a *ḥaqq* against you, your Lord has a *ḥaqq* against you, your guest has a *ḥaqq* against you, and your spouse has a *ḥaqq* against you; so give to each that has a *ḥaqq* its *ḥaqq*."

In terms of the first question, "what are we?," this hadith explains that we are *ḥaqq* and that we have *ḥaqq*s pertaining to us, which is to say we and everything else has a proper situation, a correct mode of being, an appropriate manner of displaying the Real. All things do so because God *"has given each thing its creation,"* and thereby has established not only the *khalq* of a thing, but also its *ḥaqq*.

In terms of the second question, "why are we here?," the hadith tells us, "give to each that has a *ḥaqq* its *ḥaqq*." We are here to act correctly. This demands that everything we do, say, and think be right, true, appropriate, worthy, and real. Things have *ḥaqq*s against us, so we will be asked about these *ḥaqq*s and we will need to respond. Each *ḥaqq* against us represents our responsibility. Our own *ḥaqq* is our right.

Given that only human beings were taught *all* the names by God, they alone have the capacity to recognize and realize the *ḥaqq* of everything in existence. From Ibn al-ʿArabī's standpoint, man was created in the form of the Absolute *ḥaqq*, so he corresponds and correlates with all of *khalq*, that is, with "everything other than the Real," the sum total of forms that are disclosed by the Meaning that is God. Man has the capacity to know the true names of all things, and knowing the true name of a thing is tantamount to knowing its *ḥaqq*, which is not only its truth and reality, but also the rightful and appropriate claim that it has on us and our responsibility toward it. All of creation makes demands on man because he is created in God's form and has been appointed His vicegerent. He has the God-given duty, woven into his innate disposition, to recognize the *ḥaqq* of things and to act accordingly. It is this *ḥaqq* that must be known if his knowledge is to be true, right, worthy, and appropriate, for this *ḥaqq* is identical with the *khalq* that God has established.

Beneficial knowledge, therefore, is knowledge of the what and the why of ourselves and of things. In order to know a thing truly and benefit from the knowledge, we need to know what it is—its reality (*ḥaqīqa*), which is nothing but its *khalq* and its *ḥaqq*—and we need to know how we should respond to it. What exactly does it demand from us, rightly, truly, and appropriately? To put this into a formula, we can say that *taḥqīq* means knowing the *ḥaqīqa* of God and things and acting according to their *ḥaqq*. In other words, realization is to know things as they truly are and to act appropriately in every circumstance.

Given that all things manifest the Absolute *ḥaqq* and each possesses a relative *ḥaqq*, and given that man will be held responsible for the *ḥaqq*s that pertain to him, he needs a scale by which to judge the extent of his own responsibility and to learn how to deal with the *ḥaqq*s. He cannot possibly know the *ḥaqq* of things by his own lights or his own rational investigation of the world and the soul because the relative *ḥaqq* of created things is determined and defined by the Absolute *ḥaqq*, and the Absolute *ḥaqq* is unknowable except in the measure in which God chooses to reveal Himself. Hence, the scale can only come through the prophets, who are precisely the means by which the *Ḥaqq* has chosen to make Himself known. The Koran is the means that clarifies the *ḥaqq* for Muslims: *With the* ḥaqq *We have sent it down, and with the* ḥaqq *it has come down* (17:105).

One can conclude that for Ibn al-ʿArabī, the fundamental divine command—a command whereby the question, "what should we do?" is answered most directly—is expressed in the hadith of the *ḥaqq*s by the sentence, "Give to each that has a *ḥaqq* its *ḥaqq*." Giving things their *ḥaqq*s is the very definition of the human task in the cosmos, and it is precisely the meaning of *taḥqīq*.

Once man recognizes that the Absolute *ḥaqq* is God and that the *ḥaqq* of all things depends utterly on God, he has to employ the divine scale to recognize the realities and *ḥaqq*s of the things. The first thing in the domain of *khalq* whose reality and *ḥaqq* must be understood is the human self or soul. Notice that the hadith begins, "Your soul has a *ḥaqq* against you, your Lord has a *ḥaqq* against you," and then goes on to mention others. The order is not irrelevant. Without knowing oneself, one cannot know one's Lord. God and everything in the universe have *ḥaqq*s against us, but in order to give each thing its *ḥaqq*, we first must know who we are. Otherwise, we will not be able to discern which of the *ḥaqq*s pertain to us.

On the level of the Shariah, determining *ḥaqq*s is relatively straightforward, because it demands recognizing that we are addressed by the Law, although observing the *ḥaqq* of the relevant rulings may not be an easy task. But the Shariah pertains to a small portion of reality. What about the rest of existence? When God said, *"I am placing in the earth a vicegerent"* (2:30), did He mean that His chosen vicegerents only have to obey a few commands and prohibitions, there being no need to know Him, or the universe, or themselves? When it says, *God burdens a soul only to its capacity* (2:286), does it mean that one is free to define one's own capacity by one's understanding of biology, psychology, history, and politics? How can one decide what this "burdening" entails unless one knows the capacity of one's own soul?

To put this discussion in a slightly different way, the issue of who we are pertains not only to anthropology, psychology, and ethics, but even more deeply to ontology and cosmology. To give ourselves our *ḥaqq,* we must know who it is of whom we are the *khalq. Taḥqīq* becomes a term that designates the station of those who have achieved, by divine solicitude (*ʿināya*), the full possibilities of human knowledge and existence. The *muḥaqqiq*s have recognized the *ḥaqq* in exactly the manner in which God has established it. Through giving each thing that has a *ḥaqq* its *ḥaqq,* the *muḥaqqiq*s also give God, who has given each thing its *khalq,* His *ḥaqq,* and thus achieve, to the extent humanly possible, the fullness of God-given knowledge and God-given reality.

11

Qūnawī, Neoplatonism, and the Circle of Ascent

Ṣadr al-Dīn Qūnawī's writings present a thoroughly Islamic version of that universal metaphysics that finds one of its most perfect expressions in Neoplatonism. Qūnawī discourses on the negative theology that provides the best available means to speak about the Godhead, elaborates on the nature of the One and the various degrees of existence that issue from It, and discusses how the human soul ultimately derives from the One and returns to It. His version of the descent and reascent of the soul provides a perfect example of how the Koranic teaching summarized in such verses as *Surely we belong to God, and to Him we return* (2:156) and *As He originated you, so you will return* (7:29), was expounded in terms that parallel Neoplatonic categories.

Qūnawī and Neoplatonism

Although Qūnawī profited from the expositions of the Muslim philosophers and was certainly well read in philosophy, in his writings he makes no reference to works such as the so-called *Theology of Aristotle*—which is actually a paraphrased version of parts of the *Enneads* of Plotinus (d. 270)[1]—nor are any of them listed among the works he is known to have owned.[2] Thus, before attempting to assess the extent to which Qūnawī made use of Neoplatonic formulations, it is only fair to ask how he himself, or one of his followers, might have viewed the question.

Sufism is first and foremost a spiritual way. Only in a secondary sense does it present itself as an intellectual perspective (even though, from another point of view, the perspective precedes the way). The Sufi's first concern is to turn the whole of his attentiveness (*tawajjuh*), then the whole of his existence, toward God. The spiritual discipline he follows is Islamic, since all its essential elements are based on the Koran, the Sunnah of the Prophet, and the teachings of his companions.[3] All Sufi practice begins with the observance of the Shariah;

to follow it with a certain scrupulousness means that one performs most activities—not the least of which are the five mandatory daily prayers and the various supererogatory prayers recommended by the Sunnah—with God in mind. But the Sufis go to great lengths to intensify their awareness of God, especially through the practice of *dhikr*. This means that many if not most Sufis, whatever their outward occupation, constantly repeat a name of God in the mind or the heart. What has come down to us concerning the activities of Sufi centers, like the one directed by Qūnawī himself,[4] indicates that most outward activities were also "religious" in nature, such as the practice of certain types of vigils and retreats, recitation of the Koran, communal sessions of *dhikr* (often sung to the accompaniment of music), and the study of the religious sciences, especially those directly related to the Koran and the Hadith. Qūnawī was a master in the latter field, and a number of important divines are known to have studied it with him.

A little reflection on the "psychological" concomitants of such a way of life should make my point clear: Sufis such as Qūnawī could only think in Islamic terms. When they spoke or wrote, their words were thoroughly imbued with the modes of thought established by the Koran and the Sunnah. Moreover, from the point of view of what might be called the "psychology" developed by Sufism itself, the Islamic nature of the Sufi experience becomes even clearer: The Sufis base the formulation of many of their teachings on unveiling and tasting, that is, the direct, intuitive apprehension of realities that lie beyond the grasp of the senses and the unaided intellect. Through unveiling, they observe unseen realities clothed in sensory forms in the world of images (*ʿālam al-mithāl*), contemplate disengaged (*mujarrad*) intellectual realities in the world of the spirits (*ʿālam al-arwāḥ*), and even witness God's very knowledge of the created things "before" their creation.[5] A Sufi who desires to express his vision in human language naturally employs the language of his own religious universe, which colors his mental faculties and perceptions that directed him to the unseen worlds in the first place.

When Qūnawī speaks of the One, the emanation of all things from It, and their return to It, he is expressing the fruit of his own unveilings, the result of the spiritual travail he has undertaken. He has not "learned" these things from Neoplatonists, but in Neoplatonism he would have found striking confirmation of his own visions and a powerful and adequate formulation of the knowledge he had reached through unveiling. If asked whether Plotinus had possessed the same vision of reality, he would have answered in the affirmative. And if asked how he had attained it, he would have answered, "Through the spiritual practice issuing from another divine revelation, different from Islam but one with it in essence." From Qūnawī's point of view, Plotinus could only have been a "Sufi" or a "spiritual master" (*shaykh*) like himself; this is precisely how he would have understood the title given to Plotinus in Arabic texts, al-Shaykh al-Yūnānī or the "Greek Shaykh."

Toward the beginning of the *Theology*, Plotinus's words are paraphrased as follows:

> It sometimes happens that I become isolated within my soul and leave my body to one side. I become like a disengaged substance without body. I enter into my own essence, turning back into it, and coming out of all other things. Then I am knowledge, the knower, and the known all at once. I see such beauty, splendor, and light in my essence that I remain astonished and stunned. Then I know that I am one part of the noble, excellent, living, divine world.[6]

For Qūnawī, such language provides a vivid description of the world he himself has witnessed on innumerable occasions. A single quotation can suffice to show the common ground in mystical vision:

> On the night before Tuesday, the 17th of Shawwāl, 665 [July 19th, 1267] . . . I underwent a subtle attraction from the Lord. In it God placed me before Himself and freed me all at once, without any gradual change, to turn toward Him with the face of my heart. He gave me news of the presence of the universal knowledge of His Essence, from which every other knowledge becomes deployed and in accordance with which every description, state, and property becomes entified [*ta'ayyun*] within the levels of existence. . . .[7]

The Sufis do not consider the teachings found in the *Theology* as merely philosophy, since philosophy, as Qūnawī makes clear, deals primarily with topics that are accessible to the intellect in the limited and purely human sense of the word.[8] But unveiling draws its data from a "stage beyond the stage of the intellect," which is intimately connected with the purification of the soul and sanctity.[9]

Qūnawī states explicitly that among the Greeks, the earlier "wise men" or philosophers (*ḥukamā'*) based their teachings primarily on the unveiling or "openings" (*fatḥ*) that they received as a result of spiritual practice. But after "Aristotle" (d. 322 BCE)—he probably has the *Theology* in mind—philosophy limited itself to those things that can be discerned by the intellect. In the passage quoted here, drawn from Qūnawī's commentary on the opening chapter of the Koran, he explains his own position as being similar to that of the ancient Greeks:

> Those of you who come across this book and other works by the People of the Way should realize that if there were sufficiency and healing [*shifā'*][10] in rational proofs [*al-adilla al-fikriyya*] and disputational discussions [*al-taqrīrāt al-jadaliyya*, i.e., dialectic], neither the prophets and messengers nor their inheritors—the saints, who maintain and convey the arguments of God—would have turned away from these proofs and discussions.
>
> Other hindrances have also prevented me from following this path [of philosophical speculation] in my words. One of them is that I could not prefer to follow the way of the people of disputation and

thought in a work concerned with commenting on the Book of God, all the more so because a prophetic tradition has warned us against such things: "No people went astray after guidance without arriving at disputation." Then the Prophet recited the verse, *They do not cite him as an example to you save for disputation. Nay, they are a contentious people!* [43:58].

Another hindrance is my desire to maintain brevity. Still another is that my words are addressed primarily to the realizers [*muḥaqqiqūn*][11] and the elect among the people of God, and then to those who are beloved to them and who believe in them and their spiritual states. This latter group are those people whose breasts are illuminated and pure, whose innate disposition is sound, whose intellects are enkindled and adequate, *who call upon their Lord at morning and evening, desiring His face* [6:52], and *give ear to the Word and follow the best of it* [39:18] with pure intention and fair attentiveness, after having cleansed their locus [*maḥall,* i.e., the heart] of the attributes of disputation, quarreling, and the like.

Such men are those who expose themselves to the breaths of God's generosity[12] and watch Him vigilantly. They wait to see what will come to them from His mighty Presence, who will bring it to them, from which level of the divine names it will come, and whether it will come with a known intermediary or without one. They accept what they receive with good manners, and they weigh it with the scales of their Lord, sometimes the general scales [of reason], and sometimes the specific scales [of the Shariah]. Those who possess such attributes are qualified to benefit from the fruits of correct tasting and the sciences of direct unveilings.

We have no need for theoretical discussions and the like with anyone whose state is as we have described it. For either he will share in what we describe, so he will recognize the truth of what he is told because of that of it which he possesses in himself, that is, because his eye of spiritual insight is able to perceive the all-comprehensive principle through which and of which communication is made; or he is a believer whose faith and innate disposition are sound and whose heart is pure and purified. He perceives the truth of what he hears from behind the thin curtain that is his physical nature, despite the occupations and attachments that hinder his locus from the perfection of distinct vision, but not from perceiving what is said. Such a person is predisposed for unveiling and qualified for reception; he benefits from what he hears and ascends with the light of faith to the station of direct vision.

Thus I have contented myself with remarks and allusions, preferring them over detailed expositions and clarifications; I have chosen and preferred what God has chosen and preferred in His mighty words addressed to His messenger, by which He commanded him: *Speak the truth from your Lord; so whosoever will, let him believe; and whosoever will, let him disbelieve* [18:29]. God did not command him to perform miracles, nor to display arguments for everything he had brought.

What has been related concerning the first philosophers reveals something like this, even if they dealt with thoughts [*afkār*]. For their custom was to undergo spiritual retreats and ascetic discipline and to occupy themselves with what was required by the religious laws [*sharā'i'*] that they followed. When they were given an opening toward a particular thing, they would mention of it whatever was proper to be mentioned to their students and disciples. However, they spoke in the language of rhetoric [*khiṭāba*], not that of explanatory discourse. So if a situation arose which made them prefer to offer a demonstration of what they had been given and they were able to do so, they would discuss and demonstrate it. Otherwise they would mention what they wanted to expound to their students, and he who accepted it without quarrel would benefit from it. But when someone found an obstacle within himself, or there appeared to him a contention, these philosophers would not reply to him but would tell him to busy himself with his own soul and to turn his attention toward seeking knowledge about the true state of the problematic affair from God through ascetic practices and inward purification.

Such continued to be the situation amongst the ancient philosophers down to the time of Aristotle. After him the art of dialectic [*ṣan'at al-jadal*] arose among his followers, those who are called the "Peripatetics"; and the situation has remained the same until today.[13]

In short, Qūnawī could easily claim that any resemblance between his own teachings and those of Plotinus derive from a common ground in mystical vision. Similarities should cause no more surprise than the fact that Greek and Muslim astronomers describe the visible heavens in similar terms, while differences point to the varying receptivities of individual human beings toward the perception of spiritual realities, the difference in viewpoint between the ancient Greek religions and Islam, and the inherent weakness of human language to express realities that transcend the realm of thought.[14]

The Circle of Being

Despite the numerous parallels between certain aspects of Qūnawī's way of realization and Neoplatonism, his primary means of explaining the nature of God and the world is Koranic, that is, the doctrine of God's names and attributes (*al-asmā' wa-l-ṣifāt*; two terms that, for Ibn al-'Arabī and his followers, are largely synonymous).

Although unknowable in His nondelimited and nonentified (*ghayr muta'ayyan*) Essence, God gives knowledge of Himself to mankind through revelation, a knowledge that is summarized by the names and attributes sanctified by the Koran and the Hadith. The One Essence is viewed from different perspectives, each of which is represented by an attribute. The plurality of the attributes then becomes, *in divinis*, the ultimate source of the multiplicity of the creatures. The creative process takes place because of the inherent demands of certain names, such as "Light," "Creator," and, perhaps most important of all, "Lover," for, according to the famous *ḥadīth qudsī*, God says, "I loved to be known, so I created the world."

The creatures are possibilities of outward manifestation inherent within the nonentified Essence and known by God in all their particularized details (*tafṣīl*) from eternity without beginning (*azal*). His desire to become known brings these inherent properties of His own Self into manifestation. At the same time, He remains eternally transcendent in relation to His creatures, which become ranged in a scale extending from the uppermost limits of the spiritual world to the lowest levels of the corporeal world. Ultimately, each and every one of them displays the properties of the names and attributes. The "emanation" of the levels of existence (*marātib al-wujūd*) from the One Essence is referred to by a number of terms, such as manifestation (*ẓuhūr*), effusion (*fayḍ*), and self-disclosure (*tajallī*), each of which has Koranic roots.

The entities, which are the eternal and fixed possibilities of outward manifestation contained in the nonmanifest Essence of God, become deployed through the exhalation of the Breath of the All-Merciful or through the unseen and visible self-disclosures (*al-tajallī al-ghaybī wa-l-shahādī*).[15] Once deployed, they can be divided into different kinds from various points of view. One of the most common classifications is that of the Five Divine Presences (*al-ḥaḍarāt al-ilāhiyya al-khams*),[16] the first of which is the uncreated knowledge of God. The next three are created: the spiritual world, the world of images or imagination, and the corporeal world. The world of imagination acts as a *barzakh* or isthmus between the other two created worlds; since it comprehends the attributes of both, it allows them to become interrelated. The fifth Presence is the Perfect Man, who is both created and uncreated since he comprehends the other four levels within himself. To the three created levels correspond man's spirit (or rational soul), animal soul, and body. Thus, man's spirit is a luminous and unitary reality totally disengaged from his tenebrous and multiple body, while his animal soul is a semi-spiritual entity possessing attributes of both sides. Without the soul's intermediary, the spirit would have no way of governing the body.

Each of the three created Presences derives its being from the Presence beyond itself. Thus the spirits are reflections or shadows of the fixed and uncreated entities, the images are reflections or shadows of the spirits, and the bodies are reflections or shadows of the images. In a similar manner, man's body displays the properties of his animal soul, which in turn displays the properties of his spirit, which is the manifestation of his fixed entity.[17] Each of the levels of existence contributes to making up the total human reality, just as each divine Presence contributes to making up the total reality of Being in Its deployment—a reality that is named the "Perfect Man."

From one point of view, Being becomes deployed among the existent entities because of God's command.[18] Not only does God's command generate the world; it also descends through heaven and earth and returns to Him. God's command descends and re-ascends in an order that can be described roughly as follows: It begins with the Reality of Realities (*ḥaqīqat al-ḥaqāʾiq*), which is also called the First Entification (*al-taʿayyun al-awwal*), the Presence of All-Comprehensiveness and Being (*ḥaḍrat al-jamʿ wa-l-wujūd*), and the Nondelimited Effusion of the Essence (*muṭlaq al-fayḍ al-dhātī*); this is God as the One. It is followed by the One Emanation from the One, since, as the famous axiom puts it, "None issues from the One but One" (*lā yaṣduru min al-wāḥid illā'l-wāḥid*). This emanation, known as the All-Pervasive Being effused upon the entities of the engendered existents (*al-wujūd al-ʿāmm al-mufāḍ ʿalā aʿyān al-mukawwanāt*), is often referred to as the Breath of the All-Merciful or the Cloud (*al-ʿamāʾ*). It in turn creates the universe, beginning with the First Intellect (the Supreme Pen) and the Universal Soul (the Guarded Tablet); the two of these demarcate the boundaries of the spiritual world. Between the Guarded Tablet and the Throne of the All-Merciful (*ʿarsh al-raḥmān*, the ninth heaven), which is the outer limit of the corporeal world, stands the world of imagination. Within the world of corporeal bodies, the command continues to descend through each of the heavens (beginning with the Footstool, *al-kursī*, the eighth heaven), the spheres of the elements, and the three kingdoms. It reaches the utmost limit of its descent with man, after which it ascends to the world of the *barzakh* (the isthmus between death and the resurrection), the resurrection, the worlds of hell, paradise, and the vision of God (*kathīb al-ruʾya*, "the Dune of Vision"), and finally rejoins its origin, the Reality of Realities.[19]

The Point at the Center

All of Qūnawī's teachings revolve around the concept of the Perfect Man, which can be summarized as follows: The uncreated reality of mankind is God Himself, or God as described by the Name Allah. Hence, according to the Prophet, "God [*Allāh*] created Adam [i.e., man] in His own form"; man is the outward form of God, while God is man's inward meaning. The name Allah comprehends all other names, each of which demands the existence of various loci of manifestation (*maẓāhir, majālī*) within the created world. In Qūnawī's words:

> The universal tasks [*al-shuʾūn al-kulliyya*] comprehended by the name Allah . . . are called the first names. . . . The ontological forms that become manifest through the properties of these tasks are called angels, prophets, messengers, saints, and the like. As it descends,

> the command gradually divides into a hierarchy of relative species and genera, until it reaches its limit at individuals and their states. . . . Every universal task comprises numerous other tasks subordinate to it in ontological manifestation, property, and level. The subordinated realities may sometimes be viewed only from the point of view of their entification within God's knowledge for all eternity; then they are called "realities," "entities," and so on.[20] From the point of view of the outward manifestation of the Nondelimited Real within some particular subordinating reality, the latter assumes a name in respect of its becoming clothed in existence, such as Throne, Footstool, sun, moon, animal, plant, mineral. Then as it continues to descend it is called, for example, "this person," "this horse," "this apple," "this ruby."[21]

All the above realities are subordinated to the name Allah, which comprehends all things and is the "reality" or "meaning" of mankind. That is why Qūnawī often refers to it as the human/divine reality (*al-ḥaqīqa al-insāniyya al-ilāhiyya*); it is identical with the Reality of Realities referred to above. Every single existing thing displays certain of that Reality's inherent perfections, while each individual human being reflects it as a whole: "Animal men [*al-unāsī al-ḥayawāniyyūn*] are the forms of the properties of the whole [*jumla*] of that human/divine reality in respect of outward manifestation."[22] But it is only the Perfect Men who actualize with full consciousness the human/divine reality itself and every state that manifests it in all the ontological levels. In fact:

> No attribute is ascribed to God . . . except in respect of the perfect, human, essential Reality, one of whose levels is the Divinity [*al-ulūhiyya*]. The existents are the loci of manifestation for Its qualities.[23]

If most men are not Perfect Men, this is because, even though their human form manifests the human/divine reality, they are dominated by the properties of one of the particular names that their own reality embraces. All creatures manifest certain names—ultimately, as Ibn al-ʿArabī and his followers state explicitly, each creature may itself be considered a name of God. But when man takes on the color of a particular name, he moves away from the centrality (*wasaṭiyya, markaziyya*) and equilibrium (*iʿtidāl*) peculiar to the all-comprehensive human condition:

> Man is a *barzakh* between the Presence of Divinity and the Presence of engendered existence, a transcription [*nuskha*] comprehending both Presences. So, every single thing is delineated within his level, which consists of his all-comprehensiveness. From the myriad realities embraced by his transcription of Being, certain things become

entified in each time, state, condition, location, and abode; these are determined by his particular affinity with that time, state, condition, and so on.

As long as man is not delivered from the limiting nooses of particular attributes and engendered properties, his perception will be delimited by the particular attribute that rules over him. Hence he will only perceive things that correspond to that attribute and are encompassed by its scope. But if he becomes disengaged from the properties of deviated, one-sided, and particular limitations, inclinations, and attractions, and if he attains to the Central, All-Comprehensive Station, which is the Point of Universal Contraposition [*nuqṭat al-musāmata al-kulliyya*] and the Center of the Circle that comprehends all the levels of equilibrium, that is, the supraformal [i.e., at the level of the fixed entities], the spiritual, the imaginal, and the sensory . . . then he will stand up before the two Presences in the station of his supraformal, *barzakh*-like opposure [*muḥādhāt*]. He will face the two of them in his essence, just as the central point of a circle faces each point of the circumference. He will stand opposite each of the divine and engendered realities through what he possesses of each of them, since he is a transcription of them all.[24]

In outward form every human being displays the human/divine reality as a whole; all other existents display parts or aspects of it. To stop short before traversing the Circle of Being and actualizing the fullness of that reality is to remain below the human potential:

The attractors, my brother, are attracting you from every side; the callers invite you in the language of love, because man is the beloved of all, and all things have come under the sway of his lordship. In keeping with what attracts you and with your affinities, the callers invite you to accept their call and be attracted. And you are the servant of that which you love and to which you become attracted.

In every station, state, and so forth, equilibrium is the center. He who deviates from it enters into disequilibrium [*inḥirāf*]. But no one loses his equilibrium except him who is attracted with his whole self, or with most of it, to that which is less than he. However, if the sides of the circle of every station at which a person alights or through which he passes are equal, so that he becomes fixed at its center in total undifferentiation, free of the limitations of properties and delineations, and so that he gives each attractor and caller only its just due and portion . . . then he is the Man who follows his Lord in His tasks, since *"He has given each thing its creation, then guided"* [20:50].[25]

The outward manifestation of man's form depends upon God's total attentiveness toward him at the time of bringing him into

> existence; it also depends upon both of His hands, as He has given news [see Koran 38:75]. To one of these two hands pertains the unseen and to the other the visible; from one become manifest holy spirits, and from the other nature, corporeal bodies, and forms. That is why man comprehends all the names in knowledge. . . .
>
> So, once the True Man [*al-insān al-ḥaqīqī*] has been freed from the bondage of the stations, risen spiritually, and been delivered by the central perfection's equilibrium from the attracting properties of the sides and from disequilibrium, then his attentiveness will turn toward the Presence of the Ipseity [*al-huwiyya*], namely, the Exclusive Unity of the All-Comprehensiveness of All-Comprehensiveness [*aḥadiyyat jamʿ al-jamʿ*], which is described by manifestation and nonmanifestation, priority and posteriority, all-comprehensiveness and differentiation. . . .
>
> But, if man veers away from the Center to one side because of an attracting and overpowering affinity, and if the property of certain names and levels predominates so that he leaves the equilibrium, then he will become established within the circle of that predominating name and be related and ascribed to it; he will worship God from the standpoint of the name's level and depend upon that name. It will become the utmost limit of his hopes, the goal of his desires, and his aim in respect of his states and stations, unless he passes beyond it.[26]

The ultimate station of human perfection is actualized by the Perfect Men, who follow the ascending arc of the command from the human state to the Reality of Realities. Having actualized the Circle of Being, they take up residence at the Central Point. Between the Perfect Men and those human individuals who are entrapped by the lowest of the "callers" and "attractors" (i.e., Satan and his hosts) stands the whole range of possible human types:

> Whoever leaves the equilibrium of the Central Point—which is the point of perfection at the Presence of All-Comprehensive Exclusive Unity [i.e., the Reality of Realities]—will be judged for or against in keeping with his level's proximity to or distance from the Center. Some are near, some nearer; some far, some farther. Between the total disequilibrium that pertains to satanity [*shayṭana*] and this divine, name-derived, perfect equilibrium, all the levels of the people of felicity [in paradise] and wretchedness [in hell] become entified.[27]

The Circular Ascent

On the one hand the engendering command descends from the Reality of Realities, brings the created worlds and all creatures into existence, and then returns to its Origin by way of the worlds that follow death; on the other hand the Perfect Man traverses the Circle of Being. Obviously, these two processes are related; in fact, they are basically the same process seen from two different points of view, for nothing stands outside the human/divine reality. The concept of the command is simply the way of expressing—in Koranic terms—how this reality becomes actualized in outward manifestation.

In a long passage in the *Miftāḥ al-ghayb* ("The Key to the Unseen") Qūnawī refers to a "mystery" (*sirr*) that was unveiled to him in the year 630/1233 or 631/1234 (when he was still in his twenties), seven or eight years before Ibn al-ʿArabī's death: "On that day I tasted this mystery's universal principles and general outline, with a certain amount of detailed exposition. But the explanation I give now follows my present state."[28] Qūnawī's vision provided him with the answers to the following questions:

> What is man's reality? From what does he come into existence? In what does he come into existence? How does he come into existence? Who brings him into existence? Why is he brought into existence? What is his ultimate end in coming? Is his return to the very thing from which he issued, or to its like, if it is correct to speak of likeness? What is desired from him in an absolute sense, in regard only to the universal divine desire? What is desired from him at each particular moment?[29]

In answering the question of how man comes into existence, Qūnawī describes in detail how the human/divine reality becomes clothed successively in all the possibilities of manifestation contained within itself. Because this reality embraces the whole range of existent things, each of which becomes manifest in an ontological level appropriate to its own reality, the realities encompassed by the human reality are displayed successively (although not necessarily in a temporal order) in keeping with the Circle of Being. And because each successive manifestation of an ontological reality represents the actualization of a perfection latent in the human reality, this reality's apparent "descent"—which from one point of view manifests itself as the descent of the soul into the body—is in fact an ascent toward the realization of the full perfection of the True Man.

In answering the fifth question, "Who brings him into existence?," Qūnawī first recalls that man's origin lies at the level of the beginningless divine knowledge, where he is entified as one possibility of manifestation. However,

> From the moment that man becomes a receptacle for his first ontological form . . . by undergoing supraformal transferal [*al-tanaqqul al-maʿnawī*] from existence within knowledge to existence within the entified universe, he experiences transmutations [*taqallubāt*] within the forms of the existent things stage after stage, and he is transferred from form to form. For man, these transferals and transformations are

> an ascent [*ʿurūj*] and a wayfaring [*sulūk*], starting from the Presence of the Divine Unseen, that is . . . the station of the divine knowledge. Through them man achieves the perfection for which he was made worthy and which is required by his fixed entity's universal preparedness [*al-istiʿdād al-kulliyya*].[30]

After discussing the role of the divine names in causing the descent of the engendering command, Qūnawī describes how "that thing whose existence is desired [by the divine desire] [*al-shayʾ al-murād wujūduhu*]" appears first at the level of the Pen, and then at that of the Tablet. "That thing" is referred to, not "man," since what becomes outwardly manifest is not man himself but a particular reality embraced by his universal reality:

> Then [that thing] continues to descend, passing over each Presence, borrowing the descriptions of each and becoming colored by its property; all the while it maintains its own essential, unseen, entified attributes that it actualized through its first existence [in God's knowledge]. Thus it continues to ascend by means of descent until the form of its materia becomes entified within the womb. Here its configuration [*intishāʾ*] and differentiation [*tamayyuz*] achieve totality. But it never ceases to undergo transferal in various states in this manner until its configuration is perfected and its full stature is achieved.[31]

Through this descent into the ontological levels, the reality that is becoming outwardly manifest gradually leaves the world of luminosity (*nūrāniyya*) and simplicity (*basāṭa*), which is that of spiritual existence, and enters into the darkness (*ẓulma*) and composition (*tarkīb*) that pertain to the sensory world. The world of images is still luminous and subtle (*laṭīf*) in relation to the density (*kathāfa*) of what lies below, but in order to act as an intermediary between the spirits and the bodies it must possess a certain degree of composition like the latter. Then the celestial spheres are still more composite, while the four elements and the minerals, plants, and animals represent succeeding stages of greater composition and complexity. Hence, the journey through these levels is called the "ascent of composition" (*ʿurūj al-tarkīb*). Once this is completed, the journey reverses direction:

> Then, through the process of casting off [*insilākh*, i.e., discarding the accidents, states, and attributes it had acquired through formal composition], the thing [whose existence is desired] turns back in its ascent toward the supraformal composition that the gnostics attain in their wayfaring. . . . This is called the "ascent of decomposition" [*miʿrāj al-taḥlīl*]. For the gnostic travels toward the upper world, and from the time he separates himself from the earth he never passes by any element, Presence, or celestial sphere without discarding within

it the corresponding part, i.e., the part that he had acquired when he first came. Thus he obeys God's words, *God commands you to deliver trusts back to their owners* [4:58].

He discards these parts as follows: His spirit turns away from the part and from loving attachment to governing it[32]; the property of the affinity [*munāsaba*] between him and that thing is weakened because the essential relationship between him and God predominates—for he is ascending toward Him and in the process he turns the face of his heart in His direction.

Then, when he attains to union with the Presence of the Divine Essence without having travelled any distance,[33] . . . nothing remains with him but the divine mystery [*al-sirr al-ilāhī*, i.e., his fixed entity], which became actualized and established when God first turned His attentiveness toward him.[34]

Following Ibn al-ʿArabī, Qūnawī sometimes refers to the divine mystery as the "specific face" (*al-wajh al-khāṣṣ*), that is, the specific face of God turned toward a given existent. Thus, one meaning of the verse, *All things are perishing except His face* (28:88) is that all the outward manifestations of man's fixed entity, everything other than God, will ultimately pass away, while man's reality with God remains eternally. The specific face turned toward man represents a direct ontological nexus with God that never changes, whereas the "orderly chain of intermediaries" (*silsilat al-tartīb wa-l-wasāʾiṭ*) signifies man's indirect connection to God by means of the Circle of Being.

Having returned to his Origin through the spiritual path, man may now be sent back into the world as a guide for others through a "supraformal composition corresponding to the decomposition" that he underwent in his ascent. In any case, his earthly configuration will be dissolved at the death of his body so that the next world may come into being from it.[35]

In a passage surprising for the length to which he takes the analysis, Qūnawī contrasts the journey of the Perfect Men through the Circle of Being with that of those human beings who do not actualize the full range of potentialities embraced by the divine/human reality. It must be remembered here that Qūnawī is discussing the manifestation of the divine mystery, or the particular level appropriate to that perfection. Thus, for example, the divine mystery becomes manifest at the level of each of the descending heavens and even at the level of the elements; its journey "courses through the elements in a manner that has an affinity to them"[36]:

If he is a Perfect Man, when he enters the world of the three kingdoms, his journey will be unitary [*aḥadī*]. In other words, the first plant, for example, within which he becomes manifest, will be free of all corrupting impediments until it reaches its full growth at its own level. Or rather, he would normally become manifest in the most perfect species of plant that exists in the place appropriate to his spiritual reality and his station, or in the place which is the residence of his parents. Then God will send to the plant whomsoever He will. This person will pick it, for example, and cause it to reach the parents or one of them. Or else the parents themselves will pick it from the first. Then they will eat that plant's form in the time appropriate to his level and to the level of the command within which he is included. . . .

Then that plant will be transformed into digested food, then blood, then sperm. It will become connected to the bodies of the parents in a manner that causes it to rise from the level of the plant kingdom and the mineral kingdom to the level of the animal kingdom. Finally, the material of his form will become entified and transferred from the loins to the womb. This is the first all-comprehensive entification which he undergoes, the first instance in which the All-Comprehensive Name manifests its properties within him by dominating over him. In the speed of his transferal from the plant to the animal kingdom, you can behold the speed of his transferal from the mineral to the plant kingdom. The levels are interrelated; no barriers separate them except *barzakh*s conceived by the mind.

The Holy Book refers to these stages with its words, *Then a lodging-place, and a temporary deposit* [6:98]. The beginning of the lodging-place is the womb, while what precedes it pertains to the station of the temporary deposit. In a similar manner, God says, *And We lodge within the wombs what We will, till a stated term* [22:5].

Then he will grow in the womb and be transferred in the manner well-known and described in the formal sciences, until he appears within the world of the visible. Then he rises until he reaches the station of perfection in the manner that was mentioned.

But if destiny places obstacles in his path, after entering the plant kingdom afflictions will overcome him and the plant will be ruined before it reaches completion or is eaten. So he will be separated from the plant kingdom. Then he will return to it at another time, sooner or later. Or he may be afflicted because he becomes joined to a base plant, far from equilibrium, which would never be eaten by any animal. Or, if an animal eats it, then perhaps the animal will perish, so he can also be separated from the plant kingdom in this way. Or he could be overcome by some affliction after becoming connected to the world of plants in the sense that an animal eats the plant, but then the animal perishes before it is eaten by a man. Or he will be prevented from transferring from that animal to the human stage by some obstacle. Or the human who eats it may die before a material becomes entified within him, so it will be dissolved and lost. Then it will return to the animal level.

Such will be his case for a second time, or for many times. If his entering and leaving is repeated a great deal and he continues to clash with the faculties and characteristics deposited within the levels through which he passes and the materials in which he becomes clothed—that is, as a result of the corruption of the various forms he assumes and the repetition of his coming and going—then he acquires the supraformal qualities deposited within these things [that is, he will be dominated by the particular names that determine these things]. If the characteristic that predominates is the most praiseworthy and appropriate, he will profit from this, but in what follows he will meet hardship and difficult struggle. But if the predominating property is not praiseworthy or appropriate, his knowledge and remembrance [*tadhakkur*] of the levels of his existence and his transformations will be less. Or rather, these things often will be completely hidden from him. But to the extent that repetition and opposing qualities are less, remembrance will be returned to him more quickly, and opening and the way will be made easy for him. The divine mystery referred to as the "*sure foot*" [10:2], "beginningless solicitude," the "appearance of self-disclosure" and the like is fundamental in all of this.

If the properties of the levels have not colored him to the extent that they conceal the mystery of unity and the property of the aforementioned appearance, then that mystery will dominate over him. This is referred to in God's words, *God dominates over His command* [12:21]. But if the coloring of the levels and Presences veil the divine mystery and its property, then his situation will be ruled by the property that dominates in this state. For, as you have already come to know, man is composed of different and disparate parts and from harmonious realities and faculties. But the most excellent thing within him is the divine mystery, which is the self-disclosure of the specific face. . . .[37]

When the divine mystery becomes colored by the properties it passes through, it divides in one respect into three kinds:

1. In the first kind, the qualities and garments [i.e., the properties of the levels] are related to it in the same way that accidental attributes are related to the object to which they are ascribed. This is because the mystery possesses an excellent and strong priority in God's Presence, a priority called the "sure foot," "solicitude," and so on. If this solicitude prepares the mystery to gain a balanced relationship with the states of what it passes through, and if the states of the spiritual Presences and the celestial faculties turn their attentiveness toward the mystery in a manner that is in equilibrium and harmonious, free from

the properties of both sides—then the person who is the form and locus of manifestation for the mystery will become one of the attracted [*al-majdhūbīn*], or someone not in need of many works and difficult ascetic practices, like the Prophet and whomsoever God wants of his family, and the saints.

2. In the second kind, the qualities [and properties of the levels that the divine mystery passes through] are related to their possessor like established accidents and intrinsic attributes. This is because, during its journey, the command comes to be dominated by the property of the name "Lord" [*rabb*, which nourishes—*tarbiya*—whatever it touches], in contrast to the first case [where the All-Comprehensive Name dominates]. The second kind's priority in God's Presence possesses a high excellence and strong power, while it has a certain balance in the states and properties referred to. If a person of the second kind is helped by the divine solicitude and the determining decree, he may become one of the Perfect Men; otherwise he will become a person of intermediate rank [*mutawassiṭ*]. But he can attain these ranks only after great effort and painful asceticism, if God wills.

3. In the third kind, the properties of the garments and qualities become firmly rooted, while at the beginning of entification in the Presence of God there will be no coloring by the property of solicitude. He will meet and become colored by the properties of the Presences he passes through in an incomplete manner. The properties that accrue to him from the spirits and the celestial spheres will be unbalanced, for the moment will not help him to travel the path, and he will exert little effort in purifying himself from veiling attributes and nonharmonious accidents. So he will become one of the veiled and the wretched, outside of the circle of the people of solicitude.

When a person of either of the first two kinds reaches maturity and full stature, his ascent will reverse itself to begin the casting off [of properties and attributes] in the ascent of decomposition so that he can undertake the second composition, which the gnostics attain here after opening. When man passes beyond the first ascent—which seems outwardly to be a decline and debasement in relation to what is understood by the words *the fairest stature* [95:4]—he is transferred to the second [i.e., that of composition].

So, through his Lord, man produces for himself other configurations, the first universal one of which is the configuration of the *barzakh*. That is followed by the two configurations of the Mustering and the endless Garden. Each of these four configurations [i.e., these three and the elemental configuration of the world] is in a certain respect the result of that which preceded it. This fact is alluded to by the words, *You shall surely ride stage after stage* [84:19], that is, each state is born from the one preceding it. I said "in a certain respect" because in all the configurations there is a permanent and unchanging command within which these changes take place; it is the reality of man, the substance and leaven of his configurations, the locus of manifestation for God's Fixed Being, and the divine mystery.

The journey and ascent that people undergo—sometimes from stage to stage and configuration to configuration, and sometimes within a certain configuration in keeping with their interrelationship with it . . . is of several kinds:

Some people do not complete the ontological circle because of the insufficiency of their preparedness. Such a person is referred to by the words, *We restored him to the lowest of the low* [95:5], because he traveled half the circle, or only part of it.

The first group of those who complete the circle *shall have a wage unfailing* [95:6] because the end of their supraformal ascent—which appears outwardly to be a decline—becomes joined with the second, decompositional ascent in order that their second configuration may become compounded from and within this world. For the configuration of the *barzakh* is the result of the state of this world, as we have already indicated; it makes no difference whether the person who produces this configuration through his states understands this fact or not.

But the contemplative gnostic who achieves realization is provided with complete and correct presence [with God]; he is totally alive to and aware of the abodes to which he is transferred and within which he moves from stage to stage. He truly knows their properties and all the configurations that God produces for him and through him in the worlds.

As for him whose soul is interrelated within his body in such a way that he is prevented from actualizing the perfection for the sake of which man was given a human preparedness . . . he will remain in the "lowest of the low." His transferal and journey will take place in the abodes through which he was destined to pass. He will become clothed in attributes and states in keeping with the characteristics that God deposited in those abodes and worlds and in keeping with the characteristics of his own configuration and its effects upon him. In all of this he will not know the transformation he is undergoing, nor that to which his command will return. The perfection specific to him within this worldly abode will be that at which he arrives with his last breath before he dies. . . .

So the command is a circle, and the journey is circular, not linear. Whoever is destined to complete it will complete and perfect his wayfaring. Then he will begin to travel a second, divine cycle, which begins from the time he views things in God and truly knows the One Being of God after direct vision. This is the first degree of sanctity. . . .[38]

Next, Qūnawī discusses in detail the various kinds of saints in keeping with the level of perfection that they realize. Finally, he returns to those who remain imperfect:

> The incomplete journeying which we mentioned is of two kinds: the first is an imperfection before the completion and perfection of the journey in the first circle; such a person is an "animal man." The second is an imperfection specific to the intermediaries, those who have been given a certain measure of perfection but have not yet attained to its completion. Between these two are diverse degrees. . . .[39]

The Human Soul

Qūnawī devotes relatively little attention to the nature of the human or rational soul as such (*al-nafs al-insāniyya/al-nāṭiqa*). One of the few passages where he does discuss the soul in some detail is in his reply to Ṭūsī, where he states that the inability of the Peripatetic philosophers to grasp the soul's true nature derives from the limitations of rational speculation. When he expresses his views on the soul, he usually refers to it in terms of the various levels of man's spiritual perfection. The following passage from the *Nafaḥāt* provides the gist of his remarks to Ṭūsī:

> The first perfection of the animal spirit is for it to become colored by the attributes of the rational soul. The first perfection of the particular rational soul is to actualize the description [*waṣf*] of the guardian of the first heaven, who is called "Ismāʿīl" in religious language and the "Agent Intellect" in philosophy. The particular soul's intermediate perfection is to actualize the description and gain the properties of the Universal Soul in a manner that will allow it to pass beyond it to the level of the First Intellect or Universal Spirit; finally, it reaches union [*ittiṣāl*] with and absorption [*istihlāk*] by the Presence of God. This occurs when the property of realness [*ḥaqqiyya*, i.e., the specific face] dominates over createdness [*khalqiyya*], and the characteristic of possibility [*imkān*] and delimitation are overcome by the properties of Necessity [*wujūb*].[40]

Only once in his works does Qūnawī describe the soul's descent in terms thoroughly reminiscent of Neoplatonic teachings. In the passage in question, he explains the symbolism of Jonah and the "fish" (the soul and the body) in connection with his commentary on Chapter 18 of Ibn al-ʿArabī's *Fuṣūṣ*. The key to understanding the connection between this passage and man's circular ascent lies in the concept of "preparedness," a term that denotes the extent to which an entity is able to act as a receptacle for the ontological perfections represented by the divine names. In Chapter 15 of the *Fuṣūṣ*, Ibn al-ʿArabī discusses preparedness in the context of the manifestation of the spirit, whose outstanding ontological attribute is life (here it should be recalled that Ibn al-ʿArabī and his followers consider the name "Living" as the first of the "Seven Leaders" (*al-aʾimma al-sabʿa*), or the primary names of the Divinity, the others being "Knowing," "Desiring," "Powerful," "Speaking," "Generous," and "Just"). Spirit—or life—can only display its perfections within existence when a receptacle has acquired a sufficient preparedness: "Do you not see that God's breathing [of the spirit] into bodies made ready [to receive it] . . . is to the measure of that which is breathed into?"[41]

Once the scattered reflections of the divine mystery have been gathered together into a certain equilibrium through the ascent of composition, they act as a receptacle for the spirit, first in its vegetal and then in its animal mode. Finally, when the outward human form becomes actualized, the spirit is able to manifest itself in a relatively complete sense. All the varying degrees of human perfection represent ascending degrees of the spirit's manifestation and realization. Ultimately, man may even pass beyond the spirit's ontological level.

But from the point of view of the soul considered as a spiritual entity possessing self-awareness before its attachment to the body, the situation is seen in another light; this is one of the points that Qūnawī wants to explain below. It should be noted that the soul is necessarily limited in its knowledge because it has not yet actualized the all-comprehensiveness of the human state. In this respect, its situation is similar to that of the angels, whose curtailed vision caused them to protest at God's creation of man. He replied to them, *"Surely I know what you know not"* (2:30)[42]:

> In origin human souls arose from the universal supernal spirits that the philosophers call "intellects," which the souls strongly resemble in diverse respects, including simplicity and everlasting subsistence. Hence the souls think that once they become connected [*taʿalluq*] to the corporeal bodies in respect of governance [*tadbīr*] and control [*taḥakkum*], they will not become delimited [*taqyīd*] or lovingly attached, and, whenever they desire, they can turn away from governing by their attribute of independence, like the spirits from which they arose. But in this affair they neglect the decline [*nuzūl*] of their own degree from that of those spirits and also their lack of independence from connection and governing. So, they grow accustomed to their bodies and become colored by the properties of their constitutions to the extent that the latter effect them, just as they have had an effect upon the latter. They develop a loving attachment to their bodies, and their companionship with them increases their delimitation.
>
> Then God shows them their incapacity and inadequacy to reach the degree of the spirits by means of whom He had brought them into existence. They see their own poverty and loving attachment, so

they turn back, betaking themselves to God in humility and inherent need from the direction in which there is no intermediary between Him and them. God answers their call and gives them succor from Himself with a strength and a light by which they raise their view to that which God wants to disclose to them of His sacred Presences and the subtleties of His sublime mysteries. Their loving attachment is reflected back upon that Most Sacred Presence, and they become united with It. By means of this union, which removes the properties of intermediaries, they actualize something that allows them to be ranked among the possessors of strength and vision. A closed door is opened to them, and their governance becomes absolute and not delimited by any specific form exclusive of another. On the contrary, they actualize a power and perfection enabling them to govern diverse forms at one time without loving attachment or delimitation.[43]

Solicitude may even bestow upon them such mighty rank that they disdain stopping within the levels of the sublime spirits to be like them; for they observe a beauty manifesting itself to them from behind the gate of the specific face, the gate that has been opened for them between themselves and their Creator, and they gain certain things from their Lord in this respect. From the blessing of what they attain there courses through their outward forms—by whose governance they had been delimited—powers and lights that pervade and extend into all the existent things of the lower and upper worlds. Through their all-comprehensive unity they begin to maintain—in respect of that outward form through whose governance they had been delimited—the formal disparity actualized and established among all the existent things, at the level of form and meaning and of spirits and imagination.[44]

12

Farghānī on Oneness and Manyness

When we look at those Muslims who have been called Sufis, we see that their role in Islam has often been understood by placing them on one side of a dichotomy. Thus, for example, we are told that the Sufis take one position, while the jurists and proponents of Kalam take the opposite position. The Shariah is one thing, whereas the Tariqah is something else. The Sufis look at the inward meaning, while the jurists look at the outward form. The Sufis have an esoteric perspective on things, whereas the mullahs have an exoteric perspective. The Sufis are spiritualizing and nondogmatic mystics, whereas the jurists are literal-minded and dogmatic legalists.

Setting up sharp dichotomies between Sufism and legalistic Islam has certainly made life easier for many historians. But as long as scholars persist in taking one side or the other as "orthodox" Islam, they will not necessarily provide helpful models for understanding what has actually been going on in Islamic history. Of course, dichotomies and divergences do exist and are constantly stressed in many of the original texts. We have to be aware of these dichotomies and take them seriously, but we also have to keep in mind the rhetorical usefulness of stressing differences. When we get to the task of describing what was actually being said, it may prove to be more helpful to picture the differing positions in terms of spectrums of differing shades and hues, rather than sharply defined dualities. When one is faced with an issue in Islamic thought, one could then suggest what the two extremes of the spectrum might be, and analyze the various positions in terms of the relative stress placed on particular points. In any given issue, some authors will fall on the red side of things, some on the violet side, and the vast majority will take up positions in between. On the next issue, the various authors might well take up different colors of the spectrum, not corresponding to their relative place in the previous issue.

This sort of analysis would mean that we can no longer make the sweeping generalizations that many of us have long indulged in without adding numerous qualifications. By taking this approach, we can also help dispel the still-current myths about Islam as a monolithic system with little historical and regional variation. Not that it is necessary to go as far as some anthropologists, claiming, in effect, that there has been nothing but a series of local Islams with practically no unifying factors. Rather, we may be able to provide a more accurate picture of the unity *and* diversity of Islamic civilization.

One of the more interesting sets of dichotomies discussed in both the original texts and the secondary literature has to do precisely with those factors that differentiate the Sufis from the jurists and theologians, consequently providing a good example of a spectrum of positions.[1] Before modern times, a certain balance between the outward and inward, or the "exoteric" and the "esoteric" was the general rule, although this would not necessarily be obvious if we were to limit ourselves to reading those authors who are critical of positions supposedly taken by their opponents. In fact, Islam has witnessed a constant creative tension between those who stress one side of an issue and those who stress the other. The discussions do frequently degenerate into polemics, but the upshot has been to make available to Muslims a vast range of approaches to the basic teachings of the Koran and the Sunnah. The Sufis sometimes cite hadiths and sayings that seem to allude to the positive results of this diversity of opinion: "There are as many ways to God as there are human souls," and "The divergence of the ulama is a mercy."

One of the best-known cases of divergent interpretations among Muslim thinkers arose in the wake of Ibn al-ʿArabī's grand synthesis of Islamic teachings. But, if anything characterizes the great masters of Sufism, and especially Ibn al-ʿArabī, it is certainly not that they consider their own position to mark one of the extremes. Quite the contrary, they usually view themselves as taking up an intermediate stance among the conflicting perspectives of Islamic thought and practice. Typically, they recognize and even validate the fact that there are deep dichotomies in approaches to various issues. Then they attempt to overcome not the dichotomies themselves, but the absoluteness accorded to them. They affirm the reality of difference and distinction, but they maintain that a view of things that sees interrelationship, complementarity, and polarity corresponds more closely to the Islamic ideal. Through asserting the underlying unity of the Real, they establish a framework within which all diversity can be situated.

The One and the Many

Saʿīd al-Dīn Farghānī is one of many Sufi authors who provide theoretical frameworks for overcoming dichotomies and integrating dispersed realities. Although at first sight his discussion may seem to pertain exclusively to an abstract philosophical level, one soon sees that he provides many helpful correlations among the divergent positions in Islamic thought.

In order to suggest something of Farghānī's significance and the approach he takes to Sufi thought, I want to investigate his formulation of two contrasting approaches to reality—approaches that might tentatively be called the way of love and the way of knowledge, or the way of affirming oneness and the way of discerning manyness.

As was noted in Chapter 8, since God is one in Being and also many in knowledge, Farghānī sees the Oneness of Being (*waḥdat al-wujūd*) as the polar opposite of the Manyness of Knowledge (*kathrat al-ʿilm*). This corresponds to the most basic dichotomy in reality. However, at this point I will stop using the term "dichotomy," with its suggestion that there is something deep and irremediable about difference, and use the term "polarity" because Farghānī's position demands that there be no absolute distinctions in God or the cosmos. Being and knowledge should not be looked upon as distinct and separate, but as polar and complementary.

At the highest level of Reality, Being and knowledge are identical and no distinction can be drawn between the two. At this level, one might speak of an absolute oneness prior to any manyness. This is the level of the Unknown Essence, which cannot be discussed in positive terms. As soon as we conceive of a Reality about which positive statements can be made, we are faced with the distinction between Being and knowledge. Knowledge—which is identical with consciousness and awareness—belongs to the very Essence of God. The Divine Reality, or Being, knows Itself with a knowledge that is identical with Itself, so there is no difference between the Knower (*ʿālim*) and the Known (*maʿlūm*). However, when we speak of knowing, we necessarily set up a subject–object relationship, even if we cannot draw an ontological distinction between the two sides. This perceived relationship in turn makes it possible to distinguish among the divine names. For example, one can say that since God knows His own Reality, He knows all the concomitants and characteristics of His own Reality and thus knows Himself as Alive, Knowing, Desiring, Powerful, Speaking, Generous, and Just. For Farghānī—as is the case with Ibn al-ʿArabī—one of the most important statements we can make about the Real is that His Being is one while His knowledge has many objects, even if those objects possess no ontological plurality of any sort. The multiplicity of the objects of knowledge has no effect on the oneness of God's Being. In an analogous way, a human mind is not split up into many minds by the fact that it is aware of many things.

It is extremely important to grasp the nature of the polarity that Farghānī sets up when he speaks of oneness and manyness at this primary level of reality, since he finds corresponding polarities throughout the created world. Oneness and manyness cannot be distinguished from one another in any absolute way because both qualities belong to the reality of God. Whether we look at the Real as one or many depends on our perspective, even if the point of view that considers God's oneness is more fundamental. Hence, the universe, inasmuch as it reflects its Origin, can only be understood in terms of relative qualities, and these, since they are relative, change when the point of view changes. There are no absolute dichotomies within the created universe, nor in our formulations and expressions of the nature of things. This means that from the outset,

Farghānī gives us a position that not only allows for, but even demands, other contrasting positions. Every reality demands its polar opposite. Mention of one side implies the other side, just as mention of yin implies yang.

In order to show that no absolute distinction can be drawn between Being and knowledge, Farghānī states that Being possesses a true oneness (*waḥda ḥaqīqiyya*) and a relative manyness (*kathra nisbiyya*), while knowledge possesses a true manyness and a relative oneness. Hence, both Being and knowledge are one and many, but the quality of oneness predominates in Being, whereas the quality of manyness predominates in knowledge.

Farghānī describes the true oneness and relative manyness of Being in the following terms:

> Each divine name is nothing but the manifest aspect of Being, which is the Essence Itself, but in respect of Its entification [*ta'ayyun*] and delimitation [*taqayyud*] by a meaning, or call it an "attribute" [*ṣifa*]. For example, "Living" is a name of the entified, manifest Being, but in respect of Its entification and delimitation by a meaning, which is life. Hence, in respect of Being Itself and the entification itself, Being is identical with the Essence, and Its oneness is true. But in respect of the delimitation by that meaning and this meaning's distinction from other meanings . . . Being is different from what is named. Hence It possesses a relative manyness through those entifications.[2]

In contrast, the divine knowledge possesses true manyness and relative oneness because God knows the divine names and their concomitants, and these many objects of knowledge demand that knowledge be truly differentiated, or else the manyness could not be known for what it is. At the same time, knowledge is a single reality that pertains to the One Being.[3]

When Farghānī turns his attention to discussions more familiar to Muslim philosophers, he elucidates one of the many corollaries of the fact that oneness precedes manyness by explaining the relationship between necessity and possibility. Being in Its oneness possesses the quality of necessity because It cannot not be. But Being's knowledge pertains to what is possible because each object of knowledge correlates with a possible thing, something that may or may not exist in the cosmos. The multiplicity of the cosmos externalizes the true manyness of the divine knowledge, while the underlying unity of the cosmos—present most obviously in the fact that each part of it shares in existence—reflects the Oneness of Being. That which is closer to the Oneness of Being possesses a preponderance of properties pertaining to necessity, whereas that which reflects the Manyness of Knowledge is dominated by possibility.

On the basis of this distinction between necessity and possibility, Farghānī divides the cosmos into three worlds: high, low, and intermediate. Everything that is dominated by the side of oneness and necessity, such as the angels and spirits, pertains to the high world. Everything that is dominated by the side of manyness and possibility, such as inanimate objects, plants, and animals, pertains to the low world. But human beings pertain to the middle realm, where oneness and manyness are balanced.[4] In a parallel way, human beings can be divided into three basic categories depending on the relationship established between the properties of necessity and those of possibility. People in whom necessity predominates are the prophets and friends of God. Those in whom possibility dominates are the unbelievers. And those in whom necessity and possibility are more or less equal are the faithful. So also, the human psyche can be analyzed in terms of three fundamental tendencies: ascending, descending, and in-between. To these is connected the Koranic distinction made among the three basic levels of the soul: the soul at peace with God, the soul that commands to evil, and the intermediate, blaming soul.

Other implications of the distinction between oneness and manyness or necessity and possibility become apparent as soon as we look at those divine qualities that have a personal dimension. For example, since the One precedes the many, God's mercy takes precedence over His wrath. The reality of mercy is Being Itself; to exist in the cosmos is to participate in the existentiating mercy known as the Breath of the All-Merciful. Wrath is connected in some way to the multiplicity and possibility prefigured in the divine knowledge. When one thing is differentiated from another thing, each of the two things must be lacking in certain qualities that pertain to the unity and all-comprehensiveness of Being. This deficiency in the qualities of Being demands a certain lack of mercy, or a certain domination by properties that pertain not to Being Itself but to nothingness. Hence, any situation that is deficient in existence is related to the divine wrath, though again, there can be nothing absolute about this deficiency.

The relationship between mercy and wrath correlates with the two basic categories of divine names that bring the cosmos into existence. These are called the names of mercy and wrath, or beauty (*jamāl*) and majesty (*jalāl*), or bounty (*faḍl*) and justice (*ʿadl*), or gentleness (*luṭf*) and severity (*qahr*). These pairs of qualities are in turn connected with a large number of polarities or dichotomies. For example, mercy and gentleness are associated with nearness to God, while wrath and severity with distance from Him. The people of the Garden enter into mercy, whereas the people of the Fire taste chastisement because they are distant and *veiled from their Lord* (83:15).

On the human level, the polarities expressed in the merciful and wrathful names are closely related to the basic distinction that is drawn between the spirit and the body, or between the upward and unifying tendency of the soul and its downward and dispersive tendency. The spirit is luminous and relatively close to the oneness of God, while the body is dark and relatively dominated by the properties of manyness and possibility. Hence, the spirit correlates with nearness and mercy, while the body correlates with distance and wrath. Again, these are not absolute distinctions, but rather a question of predominant attributes.

In short, wherever we can speak of two contrasting names of God—such as Forgiving and Vengeful, Gentle and Severe, Exalting and Abasing—one of the two terms will be more closely connected to the oneness and necessity of Being and the other to the manyness and possibility of knowledge. At the same time, manyness is found in oneness and oneness in manyness, so the relationships can be reversed in appropriate circumstances. This has all sorts of repercussions on the level of the "signs" (*āyāt*) of God, or those manifestations of the Divine Reality that make up the cosmos.[5]

Duality in the Cosmos

In Farghānī's formulation, the typical qualities that pertain to the Oneness of Being are unity, all-comprehensiveness, realness, freedom from distinction and otherness, and freedom from contamination by what is unreal. But created things are dominated by the manyness that pertains to the divine knowledge. Hence they are characterized by qualities such as multiplicity, dispersion, diversity, strife, otherness, and contamination by the unreal. The true manyness of the things conceals their relative oneness.

Any creature in the universe has two fundamental faces, one of which manifests the Oneness of Being and the other the Manyness of Knowledge.[6] The reality of each thing is in fact defined by the relationship set up between these two faces. Without both faces, the thing could not possibly exist. Pure oneness without manyness is an attribute of the Real alone, while pure manyness without oneness could provide no basis for an existent thing.

The first face of each created thing is turned toward the Real Being. This face demands that the thing manifest properties of oneness such as balance (*ʿadāla*), all-comprehensiveness, luminosity, and realness. On the human level, this face is receptive to God's mercy, compassion, and guidance, hence to the names of gentleness and beauty.

The second face of each created thing is turned toward the thing itself and everything that is demanded by the thing's own separate, individual reality. Since this face is veiled from the oneness of the Real, it manifests the opposite qualities: manyness, distance from the Real, darkness, unreality, deviation, and domination of the veil. On the human level, this second face is connected to the rejection of divine compassion, misguidance, and wrath, hence to the names of severity and majesty.

Psychologically speaking, each face has specific effects within the human being. The effect of the face turned toward oneness is submission to God's will and faith in Him, His prophets, and the Last Day. In short, domination by this face becomes manifest as harmony with the names of mercy and the divine guidance. Domination by the second face brings about the opposite qualities, such as immersion in misguidance.

On this first level of analysis, the Oneness of Being and the Manyness of Knowledge give rise to a world of tremendous diversity within which two tendencies can be observed among the creatures: the tendency toward oneness, harmony, wholeness, and nearness to God, manifesting the names of gentleness and mercy; and the tendency toward manyness, disequilibrium, dispersion, and distance from God, manifesting the names of severity and wrath.

This analysis may suggest that oneness is good and manyness bad. But of course this is not the implication. On the contrary, both oneness and manyness are present in the Real, since they are polar attributes. Hence, both have positive roles to play. The key is to always establish balance and equilibrium between the two.

The Two Extremes

Farghānī frequently discusses various human dangers inherent in allowing oneself to be dominated by either the face that manifests the Oneness of Being or the face that reflects the Manyness of Knowledge. Each human being has to strive to keep the two faces in equilibrium. If a person fails to do so, distortions will prevent the full development of the soul, which is defined by its infinite capacity as an image of the Divine Reality. In the process of describing these dangers, Farghānī mentions a number of key concepts that allow us to tie his discussion into the issues mentioned at the beginning of this chapter.

When the face turned toward the One Being dominates, a person will be attracted toward oneness and move away from manyness. Distinctions and differentiations will play less and less of a role in that person's personality. This movement can become so overwhelming that all manyness will be obliterated from the person's view. And this movement is intimately connected with love. Like all positive qualities, love is first a divine attribute. As such, it is closely allied with the names of beauty and gentleness. The basic characteristic of love is a tendency toward union and the erasure of distinctions. As Farghānī remarks, the reality of love bridges the gap between lover and beloved, seeker and sought. By its very nature, it is unitary (*waḥdānī*) and establishes unity (*muwaḥḥid*). Through love, the qualities that are shared by the two sides come to dominate. The ultimate result of love is the elimination of everything that keeps lover and beloved apart. Since the Beloved is the One Being, the single Reality of God, love tends toward the lifting of manyness and difference.[7]

As a unifying movement, love can be contrasted with knowledge, which separates, discerns, distinguishes, differentiates, and classifies.[8] Knowledge perceives differences between good and evil, true and false, right and wrong. It provides the basis for all the injunctions of the Shariah, which are founded on strict definitions and placing things in different categories. Thus human knowledge, like divine knowledge, affirms manyness and establishes its reality. It maintains the difference between God and the servant. To say this, however, is not to deny that there is a mode of visionary knowledge that unveils the underlying Oneness of Being. But in the first evaluation, knowledge differentiates.

Farghānī tells us that every sane person is bound by the laws established by discernment through knowledge. As he puts it, as long as people remain in the present world, they are "captive to the property of the world of wisdom, the manyness of its requirements, and the requirements of the two faces of created realities."[9] The world of everyday experience pertains to wisdom because the divine wisdom itself has set up the distinctions inherent in existence.[10] Each of the two faces of created reality is determined by the very nature of Uncreated Reality, or by the true Oneness of Being and the true Manyness of Knowledge. As long as people are present in this world, they have to observe the requirements of both faces and maintain the distinctions between the tendencies that each face manifests. These distinctions, set up by the divine wisdom itself, demand that there be two basic movements in existence: one toward mercy and union and the other toward wrath and separation. These distinctions are unavoidable because they define the nature of reality itself. As a result, says Farghānī, people "will be subject to the properties of reward, punishment, calling to account, responsibility, and reckoning in both this world and the next."[11]

The Manyness of Knowledge establishes all the distinctions and differences found in the world of wisdom. It determines the difference between guidance and misguidance and establishes the distinction between mercy and wrath, gentleness and severity. This is all positive and good. But the upshot is that the travelers on the path to God find themselves far from their Beloved, since manyness gives rise to distance and separation.

The Oneness of Being also gives rise to specific effects within the cosmos. It manifests Itself in the face that marks the direction of the ascending path, the path back to mercy and gentleness. It brings about the movement of love that erases the distinction between the two sides. Nevertheless, the Oneness of Being cannot be allowed to completely erase the Manyness of Knowledge any more than the Manyness of Knowledge can be allowed to obliterate the Oneness of Being. Exclusive attention to one side or the other can lead to deviation and disequilibrium. Both need to be kept in balance, just as they are balanced in the Real Himself, who is one in His Being and many through His names.

In discussing the dangers of placing too much emphasis on the Oneness of Being, Farghānī turns to certain types of mystical awareness that erase distinctions. In his own words, travelers on the path to God

> may become joined with the vast expanse of the world of Oneness such that they live in that Presence and gaze upon It, having realized It. They remain forgetful and negligent of created existence, its levels, and all the realities that it contains. They may have no awareness of themselves, their existence, and all the attributes, accidents, and concomitants that are seen to pertain to themselves. They witness and see the One Real Being through the Real Himself, not through themselves or through their own vision.[12]

But this is not necessarily good. For example, this sort of perception is found in *majdhūb*s, those spiritual mad men who have been overcome by the divine attraction. As long as this state remains, it represents imperfection. Such mystical awareness of the Oneness of Being is usually limited in duration. The travelers return to normal consciousness and once again follow the prophetic Sunnah and the Shariah. They put into practice the requirements of knowledge and wisdom. They observe the necessities of the Manyness of Knowledge, which distinguishes between the names of guidance and misguidance. However, some people, having experienced the world of the Oneness of Being, may now consider themselves exempt from the concomitants of the Manyness of Knowledge. They reject the requirements of the world of wisdom and have no concern for good and evil, right and wrong, command and prohibition, or the rulings of the Shariah. Once the discernment connected with knowledge disappears, so do all the rulings of the Shariah. In Farghānī's words, such people say, "In the world of Oneness I saw all things as a single thing. Hence for me there is no more command and prohibition, no more lawful and unlawful, no more distinction among things. For me everything is one, with no difference between lawful and unlawful."[13]

Farghānī then adds that such people are heretics, and by saying so he places himself squarely in the mainstream of Sufism, which strives to maintain the balance between the norms of the Shariah and the Tariqah.[14]

In this particular passage, Farghānī does not enter into the dangers of placing too much stress upon knowledge. But he does deal with it elsewhere in his works, and in any case it is a well-known theme in Sufi writings. In short, exclusive emphasis on knowledge that differentiates and separates leads to a rationalism that is unable to see beyond surface appearances. It results in excessive stress upon the differentiations set up by legalistic and literalistic interpretations of the Koran and the Sunnah. Rational thought becomes a veil that maintains difference and prevents the realization of the face turned toward oneness. In speaking of the dangers of this extreme, Farghānī writes:

> The greatest factor bringing about the dispersion that prevents your realization of the reality of all-comprehensiveness is your inclination toward the sciences of philosophy and Kalam. . . . The veils brought about by these sciences are thicker and denser than all other veils.[15]

The Actual Situation

If love and knowledge can be set up as mutually exclusive opposites, this surely has to do with extreme forms in each case. The extreme or exclusive stress upon love overpowers the discernment and distance demanded by God's knowledge of the realities of all things. Correspondingly, extreme or exclusive stress upon the differentiations of knowledge veils the union and nearness demanded by the oneness of God's Being.

One can find examples of extreme expressions of love in some of the more ecstatic verses of Sufi poetry. If such expressions of unification between God and the creature are taken simply as the vision of one of the two faces of each thing, no objections can be raised. But at different times and places we meet instances where there seems to be an exclusive reliance on the face of oneness, as evidenced by the harsh criticisms of certain types of Sufism found in the writings of the Sufis themselves. If the Oneness of Being is affirmed and the Manyness of Knowledge denied, then we have an extreme that threatens the balance set up by *tawḥīd*.

Another example of an extreme expression of the Oneness of Being is found in the *shaṭḥiyyāt* or "ecstatic utterances" attributed to many Sufis. In contrast, the various interpretations offered for these utterances by later authors attempt to reestablish a balance by discerning the right relationships through knowledge. In this same arena one finds the reason for the numerous attacks that were made on *waḥdat al-wujūd*, both by Sufis and non-Sufis. When this concept was criticized, it was invariably interpreted as negating the effects of the world of wisdom or the Manyness of Knowledge.

It must always be kept in mind that exclusive attention paid to the Manyness of Knowledge or the plurality of the divine names has a parallel negative outcome. Those who continue to stress manyness and difference end up by establishing absolute distinctions between God and the world. They value a knowledge that differentiates and separates above everything that unifies and unites. The result is a cold literalism that kills the spirit of love and compassion.

One can reformulate this discussion in terms of "exoteric" and "esoteric" approaches to Islam. But here the terminology is problematic because it is difficult to find the corresponding terms in the texts themselves.[16] What we see happening is that expressions of Islam tended in two directions, toward expressing oneness and sameness or affirming manyness and difference. In both cases we find extreme examples that delimit the range of a spectrum of positions. Excessive emphasis on unity and oneness led to an antinomian approach to Islam, and, in its extreme forms, to those movements in Sufism known as *bī-sharʿ* or "without Shariah." Excessive emphasis on the face that manifests the Manyness of Knowledge led to a literalistic and rationalistic approach to Islam and a denial that "oneness" of any sort could be established between Lord and servant. The vast majority of Sufis who wrote theoretical works attempted to establish a balance between the two sides—between love and knowledge, oneness and manyness, mercy and wrath, "esoteric" and "exoteric."

Among the advantages of Farghānī's approach is the fact that it allows for a description of the actual situation that does not fall into the typical dualities that result when we start employing dichotomous categories like "exoteric" and "esoteric," especially when we impose these categories from the outside. Although at first sight Farghānī's discussion presents itself in the rhetoric of two extremes, they are set up as the two poles of a relationship with the explicit awareness that neither pole can ever be empty of the other side. As a result, the actual situation is presented as a range of positions over a broad spectrum. And it is not difficult to see that the extreme positions hardly ever exist in reality, but rather only in the minds of those who set up "ideal" situations.

13

Jāmī on the Perfect Man

The Perfect Man is the ontological prototype of both man and the cosmos. He is the first creation of God or, rather, the primordial and original self-disclosure of the Essence, and thus the first point in the descending arc (*al-qaws al-nuzūlī*) of the manifestation or effusion of existence. But the descending arc must reach its lowest point, which is the corporeal world (*ʿālam al-ajsām*) or the world of sense perception (*ʿālam al-ḥiss, ʿālam al-shahāda*). Then the circle closes upon itself. The goal of the ascending arc (*al-qaws al-ṣuʿūdī*)—the return to the Principle—is likewise the state of the Perfect Man. Hence, the Perfect Man has two dimensions: First, he is the ontological prototype of man and the cosmos, or the origin of the descending arc of creation. Second, he is the exemplar to be emulated, or the goal of the ascending arc of creation. Here I confine myself to an analysis of ʿAbd al-Raḥmān Jāmī's treatment of the first dimension of the Perfect Man. I rely solely on Jāmī's Persian work, *Naqd al-nuṣūṣ* ("Selected Texts"), which is his most detailed theoretical explication of the major teachings of the school of Ibn al-ʿArabī.[1]

In proposing to discuss Jāmī's concept of the Perfect Man, we need to be aware of what this signifies: Jāmī is not an original thinker in the sense that he has his own peculiar concept of the Perfect Man and other Sufi doctrines. His concepts are those of the school of Ibn al-ʿArabī and his special role is to represent a culmination of that school in the history of Sufism. There is no doubt that Jāmī himself saw this school as a unified and harmonious whole, with differences of opinion only in minor points. His continuous quotations in the *Naqd* from figures who composed their works at various times over a period of two hundred years reveal this harmony, and, other than minor differences of point of view and variations in prose style, few discrepancies can be seen among these writings.

Jāmī's "originality," therefore, lies in the fact that he summarizes a whole school of thought and brings it to a climax. He carries this out in a language often clearer and more eloquent and beautiful than that of his predecessors, and thus more readily accessible to a larger audience. This is true both of his prose and poetry. Of the other Sufi poets and authors who reflected Ibn al-ʿArabī's doctrines in their verses and writings, with the possible exception of Shabistarī, none was able to express the teachings of Ibn al-ʿArabī as directly, beautifully, and simply as Jāmī. Certainly the tremendous popularity of Jāmī's writings in the Indian Subcontinent is one of the major reasons for the spread of Ibn al-ʿArabī school in that region.[2]

Jāmī discusses three major aspects of the Perfect Man as the ontological prototype of creation: First, the Perfect Man as the locus of manifestation for the name Allah; second, as the goal of creation; third, as God's vicegerent. Each of these concepts needs to be examined separately.

The All-Comprehensive Name

Practically all of Islamic religious thought goes back to the names and attributes of God. God in His Essence cannot be known, but we can know Him in so far as He has revealed His names, and therefore His attributes, in the Koran. The primary knowledge of God revealed through the Book becomes the basis for all other knowledge. Without knowledge of the names and attributes we cannot know the cosmos. The whole of the cosmos in fact is nothing but the manifestation or self-disclosure of God's names. To say that "God created the world" means in this context that the world derives its relative and limited existence from the absolute and infinite being of God, and that the characteristics and properties which we observe in the world are nothing but dim reflections of God's attributes. If certain things possess the property of life, this is because God is the Living and they receive effusion and succor (*madad*) from that name. If certain things see, that is because God is the Seeing, and so forth.

In the context of the Islamic teachings themselves, then, the key to understanding the Perfect Man lies in the doctrine of the names and attributes. According to the school of Ibn al-ʿArabī, the relationship between the names and the Perfect Man is that he is the locus of manifestation for the name Allah. Allah is the All-Comprehensive Name (*ism jāmiʿ*), and is often called the Greatest Name (*al-ism al-aʿẓam*) in which all of the names of God are contained. In Jāmī's words, "The name Allah is a unity in which is comprised all the divine names. Therefore, any heart that knows it knows all the names. This is in contrast to the other names, for the knowledge of not one of them entails the knowledge of the name Allah."[3]

The Koran says that God *taught Adam the names, all of them* (2:31). At first sight, these names seem to be the names of the created things, including the angels, but, as explained above, the created things themselves are manifestations of the divine names. So the Sufis are quite justified in saying that according to the Koran Adam was taught all of God's names, since the names of the created things are the names of God inasmuch as they are manifested in this world. Since Adam or man was taught all the names, this is equivalent to saying that he was taught the knowledge of the name Allah, which is precisely the name that embraces all the others. So Adam as the knower of Allah is the first locus of manifestation for that name in the world and the first corporeal manifestation of the eternal reality of the Perfect Man. This is why, as an individual, Adam was the first prophet.

A second Koranic verse that is taken to refer to man's all-comprehensive nature as the locus of manifestation for the name Allah occurs also in the story of the creation of Adam. After God created Adam and taught him all the names, He commanded the angels to prostrate themselves to him—for Adam also knew their names and thus possessed power over them, while they themselves did not know the names that Adam had been taught (2:31). But Iblīs refused to prostrate himself. Then God asked him, *"What prevented you from prostrating yourself to him whom I have created with My two hands?"* (38:75). Jāmī points out that what distinguishes man is that he was created with *two* hands, whereas everything else was created with only *one* hand. The two hands refer to the division of God's attributes into two categories, the attributes of beauty and those of majesty. Everything other than man is only a locus of manifestation of the attributes of divine beauty, or only those of divine majesty. Nothing else was created embracing all the attributes.[4]

Jāmī's interpretation of the hadith, "God created Adam in His own form," illustrates more fully how he understands man as the locus of manifestation for the name Allah. After remarking that the exoteric authorities simply understand from the hadith that man partakes of all of God's attributes, he states that the Sufis understand "form" to signify the means whereby unseen realities—which are disengaged from and transcend physical realities—can be conceived or understood.[5] In other words, the "form" of a transcendent reality is the means whereby that reality manifests itself in the physical world. Without man the name Allah would have no single locus of manifestation.

Of course, it is also true that since the name Allah embraces all the names, we can say that the manifestation of all the names, which is equivalent to the cosmos as a whole, is a manifestation of the name Allah in man and its particularized (*mufaṣṣal*) and multiple manifestation throughout the whole cosmos.[6]

This "two-pronged" self-disclosure of the name Allah is the basis for Jāmī's exposition of man's relation to the cosmos. Man the microcosm (*al-ʿālam al-ṣaghīr*) is the mirror of the macrocosm (*al-ʿālam al-kabīr*). But in man the name Allah is manifested in such a way that each one of the individual names that are comprehended by it is equivalent to all the others. In other words, the divine unity is manifested directly in man in the midst of the multiplicity of the world. But the world itself, though also a reflection of the name Allah, is so in a particularized mode and manifests the relative multiplicity inherent in that name. Each of the individual names embraced by the name Allah finds its own separate and independent locus of manifestation only in the external world.

This same point can be explained by saying that man is more directly a manifestation of the First Entification of the level of Exclusive Unity (*aḥadiyya*), while the cosmos is more directly a manifestation of the second entification or level of Inclusive Unity (*wāḥidiyya*). As Jāmī explains in detail,[7] at the level of Exclusive Unity the Divine Essence is nonmanifest and all relations (*nisab, iʿtibārāt, iḍāfāt*) and attributes are negated from It. At this level, one can say that each name is equivalent to all other names. God as the Nonmanifest is the same as God as the Manifest, and God as the Life-Giver is identical to God as the Death-Giver. But at the level of Inclusive Unity, each name can be envisaged as a separate reality. There is a certain relative manyness that can be discerned in the Divine, since to envisage God as the Hearing, for example, is to understand Him in a different aspect from God as the Seeing. Hence, the Perfect Man reflects more directly the First Entification, because all of the divine attributes are integrated into his own essence and are equivalent to it.[8] Yet the world contains a definite multiplicity, which confirms concretely and in a particularized mode the separate and individual—albeit relative—reality of each of the attributes.

The key term that is ascribed to man as the manifestation of the name Allah is the Arabic word *jāmiʿ*, meaning "all-comprehensive," or "that which brings all things together into a unified whole." The state thus described is called *jamʿ* or *jamʿiyya*, "all-comprehensiveness." It is a state that can be symbolized by a cross, the vertical axis indicating that the Perfect Man encompasses all the ontological levels or Divine Presences, and the horizontal axis indicating that he embraces each of these worlds or levels in its full extension. Thus, when Jāmī enumerates the vertical levels of existence from the Divine Essence to the corporeal world (that is, the First Entification, the second entification, the world of the spirits, the world of images, and the world of bodies) he states that the sixth level is the Perfect Man, who comprehends all levels. It is clear that the Perfect Man, because he embraces all of the divine names (whether we consider them to be 99, 1,001 or infinite in number[9]), also embraces myriad manifestations of names on each of the horizontal levels. For example, in the physical world all the celestial spheres, the elements, the animals, vegetables, and minerals are included within him.[10]

There is another manner in which the reality of man as the locus of manifestation for the name Allah can be expressed: Pure and undefiled existence whose source is the Necessary Being is characterized by certain attributes, and whatever exists, by the mere fact of its existence, must possess these attributes at least potentially. These attributes can be summarized by the Seven Leaders—the names Living, Knowing, Desiring, Powerful, Speaking, Hearing, and Seeing.[11] Wherever existence is found, these attributes are also found, but in most beings one or more of these attributes is potential and not actual. Only in man can all of the attributes of existence actually be manifested. Other creatures, even if they attain the fullness of their own actuality, cannot manifest all of the names and attributes. Thus, to say that man is the locus of manifestation for the name Allah is equivalent to saying that in him all the attributes of the Divine Being are actualized in external existence. In Jāmī's words:

> The name Living is the Leader of the Seven Leaders, since the other attributes, such as knowledge, desire, power, and so on cannot be

imagined to exist except after life. . . . Everything has a particular kind of life in keeping with its own nature, such that life and its concomitances—that is, knowledge, power, desire, and so on—appear within it in keeping with its own constitution. Hence if its constitution is near equilibrium, as is the case with man, all of these attributes, or most of them, will appear; but if it is far from equilibrium, as is the case with inanimate objects and minerals, life and its concomitants will remain hidden within it.[12]

Since man is a unity which brings together all of the loci of manifestation, all perfections appear within him in actuality and individually. . . . It is this all-comprehensiveness [*jamʿiyya*] that is peculiar to man.[13]

The Hidden Treasure

It might be asked why the name Allah needs a locus of manifestation. This is almost the same as asking why there is a need for any name to have a locus of manifestation. In other words, "Why did God create the world?" When making use of the mythic language of the Koranic revelation, the Sufis often answer this question by referring to the famous *ḥadīth qudsī* where God says, "I was a Hidden Treasure and I loved to be known, so I created the world." Jāmī explains the meaning of this hadith in more explicitly metaphysical language:

> In the inherent perfection of His Essence and in His unitary self-subsistence, God gazed upon His own Self by means of a vision that was in no way superadded to Himself or distinguished from Himself. He saw His names and His attributes as relations inherent in Himself, or as unseen states whose properties had been annihilated by the all-subjugating power of His unity. Their effects were in no way distinguished from one another. But God wanted to manifest these relations and states in order to display the complete perfection of His names and to gaze upon them in their loci of manifestation in such a way that their realities and effects would be distinguished.[14]

For Jāmī, the meaning of the sentence "I was a Hidden Treasure" is that in the Essence Itself, the attributes of God are nowise manifest or distinguished from one another, and therefore none of them exists separately. The door to the Treasure is locked and the precious jewels within (i.e., the attributes) are hidden from sight. The words "I loved to be known" refer to the Divine Infinity and Perfection, which require that no mode of existence be denied to Absolute Reality, not even limited and finite existence. This finite existence itself adds a new dimension of knowledge to the nonmanifest Essence, for the names and attributes that in the Essence are known only inasmuch as they are one with the Essence, are known in manifestation or creation as separate and distinct realities in the midst of multiplicity. Each of the jewels within the Treasure comes to be seen as an independent entity. To deny this separative and pluralized reality to the Essence would be, in effect, to limit It and negate from It one of the dimensions of Its infinite Perfection.

The hadith of the Hidden Treasure therefore means that God knows Himself in Himself in undifferentiated (*mujmal*) and unitary form, whereas He also must have a particularized (*mufaṣṣal*) and pluralized knowledge of Himself, which can only come about through the externalization of His attributes and their "separation" from Him. As a result of this externalization, this transfer from unity to multiplicity, each of the attributes can be contemplated in all of its individual traits and in a separative mode. "Sight," for example, which on the one hand manifests itself in God's vision of Himself, becomes manifested in all of the myriad possible forms it can assume as an independent—or rather, semi-independent—reality. In the physical world it manifests itself in countless individuals as the sight of man and animals, the photosensitivity of plants, the vision of the sages, and so on. Each mode of manifestation exists potentially within the reality of sight within God's knowledge, but it exists in actuality only through separative existence in the manifest cosmos.

What has just been explained answers only part of our question concerning the reason behind God's creating the world. Although the world is the locus of manifestation for all the names, and thus in its totality for the name Allah as well, we still want to know why the name Allah should manifest itself specifically and even uniquely in man.

Jāmī answers this question in a long passage that is worth quoting in its entirety. When the One Essence manifests Itself in the diverse loci of manifestation that make up the world,

> Its manifestation is in a mode that does not allow for the appearance of all-comprehensiveness. These loci are the various levels of existence, which particularize and disperse the One Reality. Hence, the properties of multiplicity gain sway over the properties of unity, and the reality of unity becomes hidden in accordance with the requirements of actualized diversification and objectified particularization. Hence, the One Essence desires to manifest Itself in a single, perfect locus of manifestation that will embrace all of the loci of manifestation (whether they be of the nature of light or of darkness), and which will encompass all of the hidden and open realities of the cosmos and all the manifest and nonmanifest intricacies of creation.
>
> This is because the One Necessary Essence perceives Its own Self through a perception in no way superadded to Itself or distinguished from Itself. . . . Likewise, It perceives Its attributes and Its names as inherent and nonmanifest relations whose realities are in no sense separate from one another. Then, when It manifests Itself upon the basis of the exigencies of the divine desire, in keeping with the

> diverse preparednesses of the loci of manifestation and in accordance with the multiple intermediaries between Itself and the creatures in such a manner that It becomes particularized in the diversified loci of the various levels of existence, It does not perceive Its own reality in a manner that unites all the objectified and externalized perfections with the totality of the divine names and attributes. The reason for this is that Its self-disclosure in any given locus of manifestation is in accordance with that locus only. Do you not see that the self-disclosure of God in the spiritual world is different from His self-disclosure in the corporeal world? For in the first, His self-disclosure is simple, active and luminous; while in the second, it is composite, passive and tenebrous.
>
> Therefore, the One Essence desired to manifest Itself in the universal locus of manifestation, the all-comprehensive engendered being [*al-kawn al-jāmiʿ*] that also encompasses the Divine Reality. This is the Perfect Man, for he is a locus of manifestation for both the Absolute Essence and the names, attributes, and acts, because of the all-comprehensiveness and equilibrium of his universal mode of existence and because of the scope and perfection of his state of being a locus. Moreover, he unites the realities of the Necessary Being and the relations pertaining to the divine names with the realities of the possible beings and the attributes of creatures. So he brings together the level of All-Comprehensive Unity with that of particularization, and embraces all that there is from the beginning to the end of the chain of being.[15]

Thus, only through man does God gaze upon unity in multiplicity. In Himself He sees nothing but unity, and in the world nothing but multiplicity. But in man unity and multiplicity are combined in such a way that all of God's attributes—in other words the name Allah—are manifested within one unitary locus of manifestation in the midst of the plurality of the world. Without man, a certain mode of divine knowledge would not exist and the infinity of God would be limited. This is the same as saying that man must exist.

In Itself the Hidden Treasure knows Its own Essence in a unitary mode such that every attribute is equivalent to every other. In the world, the Hidden Treasure observes each of Its attributes manifested in various combinations as semi-independent realities. Only in man does the Hidden Treasure know Itself as a unity objectified and externalized within the heart of multiplicity.

God's Vicegerent

That the Perfect Man is the locus of manifestation for the name Allah is indicated by the Koran when it states that man is God's vicegerent (*khalīfa*). Jāmī interprets this key term to mean that man is precisely the vicegerent of the name Allah and no other name, and that, since he manifests the all-comprehensive name within the world, he has been given responsibility for the whole of creation. By encompassing all of the names, man contains the principles of all creatures. He is the microcosm (or small world) as opposed to the macrocosm (or great world), since all that is contained in the world is also contained in him. In reality, however, and in terms of his rank, "Man is the great world and the world is the small man, because the vicegerent is superior to his subjects."[16]

Envisaged as the vicegerent of the name Allah, the Perfect Man has the key function of acting as the isthmus between God and the world and thereby maintaining the existence of the world. Jāmī quotes Ibn al-ʿArabī as follows: Man is like

> an isthmus between the world and God, bringing together and embracing both the creatures and Him. Man is the dividing line between the shadow and the sun. This is his reality. So he has absolute perfection in temporality and eternality. But God has absolute perfection in eternality, and He does not enter into temporality. . . . And the world has absolute perfection in temporality; it does not enter eternality. Thus man has brought together and embraced all that exists.[17]

It is precisely man's quality of being an isthmus that has made him worthy of being God's vicegerent. Since he is an isthmus, he comprises the attributes of both lordship and servanthood. Through his attributes of lordship—that is, his divine nature—he takes from God what the creatures demand. And through his attribute of servanthood, he is able to establish contact with the other creatures and to see that they receive what they need from God.[18]

Expressed differently, the Perfect Man is the means whereby the world is maintained. The Perfect Man in his aspect of lordship, or inasmuch as he embraces the divine realities, receives the effusion of God (i.e., of the name Allah). Then the reflection of the lights of God's self-disclosure overflows into the world, which subsists by receiving this reflection.[19] The beings of the world are the loci of manifestation for the names and attributes, or their forms, symbols, or "seats" (*maḥall al-istiwāʾ*). Because each being is the locus within which certain particular names are manifested, it remains under the sway of the Perfect Man, who is the locus of manifestation for the universal name that contains in itself all the others.

It follows that without man, there would be no world. Here Jāmī quotes Qūnawī:

> The true Perfect Man is the isthmus between Necessity and possibility and the mirror that unites the attributes of Eternity with those of temporal events. . . . He is the intermediary between God and creation. Through him and from his level of existence, the effusion of

> God and the succor that is the cause of the subsistence of other than God reach the world—all of it, both its celestial and terrestrial parts. If it were not for the fact that he acts as the isthmus unopposed to either of the two sides, nothing in the world could be the receptacle for the unique divine succor, because of the lack of correspondence and relationship. The succor would not reach the world and the world would cease to exist. The Perfect Man is the pillar of the heavens and the earth. Because of this mystery, when he leaves the center of the earth, which is . . . the station of Allah's vicegerency . . . the order of the earth and the heavens will be destroyed and they will be changed into other than themselves.[20]

Jāmī anticipates an objection that might occur to many people at this point: Before the actualization of the human form the world existed and the planets revolved. So how can you call man the Pole (*quṭb*) of the cosmos and the means whereby it is maintained? Jāmī replies that although man did not exist in the sensory world, he did exist in the spiritual world, and the effect of his existence was manifest in the lower world. To prove this point he refers to the hadith of the Hidden Treasure. If God's Essence were not to be manifested, He would remain a Hidden Treasure. This self-disclosure of God takes place in two modes: the mode of differentiation and multiplicity, that is, in the form of the cosmos as a whole; and the mode of undifferentiation and unity, that is, in man's form. In the elemental form of man, It discloses Itself as It is in Itself, that is, in Its unity and as embracing all attributes at once. In the world as such, the Essence manifests Itself as dispersion and multiplicity.

Thus man perfects the self-disclosure of God. This is referred to in the Koran in the famous verse of the "Trust" (*amāna*): *We offered the Trust to the heavens, the earth, and the mountains, but they refused to carry it . . . ; and man carried it* (33:72). In this verse, "heavens" refer to the celestial parts of creation, while "earth" refers to the physical world. "Mountains" are an allusion to the worlds and levels of existence that lie in between. All of these levels of existence refused to carry the Trust because they are loci of manifestation for only certain names of God. Thus they do not possess the necessary receptivity (*qābiliyya*) to be the loci of manifestation for the divine all-comprehensiveness, that is, for all of the names embraced by the name Allah. But man did carry the Trust because he possesses a perfect and total receptivity to all of the names. Hence, the divine goal in creation—the self-disclosure of God—only became actualized through man's form. Therefore, even before man was created in the physical world, the world could only exist through the effusion of existence carried out through him and directed toward his actualization in the external world.[21]

In sum, the Perfect Man, as the ontological prototype of the human self—or as the Self in its ultimate state of perfection and realization—is the locus within which the greatest name of God, which includes in itself all other names, is manifested directly. Thus, the Perfect Man is the goal of creation, for through him the self-disclosure and self-unfolding of the Infinite Ipseity is actualized. Since he is the goal of creation, all other creatures depend on him, for "without the fruit in mind the Gardener would never have planted the tree."[22] In other words, the individual and particularized names of God, whose loci of manifestation are symbolized by the tree with its myriad branches, are only manifested under the sway of the universal and All-Comprehensive Name, whose locus of manifestation is symbolized by the fruit, which contains in itself the principle of the whole tree.

14

Two Treatises by Khwāja Khurd

During the reigns of Akbar and Jahāngīr (963–1037/1556–1628), numerous Indian Sufis were writing books and treatises that one might classify as belonging to the school of Ibn al-ʿArabī.[1] Indeed, by this time, it was difficult to write anything on Sufi theory without employing the technical terminology of this school. This is not to say that all these authors had necessarily read any of Ibn al-ʿArabī's works or considered themselves his followers, but rather that this school of thought had played a major role in shaping the intellectual language of the day. Shaykh Aḥmad Sirhindī is a case in point. Although he was critical of certain ideas that he attributed to Ibn al-ʿArabī, his own writings are full of the terminology and concepts drawn from Ibn al-ʿArabī's perspective, as he often acknowledges.

Although Sirhindī may be the best known Sufi author of this period, this should not lead us to think that he was also the most important or the most representative. "Importance" depends on one's choice of criteria. In terms of certain political and nationalistic ideas that came to play a role in establishing Muslim identity in the fourteenth/twentieth century, Sirhindī may indeed be considered to have special importance. But, if we are to judge by criteria internal to the Islamic tradition in general and the Sufi tradition in particular, we will find many other authors of the same period deserving serious study, who are perhaps much more worthy of being considered important. Once the works of these authors have been published and analyzed, and once their influence on later Sufis has been traced, we might well find that Sirhindī had little to offer to the tradition and that he was unknown except in a relatively small circle. In any case, the necessary research has not yet been carried out, so at this point I can only offer this as a hypothesis.

One of the major reasons for the fact that most of the Indian Sufi writings have remained unstudied is that modern scholars have focused on social and political history and have had little interest in the goals and intentions of the Sufi authors themselves. As Carl Ernst has illustrated so well, three competing historiographical schools—the British, the Muslim, and the Hindu—with three distinct agendas, have provided us with a diversity of interpretations of the significance of the Indian Subcontinent's past in terms of modern social and political concerns.[2] One of the results of the specific preoccupations of these scholars is that, by and large—and with certain obvious and important exceptions—they have made assumptions about these traditions and ignored the actual works of the authors. Very few have had the interest or the training to situate the Sufi writings in the context of Islamic intellectual history. When statements are made about content, these are typically based not on a study of the works, but rather on a superficial understanding of the Sufi tradition as found in the central Islamic lands.[3]

Khwāja Khurd

Among the many Indian Sufi authors who remain practically unknown is ʿAbd Allāh b. Muḥammad Bāqī Billāh. Bāqī Billāh, a shaykh who was instrumental in establishing the Naqshbandī order in the Indian Subcontinent, died at the age of forty in 1012/1603, when his son ʿAbd Allāh (who came to be known as Khwāja Khurd) (b. 1010/1601), was two years old. Bāqī Billāh was the master of Aḥmad Sirhindī and entrusted his student to the upbringing of Khwāja Khurd. However, as Khwāja Khurd's writings reveal, he continued to uphold the superiority of *waḥdat al-wujūd* over Sirhindī's proposed *waḥdat al-shuhūd*.[4]

Khwāja Khurd's major work seems to be the Arabic *al-Fawāʾiḥ*[5] ("The Fragrances"), whose title is more likely inspired by Jāmī's *Lawāʾiḥ* than Kubrā's *Fawāʾiḥ al-jamāl* ("The Fragrances of Beauty"), given the Naqshbandī lineage of both Jāmī and Khwāja Khurd and the *Fawāʾiḥ*'s similarities in both form and subject matter with the *Lawāʾiḥ*. The author explains that he called the work *Fawāʾiḥ* "because its gnostic sciences spread their fragrance from the gardens of holiness to the nostrils of hearts intimate with God." The reference to intimacy (*uns*) recalls Jāmī's *Nafaḥāt al-uns* ("The Breaths of Intimacy").

About half of the *Fawāʾiḥ*, which fills forty-seven folios of fifteen lines, deals in short sections with the basic metaphysical teachings of Ibn al-ʿArabī's school. Khwāja Khurd also devotes four folios to his father's disciples from whom he took spiritual benefit and to his *silsila*, and finally turns to explaining the eight principles of Naqshbandī practice. Many of the details of the last section are derived from his father's teachings, though he mentions others as well, including Ibn al-ʿArabī.

The main body of the *Fawāʾiḥ* follows the tone established in the first few sections:

> Fragrance: The heart is a reality that collects together all realities, which are like the shadows and effects of its all-collecting reality. Your I-ness is the spirit of the cosmos. If you are delivered from delimita-

tion and the outward boundaries of Adam's manifestation, then you will reach nondelimitation.

Fragrance: Collectedness [*jamʿ*] is permanent awareness of the Essence, or witnessing the Essence in the many things. The former pertains to the beginning [of the spiritual path], and the latter to the end. As for witnessing only manyness, even if Oneness or witnessing manyness and Oneness together without witnessing the relationship between them are intelligible within it, both are dispersion [*tafriqa*].

Fragrance: A group has supposed that *tawḥīd* is in *shuhūd*, not *wujūd*, but they have not reached the reality of the station. Another group has verified that *wujūd* is the same as *shuhūd* and that the *shuhūd* that opposes *wujūd* is of no account. So free yourself from the vision of duality at the outset.

This third Fragrance rejects Aḥmad Sirhindī's position rather explicitly. In case there is any doubt that this is what is at issue, the second section of the work provides more evidence. There, Khwāja Khurd first praises his father's spiritual rank, and then mentions a long list of his disciples. He begins by mentioning the person whom he considered his own shaykh, Ḥusām al-Dīn Aḥmad. S. A. A. Rizvi tells us that this well-known shaykh showed little interest in Sirhindī's *waḥdat al-shuhūd*, but that he nevertheless got along well with Sirhindī since, in contrast to him, he had no ambition.[6] The clear distinction that Khwāja Khurd draws between Shaykh Ḥusām al-Dīn and Shaykh Aḥmad suggests that he was also not impressed by Sirhindī's claims:

> Among this elevated group is the great and established shaykh, the Pole, our master and shaykh, Shaykh Ḥusām al-Dīn Aḥmad. He is the true successor [*khalīfa*] of the greatest shaykh and imam [i.e., Bāqī Billāh]. He is the most perfect of his companions and, after him, undertook to train his children and his companions. He aided the right religion and strengthened the elect path. In secret and in hiding, he resided in the highest level and the most perfect degree. He ascended to the Divinity [*al-lāhūt*] in the year 1043 [1633] and was buried behind and facing our shaykh. . . . From the beginning of my life to the end of his life I was looked upon by his solicitude, and I became the object of divine solicitude through his aspiration [*himma*]. He is my spiritual guide, my kiblah, and my shaykh in reality.
>
> Among them was the knowing, gnostic, pious shaykh, the possessor of stations and states, the propagator of the Shariah and the Tariqah, our shaykh and master Aḥmad ibn ʿAbd al-Aḥad al-Fārūqī. I reached a number of levels through his presence. He imparted the Tariqah and the invocation [*dhikr*] to me and gave me permission to teach them. He died in the year 1034 [1624] and was buried in Sirhind.

Khwāja Khurd wrote a number of short Persian works. Two of them, *Partaw-i ʿishq* ("The Radiance of Love") and *Nūr-i waḥdat* ("The Light of Oneness"), were published together in Delhi more than a hundred years ago.[7] The former work deals with the mysteries of the divine and human lover and beloved, while the latter guides the seeker in establishing oneness. The Persian of both is simple and poetical, although the author cites practically no poetry. His often ecstatic style and his love for paradoxes are sometimes reminiscent of works slightly peripheral to Ibn al-ʿArabī's school, such as Balyānī's *Risāla*. But, in contrast to Balyānī, Khwāja Khurd combines a vigorous assertion of the oneness of all things with an equally vigorous assertion of the necessity of observing all the details of the Shariah, the Tariqah, and ethical behavior in general.

Khwāja Khurd begins each short section of both treatises with the words "O Sayyid." In *Partaw-i ʿishq*, he seems to be addressing God as Beloved. But in *Nūr-i waḥdat*, he has in mind the reader, who should dedicate his life to achieving oneness and actualizing the true state of being a "master" of the human situation. Thus he writes in *Nūr-i waḥdat*: "O Sayyid! If you want mastery [*siyāda*], become one and be one."

The printed edition of *Partaw-i ʿishq* has too many mistakes to allow for anything but a tentative translation. In order to suggest the flavor of the text, I quote its first few paragraphs:

> Praise belongs to God! Praise belongs to God, for my soul's Beloved and my Companion in the two worlds is related to me through unity. He sees none but Himself in me and does not consider me anything other than Himself. Now that this vision and knowledge have reached perfection, He wants to speak within the curtain of me. He reports on the states of loverness and belovedness. He prepares a treatise explaining the mysteries that are both hidden and open. The hidden mysteries are the mysteries of belovedness, while the open mysteries are the mysteries of loverness. Before finishing, He calls this treatise, "The Radiance of Love."
>
> The first words that the lover says to his Beloved and the slave says to his Companion are these: "O true and metaphorical lover! O companion of religion and this world! The business I have with you cannot be put in order through writing, nor can it be finished through speaking. Now you must write and speak."
>
> O Sayyid! I am not I, nor are You You. For I am You and You are I. When in eternity without beginning You wanted to disclose Yourself through loverness and companionship, You became manifest within the curtain of me through loverness and slavehood so that your belovedness and companionship might become manifest. In this manner, I am your beloved, since your belovedness appears through me. And You are my lover, since my loverness comes to be through Your love. How could You be the beloved? I am bewildered. Are You beloved or am I? Am I lover or are You? Beware, beware! What kind

of words are these? I am nothing. Whatever exists is You. Both Lover and Beloved are You. . . .

O Sayyid! I remember the time when the relationship of unity [*ittiḥād*] dominated over the relationship of love. The relationship of love had no manifestation whatsoever; it was contained and concealed within the relationship of my unity. Suddenly a dividing line appeared within the circle of unity. I became I, and You You. When this state appeared, my glance fell upon You, and Yours upon me. Until You desired, this glance remained behind the curtain. But when the time arrived for the return of the shadow to its root and the arrival of the lover at the Beloved, the relationship of love came to dominate and the relationship of unity was concealed. A situation arose that cannot be expressed in words. So much agony and pain appeared that it spread from the lover to the Beloved and made the Beloved appear in the form of loverness. Little by little the business reached a place where the previous unity became manifest, and the dividing line began to move off to the side. If there is pain, it is this: This state cannot be permanent, since it has been established that the self-disclosure of the Essence passes like a flash of lightning and does not remain. O, the infinite pain, the endless agony!

O Sayyid! Let no one suppose that these words derive from the world of reality. On the contrary, they come from the world of metaphor, which is free of reality. And let no one suppose that these words derive from the world of metaphor. On the contrary, they come from reality and have been disclosed within the curtain of metaphor.

O Sayyid! Reality is identical with metaphor, and metaphor is identical with Reality.

O Sayyid! One of your names is Reality, and your other name is Metaphor. By whatever name You call me, You also call Yourself.

Since I have been able to establish a good text for *Nūr-i waḥdat* with the help of several manuscript copies,[8] I provide a complete translation of it below. Preceding this text is a translation of another one of Khwāja Khurd's Persian treatises, namely *Risāla-yi ʿārif* ("The Treatise on the Gnostic").[9] In a sense, this short work presents an epitome of Khwāja Khurd's views, and thus serves as an effective lead-in to his more detailed *Nūr-i waḥdat*.

The Treatise on the Gnostic

Brother, the gnostic does all good works, without any desire on his part, and he avoids all bad works, without denying any bad work. He mixes with everyone, without becoming attached, and he is far from everyone, without any distaste. He considers God the same as all things and sees Him in all, without calling any of them God, and he finds God beyond all things, without the entrance of duality. The gnostic's persuasion is different from all persuasions, without his considering any persuasion as being other than his own persuasion. He maintains all persuasions without becoming sullied by any. He desires God without suffering pain, and he sometimes becomes heedless of God without finding heedlessness in anything other than presence. In heedlessness itself he is present, and in presence itself he is heedless.

The gnostic's contemplation in women is greater than his contemplation in other loci of manifestation. The property of following the most perfect Prophet, Muhammad—God bless him and his family and give them peace—has a complete joy, without pain, in the state and persuasion of the gnostic, in all situations and all works. In all pains he has complete enjoyment without enjoyment. The gnostic is both the Real and the creature. He finds God in servanthood itself, and he finds that God is servanthood itself. The gnostic has nothing to do with servanthood or with Godhood, since his reality lies beyond Godhood and servanthood.

If you should ask the gnostic, "Do you know anything and do you find anything?," he will answer, "I find nothing and I know nothing." If you say, "Is anything unknown to you and is anything sought by you?" He will answer, "Nothing is unknown to me and nothing is sought by me. Everything is known to me and in me." The gnostic knows everything and knows nothing.

The whole business of the gnostic is opposite within opposite and bewilderment within bewilderment, and concerning this opposite within opposite and bewilderment within bewilderment he has no thoughts or ideas. He is self in self, self from self, and self to self, there being no free choice in the midst. Whatever happens in the cosmos is neither according to the gnostics's desire nor against his desire, neither sought by the gnostic nor rejected by him.

"Gnostic" is no more than a name. Rather, he is identical with the object of gnosis. "Object of gnosis" is no more than a name. Rather, it is the gnostic himself, while "gnostic" and "object of gnosis" are no more than two illusory names. Where is the gnostic? Where is the object of gnosis? This is the reality of the state—it has no reality. This is the final end of the object of gnosis—it is identical with bewilderment and ignorance. Where is the gnosis? Where is the bewilderment? Both are lost in the reality of the essence of the gnostic. That which is known from the gnostic is g, n, o, s, t, i, c. The rest is all he, for he is both known and unknown, neither known nor unknown. Since the gnostic has left the reckoning of space and time, this world and the next world are one to him; heaven and hell are one in his eyes.

Listen, for brief words will now be spoken. There is no room for details. The brief of it is this: Remember God without making God your idol. Forget yourself without becoming heedless of yourself. Put the Shariah into practice without considering any individual desire or goal. Avoid the works forbidden by the Shariah without having any doubt about them, and without finding dislike for them in yourself. Acquire praiseworthy and beautiful attributes without being attached to them. Be content with whatever happens without being attached to anything. Take advantage of the joys allowed by the Shariah without being heedless of the manifestation of the Reality, or claiming gnosis and contemplation. Be neither present nor heedless. Be neither servant nor God. Be neither existent nor nonexistent. Hold fast to following the most perfect Prophet, Muhammad, the Messenger of God—God bless him and his family and give them peace—without considering Muhammad other than the Real or restricting the Real to Muhammad. Know that Muhammad is the Real and that the Real is Muhammad. The Real, the Real, the Real! Muhammad, Muhammad, Muhammad! This is perfection, perfection, perfection! And God knows the reality of the state, and He is identical with the reality of the state. Peace, and completion.

The Light of Oneness

In the Name of God,
the All-Merciful, the All-Compassionate

[On the blessed Friday night of the *ʿurs* of Bahāʾ al-Dīn Naqshband (i.e., his death anniversary), the third of Rabīʿ al-Awwal in the year 1053 (May 12, 1643), the manifestation of these mysteries began:][10]

Praise belongs to God! Praise belongs to God, for the Reality is brighter than the sun, and in every state the beauty of Oneness is seen in the mirror of manyness.

O Sayyid! This is a message to you from your own reality. I know that if you study it with the eye of aspiration, you will reach the reality from the form, and then the illusion of distance will disappear.

O Sayyid! One person gives news of distance, and that has a reason; another brings signs of nearness, and that also has a cause. Your reality, which speaks to you with the tongue of this message, informs of Oneness, where there is neither distance nor nearness. When Oneness dawns, distance and nearness are the same as Oneness.

O Sayyid! Each sect quarrels and debates with the other sects, except for the People of Oneness, for they are one with everyone, even though no one is one with them.

O Sayyid! From the conflicting and diverse paths and the contradictory and disparate schools the People of Oneness have extracted a sweet, subtle, spiritual school and a broad, all-inclusive, sapiential path. Other than this specific path and special school, they also have a school that can be discussed. Hence it is said that the theologians say this, the philosophers say that, and the Sufis say such and such.

O Sayyid! Oneness is the inner dimension of manyness, while manyness is the outer dimension of Oneness. The reality of both is one.

O Sayyid! The Existent [*mawjūd*] is one and appears in the form of illusory manyness.

O Sayyid! You have been brought from Oneness to manyness and shown the way from Unity to duality for the sake of a wisdom that He knows—glory be to Him! And His special servants also know it through His giving them knowledge. You have been made such that you have no news of the precedent Oneness—no trace of that state is found in you. Or rather, the Real has brought the whole cosmos from Oneness into manyness. After that, He acquainted a few of His servants with Himself without intermediary. He took them from manyness to Oneness, taught them the path of reaching Oneness from manyness, and sent them to manyness such that they saw Oneness in manyness. He told them to teach others this path. They obeyed His command and made the path known. Everyone who acted according to that road and followed that group reached Oneness from manyness and Unity from duality. Those great men are the prophets, and that road of arrival is the Shariah and the Tariqah.

O Sayyid! The Shariah consists of a few acts to perform and a few to be avoided, as explained in the books on jurisprudence. The Tariqah consists of the refinement of character traits, that is, transforming blameworthy attributes into praiseworthy attributes. It is also called "traveling in the homeland" [*safar dar waṭan*] and "wayfaring" [*sulūk*].[11] It has been mentioned in detail in the books of the shaykhs, especially those of Imam Muḥammad Ghazālī. Some of the rules of conduct [*ādāb*] and occupations [*ashghāl*] that the shaykhs have devised are included in the Tariqah.

O Sayyid! The rulings of the Shariah, which are based on duality, bring about the arrival at Oneness through their specific characteristics. Their mystery is known only to God and His elect. The fact that practices related to manyness bring about the arrival at Oneness provides an allusion to the fact that manyness is identical with Oneness. Understand!

O Sayyid! The ritual prayer, fasting, alms-giving, *ḥajj,* and their like bring about the arrival at Oneness through their specific characteristics. They cause the arrival at Oneness on condition that they be performed sincerely for God, as the authorities have explained. In this connection the meaning of "for God" does not enter into everyone's understanding, and something different will occur to each person's mind. However, it is necessary for the seeker of Oneness to think as follows: "I make the intention to pray or fast," for example, "for the sake of my own reality and its *wujūd,* that is, finding [*yāft*] my own reality, since I have lost it; through this act of worship, my desire is that Oneness—which is identical with God—should become manifest."

O Sayyid! The Worshiper is He and the Worshiped is He. He is the Worshiper at the level of delimitation and the Worshiped at the level of Nondelimitation. The levels as well as the distinctions within the levels are intelligible affairs. Nothing is found [*mawjūd*] but one Reality, which is Pure Being [*hastī-yi ṣirf*]. Understand!

O Sayyid! When you look carefully, you will see that blameworthy character traits, which must be eliminated through the Tariqah, are all based upon and impart awareness of alienation [*bīgānagī*] and duality, while praiseworthy character traits, which must be acquired, all provide news and knowledge of acquaintance and Unity. Hence the seeker of Oneness cannot escape from the Shariah and the Tariqah, even if he does not know at the outset the secret of how they bring about arrival. But provided he has the affinity and thinks carefully, he will usually come to understand in the manner that I have indicated.[12]

O Sayyid! All these occupations, invocations, meditations, acts of turning the attention, and paths of wayfaring that have been devised by the shaykhs are meant to eliminate illusory duality. Hence you should know that what separates Oneness (the Real) from manyness (creation) is nothing but illusion and imagination. In reality, it is Oneness that appears in the form of manyness and the One that enters vision as the many. In the same way, a cross-eyed person sees one as two, a spinning point is seen in the form of a circle, and drops of falling rain enter vision in the shape of lines.[13]

O Sayyid! A gnostic of high degree used to say, "Being a dervish is to correct the imagination." In other words, nothing other than the Real should remain in the heart. In truth, he spoke well.

O Sayyid! Since the veil is nothing but imagination, the veil must be lifted through imagination. Night and day you must dwell in imagining Oneness.

O Sayyid! If you want mastery, become one and be one. "To become one" is that you come out of the illusion of duality, and "to be one" is that you always remain upon Oneness and in Oneness. Dispersion of thoughts, heartache, and grief all derive from duality. When duality leaves the gaze, ease and stability become possible. Then you will never be afflicted with heartache and will acquire ease in the two worlds, since ease lies in nonexistence.

O Sayyid! When you reach the reality of *tawḥīd* and when Oneness becomes your attribute, you will know that your relationship to the Real after wayfaring has not increased in any way. It is the same relationship that you had before wayfaring. Or rather, your relationship before existence and after coming into existence are also the same. Indeed, you have found a knowledge and acquired a certainty that will never be erased by water or fire. From eternity without beginning to eternity without end the Real exists and none other. Never did any other come into existence. No credit can be given to an unreal illusion.

Zayd became ill by thinking that he was ʿAmr and hearing about the attributes of Zayd from the people. He set out searching for Zayd. When his illness was eliminated through good cures, ʿAmr was nowhere to be found; there was only Zayd.

Thirty birds [*sī murgh*] set out looking for the Sīmurgh. When they reached the way station, they saw that they were the Sīmurgh.[14]

The Real knew Himself through His own attributes. These are the realities of the things. Then He showed Himself to Himself through those attributes. This is the cosmos. Where is the other? How should the other have come into existence?

O Sayyid! When you have recognized the reality of the affair as being like this, you will have come to know that nearness, distance, and equidistance all derive from illusion. When was there distance that nearness should come into being? When was there separation that connection should be achieved? If you meditate upon the world for a thousand years, you will never find anything other than Nondelimited Reality, which is identical with Oneness. Or rather, no essence, no attribute, no genus, and no direction, whether external, mental, or illusory, will be found that is other than He. All is He and He is all.

O Sayyid! Whatever enters perception is He, and whatever does not enter perception is also He. That which is called "existence" is His manifestation, and that which is called "nonexistence" is His nonmanifestation. The First is He, the Last is He, the Nonmanifest is He, the Manifest is He, the nondelimited is He, the delimited is He, the universal is He, the particular is He, the incomparable is He, the similar is He.

O Sayyid! Though He is all, He is pure of all. This nondelimitation of His has another relationship, different from the nondelimitation in respect to which He is identical with all. No unveiling, rational perception, or understanding attains to this nondelimitation. This is the meaning of *God warns you of Himself* [3:28].

O Sayyid! Witnessing Him takes place in the levels of manifestation. Sometimes it takes place outside the levels of manifestation, and this witnessing is like a flash of lightning. It cannot last. Both reaching it and its not lasting are requirements of human all-comprehensiveness, which is the most complete locus of manifestation.

O Sayyid! The gnostic has no higher station than this. In this station there is universal annihilation and sheer nonexistence. This is one of the universal kinds of resurrection.

O Sayyid! These gnostic sciences in this station have been written in approximation. What the wayfarer must have is the thought of Oneness that we mentioned. He must strive in it night and day in order that the illusory manyness, which enters the gaze as otherness, be eliminated from his gaze and become the mirror of Oneness. Then the wayfarer will see none but One, know none but One, and call upon none but One.

O Sayyid! The path of invocation is as follows: "No god," that is, all things that are witnessed are not, in the sense that they are lost in the Oneness of the Essence and absorbed within Him. "But God," that is, the Oneness of the Essence is manifest in the form of these things and witnessed by the gaze. Hence the things are nonmanifest in Him and He is manifest in the things. So He is both the manifest dimension of the things and their nonmanifest dimension. In the things, there is nothing but the manifest and the nonmanifest. Hence, the things are not the things; rather, they are the Real. The names of things given to the things depend upon the viewpoint, and that also is identical with the Real.

O Sayyid! The path of meditation [*murāqaba*] can be understood from the preceding discussion in diverse ways. Meditation is the observation of the meaning of Oneness in any way that this can be done. If contemplating and imagining words becomes the means for the intellection of meanings, this is called "invocation," whatever the words may be, whether "No god but God" or the word "Allah" alone. If the intellection of meanings takes place without imagining words, this is "meditation" or "attentiveness" [*tawajjuh*]. The modes of this latter are many, as can be learned from the books of the great masters. The goal is for the meaning of Oneness to become established in the heart.

The invocation of the word Allah is as follows: The person turns his attention toward the heart reality [*ḥaqīqat-i qalbiyya*] through the visualization [*taṣawwur*] of the lump of flesh inasmuch as this heart reality is the locus of manifestation for the Real; he imagines the word Allah and applies it to the heart reality.

O Sayyid! If you turn your attention toward yourself and are able to put this attention in right order, then this business will easily be taken care of.

O Sayyid! Your body is the form and locus of manifestation for your spirit and is not other than it. Your spirit is the locus of manifestation and form of the Real and is not other than He. Both of these forms—the corporeal and the spiritual—are illusory. When you say the word Allah in your imagination, turn your attention toward the reality that is manifest in the form of these two illusions and know that "I am exactly that." Then there is hope that you will be able to witness Oneness in manyness.

You have to know that whatever enters your gaze has a form, a spirit, and a reality. Its form is its "kingdom" [*mulk*] and "human domain" [*nāsūt*], its spirit is its "sovereignty" [*malakūt*], and its reality is its "invincibility" [*jabarūt*] and "Divinity" [*lāhūt*], which consists of the Essence and attributes of the Real, that is, the "specific face" [*wajh-i khāṣṣ*] of that thing, which is identical with nondelimited Reality.

O Sayyid! The "invincibility" is the attributes, and the "divine domain" is the Essence. The attributes are not other than the Essence. Of course, in unveiling and witnessing, the viewpoint of difference appears. This takes place in the station of actualizing the self-disclosures of both the attributes and the Essence. But until now we have viewed the Essence and the attributes as a single level because of the identity.

O Sayyid! The cosmos is the Real's knowledge. It has become manifest through the self-disclosure of the Essence, which is alluded to as *alif*. And knowledge is identical with the Essence.

O Sayyid! Nondelimited Reality has infinite manifestations, but its universal categories [*kulliyyāt*] are five. The first manifestation is that of undifferentiated knowledge. The second manifestation is that of differentiated knowledge. The third manifestation is that of spiritual forms. The fourth manifestation is that of imaginal forms. The fifth manifestation is that of corporeal forms. If you take the manifestation of the human being separately, the universal manifestations are six. These manifestations are called the five or six "Descents" or "Presences."

O Sayyid! The human being comprehends all manifestations, and this all-comprehensiveness can be explained in many ways.

O Sayyid! You should know that the human reality has a manifestation within all levels in a form appropriate to the levels. All realities are the forms of the human reality, and this reality is prior in level to all realities, even if its manifestation takes place after all levels.

[O Sayyid! In the Sura of the Opening, the beginning of the majestic Koran, is found *Praise belongs to God* [1:2]. Its meaning is that being the Praiser and being the Praised belong exclusively to Him. In other words, He is the Praiser and He is the Praised. In every state, in every attribute, in every place, and in every form, there is no Praiser or Praised other than He.][15]

O Sayyid! At the beginning of the Sura of the Cow is found *Alif, Lām, Mīm* [2:1]. *Alif* alludes to *aḥadiyya* [unity], the first letter of which is *alif*. *Lām* alludes to *ʿilm* [knowledge], the middle letter of which is *lām*. *Mīm* alludes to *ʿālam* [cosmos], the last letter of which is *mīm*. In other words, unity took the form of knowledge, and knowledge the form of the cosmos.

O Sayyid! What is necessary for you is the intellection of the meaning of Oneness, continual meditation upon it, and reaching the differentiated details of these gnostic sciences. At the beginning, nothing will be of any use. When, through the divine solicitude, the meaning of Oneness sits in the heart and the image of duality is lifted, a limpid purity will come to you such that all forms of knowledge and realities will be unveiled to you, and nothing will remain hidden. As long as manyness has not left your gaze and the illusion of duality remains, correct forms of knowledge will appear only with difficulty.

O Sayyid! You have to put yourself through a few days of discipline [*riyāḍa*]. You must spend your breaths in this thought: that the image of the unreal should depart from the midst and the image of the Real sit in its place.

O Sayyid! Until this image has been established within you and has overtaken your outward and inward dimensions, you must not turn your attention toward anything. Once this image has been established and dispersion and duality are eliminated, nothing will be able to trouble you, since unreal illusion does not trouble the Real Existent.

O Sayyid! The relationship of the Real to the cosmos is like the relationship of water to snow, or rather, it must be considered even closer than that. Or, it is like the relationship of gold to the ornaments that are made from it, or like the relationship of clay to the vessels that are made from it. All of these are one.

O Sayyid! The relationship between the cosmos and the Real appears:

In the word "from," since the cosmos is configured and appears *from* Him.

In the word "to," since the cosmos returns *to* Him. This issuing forth and returning take place in eternity without beginning, eternity without end, and in all temporal moments, since at each moment the cosmos goes back to the Reality and comes out from the Reality, like the waves of the ocean.

In the word "in," since the cosmos is *in* the Real and the Real is *in* the cosmos. In one respect one of them is the locus of manifestation, and in another respect the other.

In the word "with," since without doubt the *withness* of the Essence, the attributes, and the acts is actualized.

In the word "is identical," since the cosmos *is identical* with the Real and the Real *is identical* with the cosmos.

In the word "is not," since in one respect the cosmos is the cosmos and the Real is the Real; the cosmos *is not* the Real, and the Real *is not* the cosmos.

O Sayyid! In one respect, He is incomparable with all interrelationships, and between the cosmos and the Real there is no interrelationship. This viewpoint is called "nonentification" [*lā taʿayyun*].

O Sayyid! First the traveler must turn his attention toward the name Manifest. He must know with certainty that it is He who appears in all forms and meanings and that there is no form and no meaning that is other than He. I have written this repeatedly, for emphasis, and I will write it again. The point is this: You must keep the thought of Oneness with yourself, and you must lose yourself in that thought. Once you have become drowned in that thought, you will also take a share from the name Nonmanifest.

O Sayyid! If you busy yourself for years with worship, obedience, and invocations and remain heedless of Oneness, you will be deprived of union [*waṣl*], even if wondrous states and qualities show themselves and lights and visionary events are disclosed.

O Sayyid! A state that you imagine to be union and whose fruit is not the science of Oneness is not union in reality. That which has manifested itself is one of the levels of manifestation, not the true goal. For the goal has no delimitations; it is manifest in all and identical with all. When something becomes manifest that is different in any respect from another thing, it is not the station and goal.

O Sayyid! Since the reality of the situation is like this, you must from the first meditate upon the Nondelimited, so that no distance will remain.

O Sayyid! Dispersion and duality will stay so long as you do not see all as One and know all as One. When you see all as One and know all as One, you will be delivered from dispersion and duality, and naked union will be achieved.

O Sayyid! When you see all as One, all will no longer remain. On the contrary, One will remain, nothing else.

O Sayyid! Between you and the goal there is no road. The road that appears is simply that you consider Him as separate from yourself and other than yourself. When you come to know that you are not, then there is He, nothing else. No road remains. The collectedness of the heart, freedom, knowledge of self, knowledge of the Real, annihilation, union, and the perfection of nearness are here achieved, and the work is done.

O Sayyid! When you reach the station where you do not see yourself and you see Him, you can rest. In respect to you, this world and the next world will be one. Annihilation and subsistence, good and evil, existence and nonexistence, unbelief and Islam, death and life, obedience and disobedience, will all remain behind. The carpet of time and space will be rolled up.

O Sayyid! When you no longer remain, nothing remains, since everything is tied to you and your thoughts.

O Sayyid! Know that everything is in you, and everything outside of you has no existence. When you empty yourself of all things, nothing remains.

O Sayyid! You have no existence save in the Real, while all things exist in you. When you take yourself to the Real and you throw yourself into that shoreless ocean, this means that you have gained awareness of this attribute. All things become lost with you in that ocean.

O Sayyid! If you look carefully, you will know that the I-ness that appears from you does not derive from you and that you are not this body and spirit. In the whole universe, there is only One who says "I." His I-ness is disclosed everywhere.

O Sayyid! The sign of reaching Nondelimited Reality is that the I-ness that appears from you can be applied to all things without effort, and that you can say "I" for all things. Here it is known that the veil is nothing but the entification of I-ness.

O Sayyid! There is One Essence and the whole cosmos is His attribute and stands through Him. That Essence is manifest and found through this attribute.

O Sayyid! It is that Essence Itself which became the essences, and it is that Essence Itself which first became Its own knowledge and then assumed the form of the science of the world. It is that Essence Itself which is Its own power and all powers. It is that Essence Itself which is Its own desire and all desires. It is that Essence Itself which is Its own hearing and all hearings, Its own seeing and all seeings, Its own life and all lives, Its own act and all acts, Its own speech and all speech, and so on. It is that Essence Itself which is Its own Being and all beings.

O Sayyid! Whatever has come into the world of manifestation was hidden in the Essence. Then the Essence disclosed Itself in its form, first in Its knowledge, then in Its entified existence. The Essence took on its color, and it took on the color of the Essence. That which was hidden in the Essence was certainly identical with the Essence, since other than a thing cannot be in a thing. So that Essence Itself dealt with Itself. It exercised loverness, brought servanthood and Godhood into the midst, and set up the workshops of eternity without beginning and eternity without end.

O Sayyid! Imagine that you are still there where you were in eternity without beginning, so that you may become free and never again see the face of dispersion, grief, and affliction.

O Sayyid! Your spirit is He, for you live through Him. Your heart is He, for you know through Him. Your sight is He, for you see through Him. Your hearing is He, for you hear through Him. Your hand is He, for you grasp through Him. Your foot is He, for you walk through Him.[16]

O Sayyid! Every one of your outward and inward parts and organs is He, since the work of that part and organ is performed by Him. The totality of your organs and parts is He, since you are you through Him.

O Sayyid! He-ness, You-ness, and I-ness are all His attributes. There is no one else.

O Sayyid! *Tawḥīd* is the attribute of the One, not of the I or the you. As long as I and you remain, there is association, not *tawḥīd*.

O Sayyid! When you go, that is "annihilation" [*fanā'*]. When He comes, that is "subsistence" [*baqā'*].

O Sayyid! "Wayfaring" is your effort and the elimination of duality. "Attraction" is your going to Oneness.

O Sayyid! Through wayfaring and attraction, annihilation and subsistence, the name of "friendship with God" [*walāya*] is realized.

O Sayyid! Display need for all things, for they are identical with the object of your search. Show friendship to your enemy, since he is also your goal.

O Sayyid! Look upon yourself with the gaze of love, for you are identical with the Beloved.

O Sayyid! All these are necessary in wayfaring.

O Sayyid! Throw good and bad into the ocean of Oneness so that you may become acquainted with Reality.

O Sayyid! If I say Oneness much, it is little, and if I say it little, it is much. The beginning of this knowledge is contained in the end, and the end is included in the beginning. It has neither beginning nor end. How long should I speak? How long should I write? I do not speak, nor do I write. Reality Itself is conversing with Itself.

O Sayyid! When you go to sleep, make this intention: "I am going to the world of nonmanifestation and returning to my own reality." When you wake up, know this: "I have returned to the world of manifestation and have descended from nonmanifestation to manifestation." You must arise before dawn and ask forgiveness. Say, "O my Reality, pull me to Yourself, conceal me from myself, and bring me out of duality." Perform the prayer [*namāz*] of *tahajjud* [i.e., the supererogatory night prayer] and, if you have memorized the Sura Yāsīn, recite it in your prayer. For this is the choice of the Khwājagān[17] of this world and the next. Then busy yourself with thinking about Oneness, until it is time for the morning prayer. When you finish the prayer, you must sit, whether you want to or not, facing the *qibla* meditating upon Oneness, except in unavoidable circumstances. When the sun rises, perform four *rak'as* to greet it, reciting Sura Yāsīn once. If you can recite it in all four *rak'as*, that is better. In the same way, recite Sura Yāsīn once after each prayer, since it has many benefits. When you recite the prayer and the Koran, you must not lose the thought of Oneness. You should know that He Himself worships Himself and He Himself recites His own speech.

O Sayyid! It is necessary for the wayfarer to observe all the Tariqah's rules of conduct. There is no room for the details of these rules in this treatise, since brevity is desired. That which can be written for the seeker is as follows: he must sleep less. When sleep becomes necessary and overcomes him, he must sleep in the thought that I wrote. Food and drink must be little—once in a night and day. But if he fasts, that is better. He must avoid eating unlawful food [*luqma-parīshānī*],[18] since this is one of the causes of duality, alienation, and false imaginings. Everything forbidden by the Shariah and considered bad by the Tariqah is the same. Learn this principle well, since it is absolutely necessary.

O Sayyid! You must speak less and go alone to meditate upon and contemplate Oneness in retreats and deserts.

O Sayyid! Speaking brings the heart into motion, gives rise to dispersion, and makes you heedless of achieving Oneness and Unity. Do not speak except when necessary, and when you say something, speak briefly. Do not separate Oneness from your thoughts for an instant. When you sit in gatherings, be even more strict. Beware of letting heedlessness overcome you. Try to make that manyness the mirror and strengthener of Oneness.

O Sayyid! At the beginning you must try to the extent possible to conceal these thoughts of yours. You must not show these words to everyone, only your special friends.

O Sayyid! You must make maids and servants, acquaintances and strangers, enemies and friends acquainted with Oneness. You must look upon everyone with the gaze of sincerity and the eye that sees Reality.

O Sayyid! Eliminate dispute and quarrels completely and place denial totally off to the side so that Oneness may manifest itself. You must try hard not to allow anger and wrath to appear—how could there be any room for you to strike or beat? You must consider everyone excused, whether inside the house or outside the house. With children, relatives, and strangers you must be like the water of life. If someone should do bad to you, beware! Do not let your heart turn bad toward him or become upset. Keep him happy and content with you. Reward evil with good, for this is a universal principle in the Tariqah.

O Sayyid! Being alone and sitting alone greatly benefit collectedness.

O Sayyid! The seeker has one of two states: either he has outward attachments or he does not. If he does not, his business will be easy. He must cut himself off from everyone, sit in retreat or in the desert, and turn his attention toward his own reality until the Reality discloses Itself and the illusion of duality disappears. Then whatever he does is fine.

If he has outward attachments and Shariah-related obligations, he must take care of them to the extent necessary. However, he must be extremely careful to do everything in accordance with the Shariah and the Tariqah and to avoid becoming heedless of contemplating Oneness, which is the Reality. He must strive hard in this work at night and busy himself with meditating upon Oneness. In daytime also he must set aside several hours for this business. He must increase it day by day until this meaning overcomes him and he is freed from all things.

O Sayyid! When the meaning of Oneness dominates and the divine gentleness manifests itself, all your obligations will be performed by you and you will have nothing to do with anyone or anything. God will be your representative and will take your place, while you will not be found in the midst.

O Sayyid! The companionship of this world and of the people of this world is harmful in the path of wayfaring. But if someone is entangled and is not able to cut himself off, then he must exercise extreme caution so that nothing will take place involving war with the Shariah, the Tariqah, and the Haqiqah. If he should fall short, he must return and make up for it.

O Sayyid! Never move around in the clothing of artificial formality [*takalluf*], and always keep something of the clothing of poverty.

O Sayyid! Always have presence of heart. Think not of the past or the future, and never let go of the observation of Oneness.

O Sayyid! Know that no death is worse than the death of not heeding Oneness, and no chastisement more difficult than the chastisement of distance from your own reality. Fear neither this death nor this chastisement, but turn your attention toward Oneness. Know for certain that all is One and that other than One does not exist. To the extent that this thought dominates, it brings felicity. When duality leaves a person's imagination, the resurrection takes place for him and he witnesses the Garden. He will be at ease for all eternity.

O Sayyid! Since such good fortune can be achieved in this world, why not try for it? Why are you heedless?

O Sayyid! A resurrection is coming for everyone and everything, and that is the return of all to Oneness. After the manifestation of the Whole takes place, all will have come forth to their own Root, but the joy that is appropriate will not appear to everyone, only to those people for whom the resurrection has taken place here. Hence you must strive so that the meaning that is promised to you will appear for you here. Then you will attain ease, and the joy that is appropriate will appear.

O Sayyid! The goal is simply that the illusion of duality disappear and that you not remain, that He remain, and no one else. All the prophets and the friends of God have agreed on this. In the divine scriptures, the prophetic hadiths, and the writings of the friends, there are many proofs of this. The great ones of each sect have upheld Oneness and all have said with one tongue that none exists but the Real. The cosmos is His form and His manifestation, nothing else. I have in mind to write the evidence for these matters in another book, bringing also a few of the arguments that sound reason has deduced, God willing.

O Sayyid! Today is the end of time and soon the sun of Reality will rise from the West of createdness. Before the rising of the sun, its lights and effects will become manifest; the mysteries of *tawḥīd* will appear on the tongues of the elect and the common people, by their choice and without it, understood and not understood. So the seeker must collect himself and conceal himself from himself. The reality of Oneness must disclose itself to him as is proper. He must not be satisfied with words spoken by the tongue.

O Sayyid! God is the Nondelimited and Muhammad has brought the truth.

15

A Debate Between the Soul and the Spirit

ʿAbd al-Jalīl Ilāhābādī, who is likely the same person as the Chishtī shaykh ʿAbd al-Jalīl Laknawī (d. 1043/1633–1634),[1] first attracted my attention in 1988 when I came across one of his Persian works in the library of the Institute of Islamic Studies in New Delhi. The short treatise, entitled *Suʾāl wa-jawāb* ("Question and Answer"),[2] describes a visionary conversation ʿAbd al-Jalīl had with Ibn al-ʿArabī. During the discussion, Ibn al-ʿArabī answers a number of questions connected with difficult passages in his works, mainly the *Futūḥāt*. Most of the questions have in view the long-standing current of criticisms directed against some of the technical terminology and phraseology of this work.

The manuscript that I discuss here, namely *Rūḥ wa-nafs* ("The Spirit and the Soul"),[3] is similar to *Suʾāl wa-jawāb* in both length and the fact that it is presented as a visionary conversation, although the two participants are the spirit (*rūḥ*) and the soul or self (*nafs*). The work discusses many of Ibn al-ʿArabī's ideas on *wujūd* and its levels, the fixed entities, the unknowability of the Divine Essence, and the experiences that take place in the afterlife. It also provides an interesting example of spiritual psychology. This is because it analyzes the forces at work within the inward dimension of the human microcosm in terms that recall earlier currents of Sufi teachings, while reflecting the developments and debates going on in the Indian Subcontinent during ʿAbd al-Jalīl's lifetime. It is the treatise's psychological theme that I focus on here.

Given the current dismal state of our knowledge of the development of Islamic thought in the Indian Subcontinent, it would be impossible to trace the numerous Sufis, theologians, and philosophers whose views may be reflected in the treatise. The best I can do here is to suggest that many of the ideas are rooted in the writings of Ibn al-ʿArabī and other relatively early figures. It would be difficult to say to what extent ʿAbd al-Jalīl is drawing on a direct knowledge of Ibn al-ʿArabī's writings here, since he may have known them through the tradition of criticism and commentary. The one book that he almost certainly had read, although he refers neither to its title nor to its author, is Jāmī's *Naqd*. In the *Rūḥ*, this work is quoted or paraphrased at least twice, and in one instance where a passage is attributed to "one of them," it is taken from Qūnawī's *Fukūk*, most likely through the intermediary of the *Naqd*.[4]

The Setting

Much of Sufi theoretical teaching has to do with the invisible dimension of the human being, the ambiguous "something" that fills the vast "space" between the body and the Essence of God. In referring to this something, the earlier texts employ various terms derived from the Koran and the Hadith—such as soul, spirit, heart, intellect, and mystery—without much elaboration or explanation. Already by the third/ninth century, Sufi authors like al-Ḥakīm al-Tirmidhī (d. ca. 300/912)[5]—not to mention the early Muslim philosophers—employ such terms to describe a hierarchy of increasingly invisible levels, realms, or dimensions reaching as far as the Divine Reality. In the theoretical discussions provided by Tirmidhī, Ghazālī,[6] ʿIzz al-Dīn Kāshānī (d. 735/1335),[7] and many others, it is clear that the multiplicity of terms does not imply a multiplicity of independent entities. Instead, the terms represent various names given to a single reality—the unseen dimension of the human being—in respect of the attributes that it possesses or can assume.[8]

For the Sufis, the discussion of the different dimensions of the human being was by no means simply theoretical. The unseen realities were defined so that they could be differentiated and experienced by the traveler on the path to God. Without the theoretical and linguistic "embodiment" of the tendencies of the soul, it was impossible to come to grips with one's own inward nature. The descriptions made it possible for the spiritual traveler to picture, localize, and personify his own psychic or spiritual tendencies within the infinite imaginal universe that is sometimes called the "ocean of the soul" (*daryā-yi jān*). Once this was accomplished, it was possible to strengthen the tendencies if they needed strengthening, or pass beyond them if they needed to be overcome.

Although ʿAbd al-Jalīl's treatise deals with two major dimensions of Sufi teachings—the psychological and the metaphysical—the development of the narrative emphasizes psychology. The text reaches a climax with an integration of the diverse dimensions of the human reality and a vision of the oneness of all things with God. In the historical background lie the long-standing debates in the Indian Subcontinent and elsewhere over the status of the individual soul in relation to God. More specifically, what are the practical results of the spiritual realization of the gnostic? Once the state of supreme union is achieved, can any distinction be drawn between God and the world? Granted that "All is He," of what relevance to the gnostic are the commands and prohibitions of the Shariah? Shaykh Aḥmad Sirhindī's criticisms of Ibn al-ʿArabī arose out of this same background. In fact, Sirhindī was not criticizing Ibn al-ʿArabī himself—there is little evidence that he had ever studied his works. Instead, he was attacking the position ascribed to Ibn al-ʿArabī by certain groups of Muslims who then used this position to justify their own neglect of the Shariah, or of doctrinal teachings that Sirhindī considered essential. It is clear that ʿAbd al-Jalīl had this same background in view, since he goes to great lengths to disprove some of the important arguments of those who maintain the commonly accepted misconceptions concerning Ibn al-ʿArabī's position, what one might call the "religion of 'All is He,'" or "popularized *waḥdat al-wujūd.*"

ʿAbd al-Jalīl's treatise begins as follows: ʿAbd al-Jalīl is sitting in meditation when two forms appear to him, one luminous and one dark. The two forms greet each other and then introduce themselves. The dark one calls itself the governing power of the whole universe, a power so intermixed with the creatures that they refer to it as their own "self" or "soul" (*nafs*). The luminous form explains that it is the power through which all things have life; it is called "spirit" (*rūḥ*) because within it all creatures find their "rest" (*rawḥ*) and "repose" (*rayḥān*).

The forms then speak about their respective religions. The soul says that it follows the great lover Iblīs, who is the locus of manifestation for the divine name Misguider (*al-muḍill*). The spirit says that it follows him who carried God's trust and became His vicegerent, the Prophet Muhammad, who is the locus of manifestation for the name Allah. The spirit adds that the Prophet is also the locus of manifestation for the name Guide (*al-hādī*), the function of which is to spread God's specific and salvific mercy among the creatures and to open them up to ultimate felicity.

The opposite of the Guide is the Misguider, a divine name that is not always found in the traditional lists of the ninety-nine names but that is implied by several passages in the Koran where God is the subject of the verb "to misguide." The Koran 28:15 attributes this name specifically to Satan. That the soul or self is connected to satanic forces is suggested by a number of Koranic verses and made more explicit in the hadith literature.[9]

ʿAbd al-Jalīl's description of the soul and spirit reaffirms the well-known opposition between the ascending, luminous, and angelic tendency of the human being, and the descending, dark, and satanic tendency. Hence, he has prepared us for a replay of the struggle between guidance and misguidance, the prophets and the satans. But we are also dealing here with Ibn al-ʿArabī's intellectual universe, so both the Prophet and Satan are presented as loci of manifestation for the divine names. *Waḥdat al-wujūd* does not allow the discussion to take an exclusively dualistic and oppositional form in the manner of jurisprudence and Kalam. Rather, it demands that the opposition among the loci of manifestation for the divine names should be harmonized and made complementary through unity, or, in other words, through the fact that the name Allah is the coincidence of all opposites (*jamʿ al-aḍdād*).

The Debate

The main part of the text, detailing the contents of the debate between the spirit and the soul, reflects ʿAbd al-Jalīl's perception of the controversies over many important doctrinal issues in Sufism. Many of these issues are still relevant on the contemporary scene, where there is a renewed interest in the type of spirituality represented by Ibn al-ʿArabī's school and where one often meets contrary positions similar to those maintained by the spirit and the soul. But in the "New Age," the position represented by the soul seems to have gained the upper hand, while the spirit's perspective appears to be increasingly unpopular, since it reaffirms the necessity of the practice of the Shariah as the *sine qua non* for understanding and affirming unity.

The soul is depicted as a rather clever and crafty character, skillful in the intricacies of debate and not afraid to change its position when opportune. The spirit is much more stable and somewhat stolid, reflecting the far-seeing prophetic wisdom that it manifests. At the outset, the soul mentions Iblīs as its guide, so the spirit feels duty-bound to warn it of Iblīs's shortcomings. The soul replies by having recourse to the esoteric knowledge of the Tariqah, which transcends the Shariah mentioned by the spirit, and by claiming—in the manner of the well-known Sufi defenses of Iblīs[10]—that Iblīs was the great lover of God whose secret pact with his Beloved would not allow him to bow to anyone else.

The soul appeals to a privileged, esoteric knowledge in several more passages in the ensuing debate, most of which focuses on the nature of oneness and that of *wujūd,* although the expression *waḥdat al-wujūd* is never mentioned. In brief, the soul wants to claim an absolute oneness that obliterates distinctions within *wujūd* and at the same time to maintain its own privileged identity with *wujūd*. Thereby, it shows that distinctions among things are sheer illusion, so the Shariah is a veil that misleads the stupid. Those who are truly enlightened follow their own inner light, which is God Himself. The spirit protests that this appeal to absolute oneness is in fact an appeal to one of *wujūd*'s many levels, thereby distorting *wujūd*'s reality. It is contradictory to affirm the absolute oneness of God's Essence and then to deny His many attributes. Both have to be affirmed, and then it will be seen that the divine attributes demand the relative reality of the cosmos. The necessity of the Shariah follows from the reality of the cosmos and the real distinctions among the levels of *wujūd*.

In the first part of the treatise, the soul makes a rather good case for an individualistic type of spirituality shorn from traditional supports. In the second part, where the soul has taken another tack, the arguments attempt to claim the independence of the material world from any first principle. In both cases, the practical result is that the Shariah is useless if not positively harmful.

By the end of the debate, it is not completely clear who has won. Certainly anyone who inclines toward the religious universe of Islam will read the text as giving victory to the spirit, since all the soul's arguments have been neatly answered from within the perspective of the Shariah in general and Ibn al-ʿArabī's school in particular. But much of what the soul has said would be quite convincing to those who incline toward a Sufi esoterism cut off from the Shariah and alien to scholastic philosophizing.

Despite the fact that ʿAbd al-Jalīl means to support the spirit's arguments over the soul, he also wants to acknowledge the relative validity of the soul's positions. The soul is a locus of manifestation for a divine name, and that name has its rights. The name Misguider cannot be negated, but must be harmonized with the higher names from which it derives. Although "God's mercy precedes His wrath," and, therefore, by analogy, "God's guidance precedes His misguidance," both wrath and misguidance are divine attributes and have a positive, if limited, role to play in the total constellation of existence.

The beginning of the process whereby ʿAbd al-Jalīl will harmonize the positions of soul and spirit is announced at the end of the debate proper, when the spirit realizes that its words have had no discernible effect on the soul. Hence, it proposes that they take their dispute to a third person to decide between them.

The Mystery's Judgment

The "third person" to whom the soul and spirit have recourse is the "mystery" (*sirr*), a still more inward dimension of the human reality. ʿAbd al-Jalīl has in mind a seven-part hierarchy of the human being which by this period had become commonplace in Sufi writings: body, soul, spirit, heart, mystery, hidden, and most hidden.

The mystery enters the discussion by first addressing the soul and then the spirit. It criticizes the soul for ruining the world of obedience and bringing Adam down from the Garden, but it praises the soul's grasp of the station of Oneness and its description of God's self-disclosure in all things. Then the mystery says to the soul:

> It is clear to me that Oneness has become manifest to you in the station of nature. That is why your love is completely fixed upon the world of form. You love absorption in sensory passions and immersion in the illusory pleasures that darken the mirror of the heart and bring about punishment and disaster in the next world. If the appropriate love for form were to become established within you, you would undertake good acts and works, since forms in the next world will last forever, while the forms of this plane are obviously perishing and have no subsistence. You must turn your attention toward the high level in order to reach the [divine] self-disclosure that is beyond the outside and inside worlds. In that self-disclosure, no name or description remains, nor expression or allusion.

The mystery compares the soul to a frog in a puddle of filthy water who thinks that the ocean belongs to it. The frog needs a stream of pure water to pass over the puddle and take it to the ocean. In concluding its address to the soul, the mystery focuses on the soul's particular problem, which is the affirmation of selfhood or "soulhood" (*nafsāniyya*). The only way to achieve the vision of the inward levels of Oneness is to negate one's selfhood, or to undergo annihilation: "There is no remedy except becoming lost and obliterated: they buy nothing there but a thing's nonexistence and annihilation."

The mystery then turns to the spirit and praises it for its obedience and its attentiveness to the good that can be gained in the next world. But it warns the spirit that it also has not yet freed itself of love for form. The danger remains that it will be so entranced by the Rosegarden that it will forget the face of the Gardener. The mystery criticizes the spirit for perceiving the station of Oneness from the point of view of the rational faculty (*ʿaql*) and for not abandoning itself to love. The soul's emphasis on self-identification with the Real is a valid one, and it can be experienced only through love.

ʿAbd al-Jalīl then summarizes the rest of the mystery's advice to the soul and spirit:

> The mystery made clear that the entity of the servant has two sides, one the side of nondelimitation [*iṭlāq*] and the other the side of delimitation. Servanthood and lordship both must be taken into account, since both are established in the entity of the servant. The soul had taken lordship into account and had desired to embrace immediate joys and pleasures, while the spirit had taken servanthood into account and had chosen the ease of obedience in order to grasp endless and everlasting deferred ease. Though both were flying in the world of *tawḥīd*, out of caprice the soul-vulture would in the end have stayed with the bones, while the spirit-nightingale would have inclined away from the Rosegarden of the Beloved's face toward the Garden's fruit.

In short, the spirit represents that dimension of the human reality that is able to see itself and its own limitations objectively and to efface itself by self-transcendence, while the soul represents the dimension that sees itself as central and affirms its own right to existence. The spirit rises beyond itself and affirms the Other, while the soul sinks within itself and affirms its own reality.

At this point in the text, ʿAbd al-Jalīl once again acknowledges the soul's rights to its mode of manifesting the Real, while admitting his own limited knowledge of the true situation: "O friend," he says, "I do not know which point of view God will take into account tomorrow." In other words, he does not know if God will treat the human being as a lord or a servant on the Day of Resurrection. However, people should exercise caution in dealing with God, and therefore they should observe the instructions brought by the prophets. They should actualize their servanthood here and wait to become lords in the next world.

The Birth of the Heart

Having given advice to the soul and the spirit, the mystery now addresses both, telling them to become one. ʿAbd al-Jalīl then makes the following remarks:

> From the unification of the two a marvelous state and wondrous shape appeared called the "heart" [*qalb*], which brings together the two sides and fluctuates [*taqallub*] between them. When the mystery found worthiness for the gathering of all meanings in the heart, it pulled the heart to itself and joined it with itself.

Once the heart is born, the mystery sees that the heart has the power to gather within itself all meanings. This point, so briefly stated here, is based on a rather complex exposition of the nature of the heart found in Ibn al-ʿArabī's works.[11] As Ibn al-ʿArabī maintains, human beings perceive the Real in two fundamental modes, that of incomparability and similarity. Neither point of view is sufficient for a total view of God or the things as they are in themselves. Incomparability is the point of view natural to the rational faculty, which innately desires to prove that *Nothing is like Him* (42:11). Similarity is the point of view of imagination, which perceives the Real only through His self-disclosures.

The spirit personifies the rational dimension of human nature that can only understand God as being incomparable, while the soul represents the imaginal dimension that can only grasp God in images and symbols. But the heart, in Ibn al-ʿArabī's perspective, is limited neither by reason nor by imagination, neither by rational thought nor by the perception of forms. The heart harmonizes the two sorts of perception, and since these cannot be maintained simultaneously, it "fluctuates" from one vision to the next. Yet the heart never denies the Real, whether in His incomparable and unknowable Essence or in His self-disclosures through the sensory forms of the cosmos.

The spirit's self-effacement is connected with reason and incomparability because the spirit grasps that "Nothing is like Him" and that all positive qualities belong to God; hence it sees that it is nothing in itself. In contrast, the soul's self-affirmation is connected to imagination and the vision of similarity, since it sees God manifesting Himself within itself; it therefore grasps that everything it possesses is similar to God and that all the divine attributes belong to it.

In short, by speaking of the heart's worthiness for "gathering all meanings," ʿAbd al-Jalīl means to say that the heart had integrated and harmonized the points of view of soul and spirit by combining nondelimitation with delimitation and incomparability with similarity. Thus, the mystery saw that the heart was able to perceive all meanings, not simply those that pertain to one side or the other. The mystery understood that the heart was worthy of knowing the level of inwardness and integration represented by itself, so it drew the heart to itself and became united with it.

But this is not the end of the story. Beyond the mystery lie the "hidden" (*khafī*) and the "most hidden" (*akhfā*). All differentiation must be eliminated before the vision of absolute unity.

Final Union

According to ʿAbd al-Jalīl, the "hidden" and the "most hidden" represent the innermost dimensions of the human being in terms of which the mystery perceives the Nondelimited Light of the Real, which is manifest both within itself and beyond itself:

> In the beginning, when the Light of Nondelimitation had shone upon the mystery, it had found a flash of that light evident in itself; it had seen a kind of hidden light outside itself, and a kind of most hidden light that its understanding and imagination could in no way reach but that it knew to be further away from itself.

At the beginning, in other words, the mystery had perceived the hidden and most hidden lights beyond itself, just as it had perceived a light within itself, and the soul and spirit below itself. Hence, it would seem that "mystery" signifies the center of human consciousness, a point that stands midway between the darkness of the body and the infinite Light of God. As the center, the mystery is flanked by two dimensions on each side. Once the two lower dimensions—soul and spirit—were joined together and became the heart, the mystery was able to integrate them into itself. Now the mystery can become integrated into the two higher dimensions, the hidden and most hidden. It is able to accomplish this integration because it has been strengthened through the two powers represented by the spirit-dimension and soul-dimension of the heart: "Through joining with the all-comprehensive heart, a strengthening appeared within the mystery."

The spirit and soul-dimensions of the heart now become the means for a twofold experience of both the hidden and most hidden lights. The spirit's attribute is self-effacement before the Other, since it tends toward annihilation in the Real. But the soul's attribute is self-affirmation, because it tends to see the divine light as its own and to perceive itself as subsisting through the divine attributes: "Through the light pertaining to the spirit, the mystery dissolved into the 'hidden' light, and through the strength of the I-ness pertaining to the soul it became identified with that hidden light."

In other words, the luminosity of the heart's spirit-nature allowed the mystery to become effaced and annihilated in that even greater light called the "hidden." But the soul-nature demanded self-affirmation, so in the midst of dissolution the mystery found itself and saw that it was now identical with the hidden light.

Next, ʿAbd al-Jalīl offers an explanation for the *shaṭḥiyyāt* of the Sufis. The mystery, like Ḥallāj and Basṭāmī, now speaks from the viewpoint of "I am the Real": "Here it became a stream joined to the ocean and called out, 'Glory be to me! How tremendous is my rank!' " At the same time, this invisible core of the human reality experiences the "fluctuation" of the heart, so its gaze shifts from the point of view of the soul to that of the spirit, from that of affirming itself to that of negating itself before the source of its own light:

> When the mystery's gaze fell upon the infinity of the Ocean, it said, "My God, though I said, 'Glory be to me! How tremendous is my rank!,' now I repent. I cut off the belt of unbelief and say, 'There is no god but God,' so that through the blessing of these words I may be obliterated in the most hidden light."

Once again, the mystery experiences annihilation, but the selfhood of the soul reasserts itself, and identity with the most hidden is established: "It lifted its head within the world of annihilation and began to say through the strength of the I-ness of the soul, 'I am the most hidden,' and it let loose the waves of claiming to be the ocean."

At each level, hidden and most hidden, a dual experience has occurred. Only after self-affirmation within the most hidden light can all traces of duality be erased so that ultimate union may be experienced. Beyond the most hidden lies the infinite light of the Unseen He-ness (*ghayb-i huwiyya*). At this point, ʿAbd al-Jalīl alludes to what is ostensibly a *ḥadīth qudsī*: "Verily within the body of the son of Adam is a lump of flesh, within the lump of flesh a heart, within the heart a spirit, within the spirit a light, and within the light a mystery; and within the mystery am I."[12] Hence, ʿAbd al-Jalīl writes concerning experiencing the level of the most hidden, "Just as this happened the voice of the He-ness shouted out, 'and within the most hidden am I.' " Thus, the Real reasserts His authority and the right relationships are established. All dimensions of the human reality experience a mode of identity with the One. Even the most hidden—the highest dimension of the human reality—finds itself negated in the Real:

> Through awe before that sound, the ocean of the most hidden became dry such that none of the water of existence remained within it. In this state, all of them became one. The most manifest and the most hidden mixed together. All of itself cried out, *Whose is the kingdom today? God's, the One, the Overwhelming!* [40:16].[13]

In the state of supreme union, every self-subsistent reality in the human being is negated only to be reaffirmed as God's self-disclosure. As a result of this vision, ʿAbd al-Jalīl loses consciousness. When he comes to, he cites a well-known prophetic formula that once again expresses the overriding reality of the servant—his nothingness before God:

> Here I had passed away from myself and become selfless. When I became slightly aware, the sound of "and within the most hidden am I" kept on falling into my ear from my own tongue. Out of the terror of this business I awoke. I said, "There is no power and no strength except in God, the High, the Tremendous."

ʿAbd al-Jalīl offers a final comment that situates the whole episode firmly within the imaginal universe described by Ibn al-ʿArabī. He tells us that everything he had witnessed had been the imaginal embodiment of unseen realities: "I understood that all of this had been I; all of these were the forms of my own knowledge. These discussions had been my own imaginal concepts [*takhayyulāt*] that had assumed form."

ʿAbd al-Jalīl's concluding prayer reestablishes his feet firmly on the ground of servanthood, the right attitude to be maintained in the present world: "I ask forgiveness from God for everything that God dislikes and I repent to Him, *'and I am the first of those who have faith'* [7:143]."

This brief treatise demonstrates a sophisticated grasp of the teachings of Ibn al-ʿArabī's school and a profound awareness of the complexity of the human reality. ʿAbd al-Jalīl presents none of the simple-minded polemics that often occurs between supporters of *waḥdat al-wujūd* and *waḥdat al-shuhūd*, but instead demonstrates that he—like many other Indian Sufis—was completely aware that the only way to present the highly nuanced structure of the human reality is to proceed by acknowledging the validity of a wide range of perspectives while recognizing the relativity of each of them, since absolute truth lies in God's Essence alone, and is therefore inaccessible to human beings.

16

A Chishtī Handbook from Bijapur

In his *Sufis of Bijapur*, Richard Eaton makes it clear—if there was any doubt—that Sufism was flourishing in Bijapur in the tenth/sixteenth and eleventh/seventeenth centuries in various forms. Among the most active Sufi groups during this period was the Chishtī order. It was centered on a famous family of Sufis that traced itself back to Shāh Mīrānjī Shams al-ʿUshshāq (d. 904/1499), who was born in Mecca and appears to have originally been a Chaghatay Turk. According to the traditional accounts, as a young man, he had a dream of the Prophet in which he was instructed to travel to Bijapur to find one Shāh Kamāl, who turned out to be Kamāl al-Dīn Biyābānī (d. 867/1462–1463), the successor, with one intermediary, of the famous Chishtī shaykh Gīsū Darāz (d. 825/1422).

Having himself become the successor of Biyābānī, Shams al-ʿUshshāq was then succeeded by his own son Burhān al-Dīn Jānam (d. 1005/1597), a prolific author of Persian works on Sufi theory and practice. Burhān al-Dīn was in turn succeeded by Shaykh Maḥmūd Khwush-Dahān (d. 1026/1617), who derived from a well-known Qādirī family in Bidar. Shaykh Maḥmūd also wrote many Persian works, one of which is *Maʿrifat al-sulūk* ("The True Knowledge of Wayfaring"). It has been described as "the summary work of all Bijapuri Chishtī teachings and a book upon which scores of later treatises were based."[1] In it, Shaykh Maḥmūd outlines, in an unusually simple and systematic manner, the basic teachings and practices that were being imparted to disciples by his shaykh, Burhān al-Dīn Jānam, and presumably by himself as well. Not only did this work play an important role in a major branch of Indian Sufism, but it also has a much wider significance, because, as far as I can judge, it is an especially clear presentation of the methods and goals of the later Sufi tradition.

Theory and Practice

It needs to be remembered that Sufi authors had produced a wealth of works on both theory and practice over the centuries, and the Indian authors continued to write prolifically, mainly in Persian. By the beginning of this period, Indian Sufis had access to a plethora of writings and oral teachings, and they could easily become aware of the differing theoretical and practical frameworks of diverse Sufi authors. More than two hundred years had passed since the enormous outpouring of Sufi writing in the sixth/twelfth and seventh/thirteenth centuries. Throughout the Indian Subcontinent, the more learned Sufis were familiar with the writings of Ghazālī and ʿAyn al-Quḍāt, not to mention the Persian Sufi poets (especially Rūmī) and the vast range of theoretical works by Ibn al-ʿArabī and his followers. Scores of important Sufis had produced works of significance, and each of the several Sufi orders flourishing in the Indian Subcontinent had its own favorite authors as well as shaykhs who themselves wrote many sorts of works on Sufi teachings. Then, as today, it was practically impossible for a single seeker to gain a complete overview of the diverse Sufi teachings that were available. Nonetheless, every seeker who made any attempt to visit Sufi shaykhs, study Sufi writings, and listen to Sufi poetry, would have been exposed to a variety of ideas and conceptual schemes that were not always easy to interrelate.

In order to organize the received lore of Sufism and Islam, Sufi authors took different approaches. Even when the teachings of two authors seem to be the same, careful analysis often shows that there are important discrepancies. There is no single "Sufi doctrine" accepted by all the Sufi teachers—other than the basic creed of Islam. What we usually see is that a given author will conceptualize the received wisdom in his own personal terms, on occasion idiosyncratically, and then offer his own theory to his students and readers as a guide to understanding the nature of things. In parallel texts written by philosophers or theologians, we may be dealing with pure theory, but in the Sufi texts, the practical applications of the teachings are either stated explicitly or implied by the context of the writings, which are not aimed at "thinkers," but at practitioners and adepts. The Sufis considered theory important—except in moments of rhetorical excess or poetical intoxication—but they always understood theory as a means to an end, not an end in itself. Hence, theory was constantly being modified in order to fit the practical circumstances.

From early times, Sufi authors had offered various overarching schemes to organize the Islamic worldview and to situate Muslim practice within this view. In many Sufi works, and in many chapters of these works, one specific scheme is employed as the organizing principle. Typically, as anyone who has looked at the secondary literature on Sufism is well aware, these schemes present us with hierarchies, in keeping with the general Islamic idea that reaching God depends on following a specific "path" or climbing a "ladder" (*miʿrāj*).

The great richness of the Sufi tradition in the Mughal period and the variety of conceptual schemes found in Sufi texts may help explain Shaykh Maḥmūd's intentions in writing the *Maʿrifat al-sulūk*. What he offers is a synthesis of various dimensions of Sufi thought and practice, or a way of correlating all the diverse technical terms that appear abundantly in the texts and the tradition. In presenting his synthesis, he makes it clear that all this conceptualization has the practical aim of guiding seekers on the path to God.

Shaykh Maḥmūd's Scheme

Shaykh Maḥmūd summarizes his book, which is relatively short—about one hundred and fifty pages—in a circle divided into eight sectors (see Figure 1). The circle represents all and everything—the One and the many, God and the world, Lord and servant, macrocosm and microcosm, and the interrelationships among the various realities that can be conceptualized in the nature of things. Each of the eight sectors has five levels, for a total of forty sections (forty being the number of completion[2]). However, the fifth level is the same reality in each case, but it is given different names depending on the sector from which one enters into it.

The first sector is arranged in terms of *wujūd,* and more particularly, according to the famous distinction between Necessary, possible, and impossible existence. This gives us only three levels, so the Shaykh adds two more, *ʿārif al-wujūd,* "the gnostic of existence," and *wāḥid al-wujūd,* "The One of Existence." This last and highest level obviously points to the doctrine of *waḥdat al-wujūd.* Shaykh Maḥmūd names the circle and the other diagrams according to the level of existence, and he puts the One of Existence at the highest level. Thus, he demonstrates that he belongs to the mainstream of Indian Sufism in terms of the central importance of *waḥdat al-wujūd.*

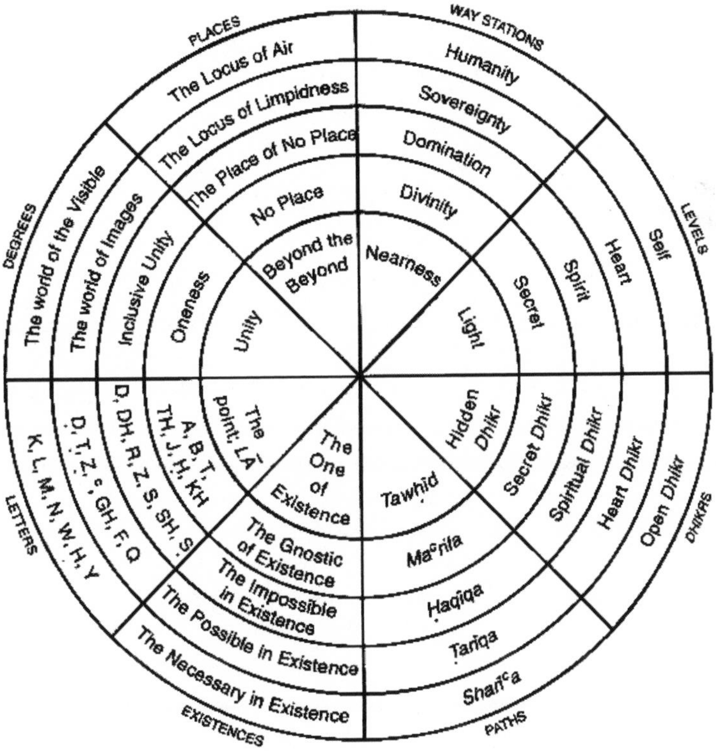

Figure 1. The One of Existence

Table 1. The Necessary in Existence

Knower *ʿālim*	The Necessary in Existence *wājib al-wujūd*	Gnostic *ʿārif*
	Entrusted angel: Michael *muwakkal*: Mīkāʾīl	
Watchfulness *murāqaba*	Growing spirit *rūḥ-i nāmī*	Annihilation *fanāʾ*
	Fleshly heart *qalb-i muḍgha*	
	Commanding soul *nafs-i ammāra*	
	Understanding: comparison *fahm-i qiyās*	
	Open remembrance *dhikr-i jalī*	
Disengagement *tajrīd*	*Tawḥīd* through words *tawḥīd-i aqwālī*	Solitude *tafrīd*
	Path of the Shariah *rāh-i sharīʿa*	
	Way station: humanity *manzil-i nāsūt*	
Witnessing *mushāhada*	Martyrdom of origin *shahādat-i mabdaʾ*	State *ḥāl*
	Seven occupations *haft shughl*	
Lover *ʿāshiq*	y, h, w, n, m, l, k	Arriver *wāṣil*

The second sector of the circle presents five "paths" (*sabīl*), beginning with the Shariah, then the Tariqah, then the Haqiqah, then *maʿrifa*, and finally *tawḥīd*.

The third sector is organized in terms of different levels of the remembrance of God, beginning with the voicing of the formula (*dhikr-i jalī*), and ending with the innermost realization of what is being remembered (*dhikr-i khafī*).

The fourth sector deals with subtle centers, which the author simply calls "levels" (*marātib*), that is, levels of the human microcosm—self or soul, heart, spirit, mystery, and light.

The fifth presents us with "way stations" (*manāzil*), and four of these are clearly inspired by standard terminology for the Five Divine Presences—*nāsūt*, *malakūt*, *jabarūt*, and *lāhūt*. The fifth, however, the author calls the way station of nearness (*qurb*)—which, according to Ibn al-ʿArabī, is the summit of the path, the highest stage attainable by anyone who is not a prophet.

The sixth sector designates "places," and here various terms are offered through which one might speak of "localization" at any level of reality. This particular scheme may have originated with the Bijapuri school, although the individual terms are well-known. The five places are the locus of air (*maḥall-i hawāʾ*), the locus of limpidness (*ṣafāʾ*), the place of no place (*makān-i lā makān*), no place itself, and "Beyond the Beyond" (*warāʾ al-warāʾ*).

The seventh sector offers us five "degrees" (*darajāt*), and here the author seems to have taken inspiration from another standard method for explaining the Five Divine Presences—the world of the visible, the world of images, inclusive unity, Oneness, and Exclusive Unity.

Finally, Shaykh Maḥmūd describes the five levels in terms of the Arabic alphabet, whose symbolism was often made use of in various contexts, such as delineating the twenty-eight degrees of the Breath of the All-Merciful that gives birth to the cosmos. The Shaykh ascribes seven letters to each of the four outer levels, beginning from the end of the alphabet. Thus, the outermost level is made up of the seven letters beginning with *yāʾ* and ending with *kāf*. The fourth level ends with the first of the twenty-eight letters, *alif*. As for the fifth and highest level, this is identified both with the point, from which the *alif* is often said to be generated, and with the *lām-alif*, which is sometimes considered the twenty-ninth letter of the alphabet. More importantly, *lām-alif* spells *lā* or "no," so it can denote the utter undifferentiation and "nonentification" (*lā taʿayyun*) of the Divine Essence—just as, mathematically, the point designates that which has no dimensions whatsoever.

To prepare the reader for the circle, Shaykh Maḥmūd first offers four tables corresponding to the four outer levels of the circle (see Tables 1–4). In the tables, however, he does not offer exactly the same scheme as he provides in the circle. He presents each table as having thirteen levels, not eight, and only five of the eight sectors are mentioned in the table, leaving eight other ways of conceptualizing the four outer levels of the circle.[3]

In the four tables, Shaykh Maḥmūd first mentions the level of existence, then the archangel who is entrusted with the level. Then he turns to the levels of the human microcosm. In the circle (Figure 1), he mentions the five subtle centers as self, heart, spirit, mystery, and light. But in the four tables (Tables 1–4), instead of this hierarchy, he provides four levels for each of spirit, heart, and soul. Thus, if the subtle centers can be viewed as specific realities from one point of view, from another point of view, each can be differentiated into levels. The four levels of spirit are the growing or plant spirit, the motile or animal spirit, the rational or human spirit, and the holy or prophetic spirit. The four levels of the heart are the lump of flesh (*muḍgha*), the repenting heart (*munīb*), the healthy heart (*salīm*), and the witnessing heart (*shahīd*). The four levels of the soul are the soul commanding (to evil), the blaming soul, the soul at peace, and the inspired soul.

Next, the Shaykh turns to the path leading to God in broad terms. First he mentions four ascending levels of *tawḥīd*—in words, acts, states, and essence—and then the mode of understanding (*fahm*) that corresponds to each level—understanding by comparison (*qiyās*), imagination (*wahm*), conjecture (*gumān*), and awareness (*āgāh*). These levels correspond to the four levels of the path, as

Table 2. The Possible in Existence

Knower	The Possible in Existence *mumkin al-wujūd*	Gnostic
	Entrusted angel: Seraphiel *muwakkal*: Isrāfīl	
Watchfulness	Motile spirit *rūḥ-i mutaḥarrik*	Annihilation
	Returning heart *qalb-i munīb*	
	Blaming soul *nafs-i lawwāma*	
	Understanding: imagination *fahm-i wahm*	
	Remembrance of the heart *dhikr-i qalbī*	
Disengagement	*Tawḥīd* through acts *tawḥīd-i afʿālī*	Solitude
	Path of the Tariqah *rāh-i ṭarīqa*	
Witnessing	Way station: sovereignty *manzil-i malakūt*	State
	Martyrdom of ecstatics *shahādat-i wujadāʾ*	
	Seven occupations	
Lover	q, f, gh, ʿ, ẓ, ṭ, ḍ	Arriver

mentioned in the circle, beginning with the Shariah. The appropriate mode of remembrance and the corresponding way stations are the same as those mentioned in the circle. Finally, Shaykh Maḥmūd mentions four levels of "bearing witness" or "martyrdom" (*shahāda*). Although the discussion and terminology here are not completely clear to me, he seems to be saying that at each level there is a specific mode of dying in the path of God, a martyrdom through which one is reborn on the next higher level.

Finally, the Shaykh mentions in each table the words "the seven occupations," and these are followed by seven letters of the alphabet. In the text, he explains that at each level, the seeker has an appropriate supplication or short prayer, each of which corresponds to a letter of the alphabet. Hence there are twenty-eight "occupations," with a twenty-ninth pertaining to the center of the circle. I have arranged the twenty-nine levels in Table 5. Most of the supplications begin with the letter to which they pertain and address the bodily member or attribute that is mentioned in the table. For example, the supplication for the

Table 3. The Impossible in Existence

Knower	The Impossible in Existence *mumtaniʿ al-wujūd*	Gnostic
	Entrusted angel: Azrael *muwakkal*: ʿAzrāʾīl	
Watchfulness	Rational spirit *rūḥ-i nāṭiqa*	Annihilation
	Healthy heart *qalb-i salīm*	
	Soul at peace *nafs-i muṭmaʾinna*	
	Understanding: conjecture *fahm-i gumān*	
	Remembrance of the spirit *dhikr-i rūḥī*	
Disengagement	*Tawḥīd* through states *tawḥīd-i aḥwālī*	Solitude
	Path of the reality *rāh-i ḥaqīqa*	
Witnessing	Way station: domination *manzil-i jabarūt*	State
	Martyrdom of intenders *shahādat-i ʿumadāʾ*	
	Seven occupations	
Lover	ṣ, sh, s, z, r, dh, d	Arriver

second level, pertaining to the letter *hāʾ* and to the knees, reads *Hadhdhib jalsatanā yā Allāh,* that is, "Refine our sitting, O God!" Shaykh Maḥmūd translates the saying into Persian and adds some commentary as follows: "O God, keep our knees sitting in this station so that they will not stand to worship anything else."

The supplication for the letter *ʿayn,* which corresponds to hearing, reads *ʿAllimnā'l-Qurʾān yā Allāh,* "Teach us the Koran, O God!" The Persian translation reads, "O God, teach us the Koran, which is Your Speech, through our hearing, so that knowledge of You may be achieved."

The supplication for the letter *zāʾ* and the attribute of adornment is *Zayyinnā fī zīnatika yā Allāh,* "Adorn us with Your adornment, O God." Shaykh Maḥmūd renders it, "O God, bestow upon our existence an adornment from Your existence."

Besides the mention of seven occupations, the four tables have other common features. They begin with one sort of existence, and the order in each case is the same. Each has a center column divided into thirteen levels. Each also has two side columns in which the same pair of terms is mentioned in the same

Table 4. The Gnostic of Existence

Knower *ʿārif al-wujūd*	The Gnostic of Existence	Gnostic
	Entrusted angel: Gabriel *muwakkal*: Jibrāʾīl	
Watchfulness	Holy spirit *rūḥ-i qudsī*	Annihilation
	Witnessing heart *qalb-i shahīd*	
	Inspired soul *nafs-i mulhama*	
	Understanding: the aware *fahm-i āgāh*	
	Remembrance of the mystery *dhikr-i sirrī*	
Disengagement	*tawḥīd* through essence *tawḥīd-i dhātī*	Solitude
	Path of gnosis *rāh-i maʿrifa*	
Witnessing	Way station: Divinity *manzil-i lāhūt*	State
	Martyrdom of witnessers *shahādat-i shuhadāʾ*	
	Seven occupations	
Lover	kh, ḥ, j, th, t, b, a	Arriver

position. Each of these pairs represents a basic relationship that has different connotations in the context of each table. The term on the left hand represents a lower stage on the spiritual journey, and the term on the right a higher stage. The left-hand term, in other words, represents a preparation for what is designated by the right-hand term.

In the first case, we have knower and gnostic. The learned knowledge of the knower will eventually turn into the tasted, witnessed knowledge of the gnostic.

Second are watchfulness and annihilation. Through the practice of watching one's own inner states in keeping with the instruction of the spiritual guide, one eventually achieves the annihilation of all individualized and self-centered attributes and the subsistence of the divine attributes, in the form of which human beings were created.

Third are disengagement and solitude. One disengages one's self from the world and the body and achieves a state of being alone with God.

Table 5. The Twenty-Nine Occupations

LETTER	REALITY
Table 1: The Necessary in Existence	
Yā’	Feet
Hā’	Knees
Wāw	Navel
Nūn	Breast
Mīm	Throat
Lām	Forehead
Kāf	Nose
Table 2: The Possible in Existence	
Qāf	Speech
Fā’	Smell
Ghayn	Eyesight
‘Ayn	Hearing
Ẓā’	Intellect
Ṭā’	Heart
Ḍād	Satisfaction
Table 3: The Impossible in Existence	
Ṣād	God’s decree
Shīn	Intercession
Sīn	Journey
Zā’	Adornment
Rā’	Mercy
Dhāl	Tasting
Dāl	Path
Table 4: The Gnostic in Existence	
Khā’	Vicegerency
Ḥā’	Love of God
Jīm	Beauty
Thā’	Laudation
Tā’	Blessing
Bā’	God’s name
Alif	God’s Essence
Figure 1: The One of Existence	
LĀ	Nonentificaton

Fourth are witnessing and state. Through witnessing the divine influxes within oneself one is transported into an altered state of consciousness.

Finally, at the bottom of the table, in the highest stage of realization for each level, are lover and arriver. The adept who is transported by love for God achieves the station of arrival at, or union with, his Beloved.

Shaykh Maḥmūd's Commentary

In the second section of the book, Shaykh Maḥmūd presents the circle as the culmination of the journey and the realization of *waḥdat al-wujūd*. The circle is the end of the first journey—the journey to God beginning from the world or the ascending arc, the upward climb on the ladder of the *miʿrāj*. The circle is also the beginning of the second journey, which is the return from God on the descending *miʿrāj* to the world from whence one began. Here, Shaykh Maḥmūd reviews the stages of the ascending journey in reverse order as stages of the descending journey inasmuch as all the stages represent different dimensions of what the seeker realizes through the One of Existence.

I will now turn my attention to Shaykh Maḥmūd's commentary on the four tables (Tables 1–4) and the circle (Figure 1). I follow his discussions of the term *wujūd* as he moves through its various stages. As is obvious from the arrangement of the tables, Shaykh Maḥmūd considers *wujūd* as the primary reality in terms of which everything else needs to be understood, and in this he is in perfect harmony with the later intellectual tradition in general.

Shaykh Maḥmūd calls the first three tables *wājib al-wujūd* (The Necessary in Existence), *mumkin al-wujūd* (The Possible in Existence), and *mumtaniʿ al-wujūd* (The Impossible in Existence). This classification of *wujūd* into three basic categories was of course standard in Islamic thought from Avicenna onward. The fourth table is that of *ʿārif al-wujūd*, "the Gnostic of Existence" or "the Knower of Existence," and this reflects the fundamental Sufi quest for the type of knowledge that is designated as *maʿrifa* (often *ʿirfān* in late texts from Persia), and which can best be understood as "self-knowledge." Shaykh Maḥmūd makes the primary importance of this self-knowledge completely explicit in his introduction to the work, immediately after citing his own *silsila* back to Gīsū Darāz. Here he explains the purpose of the Sufi path in terms of knowledge of the self, referring to the famous prophetic dictum, "He who knows [*ʿarafa*] himself knows his Lord." This knowledge is not *ʿilm*, or learned knowledge, but *maʿrifa*—tasted and realized knowledge of one's own self and one's own Lord, or, to use an English term, *gnosis*. And, of course, this is the very word that the Shaykh employs in the title of his work, *Maʿrifat al-sulūk*, "The Gnosis of the Wayfaring," or, "The Self-Knowledge Achieved by Traveling the Path." He writes:

> O traveler, the path and method mentioned [in this work] was threaded on the string by a *silsila* such as this, and this blessing was passed down, hand to hand, until it reached our own shaykh. If the seeker wants God's path and the way of the Muhammadan Shariah, he should study this treatise. Hopefully, he will lift the veil from the beauty of the object of his quest and his beloved. . . .
>
> O friend, in the path of realization, the traveler must find these four levels of existence in his own existence and he must arrive at them. He must pass, level by level, until he reaches the gnosis of the Essence of the Real—glory be to Him, and high exalted is He!

However, each existence has conditions and necessities. Therefore, each existence has been written down in a table and each has been explained. The traveler must know all the conditions and put them into practice so that he may reach his goal.

Now, if God gives success, let me elucidate the existences and explain their conditions. Thereby the reality of "He who knows himself knows his Lord" will be clarified for the seeker in the most beautiful manner.

I will depict the four existences of "He who knows himself" in four rectangular tables [i.e., Tables 1–4] to indicate directions, place, and time. Then the fifth table will be the circle of "knows his Lord." This is the circle of nonentification, nondirectionality, no-place, and no-time. This is the One of Existence, which is the Absolute Essence of the Creator.

Although the terms *necessary, possible,* and *impossible* pertain to standard philosophical and theological vocabulary, they are redefined in the work. Clearly, the Bijapur Sufis wanted to appropriate familiar terms, but they were not especially concerned to use them in the usual meanings. Thus the term *necessary in existence* normally refers to God, who *is* and cannot not be, but in the first table and in the circle, it has a completely different sense. Shaykh Maḥmūd himself explains the two meanings of the term. First, he tells us, the Necessary in Existence is God, who "abides through Himself for all eternity. He has no changing, no alteration, no new arrival, and no annihilation. He is *the Living, the Self-Abiding* [2:255], while the existence of all existent things abides through Him." Then he explains that his master, Burhān al-Dīn Jānam, applied the term to "the earthy, human existence" (*wujūd-i khākī-yi insānī*), and he explains the rationale for this as follows:

> This earthy, elemental, human existence is the necessary in existence [*wājib al-wujūd*], which is to say that it is the indispensable in existence [*lāzim al-wujūd*], because this corporeal existence is necessary and indispensable for the existence of the spirit. After all, without this corporeal existence, the spirit could not depart from the world of the unseen [*ʿālam-i ghayb*] to become manifest in the world of witnessing [*ʿālam-i shuhūd*]. If there were no corporeal existence, the spirit would remain hidden in the world of the unseen. This is because, although the spirit was created on the Day of the Covenant before this corporeal existence—for, as the hadith tells us, "God created the spirits 40,000 years before the bodies"—without this earthy existence, the spirit would not be able to gain a gnosis through which it knows the Real with all His attributes and perfections.
>
> Thus, for example, although the receptivity for the whole tree is found in the seed, if the seed is not planted in the ground, the receptivity will not become manifest and the tree will not come to

exist. Hence, God created the frame of Adam and He made the spirit of the Covenant descend into it. When the spirit and the frame were paired, the true existence became manifest from their junction as a receptacle for the Divine Essence and attributes. This is the reality of the heart's substance.

After explaining that Adam's reception of knowledge from God—when God taught him all the names—was made possible only by the heart, the Shaykh concludes this discussion by repeating that this usage of the term *necessary in existence* pertains specifically to his shaykh's technical terminology. Otherwise, he says, if someone were to say that the earthy body is the Necessary in Existence, meaning the Essence of God, that would be blatant unbelief.

The second table pertains to *mumkin al-wujūd*, the *possible in existence*. Normally, this term is applied to everything other than God that is not strictly impossible. In this sense, the term indicates that nothing but God has any claim on existence. When we consider any given thing in and of itself, we cannot say that it must exist—only God has that attribute because only God is identical with *wujūd* itself. The things, in terms of their own realities, may or may not come to exist. Their coming to be depends absolutely upon the Necessary in Existence. Here, however, Shaykh Maḥmūd applies the term "possible in existence" to the second level of the ascending arc to God. Although he refers to it as "spiritual existence," it in fact corresponds to the lower realms of the unseen world or to the "world of imagination," which lies between the world of bodies and the world of spirits. I quote Shaykh Maḥmūd's own explanation of why his shaykh, Burhān al-Dīn, employed the term *mumkin al-wujūd* in this sense:

> O friend, let me tell you the whole of the true knowledge and the reality of the possible in existence so that this existence will become plain to you. Through it you may set out on the path of the Tariqah and through this possible in existence you may give indications of the way station of the sovereignty [*malakūt*] with all its conditions.
>
> O traveler, the term "possible in existence" is used for that which does not abide through its own existence. Sometimes it is and sometimes it is not within the [creative] command of the Real. It is the existence of everything in the cosmos, from body to spirit and from [earthly] carpet to [Divine] Throne. This possible in existence abides through the Essence of the Real, but the Necessary in Existence that is God's abides through its own Essence, and He does not change, neither in His Essence nor in His attributes.
>
> Then, O friend, in his technical terminology, our shaykh named spiritual existence "the possible in existence." Within this earthy body, this spiritual existence takes the form and the shape of this same earthy body. It is this that becomes separate from the body during

sleep. It is also called the "flowing spirit" [*rūḥ-i jārī*]. Thus it has been said, "The spirit is two—the flowing spirit and the abiding spirit." This flowing spirit is precisely the possible in existence that I mentioned. It was created at the time of the Covenant. The question, *"Am I not your Lord?"* [7:172], reached this very spirit, and the answer, *"Yes indeed,"* was heard from this spirit. . . .

This spirit is called "the possible in existence" because it also does not abide through itself, but rather through the abiding spirit, and the abiding spirit is the holy spirit. The holy spirit is the ray of God's Essence, and it came to be settled at His command, as will be explained. The holy spirit abides through itself. Like the ocean, it is infinite; it does not slip and does not move. This [holy] spirit, which is the ray of the Necessary's Essence, is just like the Necessary. Hence, the possible in existence is the connection to that holy spirit.

O friend, the possible in existence is in the inner domain through form, for you will be correct to see it along with all the organs. The earthy existence has motion from this [possible] existence, and it constantly flows in a journey, without your command, going in accordance with the ancient habit.

O traveler, whatever form appears in your own inner domain—whether it is your form or the form of another—is the possible in existence. This is because the possible thing has two aspects, since it both comes into being and it turns into nothing, while it does not abide through itself. Thus it abides through the holy spirit. The holy spirit stands in the place of the Necessary, while the form stands in the place of the possible.

The place of the possible in existence is the heart, by which I mean every passing thought [*khaṭara*] that assumes form in the inner human domain, and this inner domain will be the heart since the form appears in the heart.

This place is also called "limpidness," for our shaykh said, "The elemental, necessary in existence is in the air, and the spiritual, possible in existence is in the limpidness." So, O friend, the spiritual, possible in existence journeys in the world of limpidness, just like wind, which goes through the power of Seraphiel.

At the beginning of the third table, Shaykh Maḥmūd discusses "the impossible in existence." The usual example given by the theologians for an impossible thing is an associate for God. Shaykh Maḥmūd explains that the specific meaning he has in mind for the term corresponds with what is often called the "world of the spirits"—the highest of the three created worlds—though the rationale for his use of the term in this sense is not as clear as it was in the two previous examples:

O traveler on the path, the literal reality of "the impossible in existence" is that in which nothing has existence. In other words, it withholds forms from the things. This impossible in existence is an associate for the Creator, just as has been written in the books.

It is well-known that the existences are of three sorts: first the Necessary in Existence, second the possible in existence, and third the impossible in existence. The first two were explained briefly earlier. As for the impossible in existence, it is the fact that, in eternity without beginning, nothing except the Essence of God had existence. In other words, there was only the Essence of God.

So, you should know that the Being [*hastī*] of the Real's Essence demands nonbeing [*nīstī*] since, other than God's Essence, there is nothing. This "nonbeing" is the impossible in existence, which is the existence that abides neither through itself nor through the other. It has no mode [*iʿtibār*].

It is the impossible in existence that is called "no place" [*lā makān*] and that is neither the Essence nor the relation of the attributes. It is the place of all things, since all the existent things and all the possible things of both worlds appeared within this impossible in existence.

So understand, O traveler, what this impossible in existence is within yourself in keeping with "He who knows himself knows his Lord," for our shaykh explained it after having explained the possible in existence. You must find it within yourself, while it is *not*. Once you have heard the explanation of the possible in existence, which is the moving force within the earthy body, you must cast it far from your gaze. Instead, you must gaze until you give no movement to any of your own outward or inward passing thoughts. You must remain steady, as a still witnesser [*shāhid-i sākin*]. Once this state has been turned over to you, you will have joined with the impossible in existence of yourself, which is a ray of the impossible in existence of the Real. Within this existence is the holy spirit, and this being is the ray of the Real's Being.

O traveler, the impossible in existence and the being of the spirit are not separate from each other. On the contrary, the impossible in existence is identical with the holy spirit's being, just like, for example, fire and the heat of fire, for these two are not separate from each other. Understand this, for the heat of fire does not allow anything to arrive in the fire—such as scorpions, gnats, flies, ants, and various crawling things—without burning it as soon as it arrives. So, know that the heat is the majesty [*jalāliyya*] of the fire, or rather, it is identical with the fire.

O traveler, the holy spirit has a majesty such that it lets no passing thought of the heart come into it. It is said that this majesty that belongs to being is the impossible in existence. The being of the holy spirit stands in the place of the Real's Being, while this [majesty] stands in the place of the impossible. Understand this, for it is a marvelous, subtle intimation and the allusion of the perfect spiritual guide [*murshid*]. Grasp it well within yourself, for "He who knows himself knows his Lord."

In such a way does the Essence of the Necessary abide in Itself through Itself, and through Its own "impossible in existence" It has made all the existent things appear within this impossible in existence. Understand!

The fourth table pertains to fully actualized self-knowledge and self-awareness, above even the world of the spirits. Perhaps it corresponds to what, in Ibn al-ʿArabī's terms, would be the self-knowledge gained by the greatest of the Sufis when they know their own fixed and uncreated entity, just as it is known by God for all eternity. It is this fixed entity that responds to God's command to come into existence. Then spirit, imagination, and body represent its three basic levels of manifestation. Shaykh Maḥmūd writes as follows:

> The term "gnostic in existence" is used for him who knows his own existence. In other words, it is the being [*hastī*] that knows itself. This is the being that is knowing and free from all beings. This being itself abides in God's command, while the mentioned necessary, possible, and impossible beings abide through the gnostic in existence. They have need of it, but it is totally independent of them. . . .
>
> This existence is like and similar to the nondelimitation of the being of the Real, which is free and holy beyond all the possible existences. . . . O traveler . . . find in your own existence the gnostic in existence and recognize it so that you may find and recognize God as nondelimited. This level consists of "He who knows himself knows his Lord."

In explaining the circle, which summarizes the previous four tables and adds the all-inclusive level of unity, or *waḥdat al-wujūd,* Shaykh Maḥmūd begins as follows:

> The fifth diagram is named "the One of Existence." In other words, the diagram of the previous existences was drawn from this diagram in respect of the descent and manifestation of the One Existence of the Real. This diagram is the center and circumference of all the circles, and all the circles go back to it. This is because the necessary in existence abides through the possible in existence, the possible in existence abides through the impossible in existence, the impossible in existence abides through the gnostic of existence, the gnostic of

> existence abides through the One of Existence, and the One of Existence abides through Itself. Hence, the reality of all the circles goes back to It.
>
> Every allusion written in those diagrams is also explained in this circle in keeping with the technical terminology of each sort. In order to explain in each case these technical terms, which are the language of the Sufis, the technical term of each level has been explained in eight sorts, in keeping with the eight paradises. In each term, five levels are explained, similar to the five treasures that become manifest from the storehouse of "I was a Hidden Treasure." . . .[4]
>
> Know also that each technical term is found in the path of a road through which one can reach one's own root, in keeping with "The paths to God are in the number of the breaths of the creatures." Thus each term and each road that is mentioned leads to the fifth circle, and the fifth circle is named "the One of Existence," since nothing except the Holy Essence can be called "the One of Existence," given that He is One through His own existence and He abides through His own Essence. He is One with no associate. . . .
>
> [Once the traveler passes beyond the first four circles], he reaches the fifth diagram, which is the One of Existence and which has no direction, no time, and no place. It is undelimited by any sort of binding and nonentified by any sort of entification. This is why the diagram was drawn as a circle, but those four diagrams, since they are connected with time, space, direction, and entification, were drawn as rectangles. However, when one looks at the first four diagrams from the last diagram with a gaze of nonentification, those four diagrams also appear as circular and nonentified. This is why those four circles have been drawn around the circle of the One of Existence, just like the circle of the One of Existence. Thus the traveler will be able to find the One of Existence in each circle. After all, when the traveler passes beyond the levels of the entifications and reaches the level of nonentification, he sees all the levels as nonentification. Since the form of nonentification cannot be understood save as a circle, all five tables have been drawn as circles.

After having explained why the central circle is called by eight different names, Shaykh Maḥmūd proceeds to explain each of the eight sectors in terms of the descent from the center to the circumference. Thus, concerning "existence," he writes as follows:

> Know, O traveler, that if the fifth circle is considered in terms of the technical language of existence, then it is called "the One of Existence." This is because the traveler, after wayfaring through the four

existences, will arrive at the fifth existence, which is the Essence of the Real. . . . There he will not see anything as present. All the external things, which are outside the Essence, will appear as obliterated in obliteration, annihilated in annihilation, and nonexistent in nonexistence. [Nothing will appear] save the Essence, which abides through Itself and causes all things to abide through Its attributes—whether this is called the One of Existence or the Necessary in Existence. After all, the Essence is One Being that abides in Itself through Itself, and this perfection of attribute is worthy for It.

Then, through the ray of His own One Existence, the One brought the gnostic of existence into existence. It is the Muhammadan Light, as defined earlier. Then, through the being of the gnostic of existence, a nonbeing appeared, and that nonbeing, which is the impossible in existence, made the possible in existence manifest. From the possible in existence, the necessary in existence appeared.

Thus the necessary in existence is the locus of manifestation for the possible in existence, the possible in existence the locus of manifestation for the impossible in existence, the impossible in existence the locus of manifestation for the gnostic of existence, and the gnostic of existence the locus of manifestation for the One of Existence.

O traveler, whenever someone finds the One of Existence, by the same token he will find the locus of manifestation that is the earthy, necessary in existence, as explained earlier.

Know also that although we discussed the necessary in existence that pertains to earth in terms of the human being, the verified truth is that everything included among the kinds of corporeal things is necessary in existence in keeping with the existence of that thing. This necessary in existence then entails a possible in existence, which entails an impossible in existence. Within the last a gnostic of existence is concealed—however, it is concealed in the thing in keeping with the thing's entification. Whether things be plants, inanimate objects, or animals, these four existences are within them. However, they do not become manifest save in the existence of the human individual, who is a receptacle for the Essence and attributes of the Divinity. . . .

O traveler, it was said that "The paths to God are in the number of the breaths of the creatures." This is a meaning of which nothing's existence is empty. In each thing, these four existences are concealed. When God gives this existence awareness and self-knowledge, it finds the One of Existence, which is God, in its own existence. It has no need for any other existence, for it will not see God's Essence in anything else, only in its own existence. This is the reality of "He who knows himself knows his Lord." Everyone must seek God in his own self so that he may find Him—whatever sort the seeker may be, whether jinn, human being, plant, or animal. "The paths to God are in the number of the breaths of the creatures." In every existence there is a path to God by which it can reach God.

Know, O traveler, that the encompassment of all existences by the One of Existence will be gained when the traveler reaches and recognizes the One of Existence. Just as he is the gnostic of his own existence and sees himself as encompassing all his parts, so will he see the Real as encompassing the whole universe, while no veil appears in the midst. He will gaze on nothing but the Essence of the existence of perfection, which has permeated the existence of the things through the self-disclosures in the species. Sometimes he will see the One of Existence identical with the gnostic of existence and the gnostic of existence identical with the One of Existence. Sometimes he will witness the gnostic of existence in the One of Existence, sometimes the possible in existence in the impossible in existence, the impossible in existence in the possible in existence, the possible in existence in the necessary in existence, and the necessary in existence in the possible in existence. Sometimes he will see all this as identical with the One of Existence, and sometimes he will see the One of Existence identical with all this. . . . Such is gazing upon the unity of the Essence—majestic is His majesty and all-inclusive are His gifts!

This then is a brief introduction to the elaborate and coherent synthesis of Sufi teachings offered by Shaykh Maḥmūd Khwush-Dahān. I hope that before long the opportunity will arise to provide a complete translation and analysis of the treatise. But more strongly, I hope that other scholars will take a closer look at some of the riches of the Sufi tradition that are now moldering in the libraries of the Indian Subcontinent.

III

Islamic Philosophy

17

Rūmī and the Wooden Leg of Reason

I was prompted to reflect on the role of "reason" in Rūmī's thought by the enormous popularity of his poetry in North America and the widespread habit of misinterpreting his teachings. Rūmī's popularity has its roots in the scholarly translations of Nicholson and A. J. Arberry. But the "Rūmī boom" itself is indebted to a number of talented American poets who recognized a mine of gold when they saw it. They took the ore provided by the scholars and reworked it into contemporary English poetry, often without any knowledge of the Persian language or the intellectual and spiritual tradition that Rūmī represents.

In my profession as a scholar of Islamic studies, I am often asked about the quality of these translations. I reply that most of them—although not all—are inaccurate and inept. The reason for this is simply that, generally speaking, the translators fail to bring out both the literal meaning and the deeper implications of what Rūmī is saying. It is true that they often display sparks of Rūmī's fire, and this helps explain why they have become so popular. But, for those who understand the Persian language—and even more so for those who are familiar with the worldview that animates Rūmī's poetry—the translations are lame. They remind me of a famous verse from the *Mathnawī*:

> The leg of the reasoners is wooden—
> a wooden leg is awfully unsteady.[1]

Well, the leg of the translators is much more unsteady than that of the reasoners. This is largely because the translators are unfamiliar with the universe of discourse that was articulated by the very same reasoners whose wooden leg Rūmī criticizes. When Rūmī tells us that the leg of the reasoners is wooden, notice that he is talking about their "leg." He is not saying that rational thought is useless. He is not objecting to the organized and even organismic vision of reality that was expressed in Islamic philosophy, the home of logic and systematic rational discourse. Rather, he is criticizing those who think that analysis, investigation, rational argumentation, and scientific proofs provide a leg strong enough to reach the goal of human life.

The key issue for Rūmī is "reaching the goal of human life." Here we need to remember that he was speaking within the context of the Islamic tradition, for which that goal was clear, even though the language in which it was expressed in different schools of thought could be quite diverse. The Hellenizing philosophers, who are precisely the great logicians and reasoners, had no basic disagreement with Rūmī on the issue of the goal of life.

So, what is this goal of human life? All the Muslim philosophers held that it is to reach the perfection of what is humanly possible, a perfection that stands beyond ordinary experience and awareness just as the sun stands beyond the moon. If Rūmī objects to the philosophical expression of this goal, it is simply because, in his view, rational thought and careful logic cannot provide the energizing power to achieve it. The Muslim philosophers and theologians tend to get bogged down in honing their methodologies. Too often they maintain that human perfection cannot be achieved without the specific, rationalistic tools that they themselves developed on the basis of the Greek tradition. Rūmī simply replies that their methodology is no leg with which to climb mountains. He calls Avicenna "a donkey on ice."[2] The only leg that can take the seeker to the top of the icy mountain of transcendence is the transforming fire of love.

What I stress here is that asserting the unsteadiness of the leg is not the same as denying the truth of the worldview articulated and systematized by the philosophical tradition. The proof of this is that Rūmī himself speaks for this worldview, although in a language transfigured by poetical imagery.

My foremost guide in the study of Rūmī, the late Annemarie Schimmel, has criticized me here—in print and in friendly banter—for suggesting that Rūmī considers the intellect (*ʿaql*) not only an important tool but even a necessary asset on the path to God. I reply that the proof lies in the numerous verses that Rūmī devotes to achieving the fullness of intelligence. We cannot pretend that these verses become dead letters when other verses tell us to throw away our rational thinking. Moreover, the very fact that Rūmī devotes many verses to playing down reason and playing up love indicates that intellectual understanding was a primary focus among his contemporaries and his own disciples. Rūmī was no exception to the rule that Franz Rosenthal has enunciated in his fine study of the role of knowledge and rationality in Islamic civilization, *Knowledge Triumphant*. He was not opposed to rational thought per se, as he tells us repeatedly. He simply wanted to insist that reason and intelligence cannot supply the energy needed to traverse the path to God.

Rūmī clarifies the necessary role of rationality in several passages in which he compares the intellect to the angel Gabriel, who guided the Prophet on the night journey to God. The Prophet could not have traveled up through the celestial spheres without Gabriel to show him the way. In Rūmī's depiction, Gabriel in the outside world plays the same role as the intellect in the inside world. Muhammad himself, the greatest of the prophets, needed Gabriel to guide him on the ascent to God. At the very least, this shows that others need to have some understanding of the nature of things if they are to escape from egocentricity and short-sightedness.

I do not want to deny that in Rūmī's view, love plays the most important role in the path to God. Love alone is able to provide the power to put a correct understanding of things into practice. The intellect can only take the traveler so far, and then love must take charge completely. When Gabriel took Muhammad as far as the Lote Tree of the Far Boundary, he told him that he would have to ascend the rest of the way to God by himself. If Gabriel tried to accompany him, his wings would burn off.

In short, the intellect and a correct understanding of things can take you only as far as the Lote Tree. But that is nothing to be sneezed at, because the Lote Tree symbolizes the furthest reaches of creation, understanding, awareness, and everything that can be grasped by human consciousness. If Gabriel is needed for the Prophet to reach the Lote Tree, this means that intelligence and correct understanding are needed for seekers to reach the borderline between time and eternity. Only the intellect, which is the divine light innate within each human being, makes possible the understanding that reality is one, and that everything other than God is a veil and an illusion. Nonetheless, not even intellectual vision, the highest sort of vision in the universe, can take the seeker into God's own Presence.

One more point needs to be remembered in any discussion of the intellect in Islamic texts. This is the distinction between what Rūmī frequently calls *ʿaql-i juzwī* and *ʿaql-i kullī*, the "partial intellect" and "Universal Intellect."[3] The intellect, Rūmī tells us, was created from the same light as the angels, but our intellects are only partial because they have become dimmed and obscured. Although illumined by angelic light, the partial intellect is blinded by the pride and self-interest of the human ego. The partial intellect relies upon its own cleverness, not upon God. In this it takes after its mentor, Iblīs. Iblīs is very much the self-reliant sort who figures that he does not need help from anyone—certainly not from the prophets, who are only followed by gullible believers.

If seekers of God are to escape ignorance, delusion, and egocentricity, they must find the light of the Universal Intellect, which becomes embodied in the outside world as the angel Gabriel. It is Gabriel who brings God's revelations to the prophets in the first place, and it is he who guides them and their followers on the path that takes them back to God. In the Islamic universe, Gabriel plays a central role both in revelation and in the spiritual journey, that is, both in the descent of wisdom from God and in the ascent of the soul to God. He was the means whereby the Koran was revealed, and likewise he was the Prophet's guide on the *miʿrāj*. Like other Muslims, Rūmī understands this to mean that there is no way to God except by means of the guidance that is given to the prophets. The Koran represents the divine roadmap, and the Sunnah represents the actual journey to the goal. There can be no individualistic, do-it-yourself spirituality in Rūmī's universe.

In short, Rūmī holds that the search for knowledge and understanding plays a fundamental role in any search for God. However, we need to distinguish between two sorts of knowledge. For purposes of this discussion, I label one of them *visionary* and the other *rational*. Visionary knowledge is the illumination that comes directly from the Universal Intellect. Rational knowledge is the obscured light known as the "partial intellect." There can be no ascent to God without visionary knowledge, and this is because such knowledge is identical with the divine light that is embodied in Gabriel, the source of wisdom and the guide on the path. As Rūmī says:

> Not every wing can fly across the ocean—
> only knowledge directly *from* Him takes you *to* Him.[4]

As for rational knowledge, it derives from the obscured light of the partial intellect. It acts more as a hindrance than as a help because it is deeply mired in the shortcomings of the individual ego. This is why Rūmī constantly tells his readers to forget their own ideas of the way things are and to surrender to the wisdom of the prophets and saints.[5]

Having suggested why, in Rūmī's view, a proper understanding of things is essential to human well-being, let me focus on how proper understanding comes to be articulated. The primary focus of the Muslim philosophers is to describe and explain the three fundamental domains of reality. These are God, the universe, and the human soul. The discussion of these domains goes on in three subdisciplines of philosophy, which can be called "metaphysics," "cosmology," and "psychology." Metaphysics deals with ultimate Reality, cosmology addresses the status of the universe from its beginning to its end, and psychology explains the origin and destiny of the human soul.

It needs to be kept in mind that all three of these fields have largely been abandoned in modern times. I do not mean that the words are not used. I mean that what goes by these names today has little if anything to do with what was being discussed in Rūmī's time, whether in the Islamic world or in the West (not to mention the rest of the world). Nonetheless, these disciplines inform the intellectual vision that lies behind Rūmī's depiction of God, the universe, and the human soul.

Even in the best of contemporary scholarship on Rūmī, there is often an assumption that his teachings about the universe and its intimate interrelationships with the human soul are window-dressing. The general picture drawn in the secondary literature and taken for granted in the many poetical translations is that we can ignore all the medieval ideas. After all, it is implied, not only have they been proven false from the seventeenth century onward, but Rūmī is also speaking about love, not about systematic, rationalistic knowledge.

The net result of this attitude is that many if not most interpreters of Rūmī have used his criticisms of rational knowledge to reject the whole body of metaphysical, cosmological, and psychological teachings that inform his vision of things. This might have had some justification if the interpreters were not themselves deeply rooted in a different view of the world, a view that is also systematic and rationalistic but, at the same time, profoundly antagonistic to almost everything that Rūmī held as self-evidently true.

One result of ignoring Rūmī's worldview is that many of his interpreters think that there is no contradiction between being rational and scientific (as we understand these terms today) and being "spiritual." I think Rūmī would reply that you cannot have one mental compartment for scientific knowledge and another for love of God. The human spirit—also called the "human heart"—is a single reality with no partitions. In order for the heart to open itself up to God, it must have a proper knowledge of what it is opening itself up to. You cannot love what you do not know. Moreover, all knowledge of God is built on our knowledge of the world and ourselves. If we do not understand the world and ourselves as they are, we will not be able to know God as He is, and without knowing Him, we cannot love Him.

In short, the heart needs to see things as they truly are, and this means that it must see things as Gabriel, the Universal Intellect, calls it to see them. Seeing things in terms of the cleverness of the partial intellect blocks the road of love. As Rūmī puts it:

> The partial intellect is a vulture, you poor wretch.
>   Its wings are bound up with carrion-eating.
> The intellect of the saints is like Gabriel's wing.
>   It flies, mile by mile, to the shadow of the Lote Tree.[6]

In Rūmī's view and in the view of the Islamic wisdom tradition in general, the unitary light of intelligence cannot be divided. It can only be dimmed and obscured. The spiritual quest involves successive stages of climbing the ladder to God, an ascent that is prefigured mythically in the Prophet's *miʿrāj*. At each step on the ascending ladder, the light of the Universal Intellect, which is innate in every human being, is intensified. At the earliest stages, which are infancy and childhood, the intellectual light is hardly more than a potentiality. Rūmī tells us that in actualizing the innate light, one person is like a spark, another like a candle, another like a lamp, another like a star, another like the moon, and still another like the midday sun. Only the human selfhood that has actualized the blazing sun of noon can be said to be an "intellect" in the full and proper sense of the word. This noonday sun is embodied in Gabriel, and it has been fully actualized on the human level only by the prophets and some of the saints.

In Rūmī's way of looking at things, intellect and angel are the internal and external manifestations of a single, unified reality. This single reality is God's radiance, or God's spirit. In contrast, the ego—which is our normal, everyday self-awareness—partakes of the darkness that dominates over animal nature, if not of the rebellious fire that inspires Satan. Our human situation represents the marriage of angelic light and animal darkness, or angel and devil. The purpose of life is to help the angel overcome the devil. In the *Fīhi mā fīhi*, Rūmī makes these points as follows:

> The states of human beings are as if an angel's wing were brought and stuck on a donkey's tail so that perhaps the donkey, through the radiance and companionship of the angel, may itself become an angel. It is possible for the donkey to become the same color as the angel.[7]

So, human beings are donkeys who have lost sight of their angelic nature. Their task is to see beyond asininity and find the angel's wing. Gradually, with the help of the wing, they can be transformed into something like angels. Only then can they fly, stage by stage, to the heavens. When they have become the same color as the angel itself, that is when they will have reached the top of the created realm. Only then can love work its full miracle.

In this perspective—which is common to the Islamic wisdom tradition—spiritual transformation builds on the innate light of intelligence. Given that this vision of human psychology is rejected by many (if not most) moderns and postmoderns, it is especially difficult to keep in mind that it underlies everything Rūmī is saying. According to him, our only means to happiness and salvation lies in Gabriel's wing. As long as we insist on being asses, we will have no leg with which to climb the icy mountain of transcendence and will never reach the Lote Tree of the Far Boundary, much less move on further and encounter God Himself.

As soon as we acknowledge that this is Rūmī's view of human nature, it should not be difficult to guess how Rūmī would react to the whole edifice of contemporary learning. He would see it as a grand monument to asininity. It can be nothing else, because it is built on the accumulated light of a myriad of partial intellects—or, as he might say, "vultures." No matter how many sparks you gather together, you cannot reconstruct the blazing sun of noon.

The very fact that academic disciplines are constantly being partitioned into ever narrower specialties should be enough to alert us to the fact that what we consider to be learning today has little if anything to do with the unifying light of what Rūmī calls the "Universal Intellect." In fact, the vast majority of scientists and scholars have no idea what is going on in other than their own narrow specialties. Even the best of scholars cannot have a real overview of the total situation. Those who try to do so have no authority, because they have given up all the exact and precise knowledge that bestows upon modern learning its specificity and particularity. Outside their own narrow specialties, they can only speak in vague, unscientific terms.

In contrast, the metaphysics, cosmology, and psychology of the ancients and the medievals were in fact three subdivisions of one, unitary knowledge. The more one understood any of these disciplines, the more one understood the others as well. Each of them fed into a synthetic vision. If we can take the texts at their word, that synthetic vision is simply the awareness of the nature of things, an awareness that is innate to human intelligence.

One of the many theological arguments for the unitary consciousness found in all human beings is the Koranic idea that God taught Adam all the names. As Rūmī puts it:

> The father of mankind, who is the lord of *He taught* [Adam] *the names* [2:31],
> has hundreds of thousands of sciences in every vein.
> The name of each thing, just as it is
> until its end, was given to his spirit. . . .
> Since Adam's eye saw with the pure light,
> the spirit and mystery of each name was clear to him.[8]

Having suggested some of the difficulties connected with trying to understand Rūmī in terms of current wisdom, let me turn to the issue of understanding him in terms of the sciences of his own day. We know that Rūmī considered the leg of reasoners to be wooden. Did he mean that the knowledge and learning of the reasoners was invalid, illegitimate, and, in one word, untrue? I do not think so. From the many passages that Rūmī devotes to the sciences, we can conclude that he accepted the learning of his day as a valid mode of seeing "with the pure light." However, he maintained that knowledge and learning have a clear purpose, and that purpose is certainly *not* to keep us comfortable in our everyday life. Rather, the purpose of learning is to act as a support for the real business. The real business is love, and love is total dedication to God and nothing else. The sciences were true because they provided an adequate picture of the world and the human soul. With that picture as guide, one can grasp the nature of the true object of love and devote one's energy to it.

In support of this reading, let me cite a single passage from the *Fīhi mā fīhi*. In it, Rūmī answers the concerns of certain people who are hesitating about entering the spiritual path because they fear that all of their learning will come to nothing. He says:

> These people who have studied or who are now studying imagine that if they keep on attending here, they will forget knowledge and abandon it. On the contrary, when they come here, all their sciences come to life. The sciences are all paintings. When they come to life, it is as if a lifeless body has come to life. The root of all these sciences is Up Yonder, but they have been transferred from the world without sounds and letters to the world of sounds and letters.[9]

In this passage, the word "knowledge" renders the Arabic *ʿilm*, and "sciences" renders *ʿilm-hā*, its Persian plural. A modern reader of this passage would typically assume that in Rūmī's view, there is no contradiction between love for God and science, because love gives spiritual life to all knowledge, and science is certainly knowledge. It would follow that the science and learning that we pick up from our schools, our universities, and *The New York Times* can all be given spiritual life.

However, such a reading would be superficial, because it fails to take into account what Rūmī means by *ʿilm*. I think I have said enough already to suggest that in Rūmī's view, our type of knowledge, which is based exclusively on the ingenuity and pretensions of the partial intellect, would not qualify as real knowledge. Rūmī would consider the world that we have carved out for ourselves in our scientific and academic disciplines to be just like the apple that he describes in the *Mathnawī*. That makes us the apple's worms, happy in our belief that we know ever so much more than our poor benighted ancestors.

One might reply that the learning we possess today is no tiny apple, because it embraces a vastness undreamed of by the ancients or the medievals. But, no matter how big we think the apple is, its very divisibility and physicality make it tiny in comparison to the tree of knowledge and the Gardener who planted and gives access to that tree. Moreover, our apple is even smaller than the partial intellect that sees it. After all, it is our own intelligence that has come up with this picture of knowledge. We discovered the picture in ourselves, in precisely the place where we understood it. What many of us consider "knowledge" today is a painting that we have drawn in our minds, which depicts something of our own immensity. Nonetheless, from Rūmī's point of view, no matter what the scope of the partial intellect, it cannot begin to understand the reality of the conscious, intelligent, and intelligible light that is shining in its own depths.

Rūmī has many verses in which he reminds us of a basic point of the Islamic perspective: Intelligence and thought are not derivative of the body. On the contrary, the bodily realm and indeed the whole universe are epiphenomena of the Universal Intellect. Take, for example, these verses from the *Mathnawī*:

> In your eyes the world is frightful and mighty—
> you fear and tremble at clouds, thunder, and sky.
> You stay secure and heedless from the world of thought.
> Less than an ass, you're like an unaware stone.
> You're merely a painted picture, with no share of intelligence.
> You've got no human traits, you're just a young ass.
> In ignorance you see the shadow as the object,
> so you think the object a game and a trifle.
> Wait—until the day when thought and imagination
> spread their feathers and wings without veil!
> You will see mountains become soft wool,
> and this hot and cold earth will cease to exist.
> You will see neither heaven, nor the stars, nor existence—
> only the Living, Loving, One God.[10]

What then is Rūmī talking about when he speaks of knowledge, and when he says that the sciences are paintings of what exists Up Yonder? By knowledge, he means the whole tradition of transmitted and intellectual learning that was studied among the Muslims. The transmitted learning goes back to the Koran and the sayings of Muhammad. The intellectual learning goes back to the same place, but it also builds on the philosophy and science of several other traditions, most prominently the Greek. Both the intellectual and transmitted learning are rooted in Gabriel's wing. Remember that in the Koranic view of things, God sent revelation to all peoples, which is to say Gabriel appeared among the ancients just as he appeared to Muhammad.

For Rūmī, the worldview articulated by Islamic philosophy is true, even if he would surely object to some of its tenets. To say that a worldview is true is to say that the picture it draws is an adequate representation of the objects to be found Up Yonder. "Up Yonder" is the world of the Universal Intellect, or the world of God's own omniscience. When Rūmī speaks of bringing knowledge to life by awakening the spirit within, he means to say that if the partial intellect is shaped by an adequate understanding of the nature of things, then and then alone can the angel's wing lift the donkey beyond its limitations and carry it into the infinite expanse Up Yonder, which is the realm of light, awareness, consciousness, and love.

18

Bābā Afḍal's Psychology

Bābā Afḍal, also known as Afḍal al-Dīn Kāshānī, most likely died in the year 606/1210. This makes him a contemporary of Suhrawardī, Averroes (d. 595/1198), and Ibn al-ʿArabī. He taught and died in the village of Maraq, a few kilometers distant from Kashan in central Iran. Most of what little we know about him comes from his own writings, which only contain a few autobiographical references.

What becomes clear from Bābā Afḍal's writings is that he is one of the great stylists of the Persian language. Some scholars, myself included, consider his philosophical prose to be the most concise and beautiful in the language of philosophy. But why did he write in Persian in the first place, given that he was also a master of Arabic, the philosophical language par excellence? The answer is that, in contrast to the norm, he was not writing for other philosophers or scholars, but rather for a group of dedicated students. We know this partly because he left behind six rather lengthy letters to some of his students, and these letters show that a good number of people used to come to his village to study philosophy with him.

It is this peculiarity of Bābā Afḍal—the fact that he was writing for non-philosophers—that makes him especially relevant today. Philosophers then and now are not necessarily clear and direct in what they want to say. Needing to attend to the arguments of their important predecessors and to fend off the objections of their critics, they go on and on and never quite get to the point. Bābā Afḍal, on the other hand, tries to make the reflective life available to a group of people lacking in the usual training, and he gets to the point rather quickly.

When I say that Bābā Afḍal's students were not philosophers or scholars, I do not mean that they were ignorant or uneducated. Rather, they were busy with the active life and did not have specialized training in philosophy. Why then did they come to Bābā Afḍal to study? The reason has everything to do with what philosophy was thought to be. It was lost on no one that philosophy is the search for wisdom, and that wisdom is a highly desirable trait. The Koran tells us, for example, that *He who has been given wisdom has been given much good*

(2:269). Even today, many students—whom their professors usually consider a bit naïve—take courses in philosophy because they think it will provide them with the answers to the big questions in life.

For Bābā Afḍal and those who came to him, philosophy was not simply an academic discipline. Rather, it was—to use Pierre Hadot's phrase in reference to the Greek tradition—a "spiritual exercise."[2] Wisdom (*ḥikma*) was defined as knowledge of things as they truly are along with activity appropriate to that knowledge. Wisdom, in other words, demands not only correct knowledge of things but also good and virtuous activity. This is why Bābā Afḍal stresses the practical goal of the philosophical quest in all his writings.

Although few of the better-known Muslim philosophers would have disagreed with Bābā Afḍal's basic position, they seem to have felt that the philosopher, as the knower of all things, needs to write about practically everything. Thus, after setting down the goal of philosophy, they tended to obscure it by addressing numerous preliminary steps and analyzing all the logical, linguistic, and mathematical tools that are necessary to achieve the goal.

What, then, is the goal? As I said, it is to know things as they are and to act appropriately. Bābā Afḍal takes the position that the one knowledge upon which the whole philosophical quest depends is knowledge of oneself. If seekers of wisdom can differentiate themselves from the world and situate themselves in the grand picture, it will be possible for them to actualize the perfections that are latent in the human soul and become completely human. One of the results of achieving these latent perfections will be to recognize and experience the immortality of the soul already in this life.

Immortality

That immortality was a human possibility was of course a common philosophical position among the premoderns. Generally speaking, the Aristotelians, who were enormously influential on much of Islamic philosophy, held that the soul attained immortality only inasmuch as it actualized its intellectual nature. To the degree that it remained a potential intellect, the soul was held back from everlastingness. Avicenna, however, took the position that the soul is immortal by nature, and thus he joined the mainstream of the religious tradition.

The whole discussion of immortality hangs on definitions. Especially important here are the words "body," "soul," and "intellect." For Bābā Afḍal and many others, if one can simply understand the meanings of these terms and then discern their realities within oneself, one has taken a large step toward achieving immortality. Naturally, there are numerous practical consequences that arise from this understanding, and these are discussed mostly under the heading of ethics.

Bābā Afḍal comes back repeatedly to the issue of immortality in his treatises, situating it within the broad context of metaphysics, cosmology, and psychology. One of his simplest and most straightforward analyses is found in a little treatise called *Īmanī az buṭlān-i nafs dar panāh-i khirad* ("Security from the Soul's Nullification in the Refuge of Intelligence").[3] He begins by saying that he was asked to write a treatise that "would give the seeker cognizance of the self's reality and security from the nonbeing and nullification of the human soul at the nullification of the body's life." One of his students, in other words, had asked him how the soul could be immortal, and he wrote the treatise in response.

Bābā Afḍal starts the essay by pointing out that both humans and animals seek to satisfy their needs, but that humans have a need over and above bodily needs that is not shared by animals—the need for knowledge and understanding:

> No human individuals want not to know. In every state they choose knowing over not-knowing. So much more do they love to be knowers rather than nonknowers that, when they come to know something, they do not stop at that, but they also want to know more. They never become sated with knowing. They may gather many known things, but they never suffer from this or become ill—as they do when they are held back from other forms of knowledge. On the contrary, they become more capable and stronger when there is much provision. Moreover, when they become provided for and capable through knowledge, they still see requirement and neediness.[4]

The human hunger for knowledge and understanding, in other words, although analogous to the hunger for food, is different in that it does not become sated no matter how much one knows. The body becomes full, and eventually, as its corruptibility comes to the fore, food no longer nurtures it, and it dies, because life does not pertain to its very definition. In contrast, the soul can never be full, nor can it die, because the soul is precisely life, and life is life by definition. As Bābā Afḍal puts it, "What is dead by nature comes to life through the anima, so how can what is alive by nature come to die?"[5]

The food of the soul is knowledge, and there is no end to the known things. But all knowledge goes back to a single knowledge, which is the soul's knowing itself. This is a point to which Bābā Afḍal constantly returns, explaining it with many arguments. Typical is the following from his *ʿArḍ-nāma* ("The Book of Displays"):

> The seeker of anything will not reach the object of desire unless he seeks it from its mine and locus. He who wants water and searches for it from the mine of sal ammoniac will never reach the object of desire. A cold-stricken man in need of the shine of fire and the shining of the sun who does not aim for fire and sun but turns toward running water and blowing wind will be nearer to perishment than to the object of desire. In the same way, the seeker and wanter of knowledge, wakefulness, and awareness will reach his desire only when he sets

out for the dwelling-place and mine of knowledge, wakefulness, and awareness, not when he turns his face toward the realm of ignorance and the shelter of unconsciousness.

The dwelling-place of knowledge is the knower, and the mine of awareness is the aware. Whenever the distance between you and a knower and someone aware becomes shorter, you will have more hope of finding the objective from him. No knower and no one aware is closer to you than your own intelligent anima. If you aim toward knowing it and if you bring the face of your search toward it, you will soon win the object of desire.[6]

In his *Īmanī az buṭlān-i nafs*, Bābā Afḍal tells us, in short, that one should seek for the root knowledge. In order to do this, one first needs to differentiate among body, soul, and intelligence:

> The way to reach [knowledge of self] is to think over, to enumerate for yourself, and to become aware that you have three things: [a] body, which has been woven and depicted from several diverse bodies, like bones, tendons, veins, flesh, and so on. Second, you have a soul, through which your body is alive and without which it is dead. Third, you have an intelligence, which knows both body and soul and which recognizes each of them separately.
>
> When thought comes to know all three of these, such that no doubt and mistake remain, once again you should think over and know that the body is not the soul, and the soul is not the intelligence. For the body is never held back from being a body, whether it be with the soul or without it. However, it is not continually alive; rather, it is alive through the soul. Hence the soul, through which the body is alive and without which it is dead, is not the body.
>
> In the same way, intelligence is neither the body nor the soul. Were intelligence the body, all bodies would be intelligent, and were intelligence the soul, all animals would be intelligent. Hence it is correct that the knower of the soul and the body is neither the soul nor the body.[7]

Bābā Afḍal goes on to analyze the nature of intelligence and the manner in which it assimilates into its own being everything that it knows, without thereby become colored, determined, or limited by what it knows. For intelligence has no opposite. Nothing is incompatible with it, so there is nothing that can harm it:

> When something has no opposite or incompatible, its existence will not be nullified, for everything that is destroyed and nullified is nullified and destroyed by the victory and domination of the incompatible. But the existence of intelligence is its awareness, wakefulness, and knowing from self and through self. Whatever has existence through

self and from self will not be nullified or receive destruction and corruption.[8]

After offering additional clarification on the nature of intelligence, Bābā Afḍal summarizes the argument as follows:

> Hence the path of release and security from perishment and ruin is for humans to seek refuge in intelligence and to enter under its guardianship. It is to keep the inclination and pull toward nonlasting states and the body's nonlasting enjoyments far from the nature of self. It is to be in the measure of intelligence during movement and stillness, sleep and wakefulness.[9]

Most moderns and postmoderns, of course, find Bābā Afḍal's argument unconvincing. The real problem in understanding Bābā Afḍal's concept of immortality lies in grasping the context in which his arguments make sense. In general, the barrier to any understanding of what the premoderns were saying goes back to the scientistic modes of thinking in which most of us are indoctrinated from infancy. So we are, in a sense, hamstrung from the outset.

One of the consequences of believing in the scientistic worldview is that we find it extremely difficult to think about life and awareness as anything but epiphenomena of matter. We find it natural to suppose that when the body is put together correctly, it comes to life on the basis of its constituent elements. So also, we think, living bodies develop awareness on the basis of their physical structure. The basic premodern intuition, however, is just the reverse: The body is an epiphenomenon of life and awareness. Life and awareness are utterly foundational to all of reality, and it is living awareness that gives rise to living things. However, in the physical realm, certain modes of life and awareness are more intense than others, and the most intense of these pertain to the human realm.

What I am saying is that we make sense of the world on the basis of a grand matrix of thought, and without that matrix words are empty. Philosophers like Bābā Afḍal are aware of this problem, so they make no attempt to discuss the soul and the intellect separate from other issues.

Let me then summarize the "big picture" in the context of which Bābā Afḍal's arguments gain their persuasive weight. Western historians tend to classify the Islamic philosophical worldview by calling it "Neoplatonic," and they rightly point out that it acknowledges what Arthur Lovejoy called "the Great Chain of Being." The popular perception of Neoplatonism can be summed up in a single word: "emanation." All of reality, in other words, comes forth from the One. The Muslim philosophers accept this, but they lay equal if not greater stress upon the process of the return to the One, because it is the return's trajectory that determines our individual destinies.

In this basic Neoplatonic scheme, all reality is fully present at the Origin, in the infinite consciousness and awareness of the One. The creative act is analogous to the shining of the sun, although it may be analyzed in many different ways. As the creative light moves away from its source in the One, it becomes diminished. Along with the diminishment of light comes a lessening of life, awareness, desire, power, and all the other basic qualities of the First Reality. Once the light becomes fully deployed, its dimness appears as a realm that is characterized by inanimateness, unawareness, apathy, and weakness—that is, the material world. Then, however, the flow of light reverses direction and begins to be absorbed back into the Origin.

For those of us who stand in the middle of the process, the return to the One appears as a hierarchy of beings moving from the inanimate to the living, then to the aware, and then to the self-conscious; in other words, the hierarchy appears in the minerals, plants, animals, and humans that occupy the material realm. In each higher stage, the original qualities of the One—life, awareness, desire, power—become intensified. From the human stage onward, however, the knowing subject assumes a certain responsibility for its own becoming. The quest for wisdom is the attempt to understand who that subject is and to assist it in its rise into the fullness of the human state and beyond, in the direction of the One. For the philosophers, one of the main issues was this: Do human beings achieve immortality at a certain point in the ascent toward God? Or, are they—as the Islamic religious tradition maintains—immortal by their very nature?

The Argument from *Wujūd*

Let me now turn to one of Bābā Afḍal's more original arguments concerning human immortality. It is rooted in his understanding of the single most important word in Islamic philosophy—at least from Avicenna onward. This word is *wujūd*.

A typical definition of philosophy tells us that philosophy is the study of *wujūd* qua *wujūd*. In other words, philosophers set out to understand the nature of being. They are not primarily interested in what it means to be this or to be that, but rather what it means to *be*, without qualification. What it means to be an animal might be the primary focus of a zoologist, and what it means to be a star would be an important question for an astronomer. But philosophers want to understand what it means to "be" as such. They are interested in various modalities of beings—such as animals and stars—because of the light that these throw on being per se.

When one understands what it means to be, it is then possible to understand the global significance of the various modalities of being that are studied in the diverse sciences. This helps explain why the philosophers considered their science to be the science of all sciences. Only knowledge of what it means to be allows for an all-comprehensive and all-embracing view of things.

For much of Islamic philosophy from Avicenna onward—whether the orientation was more rational or more mystical—*wujūd* was a name applied to the Ultimate Reality. Interestingly, Bābā Afḍal does not follow the mainstream here, because he discusses *wujūd* only inasmuch as the word designates everything other than the Ultimate Reality.

When the secondary literature summarizes the positions of the Muslim philosophers on *wujūd,* it usually forgets to mention that the Arabic word does not have the same connotations as the English words "existence" or "being." "Being" is perhaps a better translation than existence, because it does not imply the same coldness, concreteness, and inanimateness that "existence" does. But the literal meaning of the word *wujūd* is "to find" and "to perceive." It has always been understood to imply (if not to demand) awareness and consciousness. When Avicenna and others speak of the Necessary *wujūd*—meaning the Ultimate Reality—it is not at all strange that they should immediately say that this Being is by Its nature alive and aware. Quite the contrary, given the meaning of the word, it seems almost self-evident.

But let us turn to Bābā Afḍal. The word *wujūd* had long been used in the Persian language, so he did not have to define it. In any case, he points out—as others do—that it cannot be defined, because it is presupposed in every definition. What he does do is to make use of the Persian language to unpack the implications of using this word in global discussions of reality. He points out that it has two basic meanings. One is *hastī,* Persian for "being," and the other is *yāft,* Persian for "finding" and "perception."

Given that *wujūd* is indefinable but present in everything, the proper way to talk about it is to classify it into different varieties. When we do so, we see that "being" and "finding" designate the two basic sorts of *wujūd.* Finding is more inclusive, because everything that finds exists, but not everything that exists finds. In other words, finding is more real than simply being. The more a thing finds, perceives, understands, and knows, the more fully and actually it partakes of the qualities of reality.

Having divided *wujūd* into two basic sorts, Bābā Afḍal then uses standard Aristotelian terminology to subdivide being and finding. Both may be potential or actual. Actual being pertains to everything that exists. Potential being pertains to things that do not yet exist but which may come to exist:

> Potential being is the lowest level in being. It is the existence of material things in the matter, such as the existence of the tree in the seed and the existence of the animal in the sperm. Actual being without finding is like the existence of elemental bodies. . . .
>
> As for potential finding, it belongs to the soul. The meaning of the words *soul* and *self* is one.
>
> Actual finding belongs to the intellect. What is potential in the soul becomes actual through the intellect.[10]

Note that Bābā Afḍal defines "soul"—the Arabic word *nafs*—with the Persian word *khwud,* self, which is the reflexive pronoun. He is right to do so, not least because *nafs* is the reflexive pronoun in Arabic. However, the reflexive meaning of the word *nafs* is usually lost in Persian. And, in both Arabic and Persian, the use of the word on its own, without reference to a noun, closely parallels the use of "soul" in English. Thus, one should keep in mind that in answering the question, "What is the soul?," Bābā Afḍal and many others simply reply, "You yourself," or, "That which asked the question."

But what is it that allows oneself to recognize oneself as oneself? The answer, as we have already seen, is "intelligence" (*khirad*) or "intellect" (*ʿaql*), which is actualized self-awareness and self-consciousness. In Bābā Afḍal's terms, "intelligence" is actualized finding, realized knowing, correct and sound consciousness of oneself. And this actualized finding is the highest and fullest mode of *wujūd*: "The soul is a finder with the intellect. Just as potential being is the meanest level in existence, so actual finding is the highest level of existence, because being becomes correct through finding."[11]

In other words, existence is made real through awareness. This means that for Bābā Afḍal, the philosophical quest is for the soul to seek to actualize itself by knowing. When it comes to fully know itself, then it is no longer potential finding, but actual finding, actual being, and fully realized existence:

> When the soul seeks itself, it is potentially found and finder. When it finds itself, it is actually finder and found. As long as it knows itself potentially, it is the soul. But when it knows and finds itself actually, it is not the soul. Rather, it is the "intellect," for, when the specificity turns into something else, the name also turns into something else.[12]

In short, the highest rank of *wujūd* belongs to the intellect, which is the human self that has found itself. In terms of the cosmological scheme that I have already outlined, this is the soul that has retraced the levels of darkening and densification that became manifest when consciousness and awareness brought the material realm into existence. The self that finds itself is the soul that actualizes the original light and consciousness that gave birth to itself and to the universe.

It is in this discussion of *wujūd* that Bābā Afḍal departs from the mainstream of Islamic philosophy. For most of the Muslim philosophers, the highest level of *wujūd* is the Ultimate Reality, identical with the God of theology. For Bābā Afḍal, the highest level of *wujūd* is the actualization of human intelligence. It is to rise beyond the realm of mere being, which is the domain of generation and corruption, and enter into the realm of pure life and awareness, unsullied by the traces of death or ignorance. The fullness of finding and existing that is achieved, however, is not in fact the highest reality. In effect, he says that the Ultimate Reality lies in a realm "beyond being," although he does not use this particular expression. Hence, for Bābā Afḍal, fully actualized being—the self that knows itself—is the "radiance" or the "effulgence" of the Ultimate Reality, which he typically refers to as the "radiance of the Ipseity (*furūgh-i huwiyya*)."

In explaining the classification of *wujūd* into different sorts, Bābā Afḍal tells us that intelligence is related to the soul just as a tree is related to a seed: "The universe is a tree whose produce and fruit is man, man is a tree whose produce and fruit is the soul, the soul is a tree whose fruit is intelligence, and intelligence is a tree whose fruit is the encounter with God."[13]

Given this ontology, it is natural that immortality follows self-understanding. To the degree that intelligence—which is simply one's true selfhood—is realized, one joins with actual being. As Bābā Afḍal puts it, "The soul's being is the soul's knowledge of self, and this being belongs to it from itself. Whatever has existence from itself is secure from annihilation."[14] In other words, inasmuch as the soul knows itself, it finds itself, and "finding" is precisely "being." The very existence of the soul is awareness and finding. Finding is pure, actualized existence, unsullied by potentiality. Hence, the actualized soul is simply existence, and existence is the "radiance of the Ipseity," which shines by definition.

19

Mullā Ṣadrā on Perception

Muslim philosophers speak of perception—using the Arabic word *idrāk*—in an exceedingly broad sense. For them, perception denotes apprehension and obtaining knowledge by any agent, from animals to God, and on any level, from physical sensation to intellectual vision. In the philosophy of Mullā Ṣadrā, the concept of perception plays a crucial role both in the explanation of the nature of existence and in the analysis of the goal of human life. This follows naturally from the fact that his philosophy is oriented toward "psychology" in the premodern sense of the term. In other words, he attempts to provide an overview of the human self in all its ramifications and to map out the way for the self to achieve the highest of its own possibilities, possibilities that are rooted in its ability to perceive.

Perception

At the end of the first book of his monumental *al-Ḥikma al-mutaʿāliya fī-l-asfār al-ʿaqliyya al-arbaʿa* ("The Transcendent Philosophy: On the Four Intellective Journeys"), Ṣadrā provides definitions for some thirty words that are employed in discussing the modalities of knowledge. He lists "perception" as the first of these words. In defining it, he begins with its literal sense. As any Arabic dictionary will tell us, it has a variety of meanings, such as attaining, reaching, arriving, catching, grasping, comprehending, and discerning. Ṣadrā writes:

> *Idrāk* is encounter [*liqāʾ*] and arrival [*wuṣūl*]. When the intellective potency arrives at the quiddity of the intelligible and attains it, this is its perception in this respect. In philosophy, the meaning intended by the word coincides with the literal meaning. Or rather, true perception and encounter is only this encounter, that is, perception by knowledge. As for bodily encounter, it is not really an encounter.[1]

Before going any further, we need to allude to some of the issues raised by this definition. Like all Muslim philosophers, Ṣadrā analyzes the human self in terms of faculties. However, the Arabic word for "faculty" is *quwwa*, which is also the word for "potentiality" as contrasted with "actuality." Given that every faculty is at the same time a potentiality, *quwwa* can better be translated as "potency." Its dual meaning is especially important in Ṣadrā's writings, because his analysis of the human soul depends precisely on seeing it as a grand potentiality that encompasses every other potentiality designated by the names of the faculties.

In this definition of perception, Ṣadrā means by the "intellective potency" the power and potential of the self to know something. When this power reaches an object, it moves from potentiality to actuality. The degree of actuality that it achieves is one of the most basic issues that needs to be addressed.

In the definition, Ṣadrā says that through perception the intellective potency arrives at the "quiddity" (or "whatness") of a thing. In other words, when perception takes place, we come to know "what" the object of perception is. The fact that perception entails knowing a thing's quiddity is emphasized in the second word that Ṣadrā defines in his list of technical terms—*shuʿūr* or "awareness." Awareness, he says, is to perceive something without "achieving fixity" (*istithbāt*), that is, without ascertaining the thing's whatness. He adds, "Awareness is the first level of the arrival of knowledge at the intellective potency. It is, as it were, a shaky perception. That is why it is not said about God that He is 'aware' of a thing,"[2] although it is said about Him that He "perceives" things.

The thing that is perceived is an "intelligible," that is, an object known to intelligence. The intelligible is called the "form" (*ṣūra*) of the thing, in the Aristotelian sense of the word *form*. Hence, it is contrasted with the thing's "matter" (*mādda*), which is unintelligible in itself. The only things we can truly perceive and know are forms, not matter.

Finally, in this definition Ṣadrā insists that true *idrāk*—that is true attainment, reaching, arrival, and encounter—pertains to knowledge and not to the body. This reminds us that real perception of things can only take place if an intelligent agent encounters an intelligible object. Every bodily attainment is fleeting and evanescent. So also, any modality of perception that is sullied in any fashion by the body's materiality will be deficient in certain basic ways, because the form will be obscured both by the means of perception and by the existential situation within which it is perceived.

Levels of Perception

In the same list of important terms, Ṣadrā provides another definition that can help us understand the final goal of perception. This term is *dhihn* or "mind." He writes, "The mind is the soul's potency to acquire forms of knowledge that have not yet been attained."[3]

In keeping with the general Greco-Islamic view of things, Ṣadrā understands the human soul or self to have many powers and faculties and many corresponding levels of actualization, beginning with the plant and animal levels. The soul actualizes itself by perceiving what it has the potential to perceive. The soul's goal in its existence is to move from potential knowing to actual knowing. When its potential knowledge becomes fully actual, it is no longer called a "soul," but rather an "intellect," or an "intellect in act." In Ṣadrā's view, then, the human soul's potential to achieve actual knowledge is called the "mind."

The mind comes to know things through perception. "Perception" is simply the name given to the act whereby the soul comes to know, whatever the object may be. If we look at perception from the side of the perceiver, it has four basic varieties. In each case, the mind encounters the "form" of a thing—that is, its quiddity or intelligible reality—not its matter. However, the circumstances are different in each sort of encounter. These circumstances pertain both to the instrument that perceives and to the modality of the perceptible's existence.

The first level of perception is sense perception (*ḥiss*). At this level, the perceived form exists in matter, and the perceiver finds the form in modes specific to material embodiment. These modes are basically the Aristotelian accidents, such as quantity, quality, time, place, and situation. In its external existence as a thing, the form is inseparable from such accidental attributes, and it is precisely these attributes that allow us to perceive it with the senses. As for the matter through which the form exists, it can never be perceived in itself because it represents the furthest and darkest reaches of existence, a realm that remains almost entirely unintelligible.

The second level of perception is imagination (*khayāl, takhayyul*), which is the perception of a sensory thing, along with all its characteristics and qualities, in the same way that it is perceived by the senses. Unlike sense perception, however, imagination perceives the thing whether or not the thing's matter is present to the senses.

The third level is *wahm*. The medievals translated this Arabic word as *"estimatio,"* but modern scholars have reached no consensus on its meaning and how it should be appropriately rendered into English. I translate it as "sense intuition" in order to suggest its intermediary status between the intellect and the senses. According to Ṣadrā, it is the perception of an intelligible meaning while attributing the meaning to a particular, sensory thing. In sense intuition, the soul perceives the universal, but within a particular, rather than in the universal itself.

The highest level is intellection (*taʿaqqul*), which is the perception of something in respect of its quiddity alone, not in respect of anything else.[4]

What distinguishes the levels of perception boils down to the degree of "disengagement" (*tajarrud*), a term of fundamental importance in Ṣadrā's writings. *Tajarrud* is another word upon whose translation modern scholars have not agreed. Most commonly, it has been translated as "abstraction," a word that thoroughly obscures its basic meaning.[5] A "disengaged" thing is not only free and quit of matter, but it also dwells in a domain of intensified existence and consciousness. In Islamic philosophy in general, few concepts have been more significant than "disengagement" for describing the ultimate goal of the human quest for perfection. In the purest sense, disengagement is an attribute of God, the Necessary Being in Itself, since the Necessary Existence has no attachment to or dependence on anything other than Itself. More specifically, disengagement is the attribute of the intellect that is able to see things as they actually are, that is, without their entanglement in the obscurities of imagination and sense perception.[6] It is also the essential attribute of the forms or quiddities that the intellect perceives.

According to Ṣadrā, the four levels of perception need to be differentiated in terms of the degree of disengagement reached by the perceptibles.

The first level, that of sense perception, can be understood in terms of three conditions (*sharṭ*) that determine its nature: First, the matter is present to the instrument of perception, which is to say that the soul perceives the thing externally in its material embodiment. Second, the thing's form is concealed by the perceived qualities and characteristics. Third, the perceived thing is a particular, not a universal.

On the second level—imagination—the perceptibles are disengaged from the first of the three conditions, namely material embodiment, because there is no need for the external presence of the thing.

On the third level, sense intuition's perceptibles are disengaged both from material embodiment and from the object's specific qualities and characteristics.

On the final level, the intelligibles are disengaged from all three conditions, because the intellect perceives only universals.[7]

Ṣadrā concludes his discussion of the levels of perception by saying that the four levels can be reduced to three, because imagination and sense intuition both pertain to the intermediary domain between the intellect and the senses.[8]

Levels of Existence

The three basic levels of perception—sense perception, imagination, and intellection—correspond exactly with the three worlds that are found in the external realm. These are the world of bodies, the world of imagination, and the world of the intellect. Discussion of levels of perception is inseparable from discussion of levels of existence. If there were only one level of existence, there would be only one sort of perception. Reducing perception to sensation follows the elimination of the imaginal and spiritual domains from serious consideration.

When speaking about levels of existence, what is meant by "existence" is possible existence, or formal and delimited existence, not that existence which is necessary. Existence in itself—that is, *wujūd*—is the ultimate reality of all things, and, as such, it lies beyond the worlds and beyond the levels. In itself, existence remains forever unattainable, imperceptible, and unknowable. However, it deploys itself in degrees of strength and weakness. We come to know it indirectly by perceiving it in various conditioned modalities. The higher the realm of existence, the more it is disengaged from matter and from the conditions and characteristics of things. Correspondingly, the perception that pertains to the higher levels is more intense and more direct.

Each level of existence is typically called a "world" (*ʿālam*), and the sum total of the levels is known simply as "the cosmos" or "the universe." When speaking about worlds, we are plainly discussing knowledge and perception. In Arabic, this point is brought home by the word *ʿālam* itself. It derives from the same root as the word for knowledge, *ʿilm*. The lexicographers tell us that its primary designation of "world" is "that by means of which one knows." Thus, the "world" as a whole is a realm that is defined and designated by the fact that it can be an object of knowledge. So also, each world or level within the whole is defined by the type of perception that makes it the object of knowledge. The fact that there are three basic modes of perception derives from the fact there are three basic knowable realms.

One of Ṣadrā's more detailed expositions of the worlds comes in a chapter of the *Asfār* called "On the divisions of the sciences," that is, the modalities of knowing. There he explains that the reality of knowledge goes back to "formal existence," which is the realm of existence within which forms appear to perception. He then says that formal existence has three divisions—complete, sufficient, and deficient. Complete existence is the realm of the intelligible forms and the disengaged intellects. Sufficient existence is the realm of souls, also called "the world of imagination." Deficient existence is the domain of the sensory forms, which are "the forms that endure through matter and are attached to it."[9]

Having described the three levels of formal existence, Ṣadrā then speaks of a fourth level, that of bodily matter, which undergoes transformation and renewal at every instant. Because bodily matter is immersed in nonexistence, possibility, contingency, and darkness, it is unknowable, even if it is called by the name "existence." As examples, Ṣadrā cites time and movement.[10]

In explaining the distinctions among these four domains, Ṣadrā tells us that they differ in terms of the intensity and weakness of their existence. The stronger a thing's modality of existence, the more disengaged it is from the transient world of matter. The more disengaged it is, the more intelligible it is, because it is more purely itself. Each of the realms lower than the world of completeness and intellect is immersed to some degree in the muddiness and obscurity brought about by multiplicity, dispersion, separation, and confusion.[11]

Presence

The key to understanding Ṣadrā's concept of perception is his view of existence. Once we remember that perception and finding are already implicit in the word *wujūd* as employed by many of the philosophers, we see that any attempt to reduce existence to mere "being there" seems obtuse. Rather, existence in the full sense is not only that which is there, but also that which finds what is there. The more intensely something is there, the more intensely it finds. The fullest degree of existence is found in the fullest degree of presence, perception, and consciousness.

In a short gloss on the meaning of perception, Ṣadrā says, "Perception is the existence of the perceptible for the perceiver [*al-idrāk ʿibāra ʿan wujūd al-mudrak li-l-mudrik*]."[12] In light of the dual meaning of the word *wujūd*, this can also be translated as, "Perception is the perceptible's being found by the perceiver." In several similar glosses on the word, Ṣadrā often replaces the word *wujūd* with the word "presence" (*ḥuḍūr*) or "witnessing" (*mushāda*),[13] both of which are terms with long histories that can throw light on how he understands their nature.[14]

"Presence" is the opposite of "absence" (*ghayba*), and it is practically a synonym of "witnessing." Ṣadrā sometimes divides the universe into two basic "perceptual" (*idrākī*) domains, that is, the world of life and knowledge, which is the realm of intellects and souls, and the world of death and ignorance, which is the realm of inanimate bodies.[15] When Ṣadrā makes this division, he is likely to employ the Koranic terms for these two realms, that is, the "unseen" (*ghayb*) and the "witnessed" (*shahāda*). The "unseen" is everything that we do not ordinarily perceive. The "witnessed" is everything present to our senses.

When we ask if it is possible to perceive and witness the "unseen" world, the philosophers will reply that it certainly is. We do so precisely by perceiving those things that the senses are unable to grasp. However, in order to truly perceive the realm of unseen things, we need to strengthen our perceptual faculties and learn how to see through the darkness of the corporeal and sensory realm into the domain that lies beyond it. The unseen realm must come to *exist* for us and to be *found* by us. In other words, it must come to be *present* in the self and be *witnessed* by it.

Perception, then, is a mode of existence, or it is existence itself, which is precisely "presence"—being there and being found. Perception is the existence of the perceived object within the perceiver. It follows that in perceiving both the external and the internal worlds, the degree of perception coincides with the degree of existence. To perceive something more directly is to participate in existence more fully.

Mental Existence

When Ṣadrā says that perception is for the perceptible "to exist" or "to be found" within the perceiver, he clearly does not mean that the thing exists in the same mode internally as it does externally. He explains that when the mind perceives something, it comes from potentiality to actuality, and this actuality of the mind is the presence of the thing's intelligible form in the mind. This presence is called "mental existence" (*wujūd dhihnī*), an expression that we can also translate as "mental finding." However, as long as the soul remains the soul and has not become an intellect in act, the soul's mode of perception and existence is weak, and everything that is perceived and exists within the soul is even weaker. Ṣadrā writes that, because of this weakness,

> the specific acts and traces that are ordered upon the soul and come into existence from it have the utmost weakness of existence. Or rather, the existence of the intellective and imaginal forms that come into existence from it are shadows and apparitions of the external existences that emerge from the Creator, even if the quiddity is preserved in the two existences. Hence the traces that are ordered upon the quiddity in the external realm are not ordered upon it in respect of [its existence in the soul]. . . .
>
> This existence of a thing upon which traces are not ordered while it emerges from the soul in this modality of manifestation is named "mental" and "shadow" existence. The other, upon which traces are ordered, is named "external" and "entified" existence.[16]

In short, the things perceived by sense perception exist with a true existence in the mind, but their mental existence is a shadow of their external existence. However, as the soul gradually actualizes its potency to know the higher realms, the objects that it perceives undergo a corresponding increase in intensity. At the stage of true intellective perception, the intellect that perceives is identical in existence and consciousness with the forms that are its perceptibles.

The Potency of the Soul

Perception takes place within the soul. Discussion of self or soul begins at the level of plants and extends to the highest reaches of human perfection. The human soul can be described most simply as "all the potencies."[17] By this, Ṣadrā means that the rational soul is "the one that perceives with all the perceptions attributed to the human potencies."[18] The human soul, in other words, is pure potency, and as such it has no actuality. The actuality of the soul comes about through perception. When the soul perceives something, the thing comes to exist within the soul in the appropriate mode of existence, and the soul itself comes to actualize in itself the corresponding mode of mental existence.

The goal of human existence is to bring the soul's potentiality into actuality. At the beginning of its creation, the human self is empty of the knowledge of things. In contrast, other things are created with actualized knowledge of things, and this fixes them in their specific identities. Since the human soul is created knowing nothing, it has the potential to know everything. It is this characteristic alone that allows it to be transmuted into an intellect in act:

> God created the human spirit empty of the realization of things within it and [empty] of the knowledge of things. . . . Had He not created

> the human spirit for the sake of the knowledge of things as they are, the spirit would necessarily be, at the first of its innate disposition, one of those things in act, and it would not be empty of all. . . .
>
> Although at first . . . the human spirit is a sheer potency, empty of the intelligibles, nonetheless it is proper for it to know the realities and become conjoined [*ittiṣāl*] with all of them. It follows that true knowledge [*ʿirfān*] of God, of His spiritual realm [*malakūt*], and of His signs [*āyāt*] is the final goal. . . . Knowledge is the first and the last, the origin and the final goal.[19]

Perception actualizes a potential knowledge of the soul. Actuality demands activity, and Ṣadrā tells us that those philosophers who have spoken of perception as the soul's being imprinted by the perceptibles have missed the real nature of perception, because perception is much closer to activity and actuality than to receptivity:

> The relation of the perceived form to the knowing essence is the relation of the made thing [*majʿūl*] to the maker [*jāʿil*], not the relation of indwelling [*ḥulūl*] or imprinting [*inṭibāʿ*].[20]
>
> Relative to its imaginal and sensory perceptibles, the soul is more similar to an innovating actor [*al-fāʿil al-mubdiʿ*] than to a receptive dwelling place [*al-maḥall al-qābil*].[21]

In his discussion of vision, Ṣadrā provides a specific example of how the soul comes into act through perception. After rejecting the theories of the natural scientists, the mathematicians, and Suhrawardī, he writes:

> Vision takes place through the configuring of a form similar to the thing, by God's power, from the side of the world of the soulish, spiritual realm. The form comes to be disengaged from the external matter and present to the perceiving soul. The form endures through the soul just as an act endures through its agent, not as something received endures through its receptacle.[22]

Having said this, Ṣadrā extends the argument, showing that vision is one instance of the general rule in perception, which is that the perceiver comes to be unified with the perceptible. This is the same principle that he demonstrated previously under the rubric of "the unification of the intellect and the intelligible" (*ittiḥād al-ʿaql wa-l-maʿqūl*), which he considers one of the cornerstones of his philosophy. He is especially concerned to prove this principle because Avicenna and his followers had denied it:

> What we demonstrated concerning the unification of the intellect and the intelligible applies to all sensory, imaginal, and sense-intuitive perceptions. We called attention to this issue in the discussions of

> the intellect and the intelligible. We said that sense-perception in an unqualified sense is not as is well-known among the generality of sages, who say that sensation disengages the very form of the sensible thing from its matter and meets it along with its surrounding accidents; and, in the same way, that imagination disengages the form with a greater disengagement. . . . [23] Rather, perception in an unqualified sense is obtained only from the Bestower's effusion of another, luminous, perceptual form through which perception and awareness are obtained. It is this form that is sensate in act and sensible in act. As for the existence of the form in matter, it is neither sense-perception nor a sensible. However, it is among those things that prepare the way for the effusion of that form.[24]

Thus, the perceptible is a form that is effused upon the soul by God. Investigating Ṣadrā's elucidations of the theological implications of this statement would demand another study, so here it is sufficient to understand that God's effusion of the form actualizes the soul's potential to know. In coming forth from potency to act, the soul gains a mode of mental existence that coincides with the external existence of the perceived thing. The known thing is precisely the intellective or imaginal form, and the form's presence to the soul is its mental existence within the soul, an existence that is identical with the existence of the soul itself, since there is no plurality of existences in the soul. Rather, the soul's consciousness of the form is the same as the form's existence for the soul. In mental existence, perception and existence are one thing. It follows that, as Ṣadrā frequently tells us, the perceived object is always of the same kind as the perceiver. Through touch, taste, and vision the soul perceives objects that are of the same kind as itself, for these objects are the forms of the touched, the tasted, and the seen actualized in the soul.[25]

When Ṣadrā says that the soul is "all the potencies," he means that the human self is an unlimited potential for knowing. The soul's good lies in its actualization of its potential, and this potential cannot be circumscribed. The soul, as Aristotle says at the beginning of the *Metaphysics*, yearns for omniscience because its potential is precisely to perceive all things.[26] But *all* things can be found only in the pure intellect, where they subsist as intellective forms. Thus, the highest stage of perception is for the soul to become an intellect. In other words, the soul comes to perceive in the fullness of its own capacity, and it comes to exist in the fullness of actual finding. Once it realizes the station of full perception and full existence, all things are present to it in act. This is to say that all things are present to the intellect in the clarity of their real, intellective existence, not in the obscurity of their sensory and imaginal existence:

> When the soul becomes an intellect, it becomes all things. Right now also, it is unified with everything that it has made present in its own essence—I mean the forms of those things, not their entities that are external to it. This does not require that the soul be compounded of

> those external affairs, nor of those forms. Rather, the more perfect the soul becomes, the more it becomes a gathering of things and the more it gains in the intensity of its simplicity, because the truly simple thing is all things, as has been demonstrated.[27]

It needs to be remembered that for Ṣadrā, existence is primary, and quiddity is secondary. The quiddities are what Ibn al-ʿArabī calls the "fixed entities," and they are "fixed" because they never change. What changes is formal existence, which undergoes intensification and weakening. The levels of perception are differentiated by the weakness or strength of the existence to which they correspond. In Ṣadrā's words, only when existence reaches the level of "the simple intellect, which is entirely disengaged from the world of bodies and quantities, does it become all the intelligibles and all the things, in a manner more excellent and more eminent than the things are in themselves."[28]

At each level of perception, the soul disengages perceptible things from matter and from the other conditions of the ontological levels. Even sense perception necessarily disengages the perceptibles, because the external matter does not enter into the soul. But, when the soul disengages the perceptibles, it simultaneously becomes disengaged from the conditions of the lower worlds. The movement from sense perception, to imagination, and then to intellection is a movement from frail existence and weak perception to strong existence and intense finding. Every time the soul actualizes its own potential through knowing, it gains in the strength of its existence, and when it becomes an intellect in act, it has gained full and everlasting existence.

Ṣadrā is critical of the expositions of the earlier philosophers concerning the meaning of "disengagement." His rejection of their positions helps explain why "abstraction" is not a proper way to translate the term into English.[29] He writes:

> The meaning of disengagement in intellection and other perception is not as is well-known—that it is the elimination of certain extraneous things [*zawāʾid*]. Nor is it that the soul stands still while the perceptibles are transferred from their material substrate to sensation, from sensation to imagination, and from it to the intellect. Rather, the perceiver and the perceptible become disengaged together. Together they withdraw from one existence to another existence. Together they are transferred from one configuration to another configuration and from one world to another world, until the soul becomes an intellect, an intellecter, and an intelligible in act, after it had been potential in all this.[30]

Contrary to what was thought by some of the earlier philosophers, disengagement does not imply rejection of the body. This is because the essential reality of the body is formal, not material. The more the soul is strengthened, the more the body's intellective form is intensified and the more its existence is consolidated. Ṣadrā writes:

> Among the things that are necessary to know is that here [in this world] the human is the totality of soul and body. These two, despite their diversity in way station, are two existent things that exist through one existence. It is as if the two are one thing possessing two sides. One of the sides is altering and extinguishing, and it is like the branch. The other side is fixed and subsistent, and it is like the root. The more the soul becomes perfect in its existence, the more the body becomes limpid and subtle. It becomes more intense in conjunction with the soul, and the unification between the two becomes stronger and more intense. Finally, when intellective existence comes about, they become one thing without difference.
>
> The affair is not as is supposed by the majority—that, when the soul's this-worldly existence alters into the after-worldly existence, the soul withdraws from the body and becomes as if naked, throwing off its clothes. This is because they suppose that the natural body—which the soul governs and acts upon freely by an essential governance and a primary free-activity—is this inanimate flesh that is thrown down after death, but it is not like this. Rather, this dead flesh is outside the substrate of free-activity and governance. It is like a heaviness and dregs that drop down and are expelled from the act of nature, like filth and other such things. Or, it is like the hair, fur, horns, and hooves that are obtained by nature external to her essence for external purposes. This is like a house. A man builds it not because of existence, but to repel heat and cold, and for the other things without which it is impossible to live in this world. But, human life does not pervade the house.[31]

In conclusion, we can see that for Ṣadrā, the final goal of perception is for the human self to see things as they really are. This can only occur when the soul actualizes its unlimited potential to know. This potential is the ability to perceive all things dwelling on all levels of formal existence. The potential can be turned into actuality through a gradual disentanglement, disengagement, and separation (*mufāraqa*) from all embodiment and materiality and a return to the intelligible reality of the soul, which is nothing but the intellect in act, or the intelligence that perceives all things as they actually are in existence itself. This does not mean that the soul will no longer have any connection with the things of the external world. Rather, it means that it will have come to perceive things clearly, wherever they may be situated in the levels of existence. It will no longer fall into the nearsightedness of perceiving the forms as anchored to the various locations in which they become manifest to the perceiver, locations in which the forms appear through the dark glass of sense perception and imagination. Having perceived the self and all things for what they are and having found itself to be one with all things, the soul attains to its final goal.

20

Eschatology in Islamic Thought

The Koran discusses what occurs after death in details unparalleled by other scriptures, and the hadith literature on the subject is voluminous. Hence, scholars of Kalam, philosophers, and Sufis—not to speak of Koran commentators—all made eschatology one of their principal concerns.

The term *al-maʿād* (the "Return" or "Place of Return"), used generically for discussions of eschatological realities and events, is derived from such Koranic verses as *They will say, "Who will cause us to return?" Say: "He who created you the first time"* (17:51). Systematic discussions of the Return are often paired with a second concept, *al-mabdaʾ* (the "Origin" or "Place of Origin"), for, as the Koran affirms, *As He originated you, so you will return* (7:29). Works on the Origin and the Return deal with such questions as the nature of the human being and his relationship with God, the reason for man's creation, his ultimate good and the manner in which he can achieve it, the various types of individuals that make up the human race and their respective lodging places in the next world (*ākhira*), the ontological distinctions between this world and the next, and the interpretation of the data found in the Koran and the Hadith concerning death, resurrection, and heaven and hell. In a wider context, the topic of the Origin and the Return covers everything that touches upon the manner in which man can achieve his proper place in creation or attain to human perfection, whether moral, spiritual, or intellectual. In this sense, jurisprudence can be considered a branch of eschatology, since the Shariah is the *sine qua non* in the path of human perfection. In the domain of philosophy, ethics describes the human qualities that bring about the practical perfections of the soul, while in Sufism lengthy discussions of the spiritual stations play a similar role. Even politics, which describes the ideal human society and the means to achieve it, can be considered a branch of eschatology, since man's temporal good can be understood only in terms of his eternal good. In short, the ramifications of eschatological teachings are so broad that it is difficult to study anything Islamic without touching upon them. Here we can only allude to certain wider implications while dealing in some small detail with the science of the "last things."

Eschatology in the Koran and the Hadith

Before discussing the diverse approaches to eschatology in Islamic thought, an overview of Islam's basic teachings on the topic is in order. Drawing on relevant texts from the Koran and Hadith, I offer a commentary upon a standard statement of Muslim eschatological beliefs. The text, taken from the "Creed" of the Maturidite theologian Najm al-Dīn Nasafī (d. 537/1142), runs as follows:

> The chastisement of the grave for the unbelievers and some of the disobedient faithful, the bliss in the grave for the People of Obedience—as known and willed by God—and the questioning of Munkar and Nakīr, are established by proofs [that is, explicit revealed texts]. The Resurrection is true, the Weighing is true, the Book is true, the Questioning is true, the Pond is true, the Path is true, the Garden is true, and the Fire is true. These last two are created and exist now; they will subsist, and neither they nor their inhabitants will pass away. . . . The signs of the Hour, such as the appearance of al-Dajjāl [the Anti-Christ], the Beast of the Earth, Gog and Magog, the descent of Jesus from heaven, and the rising of the sun in the west, are true.[1]

The Prophet called death "the only preacher one needs,"[2] and its remembrance colors all of Islamic spirituality. One might say that a Muslim is not sincere until he takes to heart such Koranic verses as *What is with you is perishing, but what is with God abides* (16:96); *God is better, and more abiding* (20:73); *All things are perishing except His face* (28:88); *Every soul will taste death* (3:185); *O man! You are laboring unto your Lord laboriously, and you will encounter Him!* (84:6); and *Surely the death from which you are fleeing will meet you: then you will be returned to the Knower of the unseen and the visible, and He will tell you what you were doing* (62:8). Probably the most common epitaph in the Islamic world is this verse: *Surely we belong to God, and to Him we return* (2:156).

The Grave

Death is brought about by the intervention of the "angel of death," called ʿIzrāʾīl; giving up the soul to him is a difficult process, but it is made easy for the faithful. The dead person is aware of his body after death and observes the process of burial. On the first night in the grave, he is questioned by two angels, Munkar and Nakīr, concerning his faith. According to Jaʿfar al-Ṣādiq (d. 148/765), "The spirits of the faithful are in rooms of the Garden. They eat its food, drink its drinks, and visit one another. They say, 'Our Lord, bring the Hour to accomplish all that You have promised.' . . . The spirits of the unbelievers are in rooms of the Fire: they eat its food, drink its drinks, and visit one another. They say, 'Our Lord, do not bring the Hour to accomplish all that You have promised!' "[3]

According to the Prophet, "The grave is one of the plots of the Garden or one of the pits of the Fire."[4] As we saw in Chapter 11, the world between death and the resurrection is known as the *barzakh*. It is alluded to by this name in the Koranic verse, *Behind them is a* barzakh *until the day they are raised up* (23:100). The term *barzakh* gradually assumes major importance in discussions of eschatology, especially in Sufism and philosophy, as will be seen in the following sections.

The Resurrection

The dead remain in their graves until the Day of Resurrection, which corresponds to the end of this world: *And the Trumpet shall be blown; then behold, they are hastening from their tombs unto their Lord* (36:51). Ghazālī lists more than a hundred names for this event; among them are *the Day of Regret* (19:39); *the Day of Reckoning* (38:16); *the Day of the Earthquake* (22:1); *the Day of the Clatterer* (101:1); *the Day of the Indubitable* (69:1); *the Day of the Encounter* (40:15); *the Day of the Gathering* (42:7); *the Day wherein is no doubt* (3:9); *the Day when no soul will avail another in anything* (2:48); *the Day when eyes will stare* (14:42); *the Day a man will flee from his brother, his mother, and his father* (80:34–35); and *the Day they shall not speak* (77:35).[5]

The Weighing

Once the resurrection takes place, the works of people will be evaluated: *We will set up the Scales of Justice for the Day of Resurrection, so that no soul will be wronged anything: even if it be the weight of a grain of mustard seed, We will produce it* (21:47). According to ʿAlī, on the Day of Resurrection, "God will requite the creatures on behalf of each other through the Scales."[6]

The Book

On that day, you will be exposed, not one secret of yours concealed. Then as for him who is given his book in his right hand, he will be in a pleasing life, in a lofty Garden. . . . But as for him who is given his book in his left hand, he will say, "Would that I had not been given my book and had not known my reckoning!" (69:18–26). Concerning the verse, "*Read your book! Your soul suffices you this day as an accounter against you*" (17:14), Jaʿfar says, "The servant will remember everything he has done and is written against him, exactly as if he had done it in that hour. This is the meaning of God's words, *And the book shall be set in place; and you will see the sinners fearful of what is in it and saying, 'Alas for us! How is it with this book, that it leaves nothing behind, small or great, but has counted it?'*" (18:49).[7]

The Questioning

We shall surely question them, every one, about what they were doing (15:92–93). According to Ibn ʿAbbās (d. ca. 68/688), the questioning will not take the form of "Did you do such and such?" Rather, it will take the form of "Why did you do such and such?"[8] Asked about predestination, Jaʿfar replied, "When God gathers His servants on the Day of Resurrection, He will ask them concerning that which He entrusted to them, not that which He decreed for them."[9]

The Pond

The Prophet often spoke of the Pond that God had bestowed on him, as mentioned in the Koran, *Verily We have given you the Kawthar* [the Pond] (108:1). For example, "It is a river in the Garden, the banks of which are gold, and whose water is whiter than milk, sweeter than honey, and finer-smelling than musk. It flows over stones which are pearls, both large and small."[10] According to ʿAlī, the Prophet said, "He who does not have faith in my Pond will not be given entrance to it by God."[11]

The Path

This is a bridge that stretches over hell; for the faithful it is wide, whereas for the unbelievers it is narrow and sharper than a sword. Of the thirty-eight occurrences of the word *ṣirāṭ* in the Koran, most of them refer to the "straight-path" of Islam, and only one or two are said to refer to the bridge (cf. 37:23). Ibn ʿAbbās reports that the verse *Verily your Lord is at the Watch* (89:14) refers to the Path's seven stations, at each of which God questions men: at the first concerning the testimony of faith, at the second concerning the ritual prayer, and so on.[12] According to Jaʿfar, "People will cross the Path, which is thinner than a hair and sharper than a sword, in groups. Some will cross it like lightning, some like galloping horses, some crawling, some walking, and some while dangling from it."[13]

The Garden

Numerous Koranic verses promise the faithful the everlasting enjoyment of paradise. Among its delights will be *Gardens underneath which rivers flow* (2:25); *purified spouses* (2:25); *God's good pleasure* (3:15); *a shelter of plenteous shade* (4:57); *forgiveness and a generous provision* (8:4); *palaces* (25:10); *couches set face to face* (15:47); *abundant fruits* (38:51); *maidens restraining their glances* (37:48); *wide-eyed houris* (44:54); *immortal youth, going round about them with goblets, ewers, and a cup from a spring* (56:17–18); *platters of gold* (43:71); and *"all that your souls desire"* (41:31).

The Fire

The unbelievers' share of the next world is *the Fire, whose fuel is men and stone* (2:24). Its chastisement is *tremendous* (2:7), *painful* (2:10), *the most terrible* (2:85), *humbling* (2:90), *lasting* (5:37), *evil* (6:157), and *harsh* (35:7). The unbelievers will encounter *the curse of God, the angels, and men altogether* (2:161); *an evil cradling* (2:206); *an evil homecoming* (2:126); drinks of *boiling water* (47:15) and *oozing pus* (14:16); *garments of fire* (22:19); *hooked iron rods* (22:21), *fetters and chains on their necks* (40:71); *burning winds, boiling water, and the shadow of a smoking blaze* (56:42–43); *fetters, a furnace, and food that chokes* (73:12–13); and *a threefold shadow, unshading and giving no relief against the flames* (77:30–32). Moreover, *When they are cast, coupled in fetters, into a narrow place of the Fire, they will call out there for destruction. "Call not out today for one destruction—call for many!"* (25:13–14).

The Hour

Many verses and a number of surahs are dedicated to describing the end of this world, which takes place immediately preceding the resurrection. God alone knows the time of its arrival (7:187; 33:63), but the preparatory signs are described in detail. Gog and Magog and the Beast of the Earth are mentioned in the Koran: *when Gog and Magog are unloosed, and they slide down out of every slope* (21:96); and *When the Word falls on them, We will bring forth for them out of the earth a Beast that will speak to them* (27:82). According to ʿAlī, when the Beast appears, "he will carry Solomon's seal and Moses's staff. He will place the seal on the face of every believer, leaving the words, 'This is a believer in truth'; and on the face of every unbeliever, leaving the words, 'This is an unbeliever in truth.' . . . Then the Beast will raise its head, and everyone from east to west will see it, after the sun has risen from the west. When it lifts its head, repentance will no longer be accepted."[14]

Before the world's end, al-Dajjāl will rule for a period, and then be killed by Jesus. The Mahdī, a descendant of the Prophet who is identified in Shiʿite sources with the twelfth Imam, will also appear at the end of time, and Jesus will pray behind him. According to some hadiths, Jesus will establish a reign of justice; according to others, the Mahdī "will fill the earth with justice and equity as it had been filled with injustice and oppression."[15] We are told that as the final end approaches, God will send a cold wind from the direction of Syria, and all those on earth who have so much as single grain of good in their hearts will be taken. Then the trumpet will be blown, and everyone will perish.

The eschatological teachings outlined above have often been taken at face value. This was especially the case among theologians, traditionists, and Sufis before Ghazālī, though the philosophers from the beginning did not refrain from offering their interpretations of these teachings. Even in the eighth/fourteenth century, 250 years after Ghazālī and 100 years after Ibn al-ʿArabī, a Sufi of the stature of ʿIzz al-Dīn Kāshānī could write as follows in his classic, *Miṣbāḥ al-hidāya* ("The Lamp of Guidance"):

> It is incumbent upon everyone to have faith in the World of the Unseen and the states of the next world just as they are described in the Koran and the Hadith. . . . He must not begin to interpret and explain these for himself with his weak intellect and feeble understanding, nor try to understand how and in what manner they occur, for the human intellect cannot encompass the sciences of faith.[16]

But Ghazālī had already answered such objections in a manner that the community as a whole had to accept:

> You may say that these explanations and details are opposed to what the men of knowledge have discussed in their books, for they have said, "The affairs can only be known through imitation [*taqlīd*] and tradition [*samā*ʿ]; human insight cannot reach them." . . . But my words are not opposed to theirs, and everything they have said in explaining the next world is correct. However, it has not gone beyond the explanation of what will be perceived there. Either they have not known the spiritual realities, or they have not explained them, since most people cannot understand them. Whatever [in the next world] is of a corporeal nature can only be known through tradition and imitating the Prophet, but these other things are a branch of the knowledge of the spirit's reality, and there is a way to know that: spiritual insight and inward contemplation.[17]

Elsewhere, Ghazālī points out that the reality of death cannot be known without understanding the reality of life, and this in turn depends on knowledge of the spirit (*rūḥ*), "which is your own self" (or "soul," *nafs*).[18] The terms *rūḥ* and *nafs* are often used interchangeably to designate the ultimate human substance, though many authorities distinguish between them. In general, the theologians and Sufis prefer *rūḥ*, whereas the philosophers prefer *nafs*. Thus, in what follows, "spirit" and "soul" are essentially synonymous.

The Origin and the Return

Islamic teachings about the nature of man revolve around the fact that, according to the Prophet, God created man "upon His own Form." In the Koranic account, God made Adam his vicegerent (*khalīfa*), taught him *the names, all of them* (2:31); gave him the Trust (33:72); honored his children (17:70); and subjected to him everything in the heavens and the earth (31:20).

Ibn al-ʿArabī and his followers comment upon such verses in a manner that is harmonious with Islamic teachings in general. Thus, they say that the divine names mentioned in the Koran are the archetypes of all creatures; the heavens and the earth and all they contain, often referred to in the Koran as the signs of God, are the outward manifestations of the ontological perfections referred to by the names. In their multiplicity the individual creatures of the cosmos reflect the multiple names of God, and the cosmos as a whole reflects the All-Comprehensive Name Allah, or its near synonym, the All-Merciful. At the same time, each human being, made upon God's form, also reflects the name Allah: the microcosm and the macrocosm are mirror images, and each in turn reflects God. Man's uniqueness lies in the fact that he brings together all the realities of the cosmos in a summarized and all-comprehensive unity; he embraces within himself—at least potentially—the ontological perfections of all things.

Existence in its total deployment can be pictured as a circle. Beginning as a single point that represents the Creative Principle, the various existents become deployed in a clockwise descent that includes spiritual entities such as angels, intermediate entities connecting the spiritual and corporeal worlds, and then the whole range of corporeal entities, from the simple (the four elements) to the complex (minerals, plants, and animals). The human embryo, then, represents the lowest point of the circle. The full circle represents the outward manifestation of all the divine names (that is, the whole cosmos) in both its unseen (or spiritual) and visible (or corporeal) dimensions. The Perfect Man, who traverses the circle of being and actualizes each point, then becomes the point at the center of the circle, standing equidistant from all points on the circumference. As the actualized form of the name Allah, the Perfect Man manifests all other names equally; were one of them to dominate over him, he would fall into disequilibrium and imperfection since he would no longer be an "all-comprehensive" creature, but would manifest certain realities more than others.

When a human being is born into this world, he is, as a child of Adam, created upon the form of God, but the infinite ontological perfections alluded to by this name remain potentialities hidden within him. As he grows, he begins to actualize his potential perfections. Theological, philosophical, and Sufi texts on the soul often point out that man first gains the perfections of the vegetative soul, then those of the animal soul, and only then does he begin to become a true human being. But his entry into the human world around the time of puberty—when the practice of Islam becomes incumbent on him—marks only the first step of an infinite ascent. Man, made in God's image, knows no limits.

In a formulation somewhat different from that found in the school of Ibn al-ʿArabī, Najm al-Dīn Rāzī (d. 654/1256) speaks of five stages of man referred to in the Koran: (1) nonexistence in God's knowledge, (2) existence in the world of the spirits, (3) attachment of the spirit to the body, (4) separation from the bodily frame, and (5) return to the frame. Each stage is necessary for the actualization of the perfections required by certain divine names. Through the first stage man perceives God as Creator; through the second he comes to know Him by such attributes as desire, life, speech, sight, and power; through the third he knows Him as the Provider, the Forgiver, the Munificent, and so on; through the fourth he comes to know Him as the Slayer, and through the fifth as the Reviver.[19]

The goal of man's passage through the worlds is the acquisition of knowledge or the realization of every concomitant and concrete manifestation of the names taught to Adam. For, in the words of Jāmī, "Man in his innate disposition is plain, a receptacle for all attributes."[20] In Ṣadrā's more philosophical language, "Every human soul, because of its innate disposition given by God, is worthy to know the realities of all things."[21] This conception of the human reality is often expressed by affirming an innate knowledge of universal realities that cannot be actualized until the soul learns particulars. In Najm al-Dīn Rāzī's words:

> In the beginning the spirit had knowledge of universals, not of particulars; it had knowledge of the world of the unseen but not of the visible world. When it was joined to this world and duly trained and nurtured, it acquired knowledge of both universals and particulars, and became *knower of the unseen and the visible* [62:8] as God's vicegerent. In the world of the spirits, it did not have the strength or instruments required for the tasks of the Lord's vicegerency; it was in this (lower) world that it acquired the necessary strength and instruments, and thus attained the perfection of the degree of vicegerency.[22]

ʿAzīz al-Dīn Nasafī describes man's ascent to perfection in terms of spiritual light:

> Every individual existent possesses in itself and of itself what it must have. The spirit does not come from anywhere nor go anywhere. The spirit is light, and the cosmos is overflowing with light, for light is its spirit, moving it toward perfection. . . . At one level this light is called "nature," at another level "spirit," at another "intellect," and at still another "Nondelimited Light." . . .
>
> At the first level, life, knowledge, desire, and power [the fundamental divine attributes] do not exist in actuality. But as the existents move up through the levels, gradually life, knowledge, desire, power, hearing, sight, and speech come to exist in actuality. . . . In other words, that light which is the spirit of the cosmos and with which the cosmos is overflowing does not possess, at that level, knowledge, desire, and power in actuality; but as the light gradually moves up the levels, life, knowledge, desire, and power come to exist in actualized mode.[23]

Man's Infinite Potentiality

Avicenna, in philosophical language, provides a clear formulation of man's fundamental nature:

> The perfection peculiar to the rational soul is for it to become an intellective world within which is inscribed the form of the whole, the intelligible order of the whole, and the good that is effused into the whole; it begins with [knowledge of God, i.e.,] the Origin of the whole, moves on to [knowledge of] nondelimited, spiritual, noble substances; then to spiritual substances having a kind of attachment to bodies; and then to the celestial corporeal bodies with all their dispositions and faculties. The soul continues in this manner until it realizes fully

> within itself the disposition peculiar to existence as a whole. Hence, it is transformed into an intelligible world parallel to the entire existent cosmos; it contemplates that which is absolute comeliness, absolute good, and true beauty, and it becomes united with it.[24]

As for the form of all the names—all the ontological possibilities—the human substance is able to achieve a total correspondence with the entire cosmos. But there is no guarantee that a person will reach such a station, and in fact the vast majority of human beings stop short before realizing their full potential. In effect, they actualize only some of the ontological possibilities embraced by their all-comprehensive primordial nature; they cease to reflect all the divine names and become loci of manifestation for only some of them. They become mirrors for part of the universe instead of the whole. They leave the centrality of the human state, and instead of being all creatures and all creation, they become this creature or that. Particularly in Sufi texts, the infinite potentiality of the human state is perceived as a kind of unlimited malleability that allows man to become anything at all.

Thus, Nasafī explains that the earth cannot play the role of water, nor the grapevine that of the almond tree, nor the eye that of the ear:

> Have you not recognized that each thing fulfils its fixed function, but that man can necessarily fulfill the function of all? . . . Thus man is defined in the sense that he can assume the qualities of every other creature. . . . According to whether he assumes the qualities of this or that creature, it is this or that creature that he becomes, even though outwardly he may have the form of a man.[25]

Long before Nasafī, Sanāʾī had described man as compounded of all the worlds—material, psychic, and spiritual—and hence "molded of heart and clay." Each existent other than man assumes a single aspect, according to its fixed place in the hierarchy of existence, but man cannot be reduced to "one color."[26] Rūmī often refers to man's infinite potentiality: "God will give you what you seek. Wherever your aspiration lies, that you will become."[27] Rūmī's son, Sulṭān Walad (d. 712/1312), makes an explicit connection between this teaching and eschatology:

> Man is compounded of form and meaning, of satanic and divine; every instant the houris of paradise and the devils of hell show their faces from his inward reality so that it may be seen which vein and which attribute dominate over him. His desire takes him to that form with which he has a greater affinity [*munāsaba*]; it becomes his kiblah and beloved. Necessarily in the end he will become identical to it and be resurrected with it.[28]

Again in Rūmī's words:

> Whatever makes you tremble—know that you are worth just that!
> That is why the heart of God's lover is greater than His Throne.[29]

According to the *ḥadīth qudsī*, "Neither My heavens nor My earth embrace Me, but the heart of My believing servant does embrace Me." The servant whose heart encompasses God has become the Perfect Man by actualizing the divine form upon which he was created; having comprehended all the divine names, he contains within himself the form of every creature. This is the meaning of Ibn al-ʿArabī's famous verse:

> My heart has become a receptacle for every form,
> a pasture for gazelles and a cloister for Christian monks.[30]

In a similar vein, Ibn al-ʿArabī alludes to a hadith that says that God will appear at the resurrection in a multitude of forms, but His creatures will deny Him until He appears in a form that corresponds to their own belief. It is only the Perfect Men, whose hearts encompass all the divine names in perfect equilibrium, who will recognize God in whatever form He displays:

> He who delimits God [according to his own belief] denies Him in everything other than his own delimitation, acknowledging Him only when He reveals Himself within that delimitation. But he who frees Him from all delimitation never denies Him, acknowledging Him in every form in which He appears.[31]

Ṣadrā summarizes this discussion as follows:

> The soul is *the junction of the two seas* [18:60] of corporeal and spiritual things. . . . If you consider its substance in this world, you will find it the principle of all bodily powers, employing all the animal and vegetal forms in its service. But if you consider its substance in the world of the intellect, you will find that at the beginning of its fundamental nature it is pure potentiality without any form in that world. . . . Its initial relation to the form of that world is that of the seed to the fruit, or of the embryo to the animal: Just as the embryo is an embryo in actuality and an animal only potentially, so [at first] is the soul a mere mortal man in actuality, but a [realized] intellect potentially.[32]

Through life in this world the soul's potentialities become actualized; death is in no way an imperfection, since, as stated in the commonly quoted hadith, it is merely "transferal from one abode to another." In Ṣadrā's terms, death occurs once the soul has actualized all its potentialities. Having no more need for the material body, it discards it in order to move on to the next stage of its existence:

> The reason for physical death is that the soul reaches perfection and independence in existence, so it turns through its ingrained activity and efforts toward another world. Thus, as its essence gains strength, little by little, until it attains a new kind of existence, it cuts off its connection [with the body] by strengthening its connection to another body, which is acquired in accordance with its moral qualities and psychic dispositions. Hence, first and in essence it takes on a second life; but as an accidental corollary, its physical life comes to an end. . . .
>
> Attaining the degree of substantiality, actuality, and independence is shared by the believer and unbeliever. . . . and by many animals that have an actualized imaginal faculty. There is no contradiction between this ontological perfection and substantial independence on the one hand, and wretchedness and suffering torment through the fire of hell . . . on the other; on the contrary, these things merely confirm our conclusion. For the fact that the existence [of the individual] is strengthened and accentuated and that it departs from material coverings and veils results in an increased intensity in the perception of pains.[33]

The Role of the Body

In the above passage, Ṣadrā speaks of the soul's discarding its body through its connection to "another body." Ṣadrā, Ibn al-ʿArabī, and others maintain that a body is indispensable to the soul at all stages of its existence; in fact, they are following Koranic usage, where the word *nafs* most often refers to the whole human reality, not just to the spiritual side of man's existence.[34] In Ibn al-ʿArabī's words, "When God created the human spirit, He created it governing a natural (*ṭabīʿī*) sensory form, whether in this world, in the *barzakh*, or wherever."[35] Like Rūmī, Ibn al-ʿArabī compares the individual souls of men to patches of light thrown down into separate courtyards by the "sun," that is, the *single soul* (7:189) from which the souls were created. The individual existence of a soul thus depends on the locus within which it becomes manifested. After death, "God desires the subsistence of these lights in keeping with the disparity they have assumed," so He creates bodies for them in the *barzakh*, through which they remain distinct from other souls.[36] Mullā Ṣadrā explains that the total potentiality of the human innate disposition cannot be actualized without bodies, since man is in need of the physical senses to actualize his imaginal faculty: "Then, on the basis of correct images, the soul is able to extract disengaged meanings, and from these it can come to understand its own worlds, its Origin, and its Return."[37]

The all-comprehensive human reality has to be a potential locus of manifestation for every divine name, including those, like the "Outward," which demand a mode of existence at the outermost limit of manifestation. Otherwise, man would not encompass "all the worlds" and would cease to be man. Hence, for Ṣadrā, the resurrection of the body follows from the very definition of the human being, and he marshals his formidable powers of reasoning to prove its reality. It is impossible here to even allude to his various complicated proofs; it need be mentioned only that he maintains vehemently the fundamental identity of the resurrection body and the body man possesses in this world, despite certain differences. This is because bodily nature is determined solely by "form" (in the Aristotelian sense) and not by "matter," which is nonmanifest without form. Therefore, the resurrection body is the same body, even though the ontological conditions of the *barzakh* and the resurrection differ in certain respects from those in this world.[38]

Like the world of the spirits, the *barzakh* is immaterial, but like that of the corporeal bodies, it possesses shape, form, and number. Without it, the spiritual beings, which are luminous and disengaged from matter, could have no contact with beings of the corporeal world, which are material and tenebrous. Ibn al-ʿArabī states,

> The *barzakh* is *the junction of the two seas* [18:60]: the sea of spiritual meanings and the sea of sensory objects. The sensory things cannot be meaning, nor can the meanings be sensory. But the world of imagination, which we have called *the junction of the two seas*, gives meanings corporeal shape and makes sensory objects into subtle realities.[39]

In the same way, without the animal soul, which is the locus of imagination in man, the human spirit or "rational soul" could not govern the body.

Ibn al-ʿArabī distinguishes between the *barzakh* located on the descending arc of the circle of being and that on the ascending arc. The first of these *barzakh*s acts as the ontological nexus between spiritual and corporeal realities, whereas the second—called the "grave" in many hadiths—grows up from human acts and moral qualities as a fruit grows on a tree.[40]

In the human microcosm, the world of imagination is directly reflected in the faculty of imagination, which is experienced most clearly in dreams, when we see, hear, smell, taste, and feel without any corresponding objects outside of the mind. In Ṣadrā's view, imagination is a faculty that creates images in our mind, whether or not these correspond to objects in the outside world. Hence, even during wakefulness, the imagination creates in the mind the image of the object that the eye has "perceived." Imagination has an infinite power of conjuration because it can picture all that exists and all that does not exist. The ultimate source of his ability is the fact that man is the microcosm containing all things in himself, while his imagination is a locus of manifestation for the divine name the "Form-Giver."

Ṣadrā's conclusion is that after death man exists in the *barzakh* in an imaginal body whose very substance is produced by himself. This does not mean that the *barzakh* is "imaginary"; in fact, it is far more real than this world, since it lies at a higher point on the circle of being. In the words of the Prophet, "People are asleep, but when they die, they wake up."[41] None of what man witnesses in the next stage of existence is outside his own soul, but the reality of the soul, as the form of God, is ultimately without limits. So it should not come as a surprise that Ṣadrā calls the "imaginal" experiences of the next world "more strongly substantial, more firmly established, and more permanent in reality than material forms."[42]

Equilibrium and Deviation: Mercy and Wrath

The goal of Islam is to guide mankind to ultimate felicity by establishing equilibrium on both the individual and the social level. This means that the human substance, made upon the form of the all-comprehensive names Allah and All-Merciful, must be shown the way to actualize all the concomitants of the individual divine names. Ṣadrā summarizes the destiny and felicity of the soul in the following terms:

> In respect to its intellective essence, the felicity of the soul lies in its attaining to pure intellectual realities and becoming the locus for divine forms, for the order of existence and for the disposition of the whole, from God Himself down to the lowest levels of existence. As for the soul's perfection and felicity in respect to its companionship with the body . . . this lies in the attainment of "justice." . . . This means that it must achieve perfect balance among opposing moral qualities.[43]

By employing the term justice (*ʿadāla*), derived from the same root as the word "equilibrium" (*iʿtidāl*), Ṣadrā is alluding to the point of contact between the ultimate perfection of the human soul—sometimes called the station of the Perfect Man, who stands at the point at the center of the circle—and the science of ethics, whether considered as a branch of philosophy, Sufism, or the Shariah. In Ṭūsī's words, "Among virtues, none is more perfect than the virtue of justice, as is obvious in the discipline of ethics, for the true mid-point is justice, all else being peripheral to it and taking its reference therefrom."[44]

Ghazālī identifies justice with the straight path of Islam, being "the true mean among the opposite moral qualities."[45] He summarizes Islamic ethics in his *Iḥyāʾ* when speaking of the four basic kinds of human attributes: beastly (*bahīmī*), predatory (*sabʿī*), satanic (*shayṭānī*), and lordly or seigneurial (*rabbānī*). It is as if "the total in man's skin is a pig, a dog, a devil, and a wise man." The first three kinds of attributes must be put under the domination of the fourth, which is manifested most clearly in man's intellect. If the latter dominates, "the matter is in equilibrium, and justice appears in the kingdom of the body and all proceeds on the straight path."[46] Otherwise man will be in the service of the pig, dog, or devil, and he will fail to achieve human status. This is in fact the state of most men, and it explains their lot in the next world.

The Shariah and the Tariqah provide the framework in which the "true mean" among the moral qualities can be achieved; they allow man to follow the advice of the hadith, "Assume the character traits of Allah"; in other words, "Actualize all the divine names upon the form of which you were created." Ghazālī refers to the actualization of these names as the station of *ta'alluh* (a word derived from the same root as the name Allah), meaning "being God-like" or "theomorphism."[47] Muslim philosophers, like Avicenna, adopted this term as a definition of human perfection; thus Ṣadrā is often referred to as the "theomorphic sage" (*al-ḥakīm al-muta'allih*).

Farghānī explains that man must follow the Shariah, because only it can protect him from being overcome by the multiplicity and disequilibrium of the sensory world and facilitate his actualization of his theomorphic nature. In our present state, nature veils the spiritual world and its properties of oneness, equilibrium, and simplicity. By following the Shariah a person gains an actualized connection to certain divine names closely related to unity that formerly had only been latent within himself. Thus, God is the Guide, the Right-Guider (*al-rashīd*), the All-Compassionate, the Forgiver (*al-ghafūr*), and the Pardoner (*al-ʿafū*), but to benefit from these names a person must accept the divine guidance and compassion that are offered—that is, he must submit to the message from Heaven.[48]

It is essential to recognize the distinction between the names of mercy and gentleness, such as those mentioned above, and those of wrath and severity, such as the Vengeful, the Terrible, the Abaser, and the Almighty. According to the *ḥadīth qudsī*, "My mercy takes precedence over My wrath"; so the names of mercy take precedence over those of wrath. The reason for this is simply that mercy is the very nature of God, whereas wrath comes into play in connection with certain of His creatures. In the words of ʿAbd al-Karīm Jīlī (d. ca. 832/1428), "God said, *My mercy embraces all things* [7:156], but He did not say, 'My Wrath embraces all things,' for He created all things as a mercy from Him. . . . The secret in this is that mercy is the attribute of His Essence, but wrath is not."[49] Moreover, since man is created upon the form of the All-Merciful, the equilibrium attained by the Perfect Men relates directly to the attributes of the Essence, such as unity. But disequilibrium, deviation, and multiplicity relate to those names—the names of wrath—which are in one respect opposed to the names of mercy.

This is why theologians and jurists such as Abū Ḥanīfa often point out that evil deeds are debarred from any connection with such merciful attributes as good-pleasure (*al-riḍā'*) and guidance.[50] In expanding on such teachings, Ibn al-ʿArabī draws a clear distinction between the paths of mercy and wrath: Although all things return to God, their returns are conditioned by the particular names to which they are connected. Hence, God calls us to follow the path of justice and equilibrium, which will lead us to the names of mercy: "God calls us to worship Him according to the path which connects us to our particular felicity." As his commentator points out, all paths lead to God but each takes us to a different name.[51]

God is the Just (*al-ʿadl*), and thus He puts everything in its proper place. This means that those creatures who have actualized the form of the All-Merciful upon which they were created enjoy mercy, while those who have not actualized the human potential suffer wrath, since they remain in multiplicity and disequilibrium. The Koran makes a clear connection between wrath and the chastisement of hell. Al-Niffarī (d. 360/971) points out the relationship between the names of wrath and the Fire on the one hand, and the names of mercy and the Garden on the other; he declares that the Fire derives from "otherness," that is, being veiled by separation and plurality from God and from one's own innate disposition: "Unveiling is the Garden of the Garden, veiling the Fire of the Fire."[52] In short, "to enter the Garden" is to actualize the form upon which one was created and to attain to mercy, whereas "entering the Fire" means to be separated from one's theomorphic selfhood. As Frithjof Schuon puts it:

> The good reason for the sanctions beyond death is apparent once we are aware of human imperfection; being a disequilibrium that imperfection ineluctably calls forth its own repercussion. . . . The fire beyond the grave is definitely nothing but our own intellect actualized in opposition to our own falsehood. . . . Man therefore condemns himself; according to the Quran it is his members themselves which accuse him; once beyond the realm of lies his violations are transformed into flames.[53]

Certain Sufis maintain that after death—as before death—God reveals Himself to man primarily in the mode of mercy, but the unbeliever's corrupted nature perceives that mercy as wrath. In Niffarī's words, "That through which He blesses in the Garden is the same as that through which He chastises in the Fire."[54] Ibn al-ʿArabī is more explicit:

> Chastisement occurs through the very things that cause bliss. . . . just as a man of cold temperament enjoys the heat of the sun, while a man of hot temperament is tortured by it. In the last analysis, the very thing that causes bliss causes pain.[55]

In discussing the torments of hell, Muslim thinkers eventually come back to the precedence of God's mercy over His wrath. The names of mercy in the Koran outnumber the names of wrath by at least five to one; the name Vengeful does not occur as such, but only once in verbal form, whereas its opposite, the Forgiving, occurs about a hundred times. Considerations such as these explain why the view that hell cannot be everlasting has often prevailed, even among some exoteric theologians. For Ibn al-ʿArabī and his followers, the precedence of God's Mercy means that the chastisement (*ʿadhāb*) of the unbelievers will one day turn sweet (*ʿadhb*), even if they remain in hell forever.[56]

Death and the Barzakh

Long before Muslims began writing about an independent world of imagination identified with the *barzakh,* the community was well aware that "Sleep is the brother of death" (a saying normally cited as a hadith). The Koran states, *God takes the souls at the time of death, and those which have not died, in their sleep* (39:42); and authorities such as the exegete al-Zamakhsharī (d. 538/1143–1144) could argue that sleep and death were the same reality.[57] The science of dream interpretation is mentioned in the Koran and was practiced by the Prophet. And the vast literature that developed on the subject shows that it has been popular throughout Islamic history. Since the close connection between sleep and death was affirmed from early on, it is not surprising that the eschatological data came to be interpreted following much of the same principles that were employed for dreams.

In dreams the imaginal faculty displays ideas in forms that possess a correspondence or affinity with the underlying meaning or content. The task of the interpreter is to understand the original meaning behind the form. His task is made easier, of course, if the dream is "true" (*ṣādiq*) and derives therefore not only from the dreaming subject but also from the objective world of imagination outside and beyond him. The Prophet himself said that a true dream is "one of the forty-six parts of prophecy."[58]

Ghazālī points out that because sleep is the twin brother of death, through it "we have gained an aptitude for understanding certain states which we could not understand through wakefulness." He explains that the works of men have "spirits" and "realities" that cannot be perceived in this world but that appear after death, for in the next world, "Forms are subordinate to spirits and realities, so everything seen there will be seen in a form appropriate to its reality."[59] In the same way, the forms we see in dreams correspond closely to their meanings, as can be understood from an account of the famous dream interpreter Ibn Sīrīn (d. early second/eighth century). When asked about a man who had dreamed he was sealing the mouths and private parts of people with a seal ring, he explained that the man must be a muezzin who calls people to prayer in the early morning of Ramadan (thus announcing to them that they must commence the fast). Ghazālī explains:

> When this man became separated somewhat from the world of corporeal sensation, the spirit of his work was unveiled to him. But since he was still in the world of imagination [*ʿālam al-takhayyul*]—for a

> dreamer never ceases to imagine things—his imaginal faculty veiled the spirit [of his work] in an imaginal likeness [*mithāl mutakhayyal*], that is, the seal ring and the sealing. This likeness reveals the spirit of his work more clearly than the call to prayer itself, since the world of dreams is nearer than this lower world to the next world.[60]

"What is really strange," remarks Ghazālī, "is that you have been shown so many examples of the resurrection in sleep, yet you remain totally oblivious to its reality."[61] So dreams provide a key to understanding the Islamic teachings concerning the next world. For example, the Prophet describes the reality of the present world by saying that on the Day of Resurrection it will be brought in the form of an ugly old woman, and everyone who sees her will say, "We seek refuge from you in God." Then they will be told, "This is the world that you spent so much effort in trying to acquire."[62] Again, the Prophet speaks of the unbeliever in his grave being tormented by ninety-nine dragons (*tinnīn*), each of which is ninety-nine serpents with nine heads. These represent the unbelievers' evil qualities, such as pride, hypocrisy, envy, and greed, while the exact numbers refer to the fact that such qualities can be divided into a limited number of general principles possessing subdivisions (as can be observed, for example, in the science of ethics). As Ghazālī puts it, "It is these qualities which are mortal sins; they themselves are transformed into scorpions and serpents."[63]

Ghazālī's conclusion is clear, especially since it is repeated in numerous texts on eschatology over the centuries: In death, man finds nothing but his own attributes; no longer veiled by the corporeal body, they reveal themselves to him in forms appropriate to his new abode.[64]

Upon death, therefore, man awakens to the realities of his own words, acts, and moral qualities; his moral substance, whether good or evil, assumes corporeal shape. Everything that had been hidden in the lower world becomes outwardly manifest. This is why, in the words of Ṭūsī, "Whoever is afraid of natural death is afraid of the concomitant of his own essence and completion of his own quiddity."[65] Rūmī makes the same point:

> If you fear and flee from death, you fear
> yourself, O friend. Take heed!
> It is your own ugly face, not the face of death.
> Your spirit is like a tree, and death its leaves.[66]

Sanā'ī explains how the afterlife is where the inward becomes outward:

> When they lift the veil of sensory perception from your eyes,
> if an unbeliever you will find scorching hell, if a man of faith
> the Garden.
> Your heaven and hell are within yourself: look inside!
> See furnaces in your liver, Gardens in your heart.[67]

Rūmī asks:

How many children of your thoughts will you see in the grave,
all surrounding your soul crying, "Papa!"?
Your good thoughts give birth to youths and houris;
your ugly thoughts give birth to great demons.[68]

Such ideas explain the eschatological significance of these famous lines of Rūmī:

You are your thought, brother,
the rest of you is bones and fiber.
If you think of roses, you are a Rosegarden;
if you think of thorns, you are fuel for the Furnace.[69]

ʿAyn al-Quḍāt explains that all vision of the spiritual world or of the next world is based on the "display of images" (*tamaththul*). According to the Koran, Gabriel appeared to Mary as *a man without fault* through *tamaththul* (19:17). On this basis we can understand the questioning of Munkar and Nakīr:

> It takes place within yourself. Those of our contemporaries who are veiled from the truth have come up with this problem: How can the two angels, in one instant, visit a thousand different individuals? [They conclude that] one must accept this as an article of faith [since it contradicts reason]. But in this connection Avicenna—God have mercy on him—provided a world of explanation in two sentences: "Munkar is his evil deed, and Nakīr is his good deed." . . . The ego is the mirror of blameworthy qualities, and the intellect and heart are the mirror of praiseworthy qualities. When a man looks, he sees his own attributes revealing themselves in images [*tamaththul-garī kunad*]. His own existence is his torment, though he thinks someone else is tormenting him. . . . If you want to hear the Prophet himself say this, listen when he speaks of the chastisement of the grave: "They are only your works given back to you."[70]

The Lesser Resurrection

The experience of death for the microcosm corresponds to the coming of the Hour for the macrocosm. Hence, the Koranic accounts of the end of the world can also be understood as referring to the death of the individual. Many Koranic commentators, such as ʿAbd al-Razzāq Kashānī, understand verses referring to the resurrection in such terms. Ghazālī had already brought this type of commentary under the protective wing of mainstream Islam in his *Iḥyāʾ*: "I mean by 'lesser resurrection' the state of death, for the Prophet—God bless him and give him peace—said, 'He who has died has undergone his resurrection.'" He explains that all the terms that refer to the greater resurrection have their equal (*naẓīr*) in the lesser resurrection. Thus, the earth corresponds to the body, mountains to bones, the sky to the head, the sun to the heart, the stars to the senses, grass to hair, trees to limbs, and so on:

> So when the elements of your body are destroyed through death, *the earth will be shaken with a mighty shaking* [99:1]; when the bones are separated from the flesh, *the earth and the mountains will be lifted up and crushed with a single blow* [69:14]; when the bones decay, *the mountains will be scattered like ashes* [77:10]; when your heart is darkened through death, *the sun will be darkened* [81:1]; when your hearing, sight, and other senses cease to work, *the stars will be thrown down* [81:2]; when your brain is split, *the sky will be split asunder* [55:37]. . . . The instant you die, the lesser resurrection will take place for you; nevertheless, you will not miss anything of the greater resurrection.[71]

Bābā Ṭāhir Hamadānī (fl. fifth/eleventh century) employs a similar method of interpretation to explain the events that follow the resurrection:

> People are now standing on the Path though they are unaware, for in the eyes of the Sufis, this world is the next world. In the hereafter there will be a Path, a Scale, a Garden, and a Fire. The Path of the Sufis in this world is their way, which is "sharper than a sword." Their Scales are their hearts, which are the best of all scales; their Garden is the turning of their hearts [toward God], and their Fire is the turning of their hearts away [from Him.][72]

Like many other authors, Sayyid Ḥaydar Āmulī (d. after 787/1385) details several kinds of resurrection (see Table 6).[73] Jīlī, for his part, interprets the events that take place at the end of time in terms of the voluntary death or greatest resurrection experienced by the spiritual traveler. According to a hadith, Gog and Magog will appear on the earth, eating its fruits and drinking its seas; once they are slain, the earth will revive. In the same way, the ego's agitation and corrupt thoughts take possession of the earth of man's heart, eat its fruits, and drink its seas, so that no trace of spiritual knowledge can appear. Then God's angels annihilate these satanic whisperings with sciences from God: the earth is revived and it gives abundant harvest. This is a mark of man's gaining proximity to God. As for "the beast of the earth," it will come to tell the earth's inhabitants about the truth of the promises concerning the resurrection. In the same way, the traveler reaches a stage of unveiling where he comes to understand the inward mysteries of religion; this is a favor from God, so that "the troops of his faith will not retreat before the armies of the continuing veil." Just as people will not

Table 6. Kinds of Resurrection According to Sayyid Ḥaydar Āmulī

		Lesser	Intermediate	Greater
Microcosmic	Formal (*ṣūrī*)	Physical death	Period in the grave (*barzakh*)	Gathering on the Day of Resurrection
	Supraformal (*maʿnawī*)	Voluntary death or Spiritual awakening	Transmutation of moral Qualities	Annihilation of self and subsistence in God
Macrocosmic	Formal one view	Destruction of the world through return of compound things to the domain of simple elemental bodies	Return of simple things to the *materia prima*	Return of the souls and spirits to the First Substance
	Formal another view	Appearance of the Mahdī	Transformation of the sensory world into the *barzakh*	Bodily resurrection
	Supraformal	Return of particular souls to the Universal Soul	Return of particular spirits to the Greatest Spirit	Return of intellects to the First Intellect

be convinced of the coming of the Hour until the appearance of the beast, so too will the gnostic not understand all the requisites of Divinity until the spirit appears from out of the earth of his bodily nature. The conflict between Jesus and the Anti-Christ (Dajjāl) refers to the battle between the spirit and the ego, while the appearance of the Mahdī alludes to man's becoming "the possessor of equilibrium at the pinnacle of every perfection." Finally, the rising of the sun from the west marks the realization of the ultimate human perfection.[74]

The Greater Resurrection

Some authors, such as Maybudī, compare the *barzakh* with the womb. Ibn al-ʿArabī expands on this idea, explaining that after death man begins to reap the fruit of his life in this world: "having undergone various stages of development, he is born on the Day of Resurrection."[75] The imaginal bodies that men possess in the *barzakh* are like lamps within which the spirit is lit. Then *the Trumpet shall be blown, and whosoever is in the heavens and whosoever is in the earth shall swoon, save whom God wills.* At this first blast of the trumpet, the lamps will be extinguished and transferred into resurrection bodies. *Then it shall be blown again, and lo, they shall stand beholding* (39:68); that is, once again the lamps will be lit. Some of those newly awakened will ask, *"Who roused us out from our sleeping place?"* (36:52). People will gradually forget their situation in the *barzakh* and imagine that it had been a dream, even though, when they first entered the *barzakh,* that had been an awakening relative to their life in the world.[76] The resurrection is far more real and intense than the *barzakh,* just as the latter is more real than the world. This is why, after death, the people of Pharaoh are *exposed morning and evening* to the Fire, but they do not enter into it, since they are still in the *barzakh.* But *on the day when the Hour is come: "Admit the people of Pharaoh into the more intense chastisement"* (40:46).[77]

Although most theologians maintained that the resurrection body would be the same body as that which existed in the world, Ghazālī among others points out that even this earthly body does not stay the same, since it constantly changes throughout life. The truth of the matter is that "the body is only a mount; though the horse should change, the rider stays the same."[78] Najm al-Dīn Rāzī suggests that the difference between the earthly body and the resurrection body lies in its degrees of "subtlety" (*laṭāfa*). In both cases the body belongs to the realm of nature and is therefore compounded of the four elements; but in this world earth and water predominate, whereas in the next world fire and air predominate. Then, "when the form is subtle and luminous, it no longer interferes with the spirit." This is why people will display outwardly in the next life the realities that were latent in their hearts during their earthly lives.[79]

As already indicated, Ṣadrā holds that the resurrection body is identical with the earthly body in form. Ibn al-ʿArabī and his followers speak of a sensory resurrection at the level of nature, that is, within the domain of the four elements, but the ontological level of hell will correspond to that of this lower world, with its multiplicity and disequilibrium. Qūnawī explains that the people of wretchedness will meet all their thoughts, knowledge, states, and works in forms appropriate to their debased ontological level, while the spiritual dimensions of these things will depart from them. In contrast, the thoughts, states, and works of the people of felicity will be transformed into spiritual entities, while their resurrection bodies will subsist inside themselves. In this world, a person's inward reality is infinitely malleable and nondelimited, whereas his outward form and acts are defined and determined. In paradise, "the property of nondelimitation will pertain to the outward dimension, while the property of delimitation will belong to the inward."[80]

If it is true that the inward state of man is revealed at the lesser resurrection, this is even more true at the greater resurrection, the day when *that which is in the breasts is brought out* (100:10) and *secrets are divulged* (86:9). In the words of Sanāʾī:

> If you die with an ugly character, you will be
> resurrected in the form of a beast. . . .
> When meaning comes out of the house into the street,
> your face will be impressed with what is in your heart.
> For the sake of display, the Originator of qualities
> will put potentiality on the inside and actuality on the outside.[81]

The result of not having realized "justice" and "equilibrium" in this world becomes manifest in the very form in which the resurrection body appears. Ghazālī had spoken of the "pig" and "dog" within man, that is, the faculties of beastliness or "concupiscence" (*shahwa*) and predatoriness or "irascibility" (*ghaḍab*), which must be overcome by the intellect. A number of authors state that man will assume corporeal shape in the *barzakh* according to the character that dominated over him in this world. Thus, he will be raised up in the form of a dog if he was dominated by irascibility, a pig if dominated by concupiscence, and so on.

According to Rūmī:

> There are thousands of wolves and pigs in our existence,
> good and evil, fair and foul.
> Man's properties are determined by the trait that predominates:
> if gold is more than copper, then he is gold.
> Of necessity you will be given form at the resurrection in accordance
> with the character that predominated in your existence.[82]

Among the philosophers, al-Fārābī (d. 339/950) interprets certain teachings of Plato in similar terms,[83] and Shiʿite thinkers like Ibn Abī Jumhūr Aḥsāʾī (d. 905/1501) develop this mode of interpretation in detail, citing many Koranic verses and hadiths in support of their arguments.[84] Ṣadrā holds that the very essences of human souls will diverge in the hereafter and that they will become many species, falling into four main genera (corresponding to Ghazālī's pig, dog, devil, and wise man).[85] This is not transmigration (*tanāsukh*), say our authors, since it does not take place in this world, but on another plane of existence.[86]

Although theologians and most Sufis did not question the reality of the bodily resurrection, the early philosophers were inclined to be skeptical because they could find no rational proofs outside revelation to support it. Nonetheless, many of them considered the survival of the soul a foregone conclusion, since it belongs by nature to the domain of disengaged and incorruptible spiritual substances; then its bliss is for it to contemplate the highest realities and God Himself. According to Avicenna, if the soul attains to perfection, after death it will become connected to the Divine and be plunged into true pleasure. Imperfect souls experience various degrees of pleasure or pain according to the degree to which they have become detached from the body or remained immersed in the world. Concerning bodily resurrection, Avicenna anticipates later developments in Islamic thought by suggesting that certain souls may experience the events described in the Koran and the Hadith because these descriptions had shaped their imaginal faculties; they will then perceive what they had believed they would perceive. After all, he says, imaginal forms are stronger than sensory forms, as can be observed in dreams. But the images contemplated in the next world are more stable than those seen in dreams because the body no longer interferes with perception.[87]

Avicenna also suggests that the Islamic teachings about bodily resurrection should be interpreted allegorically. Islam is addressed to all men, not just philosophers and sages, so it has to speak a language understood by everyone, that of corporal realities: "Our Prophet—God bless him and give him peace—perfected this mode of explanation such that nothing can be added to it." Avicenna then turns the tables on those Christian missionaries who later were to criticize Islam for its "sensual" descriptions of paradise. He says that the Christians accept the bodily resurrection but fail to describe the various forms of corporeal ease and punishment; instead, they suggest that men will be like angels. But:

> Most people think—though they do not dare say so because of their fear [of the religious law]—that angels are miserable creatures who have no ease or joy. They do not eat, drink, or have sexual intercourse, and they occupy themselves constantly with unrequited worship. The common people think this way since they cannot begin to understand the nature of true felicity and spiritual joy.[88]

Many Sufis agreed that the Koranic data need not be taken literally. Sulṭān Walad writes:

> The true nature of meanings cannot be expressed in words; they do not resemble anything, nor are they opposed to anything. But some-

> thing has to be said in keeping with the understandings of people so that they will strive to reach those meanings. In the same way, one explains to a child the pleasure of kissing by comparing a woman's lips to sugar. . . . But in fact, what is the relationship between lips and sugar? There is no resemblance at all. Likewise, God explains the Garden in terms of houris, castles, trees, and rivers in order that it may be understood in these terms. But in fact, how should the Garden resemble such things? For they are transitory, while it is eternal. What relation is there between the transitory and the eternal?[89]

Ghazālī displays the concern of a theologian in affirming the bodily nature of the resurrection, but he reminds us that the soul will also be resurrected, so spiritual delights and torments must also be taken into account. The Koran refers to the latter in such verses as, *What shall teach you about the Crusher? The kindled fire of God, roaring over the hearts* (104:5–7). Ghazālī divides this spiritual fire into three kinds: (1) the fire of separation from worldly desires, which is particularly strong at death and in the *barzakh;* (2) the fire of shame and disgrace, which overcomes man at the resurrection when all his deeds are displayed; (3) the fire of regret over being deprived of the vision of God, which is the lasting torment of hell.[90]

All the inhabitants of the Garden will possess "bodies," but their spirits will dwell in different degrees of proximity to God. Already at the time of the Prophet, there are references to eight levels and a hundred degrees of paradise; many authorities rank the levels in accordance with different names employed in the Koran.[91] According to some accounts, the vision of God guaranteed to the believers in several hadiths and alluded to in the Koran (e.g., 75:23), will take place at the Dune of White Musk. Ibn al-ʿArabī states that all of the people of the Garden will take stations there, "in keeping with their degrees of knowledge of God, not the degree of their works; for works pertain to the bliss of the Garden, not to the contemplation of the All-Merciful."[92] In this context, many authorities cite the *ḥadīth qudsī,* "I have prepared for My righteous servants what no eye has seen, nor ear has heard, nor has entered the heart of any man. . . . *No soul knows what is laid up for them secretly* (32:17)." They also cite the hadith, "God has a Garden in which are no houris, castles, milk, or honey; our Lord discloses Himself, laughing.[93]

According to Basṭāmī, all the believers will see God once in the Garden, but after that only the elect will continue to see Him. For, according to the well-known hadith, "In the Garden is a market where there is no buying or selling, only the forms of men and women; when a man desires a form, he enters into it." Those who enter a form, says Basṭāmī, will never again go to visit God: "God misleads you in this life as to the market, and also in the next; you will always be enslaved to the market."[94] Ibn al-ʿArabī and his followers explain the market of the Garden as a branch of the world of nondelimited imagination from which the forms of the felicitous will be constantly renewed.[95]

At this point we can recall Koran 33:72: *We offered the Trust to the heavens, the earth, and the mountains, but they refused to carry it and were afraid of it; and man carried it.* By virtue of the fact that man was created upon the form of the All-Merciful, he has been given God's Trust. The role of Islam is to guide man on the straight path of justice and equilibrium so that he can carry the Trust and fulfill his rightful function as God's vicegerent. But the above verse continues by saying that man is *sinful, very foolish,* that is, to the extent that he fails to live up to his divine form. Hence, through the very majesty of his freedom and responsibility, he is able to cut himself off from the effusion of mercy and light that fills the universe. Whether he experiences God's mercy or wrath, the next stages of his existence depend upon his own choice.

21

The Circle of Life

Among the diverse schools of contemporary philosophy, phenomenology offers interesting parallels with traditional Islamic thought. A good example is provided by the many books of Anna-Teresa Tymieniecka, for whom both cosmos and soul are vital philosophical issues. In her perspective, life is the ultimate point of reference and the center of concern.[1] Much of what she says about life's role in the world, the emergence of variety in the living realm, and the manner in which the human condition allows for "an inventive/creative profusion of representations detached from existence"[2] would be familiar to historians of Islamic philosophy. However, traditional Muslim philosophers, faced with her views, would find her silence on many issues rather deafening. Three of these can serve as examples and at the same time illustrate the sharp points of divergence between Islamic thought and a form of contemporary philosophy that is unusually congenial with its perspectives: first, the real nature of the ultimate point of reference; second, the supra-human dimensions of human creative virtualities; and third, the role of death in the fulfillment of life.

The starting point of Islamic thought is not the world as it gives itself to a generic us, because most people are forgetful and negligent. Rather, the starting point is the world as it gives itself to those who have heard the reminder and remembered. Reminder comes from the Ultimate Principle both by way of the prophets and by way of the innate human condition. The proper response to the reminder begins with *tawḥīd*, which is the innate intuition of any healthy soul.

The philosopher or sage endeavors to bring out the implications of the oneness of the Ultimate Reality for the way in which we perceive the unfolding of the cosmos and our own selves. In a typical treatise, the author might explain how the unity of the Real demands the appearance of the universe along with human beings, elaborate upon the manner in which human beings play a unique role in the overall economy of the cosmos, and then consider how the whole process necessarily curves back on the point of origin.

The task of the thinker is not to declare the self-evident unity of the First Principle, but rather to throw light upon the qualities and characteristics of unity and to explain how these give rise to the world of appearances and impinge on our human nature. The point of the exercise is to set down guidelines for discerning human priorities and living a life worthy of our nature. The Muslim philosophers will speak in terms that recall the abstracting tendency of the Greek philosophical tradition, using the tools of Aristotelian logic and the arguments and insights of Neoplatonism. The Sufis are likely to avoid abstract terminology and discuss the Real in terms of the mythic language of the Koran and the imagery and symbols of the poetic tradition, all the while stressing the centrality of realized knowledge. The philosophers and, with even more reason, the Sufis, will speak not as theoreticians but as physicians of the soul. It is not without reason that Avicenna called his grand summa of logic, psychology, and metaphysics *al-Shifāʾ* ("The Healing").

In both Islamic philosophy and Sufism, human perfection is envisaged as the full actualization of the potentialities that are present because human beings were created as complete and total images of the Real. Not that the mere fact of being human provides the necessary discernment to experience and understand the embodied image. The Koran differentiates clearly between those who know and those who do not. The philosophers call those who know "philosophers" and those who do not "the common people." For Ibn al-ʿArabī, those who have achieved the fullness of human reality are the Perfect Men, and those who remain heedless are animal men. He writes:

> When it falls to the ears of man that he is created in the form of the Real, but when he does not differentiate between perfect men and animal men, he imagines that man is in the form of God simply because he is human, but this is not so. Rather, because he is human, he is receptive to the divine form. This means that when it is bestowed, he is not prevented from receiving it. But, only when it is bestowed is he in God's form and counted among the vicegerents of God. Such a person acts in accordance with the activity of the Real.[3]

The Sufis often discuss the achievement of perfection in terms of "union" with God, which is the discovery of one's identity with the divine image and the fulfillment of the proper human role in both cosmos and society. The philosophers stress the attainment of connection with the Universal Intellect and the actualization of the virtues latent in the soul. The language and methodologies of the two perspectives differ, but both presuppose that human beings alone, among all finite things, have the possibility of achieving a mysterious oneness with the Infinite Source of all being and a perfect congruence with the Absolute Origin of the cosmos.

While the Sufis stress the conscious and living reality of *wujūd*, several of the philosophers also assert that true knowing is nothing but *wujūd*, that is, a being-cum-awareness that finds the known object present in the self that knows. The ultimate goal of the philosophical quest was commonly known as "conjunction" with the Intellect, and it was understood to mean that the seeker finds the source of all wisdom and reality within himself. The discussion of "presential knowledge" (*ʿilm ḥuḍūrī*), which is associated with the names of Suhrawardī and Mullā Ṣadrā, is closely tied up with the understanding that the presence of the known thing in the awareness of the knower is nothing but the *wujūd* of the thing. When a thing is known, it is found by the soul and exists for the soul and in the soul.

Life and Death

Tawḥīd demands that all reality be rooted in the Ultimately Real. The moment we speak of "life," we need to recognize that it can only be grounded in Real *wujūd*. Not only that, but real, permanent, actual, and stable life can belong only to the Real, because the Real alone is alive by definition. Any other sort of life—such as the life that we experience as our own—will be unstable, impermanent, and unreliable. In other words, any life other than the Real's own life must be understood along with its opposite, which is death.

The Koran already clarifies the ambiguity of cosmic life by using the three divine names, Alive, Life-Giver, and Death-Giver. In Himself, God can only be alive, but when we speak of the life that He bestows on things, we need to speak in terms of duality and opposition, because bestowal is contingent on the bestower. The correlative names, Life-Giver and Death-Giver, express the fact that it is the Alive who gives life and then takes it away. To say that God is the Alive means that He alone is truly alive; other things, to the extent that they can be considered alive, must have derived their life from Him. And, in giving life, God also gives death.

In discussing the divine attributes that allow for the appearance of the universe, Ibn al-ʿArabī points out that each of them depends on life. To speak of God as merciful, or forgiving, or creating—as the Koran often does—only makes sense if God is first alive. As Ibn al-ʿArabī puts it:

> The attribution of life to the Divine Essence is a precondition for the correct attribution of every relation that is attributed to God, such as knowledge, desire, power, speech, hearing, seeing, and perception. If the relation of life were eliminated from Him, all those relations would also be eliminated.[4]

If "life" is an attribute of the Essence of the Real, and if all divine attributes depend upon it, then the whole universe depends on life, because the universe derives its being and attributes from the being and attributes of God. So much is this so, says Ibn al-ʿArabī, that life is inseparable from the essence and existence of each thing, just as it is inseparable from the Essence and Reality of the Real. He writes:

> The name Alive is an essential name of the Real—glory be to Him! Therefore, nothing can emerge from Him but living things. Hence, all the cosmos is alive, for indeed the nonexistence of life, or the existence in the cosmos of an existent thing that is not alive, has no divine support, whereas every contingent thing must have a support. So, what you consider to be inanimate is in fact alive.[5]

In the continuation of this passage, Ibn al-ʿArabī explains that when something "dies," this does not mean that the body is really dead, because, like all other things, it is inherently alive. Rather, God has disconnected one living thing from another living thing. What we call the "life" of an animal is the fact that an invisible, spiritual being, commonly known as a "soul" or a "spirit," has been given control over another living thing, commonly known as an "inanimate body." Ibn al-ʿArabī says the following: "As for death, it is the separation of a living, governing thing from a living, governed thing, for both the governor and the governed are alive. The separation is a relation of nonexistence, not of existence. It is merely dismissal from rulership."[6]

Ibn al-ʿArabī does not deny the existence of inanimate things. He simply wants to point out that such talk is true only from a certain point of view. Inasmuch as things and objects "exist"—that is, inasmuch as they have *wujūd*, which is being along with life and consciousness—they are in fact alive. However, inasmuch as they do not exist, they are dead. In themselves, they have no claim upon *wujūd*, so they are dead in themselves. Their cosmic situation, however, is contingent on participation in *wujūd*, so their presence in the cosmos proves that they are alive. Some, however, are more alive than others, and our understanding of the meaning of life determines where we draw the line between the living and the dead. Such lines always have something of the arbitrary about them.

We can also say that everything other than the Real is woven of *wujūd* and nonexistence, so everything other than the Real is relatively alive and relatively dead. We experience life only in relation to death, so every experience of life is also an experience of death, and every experience of death is also an experience of life. Discerning the nature of the diverse appearances of life and death becomes the task of discerning the intensity of *wujūd* in contingent things. This is Ṣadrā's project when he speaks of *tashkīk*, the "gradation" or "systematic ambiguity" of being or existence.

In talking of omnipresent life, Ibn al-ʿArabī explains that "life" is another name for the divine mercy that gives rise to the cosmos and that, according to the Koran, *embraces all things* (7:156). In many passages, he speaks of the genesis of the universe in terms of the Breath of the All-Merciful. He points out that mercy is in fact the Koranic (and hence mythic) designation for what the philosophical tradition calls *wujūd*. As for "breath," it is universally recognized as the necessary concomitant of life. The symbolic resonance of the term *breath*, however, gives it the ability to convey more directly than the word *life* the concrete, embodied reality that is at issue.[7]

In describing the Breath of the All-Merciful, Ibn al-ʿArabī says that God breathes living and compassionate *wujūd* into the virtualities of all things, which are latent in the divine omniscience, thereby giving birth to the cosmos. This inbreathing is accompanied by the traces of specific divine attributes that determine the nature of each creature. Hence, the Koran speaks of the divine inbreathing in terms of speech, which is articulated breath. God articulates each creature as a "word" in His own Breath, so its underlying substance is Breath. This Breath is simply the divine life, or the Universal Spirit, or the overflowing mercy of omniscient and omnipresent *wujūd*. As Ibn al-ʿArabī writes, "Through life He has mercy upon the cosmos, for life is the sphere of the 'mercy' that *embraces all things* [7:156]."[8]

Traversing the Circle

In the intellectual tradition, the cosmos is understood as the delimitation, concretization, and sedimentation of *wujūd*, which is Infinite Mercy and Absolute Life. When God speaks, the cosmos moves from the undifferentiation of the Breath of the All-Merciful to embodied discourse, becoming manifest as a never-ending tale, fraught with meaning. Like words emerging from a human speaker, beings and objects become articulated and then disappear, only to be renewed in the next breath, which is the next instant. The cosmos undergoes constant transmutation, eternally emerging from the Breath and eternally disappearing back from whence it came.

If we think of the cosmos—that is, "everything other than God"—as the Divine Breath within which words are constantly appearing and disappearing, we can also think of the great chain of being that structures the cosmos as a hierarchy of meaning and awareness. But there are two endless movements in the chain. In one respect, there is an emergence, beginning with words whose meanings are universal and all-comprehensive and ending with words whose meanings are particular and specific. In another respect, there is a submergence, beginning from specific and particular words and ending with the comprehensive and the universal.

The emerging movement is the descent from the Origin, or the centrifugal flight from the Center. The submerging movement is the ascent back to the Origin, or the centripetal flow to the Center. This process of flight and return is not understood in temporal terms. Rather, it is seen as an ever-present, on-going occurrence. At every time and in every place, *wujūd* is simultaneously descending and ascending, appearing and disappearing, emerging and submerging. In the midst of all this, it is the task of the philosopher to discern the relevant modality in any given situation.

In describing the trajectory of the originating and centrifugal movement, the Muslim thinkers insist that the manifestation of life begins in the fullness of unified awareness and consciousness. As this living and aware light emerges from its Source, its blinding radiance is diminished and diversified. When it becomes sufficiently dim, it appears as various realms that allow for diverse sorts of creaturely perception. The lower reaches of the descent are commonly called "heaven," "earth," and the "elements." At the lowest point, the flow of life and light reverses direction.

In the descending movement from the Origin, life remains invisible and traceless, first in the spiritual realm, then in the celestial ream, and then in the four elements, which do not exist as such in time and space. In the returning movement, the combination of the four elements gives rise to the visible and temporal realm of inanimate things, plants, and animals, and the traces of life begin to appear in the indefinite diversity of perceptible forms. The apparently inanimate world turns out to be a seedbed in which the outward forms of life sprout and grow.

Having described the several stages through which *wujūd* diminishes in intensity during its descent, Ṣadrā writes as follows concerning the lowest point on the circle:

> So it continues, until it comes to an end at a common matter in which there is no good save the potency and preparedness to receive things. You will come to know that, although this matter reaches the utmost meanness and evil in its essence, it is the means for the approach to all good things, and, because of it, *wujūd* goes back and returns to perfection after deficiency, nobility after meanness, and ascension after fall.[9]

Wujūd, then, is the effulgent and merciful life-force that animates the cosmos. Having completed its descent, it turns back toward the Origin, making itself apparent in the three kingdoms. In the inanimate realm, the infinite potentialities of life are constrained and obscured by physical conditions. If life is to show the vast range of its virtualities, it must turn back to the invisible realm. Having exhausted the possibilities of sensory manifestation through the diversity of minerals, it begins to give intimations of its true, invisible nature through the qualities and characteristics that become manifest in plants and animals. It reaches its first culmination in the human condition. At this point it turns fully inward.

In the ascending levels that lead up to the human state, life displays its virtualities only through the limited possibilities represented by the species and forms of the natural world. It cannot actualize the infinite potentialities of its own flowering in these confined and constricted realms, but can only do so in its original domain, which is internal and invisible. Nothing in the external realm has the capacity to act as a vehicle for all of its potentialities except the human form, made in the divine image.

At the surface of the human condition, relative uniformity is the rule, because all human beings belong to the same species. Life's richest and most authentic possibilities unfold not in outward human differences, activities, and productions, but in the invisible depths of human souls. Alike on the surface, people are profoundly diversified by the unseen ramifications of the infinite modalities of conscious life. It is this inner wealth that overflows into activities, arts, artifacts, and cultural productions. The outward variety of human fabrication mirrors the inner diversity of internalizing *wujūd*, moving back toward its Source.

The mineral, plant, and animal species are passive participants in the play of life, with relatively little access to the infinite resources of awareness and consciousness. In contrast, human beings present a radical *novum*, because they are fully open to the divine image and have no choice but to participate as active partners in shaping the invisible realms of true existence and real awareness. For both Islamic philosophy and Sufism, the domain of outward activity is simply the beginning of specifically human concerns. By its very nature, the returning upsurge of life moves from outwardness to inwardness, from unconsciousness to awareness, from the obscurity of death to the radiance of life, from practice to contemplation. We conform to the nature of things only by turning our attention and efforts toward the inner, invisible realm of understanding, awareness, and consciousness.

Despite the indefinite range of life and awareness that is accessible to the human species during existence in this world, an even more radical *novum* stands beyond corporeal embodiment, and that is the domain of life and awareness that is commonly called "death." In death, the infinitely diverse realm of the human soul achieves an "invisible visibility" through spiritual corporealization. The increasing internalization of life that had reached its peak in the human species undergoes a profound intensification. The realm of inner experiences that had been only dimly available to the embodied soul is brought into focus as the real, concrete realm of conscious life. Death is inextricably bound up with the opening up of consciousness and awareness.

Ibn al-ʿArabī and others tell us that after death, what had been outward, visible, and corporeal in our individual human condition is internalized to become the stable ground of our inner being, and what had been inward and hidden is externalized to become the defining landscape of our new world. As Ibn al-ʿArabī writes in one of many passages describing this reversal:

> The next world is a domain that is quickly and immediately receptive to activity, just like the inwardness of the configuration of this world at the level of thoughts. Hence, in the next world the human being is reversed in configuration, since his inwardness will be fixed in a single form, like his outwardness here, but his outwardness will undergo quick transmutation in forms, like his inwardness here.[10]

When death removes the material embodiment that obscured the imaginal realm during life, the world of imagination comes into stark focus. The senses continue to function, but are no longer hindered by bodily objects and corporeal forms. Perceptions are determined as much by the soul of the perceiver as by the imaginal objects perceived.

According to Ṣadrā's detailed eschatology, the potential infinity of the human soul blossoms only after death. In our present human condition, embodiment prevents the Imaginatio Creatrix from unfolding its wings, but in the new human condition after death, creative possibilities are fully unleashed. This is not because the body was a negative factor in the development of creativity. Quite the contrary. Ṣadrā and others insist that embodiment alone makes possible the full unfolding of the soul's potential. But, given that the body is nothing but a densification, sedimentation, and exteriorization of the spiritual realm, it must gradually be subtilized and interiorized. So vast is the soul's potential for embodiment that every human being, whether of the blessed or the damned, will create an entire, independent world in its posthumous becoming. Ṣadrā says:

> The bodies and orbs of the next world are infinite in keeping with the number of conceptions and perceptions of souls. This is because the proofs that establish the finitude of the dimensions do not apply to the next world, but only to material directions and spatial confines. In the next world there is no crowding or interference, and nothing there is located inside or outside anything else. Rather, every human being, whether felicitous or wretched, will have a world complete in itself, greater than this world, and not strung on the same string as any other world. Every one of the folk of felicity will have the kingdom that he desires, however vast he may desire it to be.[11]

22

The Goal of Philosophy

The essence of the philosophical life is perhaps best summed up in the Delphic maxim, "Know yourself." All philosophy worthy of the name must be animated by the quest for self-knowledge, and true philosophy remains inaccessible to those who do not know themselves. In other words, those who investigate and learn things that do not throw light on their own self-understanding are simply wasting their time.

What is clear is that the Muslim philosophers generally have a practical goal in mind. They are lovers of wisdom who set out to know existence per se, and, in knowing existence, to know all things that exist. But, to grasp *wujūd* in its totality is the same as to grasp the knowing self in its totality. "To be" in the full sense of the word is to have total awareness. Absolute being is absolute knowledge. The philosopher strives to know *wujūd* qua *wujūd*, but he can only do so by knowing self qua self. In other words, the philosopher is striving to know the intellect as the intellecter, or to know his own pure and disengaged (*mujarrad*) intelligence as the only true object of knowledge. This is the stage of the unification of the intellecter, the intellect, and the intellected, a position supported most vocally among Muslim philosophers by Mullā Ṣadrā.

The practical goal of the philosopher, therefore, is to know all things. But in order to know all things, the philosopher must know the principle of all things, a principle that is at one and the same time the knower of all things and the fullness of being. This knower is the "intellect," which is the fully actualized soul, or the self that is totally aware of itself, or, as Bābā Afḍal calls it, the "radiance of the Ipseity."

In the fullness of their actualization, self and existence are identical. In both, there is a clear unfolding from the lowest, inanimate level, to the highest, self-aware level, which is the fully actualized intellect, where existence and awareness are one. It follows that the disciplines of psychology and ontology both focus on the ascent from potentiality to actuality. But how do things come to exist in a state of potentiality in the first place? In discussing the Return, the Muslim philosophers elaborate upon a basic human intuition. People know innately that they have "come up" and can go up further. An adult has come up from childhood, a child from the womb, and a knowing person from ignorance. People can assist their upward climb by their own efforts. They can climb up through their aptitudes and talents, and they can set their goals as high as they wish. All concepts of education, learning, improvement, progress, evolution, and directed development are based on this fundamental understanding that things can be changed in an "upward" direction. The idea is so basic to human life that people rarely bother to reflect upon it, but simply take it for granted. In the mythic terms of the Western monotheisms, among others, the goal toward which the upward movement is oriented correlates with the celestial, starry realms as well as with paradise, or the happy domain after death. Refusal to undertake the upward movement is correlated with the lower reaches of existence and with hell.

The philosophers discuss the upward, returning movement in terms of both ontology and psychology, but they discuss the downward, originating movement mainly in terms of cosmology. The question is this: Where did this world come from and how do we happen to be here? In answering the question, the philosophers elaborate on an intuition that is as basic to premodern humanity as the perception of upward movement. This is that nothing can go up that has not come down in the first place. As Bābā Afḍal puts it in passing, "Whatever does not fall from heaven does not rise from earth."[1]

We are now down. The proof is that we aspire to higher things, and we often achieve them. But if we are down, our aspiration must correspond to something within us that knows what it means to be up. True knowledge of upness presupposes some mode of previous awareness of what upness is, and that in turn means that something of the up must have come down to us.

Mythic formulations of the precedent upness are practically universal. The scientific myths of evolution and progress may be the only examples of myths that speak of the upward movement while denying the primal descent. In modern myths, we situate ourselves at the top and look back at the bottom. The alpha is one thing, far behind and below us, and we are the omega, or at least the current omega. In premodern myths, people saw themselves as situated on a trajectory that began on high, with God or the gods. Then human beings came to be low, and now they are in the process of going back in the direction from which they came. The alpha and the omega are ultimately one.

Some versions of the modern myth suggest that the process has its own necessity—we have been forced up because of the impersonal laws of evolution, and we will keep on going up as we evolve further. The premodern myths offer no guarantee of ascent, not at least in any meaningful future. If there is to be an ascent, people must strive to achieve it. We can as easily move further away from the Ultimate Reality as we can move closer to It. We can be left in dispersion and multiplicity indefinitely. Even versions of the premodern myths that speak of an inevitable return to the personal and loving God, as does the Islamic, insist that human beings must exert their own efforts if they are to return by a route that will leave them happy with the journey. If they are not ready for the climb, they will go back under constraint, and they will suffer because of the lack of congeneity and harmony with what they meet on the way and at the destination.

The underlying rationale for the premodern myths is the perception of invisible qualities in the world and the self, that is, the understanding that there is more to existence than meets the eye, not in terms of physical inaccessibility, but in terms of spiritual distance. The myths all acknowledge a realm of superior, intelligible, and intelligent things that can be seen through the beauty and goodness that we find in ourselves and in the world. We must reach up for this realm if we are to make contact with it, and those who reach with sincerity, love, and devotion achieve it more fully than those who go through the motions perfunctorily, or those who make no attempt to undertake the journey. In short, the world is perceived as bathed in the supernal qualities, and a whole and healthy human self is understood to be one that is drawn in the direction of those qualities, which are the source of all awareness and everything that is good, beautiful, desirable, and lovable.

The rationale for modern myths seems to be the inability to see quality beyond quantity. All so-called "qualities," if real in any way, are explained away in reductionist, quantitative terms. By indefinite division and analysis—by taking things back to genes or social conditioning or atomic particles—we can explain away all the echoes of the Divine that were seen by "primitive" and "backward" peoples. We ourselves then stand in a privileged position at the peak of the evolutionary upsurge. We alone are finally able to understand the truth behind the cosmos—or, what is more likely nowadays, that there is no truth behind the cosmos.

In short, perception of quality allows people to see things as diaphanous screens within which the signs of God are displayed, but inability to see anything but quantity breeds a sort of thinking that understands only in terms of reduction to the least-common denominator.

For Islamic thinking in general, knowing the qualitative domain toward which we are aspiring demands knowing the qualitative domain from which our aspirations have descended. Those who want beauty aspire to it because they have a sense of what it means, and that sense drinks from the same well as beauty itself. But, in order to find the goal, one has to know the route by which aspiration came to us in the first place. Bābā Afḍal explains this in a letter to a student:

> You must also know that searching out and exploring things and investigating the Origin and Return of the self do not arise from bodily individuals. If searching and yearning for the meanings and the road of reality arose from human individuals inasmuch as they are individuals, this wanting would be found in every particular individual, but such is not the case. This is because the wish to encompass

> both worlds is fitting for someone for whom it is possible to encompass them. But it is impossible for any particular individual in respect of individuality to encompass another individual, especially both worlds. Hence this wish does not arise from the individual. Rather, it arises from the soul that is radiant with the divine light.[2]

The philosophers investigated the Origin in order to understand the Return. Origin and Return represent the two basic movements demanded by *tawḥīd*, the assertion of God's unity. Asserting that the Ultimate Reality is one demands recognition that It is both First (*awwal*) and Last (*ākhir*). Everything comes from the First and everything returns to It. In order to understand how we will return to the First, we need to discover how we came to be separated from the It. To do so, we must grasp the nature of our faculties and powers, including the senses and intelligence. We also need to ask if the compulsory return to the First that is now driving us toward death is sufficient for the achievement of true humanity, or if we need to employ our cognitive and practical powers to achieve that humanity, just as we employ these powers to achieve everything else that we achieve.

The Muslim philosophers considered the study of the human soul fundamental to the "quest for wisdom," which is the very definition of philosophy. And they looked for the roots of the soul in the First. They considered ethics an important science, because ethics is nothing if not a discussion of how the soul achieves harmony with the First in keeping with the manner in which it came out from the First at the beginning. The soul appeared in the world because of a compulsory descent, in the sense that none of us were asked if we wanted to come. Or, in the light of a certain Neoplatonic approach, human freedom (*ikhtiyār*) was already manifest in the choice of the human self to come into this world. Whether or not we chose to come, we have come, and now we must go back to where we came from. We have sufficient freedom to make some choices, and what freedom we have must be put to good use if there is to be any possibility of achieving ultimate happiness.

According to the philosophers, human beings in their present situation are in the process of going up, which is to say that they are moving from the potency of the fertilized egg toward the pure actuality of the disengaged (*mujarrad*) intellect. Because of the compulsory return, they have gathered together the stages of inanimate nature, the plant soul, and the animal soul, and they possess the powers and faculties of all these stages. Now they stand at the level of the human soul, so they are free to direct their own ascent. No one is forcing them to continue the upward movement. If they prefer to do so, people can stay where they are and go about actualizing the animal traits to a degree undreamed of by any non-human animal.

Unquestionably, human beings possess the power of intelligence. To deny this in any sort of meaningful way would be to contradict oneself. Given that people have this power, they can use it as they see fit. But this is not to say that how they use it is indifferent and that all will necessarily be for the good. Just as they need discipline and guidance to become pianists or soccer players, so also they need discipline and guidance to become fully intelligent, which is to say, fully human, since intelligence alone is their uniquely *human* characteristic.

I do not wish to suggest that intelligence is their only human characteristic. Rather, it is the highest human trait and the pinnacle of human possibility, because the fullness of intelligence is identical with the fullness of being. It perhaps needs to be stressed, however, that the soul has two perfections, the theoretical and the practical, and both need to be actualized. Practical perfection demands the fullness of ethical and moral being, or the actualization of all the virtues (*faḍāʾil*). Neither theoretical nor practical perfection can be achieved in isolation. Perfection of intelligence cannot be achieved without perfecting all the soul's aptitudes, and most of these are named by the names of the virtues—love, compassion, justice, forgiveness. Ethical activity and beautiful character traits are inseparable from striving for human status.

In order to move from potential intellect to actual intellect, people need to know what they are striving for. In general, the religious tradition looks for knowledge of the final goal in the Koran and the Hadith, and it looks for knowledge of the praxis that allows the goal to be reached in the Sunnah and the Shariah. But the philosophers maintain that knowledge of the final goal and of the praxis needed to achieve it require thought and reflection. To the extent that people put the power of their own intelligence to work by coming to understand the nature of things, they will actualize intelligence, and will gradually move away from potential intellect toward the fully actualized intellect.

Philosophical discussions of the Return focus on the two basic ways of going back to the First—the road that people will be compelled to follow and the road that they are free to follow if they choose to do so. Discussions of the Origin focus on how they arrived at their starting place. If they can go up to intelligence, they must have come down from intelligence. The Return is the mirror image of the Origin.

The descending route of the Origin is well-known. The basic outline is the same as that already present in Neoplatonism—Intellect, Soul, heavenly spheres, four elements. Bābā Afḍal sticks to this simplest of schemes, though some of the philosophers had developed it into several degrees, as did al-Fārābī and Avicenna.

One should not be thrown off track by the language of these discussions and think that, for example, the philosophers are reifying the concepts of Intellect and Soul, much as people today reify the concept of God; or that they are describing the planets and celestial spheres with anything like the concerns of modern astronomy. Discussions concerning the Intellect and Soul have to do with what we can retrace in our own selves, and discussions of the spheres have to do with what we can discern with the naked eye. By studying the heavens, the philosophers want to know what we can learn about what is "up" by looking in that direction. The upness of the physical domain is an analogue of the upness of the spiritual domain, which is to say that what is "up" in terms of our sense perception is a marker of realities that are "up" in respect of our intelligence and understanding. If we look up in the outside world, we see the planets and stars, and if we look up in the inside world, we see soul and intelligence. The key is looking, gazing, thinking, reflecting, pondering, meditating, contemplating.

In short, discussion of the heavens pertains to the investigation of the qualities and characteristics that are "higher" than we are in our corporeal—although not our intellective—nature. Inasmuch as the heavens pertain to the Origin, they represent descending stages through which the self, in coming down from Intellect and entering the womb, becomes more and more differentiated from other selves and immersed in multiplicity. Inasmuch as the heavens pertain to the Return, they represent stages that the self must pass through in order to actualize its potentiality, harmonize its diverse powers, unify its multiple aptitudes, and rejoin the Intellect from which it arose. The mythic model for this Return is provided by the accounts of the Prophet's *miʿrāj*.

The philosophers were able to read spiritual significance into what they saw of the celestial spheres because they were reflecting upon themselves. They saw that they themselves, beginning in the womb, had risen up from mineral, to plant, to animal, to human, and that they were now striving to rise to the fullness of self-knowledge, the Intellect that knows itself and all things. In their view, the way to achieve a truly useful knowledge of the spheres—that is, useful in the quest to become human—is to investigate how the celestial realms display the qualities and characteristics of our own intellective nature. To study the heavens is to study realities that bring together many other realities and embrace and encompass the evanescent world below. The heavens reflect much more directly than the sublunary realm the nature of the intelligent self, which is incorruptible and everlasting.

When reading historical discussions of Islamic cosmology, we are sometimes left with the impression that the First Intellect and the Universal Soul—that is, the initial stages of descent from the Origin—were concepts lifted from Neoplatonic sources without much reflection. The two can appear as rather odd suppositions that have nothing to do with the real world—although it is understandable, we may be led to believe, that the unimaginative Muslims, relying as usual on the Greeks, should borrow this notion as an easy and ostensibly "rational" explanation for the origin of the universe. But there is no reason to think that these ideas were taken over without critical assimilation on the part of those who took them over. Philosophy is nothing if not the sober consideration of what we can know, the sifting of supposition from real knowledge. It is rather a certain breed of historian that has seen the history of ideas as an unreflective collecting of ideas from the past as if they were precious artifacts.

If we are to make any sense of the Intellect and the Soul as the dual progenitors of the cosmos, we have to stop and reflect on what the philosophers were trying to say. As human beings, we know innately that all things have been born from the Soul because our own souls embrace nature along with the plant, animal, and human faculties. We know innately that the Intellect is the all-embracing Origin because it is precisely our own intelligence that knows all this, arranges all this, becomes all this, and embraces all this. If our microcosmic intelligence is able to conceive of the whole world, it can do so only because it is already, at some level of itself, an intelligence that conceives of the whole universe. What goes up must have come down in the first place.

Instead of abandoning Islamic cosmological teachings because it does not accord well with the cosmological constructs popular today, we should ask ourselves the following: What is the goal of studying the universe? What are the self-imposed limits of those who study it? One thing is for certain: Current approaches to the study of the universe and the accompanying theories all stop short at the surface of reality. Islamic cosmology, on the other hand, was always concerned with the depths of reality, and the depths of reality are inseparable from the human self.

Today, the study of the human self has been abandoned. Instead, people study subjects that allow them to go out and get things done, or at least to make money. For Islamic philosophy, to abandon the study of the self is to abandon humanity, to give up any claim to human status. Knowledge that does not help us understand who we are is not in fact knowledge. Theories that purport to provide knowledge divorced from the knowing subject are simply systematic ignorance. Such theories can be enormously useful for manipulating the world and establishing power relationships, but they do not and cannot aid in the quest for wisdom.

In the view of Islamic philosophy in general, to be human is to seek after knowledge that will increase one's humanity. Humanity's defining characteristic is the self-aware intelligence, and to know that intelligence in an intelligent and self-aware manner demands focusing one's energies on self-knowledge. The fruit of any knowledge that does not aid in the quest for self-knowledge can only be the dissolution and destruction of human nature.

IV

Reflections on Contemporary Issues

23

The Metaphysical Roots of War and Peace

Many look to religion with the idea that its help can be enlisted to establish world peace. But religion—if one can speak in generalities—does not acknowledge any principles higher than its own, not even the survival of the human race. Asked to help establish peace, it will do so in its own way or not at all.

In the general Western view, Islam is one of the most warlike of all religions. Stereotyped opinions, coupled with the fact that few people have the patience to delve into the principles and "myths" underlying surface appearances, make the task of presenting Islam's actual views on war and peace especially difficult. Only by probing deeply into Islamic ways of thinking, however, can we hope to understand Muslim views of the current situation. Once we have taken a step toward understanding Islam, perhaps we will find the appropriate language with which to "enlist" its help in establishing true peace in the world.

I would like to clarify the basic Islamic view of peace and war, on the assumption that real and effective cooperation with Muslims can only be undertaken after we have reached a genuine understanding of how they perceive the human situation. We cannot ask followers of Islam to propose "practical" and "concrete" cures for present crises unless we first listen with a sympathetic ear to their diagnosis of the disease.

It is important for the reader to realize at the outset that what is being discussed here is the religion of Islam as set down in its fundamental texts, not necessarily the opinions of contemporary Muslims. No Muslim today would claim that the community as a whole lives up to the ideals established by the Koran and the Prophet's Sunnah. All agree that a distinction must be made between what Islam teaches and what Muslims think and do. At the same time, differences of opinion among present-day Muslims as to what in fact Islam does teach—especially when it is a question of applying these teachings to the contemporary situation—run deep. Any attempt to sort out these different opinions, even in the limited domain of peace and war, would require a lengthy study. At present, we will only deal with the underlying Islamic principles that are more or less agreed upon by all Muslims, whether or not everyone would express them in the terms employed here. The question of how to deal with the present situation on a practical level will have to be answered by those Muslims who wish to live in accordance with their own tradition.

To discuss the political reality of peace and war within the Islamic context, we need to understand how Islam views these two concepts in a general sense. English dictionaries tell us that peace can be defined as "freedom from war," while war can be called "a state of hostility, conflict, opposition, or antagonism between various kinds of forces." These definitions prove a starting point from which to approach the specifically Islamic way of looking at peace and war as set down in the fundamental source for all Islamic thought and activity, that is, the Koran. Once the general Islamic sense of the two terms is clear, we can turn to the specific issue of how traditional and normative Islam would strive to establish peace in today's world.

Since all Islamic thinking begins with God, or, more specifically, with the first Shahadah (which is considered to be a unique certainty upon which all other truths depend), our initial task is to answer the following question: In the Islamic view, how do peace and war relate to God and to the Shahadah?

"Peace" *(al-salām)* is a name of God. The Koran uses the name once: *He is God; there is no god but He. He is King, Holy, Peace, Faithful, Preserver, Mighty, Compeller, Sublime. Glory be to God above everything they associate with Him. He is God, the Creator, the Maker, the Form-Giver. To Him belong the names most beautiful. All that is in the heavens and the earth glorifies Him. He is Mighty, Wise* (59:23–24).

These few sentences epitomize Islamic theology. More specifically, they express two ideas about God found throughout the Book—incomparability and similarity, or transcendence and His immanence. "Peace" fits into the category of the "negative" divine names, which assert God's incomparability. It signifies that God is free from and infinitely exalted above all defects and imperfection, because these are attributes of the creatures, not the Creator. In Himself God knows no "hostility, conflict, opposition, or antagonism." As for God's immanence, this is expressed by the mention of His creativity, the fact that He is close enough to the creatures to shape and form all things. All attributes and qualities found in the world derive from Him; so true is this that *Wherever you turn, there is the face of God* (2:115). If all that is in the heavens and the earth glorifies Him, this is not only because all things alert us to the fact that He is exalted beyond their imperfections, but also because they tell us that every positive attribute comes from Him. As the Koran constantly reminds us, everything in the universe displays God's signs.

The name "Peace" signifies that no imperfection or conflict is to be found in God. In light of the Shahadah, we can say, "There is no peace but God" and "There is no perfection but God." Moreover, everything in the universe is other than God and therefore opposed to peace in some sense. In other words, all things are imperfect by definition—*All things are perishing except His face* (28:88). True peace belongs to God alone, whereas any peace possessed by creatures can only be imperfect and perishing.

God's peace follows upon His unity. He is one in every respect, so He alone is He. There is nothing in Him that could oppose or contradict Him. His Self is totally unlike the human self, which is constantly flooded with conflicting thoughts and feelings. Human beings are never wholly at peace with themselves because they are made up of opposing faculties and energies. And this is as it must be, since real peace belongs only to God, while its opposite—war, that is, "hostility, conflict, opposition, and antagonism"—is intrinsic to everything other than God, that is, to all created things.

If God is absolute peace, is the world "absolute war"? Certainly not, because that would demand strife and conflict so deep and so far reaching that no two things in the universe could coexist. It would be total chaos if not pure nothingness. Hence, the world is only "relative war," but as such it is also "relative peace." The world's peace—the harmony and equilibrium that exist among its opposing forces—is, in Koranic terms, a "sign" or reflection of God's absolute peace. The world is a mixture of opposing forces that may conflict or harmonize depending on the situation. If its relative peace is to be increased, this can only be done by bringing it closer to the absolute peace of God.

But is "war" understood as a "state of hostility, conflict, opposition, and antagonism" necessarily bad? No, says Islam, since war in this general sense is inherent to the world, and the world is God's good creation. Hence, all conflict must be working toward God's ends, even if it appears evil in our eyes. In other words, conflict and opposition may in fact make up the different dimensions of an equilibrium that escapes our view.

It was stated above that God is Peace but not war, since this would demand conflict and opposition within God's one Self. But many Muslim theologians provide a much more sophisticated explanation of the Divine Reality. In fact, they say, conflict and opposition must ultimately derive from God, because He created the world and accomplishes His aims through all the opposing forces found within it. To understand the metaphysical roots of conflict, we need to turn to the doctrine of the divine names.

Although God in Himself is One, He assumes a variety of relationships with His creatures. He is the Life-Giver and Death-Giver, the Exalter and the Abaser, the Benefiter and the Harmer, the Forgiver and the Avenger. At any given moment every creature is related to these and other pairs of opposing divine names. Life in this world has been given to us, and before long we will be given death. We are exalted above some of our fellow creatures in wealth, power, and intelligence, but abased before others. We have received many benefits and suffered many ills. The ontological roots of every situation we experience derives from the divine nature. The fact that we undergo constant change shows that God continuously bestows on us new relationships with these and other names. Perfect equilibrium among the divine names is found only in God Himself, the Coincidence of Opposites: *He is the First and the Last, the Manifest and the Nonmanifest* (57:3). But the creation of the universe demands that the divine names display their opposite properties in unequal proportions, or else the properties would cancel each other out.

Even though a certain "disequilibrium" of the divine names allows the individual things of the world to exist in their infinite variety and constant change, it remains true that the universe as a whole represents an equilibrium among all the divine names. Each name conveys to us a mode in which the Divine Reality establishes relationships between Himself and the creatures. The modes may conflict at any given moment and in any given existent, but the totality of existence represents a harmony of all the different modes because existence gushes forth from Reality or Sheer Being, just as light comes forth from the sun. If one ray is perceived as green and another as red, this does not contradict the underlying unity of light.

The archetype of peace *in divinis* is the unity of the Divine Self, and the archetype of war as a positive reality is the multiplicity of the divine names. In God Himself the names coexist in perfect harmony and equilibrium, since the names are not different from His one Being. The Forgiver is God, and the Vengeful is God; the Life-Giver is God, and so also the Death-Giver. But once the properties of the divine names appear in the world, they often contradict each other. God as Forgiver displays Himself differently to His creatures than God as Vengeful. Nevertheless, all opposition works within the context of the divine unity that gives birth to it. Vision of things as they are in themselves is to see all things as God's creatures within the context of His one Reality. It is to see that all the colors of the spectrum manifest the same light.

It was pointed out that God is absolute peace, while creation is relative peace and relative war. The world displays a certain conflict and strife as a result of the opposition among divine names, such as the Abaser and the Exalter, even though the activities of these two names go back to the one God. This sort of opposition among the names might be called "horizontal" because neither of the opposing names dominates over the other, and each of them manifests the divine peace through its harmonious relationship with its opposite.

But there is a second kind of opposition among the names that might be called "vertical." In the present context, this means that certain names display the divine peace, while their opposites bring about opposition and conflict. For example, God is both merciful and wrathful. At first sight it might appear that these two names stand on the same level, but, as the *ḥadīth qudsī* says, "My mercy takes precedence over My wrath." Mercy is prior to wrath because mercy represents the divine nature Itself. Wrath is an attribute that God assumes only in relationship to certain creatures. In other words, God is merciful toward all creatures and wrathful only toward some. In the last analysis, His wrath must be considered an extension of His mercy, just as a father's anger toward his child displays his love.

The names and attributes of God connected to mercy represent God as He is in Himself, while the names and attributes connected to wrath represent specific attitudes that God assumes in relation to certain creatures for special reasons. Mercy is closely allied to such divine attributes as unity, beneficence, bounty, guidance, forgiveness, and equilibrium. Wrath is allied to multiplicity, harm, error, vengeance, and deviation. The eschatological fruit of mercy is paradise, which is nearness to God, and that of wrath is hell, which is distance from Him. In human history, mercy is made manifest by the prophets, who express the divine name the Guide. Wrath is made manifest by Iblīs and his attendant demons, who express the divine name the Misguider. Note that in Islam Iblīs is the ape of the prophets, not of God; all things in existence, even the negative and dispersive tendencies, come under the sway of the divine unity.

The vertical opposition between mercy and wrath is fundamentally different from the horizontal opposition between, for example, the Life-Giver and the Death-Giver. In the case of horizontal opposition, all creatures and activities that manifest it remain at the same "distance" from God; the two opposing names bring into existence a sort of yin–yang relationship between forces in the world, an opposition that is in fact complementary, since both forces work toward the same end. But mercy and wrath do not work on the same level. Everything that manifests mercy is closer to God than what manifests wrath. If a being moves from mercy to wrath, it leaves unity and harmony and enters into multiplicity and disequilibrium. If it moves in the other direction, it travels away from conflict into harmony. In other words, "peace" or freedom from conflict lies at the center of an infinite circle. The center is God, and the circumference is chaos. All creatures are situated on the radii. If they move centripetally, they travel closer to peace, unity, bounty, forgiveness, and mercy. If they move centrifugally, they journey toward war, dispersion, harm, vengeance, and wrath.

The horizontal conflict among the names is taken into account in the Koranic verse, *Everything in the heavens and the earth glorifies God* (57:1). This means that all creatures work in harmony toward the end for which they were created, even though a certain strife and opposition can be perceived on every level of created existence. Even angels dispute, as Koran 38:69 tells us. A second sort of conflict, peculiar to human beings, derives from the vertical opposition between mercy and wrath. It is alluded to in the Koranic verse, *Have you not seen how to God bow down all who are in the heavens and all who are on the earth, the sun and the moon, the stars and the mountains, the trees and the beasts, and many of mankind?* (22:18).

Not all human beings bow to God. Those who do not bow have turned away from mercy and guidance and embraced wrath and error. In other words, they have rejected the purpose for which they were brought into the world, a purpose explained in the verse, *I created jinn and mankind only to worship Me* (51:56).

The first kind of war and conflict, the horizontal sort, is inherent to the universe. It is willed by God because it displays the diverse properties and characteristics of His names. It results from the divine command "*Be!*" (2:117) that brings all creatures into existence. All conflicts and wars that derive from this command simply manifest the diverse possibilities of existence latent in the divine creativity.

But God created human beings in His own image, giving them freedom to choose between good and evil. Since He has given freedom only to mankind and the jinn, He directs at them a different kind of command: *He has commanded that you worship none but Him. That is the right religion, but most men know not* (12:40). This command differs from the first command in that it can be disobeyed by those toward whom it is directed. The creatures cannot disobey God when He commands them to enter into existence, because they have no separative existence and awareness that would allow them to disobey.

If horizontal conflict arises as a result of the creative command—if lions devour lambs and waves smash against the shore—this only shows that hostility, opposition, antagonism, and "war" are inherent to the created world. But human beings can choose to ignore the religious command, and as a result a new kind of conflict arises in existence, a vertical conflict between the creatures and the guidance desired for them by their Creator.

Given the fall of the human race and mankind's subsequent "heedlessness" (*ghafla*), this kind of war may be inherent to human nature, but it works counter to the divine command, which is to worship or serve God. It removes human beings ever farther from their own Center, which is mercy and peace, and hence it calls down on them God's wrath. In other words, it takes them ever closer to the circumference, which is dispersion, multiplicity, deviation, and disequilibrium.

When God created human beings, he made them His vicegerents in the earth. To represent God as His vicegerent means that people have a responsibility toward other creatures. Ignoring God's commandments results in evil consequences not only for those who do so but also for the whole of creation, over which mankind was given power. Disobeying God results in the corruption and ruin of the earth itself.

The closer human beings stand to the divine mercy, the more they are brought into harmony with the divine peace. When they are at peace with God, they fulfill their functions as vicegerents and thereby govern and control the earth in a manner that brings all creatures under the sway of God's peace. But if people move toward the periphery of existence—toward the circumference that is war and conflict—they fail to represent God in the earth in the proper manner. As a result, they call down disequilibrium, dispersion, and conflict upon themselves, and they call it down upon those whom they are supposed to protect, namely the creatures of the natural world.

These ideas are expressed clearly in the Koranic doctrine of the "corruption" (*fasād*) of the earth. When God told the angels, *"I am placing in the earth a vicegerent,"* they questioned Him, saying, *"What, will You set therein one who will work corruption and shed blood?"* (2:30). Working corruption in the earth is a possibility reserved for human beings, since only they can turn against the divine mercy and their own natures by disobeying God's commandments. The Koran employs various forms of the word "corruption" fifty times, and in every case where actual corruption is envisaged it results from human activity. In short,

Corruption has become manifest on the land and in the sea because of what peoples' hands have earned, so that He may let them taste some part of what they have done. Haply they may return [to Him] (30:41).

God allows corruption to appear because human beings have been given the freedom to choose their own destinies. At the same time, corruption can serve to remind them of their responsibilities as vicegerents. "Repentance" or "turning toward God" is seen as corruption's only remedy. To repair the ill results of disobedience, people must once again follow the religion that God has sent down for them. In other words, they must put *tawḥīd* into practice. This is why corruption is closely linked with the lack of unity. As the Koran puts it concerning the heavens and the earth, *Were there gods in them other than God, they would surely be corrupted* (21:22).

Human disobedience and the resulting corruption in the earth grow up out of the failure to affirm God's unity, also called the "association of other divinities with God" (*shirk*). This erroneous introduction of multiplicity into the Origin and Center leads to disequilibrium and dispersion—or an encounter with the full force of the divine wrath—since the "associator" or "idol-worshipper" (*mushrik*) negates any possibility of linking himself with the Center. Hence, he cannot possibly achieve peace, which depends on establishing harmony through unity, so he remains in conflict and war, at least within his own soul. More often than not the false divinity that a person "associates" with God is self-will, egocentric desires, or "caprice" (*hawā*). In the words of the Koran, *Have you seen the one who has taken his own caprice as his god?* (45:23).

Once people begin to obey their own whims and caprices instead of following God's revealed guidance, they are acting as if there were *gods in earth and heaven other than God*. The result can only be the earth's corruption, the dissolution of the kingdom over which they were made vicegerents. Hence, the Koran says, *Had the Real followed their caprices, the heavens and the earth and whosoever is in them would have been corrupted* (23:71). Only God's mercy keeps the universe intact despite people's rejection of the divine command and their eager attempts to embrace His wrath.

The Koranic opposite of corruption is *ṣalāḥ*, which means wholesomeness, wholeness, soundness, properness, rightness, goodness. It is commonly translated as "piety." Two derivatives are especially important in the Koran—*ṣāliḥāt*, wholesome deeds; and *ṣāliḥūn*, the wholesome ones. The Koran employs the noun *ṣalāḥ* and the adjectival form *ṣāliḥ* in more than one hundred and twenty instances to refer to an ideal activity or situation that human beings must strive to achieve. Wholesome deeds bring human beings into harmony with the divine command. The corruption of the world can only be overcome by wholesomeness, and that is achieved by wholesome people doing wholesome deeds: *"Obey not the commandment of the prodigal, who work corruption in the earth and fail to make things wholesome"* (26:151–152); *"Be my successor among my people,"* Moses says to Aaron, *"and make things wholesome; do not follow the way of the workers of corruption!"* (7:142).

There is another word from the same root as the word *ṣalāḥ* or wholesomeness that is highly significant in the present context. This is *ṣulḥ*, which is the term that is most commonly used for "peace" among nations. The literal sense of *ṣulḥ* is to set things right or to make things good, sound, whole, and wholesome. To establish *ṣulḥ* in a conflict is to bring about a reconciliation between the opposing parties. The Koran employs the word in a single instance, in the sense of reconciliation between husband and wife (4:128).

Thus, wholesomeness is activity that erases corruption and establishes peace, and it is achieved through conformity with the One, which brings about harmony, balance, equilibrium, and unity.

The Koran employs the phrase, "Those who have faith and do wholesome deeds," fifty-three times. This has become a set phrase referring to good Muslims. Through faith in the One and the concomitant wholesome deeds that they do, the faithful are able to overcome corruption and dispersion and move toward peace, harmony, and wholeness. This "vertical" movement toward God is referred to in the Koranic verse, *To Him good words go up, and the wholesome deed—He uplifts it* (35:10). Hence, those who move toward God's mercy and avoid His wrath, who strive to achieve His peace and avoid conflict with Him, will reach nearness to Him and paradise: *Surely those who have faith, and those of the Jewry, the Sabaeans, and the Christians, whosoever has faith in God and the Last Day and performs wholesome deeds—no fear shall be upon them, neither shall they sorrow* (5:69); *Whosoever, male or female, does a wholesome deed, having faith, We shall assuredly give them to live a goodly life* (16:97); *I am All-Forgiving to him who repents, has faith, does wholesome deeds, and follows guidance* (20:82).

Although opposition and strife are inherent to creation, the world remains in relative equilibrium as long as human beings attempt to carry out their duties as God's vicegerents in the earth by performing wholesome deeds. These duties are summarized by the term *islām*. The word derives from the same root as *salām*, "peace." The literal sense of the term is to become free or safe from something, or to gain peace in respect to it. The implication is that through submitting one's will to God's will, people gain safety from error, deviation, and corruption. They are integrated into the divine unity and hence put into harmony with the opposing yet complementary properties of the divine names. Faith and wholesome deeds provide the remedy for the corruption that has taken place in the land and the sea at the hands of those human beings who have not carried the Trust. Hence, submission to God brings about peace both in the sense of *salām* and *ṣulḥ*. The first sort of peace is with God, and the second with His creatures; the two sorts establish equilibrium with the Divine Origin.

Varieties of Peace

In order to understand the Islamic idea of peace (*ṣulḥ*) among nations and peoples, we need a clear conception of the primary peace (*salām*) that needs to be established with God. In the Koranic view, peace with God necessitates "war" against everything that tends toward dispersion and disequilibrium. It demands a movement toward the Center, which is Mercy and Peace, and an active opposition against forces that draw away from the Center. In other words, to be at peace with God is to be at war with heedlessness and caprice, which are the forces within ourselves that draw us away from God.

On the primary level, peace with God is necessarily a good, but peace with other than God may or may not be good, depending on the nature of the other. So also on the secondary level: Peace among peoples and nations is not necessarily good, because "peace" merely designates a certain lack of external conflict among various forces. Before we can say it is good to be at peace, we need to ask about the nature of the forces that are avoiding conflict. Peace cannot be good if it means acquiescence and submission to dispersion and disequilibrium, whether of the inward kind, which the Koran calls "caprice," or the outward kind, which it calls "this world" (*al-dunyā*). Iblīs personifies both the inward and the outward dispersive movements because he works in this world as well as in ourselves.

If peace is not necessarily good, war is not necessarily bad. War against the forces of dispersion and disequilibrium is a struggle to establish peace with God. War is good if it brings about harmony and equilibrium. Thus, the issue is not whether there is "peace" or "war." There will always be both peace and war in the world, given that the world is the domain of relativities and relationships. Absolute peace is God, and everything other than God is at peace and war at one and the same time. The question is, are they at peace with dispersive tendencies and at war with equilibrium? Or are they at war with dispersion but at peace with balance, harmony, and justice? The fact is, most people follow the natural movement of this world, the downward current of the river of forgetfulness that pulls them away from the Center.

It is important to note that "peace with this world" is not the same as "peace with creation." In fact, the two are diametrically opposed. To live in peace with this world (*dunyā*) is to harmonize with those tendencies in the created world that take human beings away from God, while to live in peace with creation (*khalq*) is to act as God's vicegerent on the basis of having been integrated into the Divine Unity and Peace. It is to contribute toward bringing all creatures under the sway of equilibrium and harmony.

In order to give a bare introduction to some of the basic Koranic ideas concerning peace and war, let me elaborate on these ideas by outlining two basic sorts of peace and two of war: peace with God and peace with caprice and this world; war for God's sake and war against God.

Peace with God

Strictly speaking, peace belongs to God alone. But nearness to God, however envisaged, results in harmony with Him and therefore relative peace. Hence, the

Koran refers to paradise as the *Abode of Peace* (6:127). According to the Koran, the Muslim greeting, "Peace be upon you," is the formula of welcome by which the angels accept the blessed into paradise, and there the blessed exchange it among themselves (7:46, 10:10, 13:24, 14:23, etc.). The formula means something like, "May you and your religion be free from defects and imperfections." Or, more simply, "May Peace—which is God—be with you." To achieve peace in this world and the next, people must follow God's guidance, which will take them back to the luminous Center, far from the shadows of dispersion and error: *There has come to you from God a light and a Book manifest, whereby God guides whosoever follows His good pleasure in the ways of Peace; He brings them forth from the shadows into the light by His leave; and He guides them to a straight path* (5:15–16).

The "straight path" is the path of Islam, that is, submission to God's will and obedience to His command, faith in Him and His prophets, and achievement of spiritual virtue and moral perfection: *"Obey God, and obey the Messenger. . . . If you obey the Messenger, you will be guided"* (24:54); *Whosoever obeys God and His Messenger, He will admit him into Gardens underneath which rivers flow, therein dwelling forever; that is the mighty triumph* (4:13); *The faithful . . . obey God and His Messenger. Those, upon them God will have mercy* (9:71); *God ever guides those who have faith to a straight path* (22:54).

Those who have been guided to God and who have reached peace with Him are called His "friends": *Surely God's friends, no fear shall be upon them, neither shall they sorrow* (10:62). Their hearts are "at rest" with God, or more specifically, with His "remembrance" (*dhikr*): *God wrought this not, except as good tidings, and that your hearts might be at rest; victory comes only from God* (8:10); *In God's remembrance are at peace the hearts of those who have faith and do wholesome deeds* (13:28–29); *O soul at rest with God, return to your Lord, well-pleased, well-pleasing!* (89:27–28).

Peace with Caprice and This World

Those who are at peace with this world are the associators and unbelievers,[1] those who have made their own caprice into a god. Paradise is the "Abode of Peace," while life in this world is *naught but a sport and a diversion; surely the next Abode is better for those who are Godwary* (6:32). One cannot take the rectification of this world's situation as the goal of human endeavors because this world in itself, considered independently of the God who gives it subsistence, has no stability, permanence, or worth: *The likeness of this life is as water that We send down out of heaven; the plants of the earth, whereof men and cattle eat, mingle with it, till, when the earth has taken on its glitter and has decked itself fair, and its inhabitants think they have power over it, Our command comes upon it by night or day, and We make it stubble, as though yesterday it flourished not* (10:24).

The unbelievers see nothing but this world and they follow their own caprice and egocentric desires. They are heedless of God and pleased with this world: *Surely those who look not to encounter Us and are well-pleased with the life of this world and are at rest in it, and those who are heedless of Our signs, those, their refuge is the Fire* (10:7–8). And the "submission" of such people is to their own lower selves: *The evildoers follow their own caprices without knowledge. . . . They have no helpers* (30:29).

War for God's Sake

"Peace with God" is a goal that the believers must strive to reach, not their actual situation. It cannot be actualized if they take a passive stance toward existence, that is, if they accept their own situation as good and desirable. Peace can only come from obedience to God and submission to His command. Hence, it demands activity. Human beings must apply God's commands and prohibitions to every dimension of life. This necessitates following the models and ideals of Islam's three dimensions. Only then can *tawḥīd* be realized. Asserting God's unity demands conforming to His nature not only in deeds and activities but also in the mind and the heart. People must strive to gain nearness to God not only through wholesome works, which eliminate corruption and establish peace in the outside world, but also through the wholesomeness and perfection of their own souls.

One Koranic term that describes human efforts to realize *tawḥīd* on all levels is *jihād*, which literally means "to struggle, to strive." This term commonly refers to the most outward and obvious kind of struggle, the war against the unbelievers on the field of battle. In this sense it has often been translated as "holy war," an expression that is unsatisfactory for a number of reasons, not least because it conjures up stereotypes in the minds of most Westerners. The word *jihād* has been used in Islamic history for practically any war fought by a Muslim king, whatever the motives for engaging in the war might have been, and whether the war was just or unjust. To suggest that these motives have been considered "holy" is to ignore the fact that in many cases the majority of the ulama did not consider these wars legitimate because the Shariah lays down stringent rules that must be followed before *jihād* can be undertaken. Moreover, kings rarely consulted with those religious authorities who might put the standards of the Shariah before the interests of the kingdom. "Holy war" can be a satisfactory translation of *jihād* only in the deepest and most inward sense of the term, that is, the struggle against God's enemies in the soul in the effort to attain perfection. In the present context I translate the term in its literal sense as "struggle" in order to bring out its broad implications.

The Koran employs the word *jihād* and its derivatives thirty-five times, often with obvious reference to specific historical situations and the outward battle (*qitāl*) against those who were hostile to the early Muslim community. But many of the verses have a clear significance transcending specific events. When the Koran says, *Struggle for God as is His due* (22:78), this has obvious relevance to the whole range of human endeavor, exterior and interior. In explaining the meaning of this verse, the commentators distinguish between the outward and inward struggles and cite the saying of the Prophet when he came back from the Battle of Tabuk, one year before his death: "We have returned from the lesser struggle to the greater struggle," that is, from the struggle against the unbelievers to the struggle against caprice and heedlessness.

The same sources cite a saying by ʿAlī, according to which struggle is of three kinds—with the hand, the tongue, and the heart.[2] When we remember that the Prophet defined faith as acknowledgment with the heart, voicing with the tongue, and action with the limbs, we can see that ʿAlī's saying refers to all three levels of human existence. Most authorities agree that the inner and greater struggle takes precedence over the outward and lesser struggle because the inner struggle is incumbent on believers at all times and in all places, but the outward struggle depends on circumstances.

The Shariah addresses the domain of action, not intentions and spirituality, which are the domain of the inward struggle. Those authorities who specialized in the inward and spiritual domain usually described the greater struggle in terms of the transformation of the soul to be achieved through spiritual practice, referring to it by the term *mujahāda,* a term from the same root as *jihād* that is grammatically equivalent; both terms are employed as the verbal noun for the verb "to struggle." Although the two words are exact synonyms, the distinction between the outer and inner struggles came to be reflected in the usage of the two terms. Whether the ulama talk about *jihād* or *mujāhada,* they cite exactly the same Koranic verses to make their points. Ghazālī, for example, hardly uses the word *jihād* in the *Ihyā*ʾ except to show that the inward struggle is more important than the outward. However, he employs the word *mujāhada* frequently and explains what it signifies in detail.[3]

In short, the path to God is to struggle against oneself and against those who are opposed to Him: *Obey not the unbelievers, but struggle against them mightily* (25:52); *Whosoever struggles, struggles only for his own self; surely God is independent of the worlds* (29:6). Like "struggle," the word "fight" is used frequently in the Koran and is interpreted in both an outward and inward sense: *So let them who sell the present life for the next world fight in the way of God. . . . Those who have faith fight in the way of God, and the unbelievers fight in the way of idols. Fight you therefore against the friends of Satan* (4:74–76).

The aim of the inner warfare is to attain the primary peace upon which all real peace depends, that is, peace with God. The aim of the outer warfare is to rectify the corruption worked in the earth by those who have failed to live up to their responsibilities as God's vicegerents. Only then can relative peace and harmony be established among the contending forces of this world. The Koran makes this point in retelling the story of David and Goliath: *And they routed them, by the leave of God. David slew Goliath and God gave him the kingship and Wisdom, and He taught him such as He willed. Had God not driven back the people, some by means of others, the earth would surely have been corrupted; but God is bounteous unto all the worlds* (2:251; cf. 5:33).

The faithful are at peace with God, and with the friends of God, but at war with His enemies: *Muhammad is the Messenger of God, and those who are with him are hard against the unbelievers, merciful to one another* (48:29); *O you who believe, whosoever of you turns from his religion, God will assuredly bring a people whom He loves and who love Him, humble toward the believers, disdainful toward the unbelievers, men who struggle in the way of God, not fearing the reproach of any reproacher* (5:54).

War Against God

War against God, like struggling in God's path, may be outward or inward. The outward war takes place with the sword, the inward with the heart. In both cases, those who fight this war have been overcome by unbelief, ingratitude, and disobedience to God's command. The unbelievers consider God their enemy (2:98, 8:60, 9:114), and their recompense is the Fire (41:28). The believers struggle in the path of God, and the unbelievers struggle to prevent people from entering the path: *Surely those who disbelieve and bar from the way of God have gone astray into far error* (4:167; cf. 9:34, 11:19, 16:88). They have taken up the work of Satan, who *desires to precipitate enmity and hatred among you . . . and to bar you from the remembrance of God and from prayer* (5:91).

A Final Word

This brief survey of Islam's understanding of war and peace could be extended indefinitely by further quotations from the Koran, the Hadith, and Islamic literature in general. But the conclusion would be the same: Islam considers peace with God and in God to be the goal of human life. It also holds that this peace cannot be achieved without war against God's enemies—in particular the caprice of the human soul. People cannot have peace as long as they remain distant from God. To be with God—and thus to become fully human—they have to struggle against everything that turns them away from their duties as God's vicegerents.

Only the greatest human beings—the prophets and those who have attained to God's good pleasure and proximity already in this life—have attained peace with God, their hearts being "at rest" with Him. But this inward peace does not contradict outward effort and strife, as the life of the Prophet Muhammad demonstrates. Long after he had won the inward and greater struggle, he had to continue with the lesser struggle. Moreover, he never for a moment gave up the outward forms of the greater struggle (namely prayer, fasting, and the like). That is why the Muslim authorities point out that *jihād*/*mujāhada* remains incumbent on human beings as long as they continue to exist within the domain where God has prescribed religious duties (*taklīf*) for them, that is, as long as they live in this world. Full and total peace will not be achieved until they reach the Abode of Peace.

War and strife accompany human beings in the present world because they and all created things are evanescent and perishing. The changing nature of all creatures brings about opposition and conflict. To make the most of this conflict, people must put themselves in harmony with Peace, the Divine Reality. In function of Peace they can struggle to bring relative harmony into the world by performing wholesome works and thereby eliminating its corruption. As long as people want to remain human, they have no choice but to engage in the greater and inward struggle. If they do not carry the Trust, they will enter into the ranks of the ungrateful and irresponsible unbelievers, and their refuge will be the "Fire," which is as good an image as any for war and for the churning maelstrom of conflicting forces that people fail to overcome when they refuse to struggle in the path of God.

The fact that this world is full of war and strife is a sign of God's mercy, which always takes precedence over His wrath. War and conflict remind human beings that God alone is Peace. If people want peace, they must struggle for God, not for themselves, no matter how grand their vision of a "better society" or a "happier world" may be. They cannot escape turmoil by seeking to overcome it on its own level. The more they try to do so, the more it will engulf them. The history of the world during the past two hundred years is all the proof this statement needs. In order to solve any of the problems plaguing the human race today, we have to solve the problem of the human race itself. In other words, we can only achieve real peace in the world when we first find it within ourselves.

24

Harmony with the Cosmos

The ecological disequilibriums caused by human wastefulness and extravagance are plain to everyone, and more and more people have become involved in discussing how to prevent worldwide disaster. Books are published by the hundreds, and international conferences are constantly being held. The rapid pollution of Islamic countries in the rush to industrialization has led many Muslim scientists and thinkers to involve themselves in these international efforts. Few of them, however, pay attention to the root cause of the problems as delineated by their own tradition.[1]

The first question we have to ask is how Islam has traditionally discussed the concept with which we are dealing. How does one say "environment" in the language of the Koran? What terminology would be used to speak of these issues in fourteenth-century Cairo or Isfahan? It is undoubtedly possible to translate the words "environment" and "ecology" in meaningful ways into the contemporary languages of the Islamic world, such as Arabic, Turkish, Persian, and Urdu, but this is not because the concepts as currently understood have always existed in these languages. The reason for this is obvious: Our view of the environment has developed along with modern science.

It is fair to say that "the problem of the environment" arose only because of the development of modern science and technology. If today there are serious environmental problems in various parts of the Muslim world, this is not because Muslims are living according to their own ideals and principles, far from it. What has happened is that non-Islamic ways of doing things have been imposed by the circumstances of the past two hundred years. In other words, Western environmental problems have been imported along with Western technology and know-how. Traditional Islam has never before been faced with major man-made ecological disasters or even with their possibility, so Islam has never had to frame the kind of concepts concerning the environment with which the West is now familiar.

With these prefatory remarks, we can ask whether any concepts are found in the Koran that indicate how traditional Muslims might have understood the

English word "environment." The best candidate for an equivalent seems to be the word *muḥīṭ*, which has the same literal meaning as environment—that which encircles and surrounds. It is an active participle from the verb *iḥāṭa*, which the Koran uses a dozen times. For example, the Koran tells us that hell "surrounds" the unbelievers. Significantly, most of the verses that use the word do so in reference to God, who *surrounds the unbelievers* (2:19), *surrounds what you are doing* (11:92), and *surrounds all things* (4:126; cf. 41:54).

If "God surrounds all things," this means that God is our environment: It is God that surrounds us. As the active participle of the verb, *muḥīṭ* is a divine name employed seven times in the Koran. It signifies that God is "He who surrounds," or is the "Environer" or the "Environment." At first glance, we can take this as a statement of God's transcendence. God surrounds all things because He is infinitely beyond the things, yet He controls the universe utterly. As the Koran puts it, He sits on His Throne, and His "Footstool," situated below the Throne, *embraces the heavens and the earth* (2:255).

Traditional Islamic cosmology often depicts the universe as a sphere encircled by the Footstool, which in turn is surrounded by the Throne, upon which God is sitting. This God who sits on the Throne is called not only the Environer, but also the All-Embracing (*wāsiʿ*). He embraces the Throne and Footstool, which in turn embrace heaven and earth—that is, all reality, no matter how far it may extend into other galaxies.

If God is our ultimate, transcendent environment, because He surrounds all reality, what is our immediate, immanent environment? One Koranic answer would be "God": *To God belong the east and the west; wherever you turn, there is the face of God; God is All-Embracing, Knowing*" (2:115); *He is the First and the Last, the Manifest and the Nonmanifest* (57:3).

The Koran often calls our immediate environment *dunyā*, which means this world or, more literally, "that which is near." It contrasts it with *ākhira*, "the next world." The meaning of the two words is inseparably intertwined. To mention one is to imply the other. In many passages the Koran points out that the next world is a far better place than this world and that there we will meet God. We entered this world after having been with God, we live in this world surrounded by God, and we will meet Him again in the next world. *God originates creation*, says the Koran, *then He brings it back again* (10:34).

Another Koranic term for our immediate environment is *arḍ*, "earth." Note that this word, like "this world," is correlative, since it is usually accompanied by, and in any case implies, "heaven" or "heavens." The phrase "heaven and earth" is taken by many commentators to refer to the two fundamental kinds of creature, the spiritual and the corporeal, or the visible and the invisible. Both these pairs of correlative terms—this world and next world, heaven and earth—refer to the cosmos. The first set of terms—this world and the next world—describes the cosmos in terms of its becoming or its temporal situation. The second set—heaven and earth—describes it in terms of its static or spatial situation.

Islam's emphasis on the primacy and ultimacy of God's reality and on His absolute power over all that He creates means that the cosmos, however envisaged, must be related back to its Creator in order for it to be understood correctly. Even if our sole concern is the environment of our planet, we can correctly understand its situation only in the context of "all things" which precisely "God surrounds." Moreover, the spiritual world comprehends and surrounds the physical world. It stands above us, or between us and God. It also stands before and behind us—again, between us and God, who is the Last as He is the First. When we leave our immediate environment through physical death, we enter into a spiritual environment that surrounds the corporeal world and is in turn surrounded by the Divine.

An Islamic perspective on the environment can only derive from Islam's perspective on God and the cosmos. Moreover, the human relationship to the environment is a basic issue, because it is human beings, not other creatures, who have upset the equilibrium of the environment. This means that it is we who no longer live in harmony with what surrounds us. We have destroyed the proper relationship between ourselves and the cosmos, and, by the same token, between ourselves and God, or between the Surrounder (*muḥīṭ*) and the surrounded (*muḥāṭ*).

What then are human beings? How is it possible for them, among all creatures, to upset the relationship between the cosmos and its Maker? In order to understand the situation of our surroundings, we first have to understand ourselves. Thus, the task of delineating the Islamic perspective on the environment would come down to explaining Islam's teachings concerning God, man, and the cosmos.

The Signs of God

In the Islamic view of the cosmos, God's signs do not represent two or more different kinds of things; the natural and the supernatural blend and become inseparable. God's self-disclosure is an intrinsic dimension of reality; it can be perceived in a religious and supernatural context, or in a non-religious and natural context, but both contexts fit into larger frameworks—first that of the cosmos and second that of God, the two primary environments that we spoke about earlier. In other words, the natural world is not fundamentally different from the supernatural world; natural things can never be looked upon as mere objects, nor can supernatural signs and miracles be considered to occur outside of natural laws. Every single thing, whether of natural or supernatural origin, is God's creation and sign; each must be treated with the appropriate reverence and remembrance.

Here it bears repeating that Islam includes in the cosmos not only the world that we can see—or in principle could see if we were in the right place at the right time and had the right instruments—but also the invisible world, which includes such supernatural beings as angels, and which lies at an ontological level closer to God than the visible world. Here again, invisible beings are so much a part of the Islamic worldview that our immediate environment is not and cannot be a closed system, shut off from invisible influences, whether angelic or divine. The visible world is a theater within which higher realities display themselves; it can never be considered apart from the demands those higher realities make upon us. Consider the following Koranic verse: *Your Lord revealed to the bees: "Take unto yourselves of the mountains, houses, and of the trees, and of what they are building. Then eat of all manner of fruit, and follow the ways of your Lord, easy to go upon." Then there comes out of their bellies a drink of diverse hues, wherein is healing for men. Surely in that is a sign for a people who reflect* (16:68–69).

Human Vicegerency

God's signs—whether those of revelation or those of the natural world—are directed toward man. In the verse quoted above and in numerous other passages, the Koran refers to these signs and then asks mankind to reflect and meditate on them, warning those who ignore and deny them of the painful chastisement of hell. God's messengers have come to remind (*tadhkīr*) man of God, and it is man's duty to remember Him (*dhikr*). In short, human beings alone among the creatures (with the sole exception of the jinn) are called to ponder the signs of God.

Man, then, may or may not take heed. He alone has the choice of whether or not to remember God. *Everything in the heavens and earth glorifies God* (57:1), says the Koran, precisely because all things are His signs. Again, *Have you not seen how to God bow all who are in the heavens and all who are in the earth, the sun and the moon, the stars and the mountains, the trees and the beasts, and many of mankind?* (22:18). So mankind alone may choose not to bow down to God—and this fact, paradoxically perhaps, is one of God's greatest signs, for only a being created in God's image could have the ability to deny Him. By sharing in God's knowledge and free will, man can set himself up as a little god. The Koran seems to be alluding to this point when it says, *To God bow all who are in the heavens and the earth, willingly or unwillingly, as do their shadows in the mornings and the evenings* (13:15; cf. 3:83). Whether or not a given human being bows willingly to God, he is still a sign of God and thereby glorifies Him.

The gift of free will is at least part of what the Koran is referring to when it speaks of the Trust that God bestowed on mankind: *We offered the Trust to the heavens, the earth, and the mountains, but they refused to carry it and were afraid of it; and man carried it. Surely he is sinful, very foolish* (33:72). The fact that man is "sinful, very foolish" obviously alludes to his mishandling of God's Trust.

Adam learned the names of all things in terms of their relationship to God, not their separation from Him. The fact that Adam was taught the names refers to the special nature of his intelligence and his ability to recognize God's signs. Many commentators point out that the names are the realities of all things, or the things as they are known by God Himself. The Islamic formulation of the concept of man as microcosm, the mirror image of the macrocosm (the sum of all things), derives in part from this view of human nature as containing the names of all things within itself. Ultimately it is these same names that man "remembers" when he recognizes and acknowledges God's signs; in effect, he is affirming the intimate relationship that exists between each thing and its Creator, or, as the Sufis would say, between the form and the meaning, the outward and the inward, or the manifest and the nonmanifest reality. At the same time, he is affirming that he himself is somehow identical with all things, since his knowledge of what is outside himself derives from what is inside himself. In other words, the fact that Adam was taught all the names shows that he somehow participates through his quality of being a divine image in God's omniscience.

One of the consequences of man's potential knowledge of all things is that he is given power over God's creation. The Koran recalls to man that God has subjected (*taskhīr*) to him the creatures of the cosmos; this subjection itself is one of God's manifest signs: *Have you not seen how God has subjected to you all that is in the earth?* (22:65); *Have you not seen how God has subjected to you whatsoever is in the heavens and earth, and has lavished upon you His blessings, outward and inward?* (31:20)

The Koran recounts how God commanded the angels to bow down before Adam (2:30); this is clearly connected with the fact that *everything* in the heavens and the earth is subjected to man, even the inhabitants of the invisible world.

The microcosm and macrocosm are united through the divine link that was established when God made man His vicegerent. The clear import of this Koranic anthropology is that, among the creatures, man alone can destroy the earth.[2] Still, man is bound to the earth in an intimate union, so that the outward state of the cosmos reflects the inward state of his consciousness. Subject and object are inseparable, although the former takes the active role. Hence the "illness" of one side of the relationship can only be a sign of the illness of the other side, while responsibility for "corruption" remains with the active partner.

At this point a key question needs to be answered: How in practice can man carry the Trust? How can he be the perfect vicegerent who does not corrupt the earth but on the contrary establishes peace and harmony? To answer this question, we have to look at another dimension of the Koranic concept of human nature.

The Servant of God

To say that the Koran singles out Adam and his descendants as God's vicegerents does not provide a complete picture of the Koran's anthropology. For one thing, it is clear that not all of Adam's children are able to function as true vicegerents; "corruption and the shedding of blood" began already with Cain. From his time onward, there have been human beings who fail to live up to the Trust and who therefore corrupt the earth. The vicegerent who rules over the earth does so not according to his own whims but according to God's command; he is able to represent God because he has passed beyond limited, individual motivations and surrendered his own will to the divine will. Hence, he is called the "servant" or "slave" of God. The Prophet Muhammad himself is mentioned in the daily canonical prayers as "His servant and His messenger" (*ʿabduhu wa-rasūluhu*). First Muhammad is God's servant; only then is he qualified to be His prophet. So also for those who follow the Prophet; they must first be God's servants, and only then can they hope to be His vicegerents. Man cannot carry God's Trust without submitting himself to Him. The fundamental importance of this idea is indicated by the literal meaning of the word "Islam" (that is, submission to God). In short, if from one point of view man was created to be God's vicegerent, from another point of view he was created to be His servant: *I created jinn and mankind,* says God in the Koran, *only to serve Me* (51:56).

What then is the "service of God" that is a prerequisite to carrying the Trust and becoming God's vicegerent? Simply put, it is submission to God's will as revealed in the Koran and in the Sunnah of the Prophet. In other words, man cannot represent God on earth without following His revealed religion. To fail to follow revelation is to ignore God's manifest signs and to become an unbeliever (*kāfir*), that is, an ingrate. Thus it brings us back to the Koranic doctrine of signs: The great sin of the ungrateful is that they cover over and conceal the signs of God by not acknowledging that the universe is His theater of activity and that the scriptures are His guidance. To treat the natural world and the religions sent by God with anything but reverence and gratitude is to enter into the ranks of the ungrateful unbelievers: *And those who disbelieve in the signs of God—for them awaits a terrible chastisement* (3:4).

According to a well-known Koranic formula, a punishment that God metes out to the unbelievers is that *they lose both this world and the world to come* (22:11). Indeed, one of the manifest signs of God to which the Koran often returns is the fact that He has destroyed unbelievers throughout history. *Journey in the land,* commands the Koran, *and behold what was the end of them that cried lies* (3:137).

When human beings fall into disbelief and ingratitude and thereby fail to render to God the service and worship that are His due, they will reap the fruit of their own works.

The Koranic message then is clear: Man can be the vicegerent of God, ruling over creation on his behalf, only on the condition of submitting his own will to God's will. If man fails to surrender to God's guidance as transmitted by the prophets, he will not be able to function as a true vicegerent. Instead of establishing peace and equilibrium, he will work corruption. More specifically, the role of Islam is precisely to establish peace and equilibrium between heaven and earth with a view toward man's ultimate good. Given the hierarchical nature of reality, it is only natural that peace with the Surrounder of our first and our last environment is a prerequisite for peace with our immediate environment. That is to say, we cannot live in harmony with the cosmos until we live in harmony with God. Man as God's vicegerent can only rule the subjects that have been entrusted to him on the condition that he accept God's rule over himself.

But if he rebels against God, the creatures will rebel against him. This explains why contemporary man is on the verge of being destroyed by the very creatures entrusted to his care.

25

Stray Camels in China

One useful way to deal with the question of Islam's attitude toward other religions would be to provide an historical survey of Islamic viewpoints. This approach would lead us to the conclusion that over history, Muslims have had diverse understandings of other religions. Having concluded that, we might then ask which of those understandings best represents Islam. Then we would face the problem of how to define Islam. And of course, over history, Muslims have had diverse understandings of what exactly Islam is and what it demands from them.

For my part, I have neither the resources nor the means to make an historical survey of Islamic views of other religions. Instead of addressing the historical issue, I want to ask a theological question, which is the following: What are Islam's resources for coming to an understanding of other religious traditions?

Here I understand the word *Islam* to refer not to any particular school of thought, but to the basic texts of the tradition—the Koran and the Hadith—and to the intellectual perspectives of the great representatives of the tradition over history. Again, I do not want to provide an historical survey, but rather a theological argument, an argument that is rooted in fundamental Islamic perspectives. It is an argument that strives to suggest how Muslims might acknowledge not only the legitimacy of religious diversity, but also its necessity and providentiality. What I have to say will be an argument *for* inclusivism (although perhaps *pluralism* is the better term) and *against* exclusivism. In other words, I show that Islam has the theological means not only to accept religious diversity, but also to appreciate it and approve of it. On the basis of their own traditional teachings, Muslims may, if they wish, look at other religious traditions as revealed ways that lead to the absolute truth of God. However, I do not want to deny the legitimacy of exclusivism, because, by excluding the exclusivists, I would join them in being exclusivist. Instead, I would say that exclusivists are perfectly free to read Islam in an exclusive manner. They may, if they wish, understand Islam—by which they usually mean their own, specific version of Islam—as the only way to the truth. The tradition certainly provides support for understanding Islam in these terms. But such a perspective is of no interest to me.

Before attempting to answer the question I posed at the start of this essay, it is necessary to ask which specific topics we wish to understand. Nowadays, topics that are discussed on the international level are typically determined by international interests, and these in turn depend largely on current events and, more specifically, on the political, economic, and social agendas of the industrialized powers. If our purpose here is to discuss "Islam" and not country X or country Y that has a majority population of Muslims, then the current issues—as designated by politicians, the media, and economic interests—should be ignored for the time being. Instead, we need to address the perennial issues of Islamic discourse, issues that have not changed over the past thousand years because human beings have not changed. These issues start with first principles, and the first of all principles is that of reality itself.

In Islamic terms, in order to discuss reality we have to discuss God. This raises immediate problems in the context of so-called contemporary issues, because people have no patience with theology, and they also have no sense that theology can have any meaning except as an ideological ploy. When God is mentioned, many immediately start to grumble about fanaticism and fundamentalism, and that ends the possibility of discussion. We are told that we need to address immediate and pressing issues—the "real" problems. However, we are then compelled to let contemporary intellectual predilections, or the lack of them, provide us with a definition of what these "real" problems may be. The "real" here has little relevance to what the Islamic tradition has always understood to be real. Hence, Muslims who want to participate in the discussion have no choice but to forget the first principles of their own tradition. Nevertheless, no discussion can have a meaningful claim to have anything to do with Islam until the participants agree on the necessity to begin with first principles.

First Principles

The first of the first principles of Islamic thought is *tawḥīd*. When we read the great Muslim thinkers of the past, we see that they had complete confidence in the universality of this principle. By "universality," I mean the idea that *tawḥīd* was known and understood by all peoples at all times and places, because it was the message of all the prophets and all the sages. The Koran asserts that God has sent a messenger to every community and that the underlying content of every divine message is *tawḥīd*. Muslim thinkers who understood this had no fear of learning about other civilizations, because the Koran taught them that the Koranic message was nothing new, but rather a confirmation of earlier messages. This attitude helps explain the great interest shown by the early Muslims toward the Greek and Iranian intellectual heritages, not to mention the Indian. Islamic thought, in its fully developed form, is inconceivable without Greek formulations in particular, but this was nothing for Muslims to be ashamed of, because it simply confirmed the Koranic teaching that wisdom is universal.

Among the many traditional expressions of the early Muslims' recognition of the universality of *tawḥīd* in the pre-Islamic heritage are two well-known sayings attributed to the Prophet: "Seek knowledge, even unto China" and "Wisdom is the believer's stray camel; wherever he finds it, he has the most right to it."[1] Such sayings suggest that the goal of Muslim intellectuals in addressing other civilizations should be to recognize the wisdom that is inherent in them. The wisdom found in traditional Chinese civilization, for example, is nothing foreign to Islam because, at root, it is the wisdom of *tawḥīd*.

But before Muslims go looking for stray camels in China, they need to examine their own herds. If they take a close look at their own intellectual resources, they will find several domains of wisdom that can be extremely helpful in addressing issues of religious diversity. These domains tend to be forgotten or glossed over in contemporary discussions. If Muslims do not recognize these domains of learning as Islamic wisdom, they will not be able to find wisdom's camels under Chinese blankets, let alone the blankets of other civilizations.

I said that, in order for a discussion to be Islamic, it must begin with first principles and that, in Islamic terms, the first of all principles is *tawḥīd*. Other first principles follow in the wake of *tawḥīd*. Traditionally, Muslims divide the domain of first principles into three topics—*tawḥīd*, prophecy, and the Return.

Given that Muslims have always taken a diversity of positions concerning the expression of first principles, we can attempt to suggest what sort of positions might be most helpful in the context of interreligious dialogue. The brief answer here is that any position recognizing a broad base for determining Islamicity will find it relatively easy to recognize the universal truths of Islam in non-Islamic forms. Those who know and appreciate the diversity of Islamic camels will have little difficulty recognizing their own camels outside the borders of the Islamic community. In contrast, those who like to think that there is one Islam and that other Islams are deviant or distorted, will find it exceedingly difficult to see Islamic truths beyond the borders of their own positions.

Two Perspectives

The two halves of the Shahadah establish two basic levels of discourse. The first level has to do with God, and the second has to do with the wisdom that God sends to His creatures. Hence, the second half of the Shahadah is an explicit expression of what came to be known as the second of Islam's first principles, that is, prophecy.

It is important to keep in mind that the Koran speaks of the universality of *tawḥīd*. In other words, it declares that *tawḥīd* has been affirmed by all prophets. Of course, the Koran also affirms the universality of prophecy, because it asserts that prophets have been sent to every people. However, the Koran makes it clear that each prophet has a specific message or historical role. In other words, the Koran affirms that *tawḥīd* is a universal truth, having applicability in every situation throughout all of history, but it does not claim that the statement "Muhammad is the messenger of God" is universal in the same sense. Before the coming of Muhammad, there were other prophets and other messages. Each prophet was given the message of *tawḥīd*, but along with it, they were also given specific teachings and laws that were not identical with the laws and teachings of other prophets. Hence, the Koranic view of things is that the prophetic messages are the same on the level of *tawḥīd*, but different on the level of specific teachings and practices.[2]

Any discussion of Islamic first principles has to begin by looking at the meaning of the two halves of the Shahadah, which establish the first two principles of faith. After all, the Shahadah gives voice, in the most succinct manner, to the teachings of the Koran. The first half of the Shahadah is the declaration of a universal truth that is understood to be present in all wisdom. The second half is the declaration of a specific set of teachings that is aimed at a specific historical community. Thus, we have the first two principles of Islam, *tawḥīd* and prophecy. The first principle tends toward inclusivism and plurality, but the second tends more toward exclusivism.

One way to understand how these two principles establish both inclusivism and exclusivism is to meditate on the implications of the two most basic names of the Koran, which are *qur'ān* itself and *furqān*. If we look at the linguistic root of the term, we find that *qur'ān* means not only "recitation," but also "gathering" and "bringing together." The Koran is understood as a bringing together because it is looked upon as containing the wisdom of all mankind. As for the word *furqān*, it comes from a root that means to separate, so it signifies "separation, differentiation, discernment, discrimination." Together, the two names *qur'ān* and *furqān* tell us that the Koran is a recitation of divine wisdom that brings together all wisdom and provides the keys for discerning between truth and falsehood, reality and unreality, right and wrong, guidance and misguidance, salvation and damnation. The divine wisdom that is brought together in the Koran is the wisdom that was given to all the 124,000 prophets who are said to have come to mankind from Adam down to Muhammad. This universal wisdom of all the prophets is summarized in one Koranic verse: *There is no god but I, so serve Me* (21:25). This is *tawḥīd* along with its diverse implications. *Furqān*, or the discerning and separating wisdom that the Koran establishes, is also *tawḥīd* because it allows people to distinguish between the One and the many, the Real and the unreal. But *furqān* also specifically refers to the diverse implications of *tawḥīd*, the many concrete teachings and guidelines that were given to the prophets over history. It is through these specific applications and concrete guidelines that separation occurs among the prophetic messages and Islam becomes distinct from other religions, even if, on the level of the first half of the Shahadah, *qur'ān*, all the messages are the same.

The first half of the Shahadah, the statement of *tawḥīd*, is often understood as summarizing the whole message, both *qur'ān* and *furqān*. Hence, the first half of the Shahadah implies within itself the second half. However, one cannot argue that it demands the second half only in the specific historical form of "Muhammad is the messenger of God." Rather, *tawḥīd* demands the reality of wisdom and prophecy, a reality that becomes manifest to all peoples. By insisting that God sends prophets to all nations, the Koran is asserting that *tawḥīd*—the unity of Reality—demands that wisdom appear only in function of the Source of all reality. In other words, wisdom is inaccessible without the initiative of the Source of all wisdom, which is the Real Itself, God, the Absolute Principle.

Let me briefly explain how the first half of the Shahadah demands both *qur'ān* and *furqān*. I begin with *furqān*, on the basis of which we can differentiate some things from other things. By saying "No god but God," people assert that God is one. This formula negates the idea of other gods and separates God from all false claimants to godhood. In order to understand this meaning from the formula, one needs to grasp the meaning of the word *god* (*ilāh*) in Arabic. The basic idea of the Arabic root has to do with service, worship, and adoration. A god is what one serves. By this definition, practically anything can be a god. Anything that one serves or sets as one's ideal is a god. Any object, any idea, any ideology can be a god. A person can, of course, have many gods, and most people do. The Koran often criticizes the worship of many gods. Among the gods it stigmatizes vehemently is caprice, that is, self-will and individual desire. In the Koranic perspective, all those who depend on themselves and make decisions on the basis of their own personal likes and dislikes are following the god that is "caprice," and this god will certainly lead them to an unwelcome destination.

In short, the first thing that one understands from the Koranic assertion, "No god but God," is that nothing is worthy of service, worship, and trust except God Himself. Thus, the Shahadah establishes the *furqān* or discernment between God, who is worthy of service, and everything other than God, which is not worthy of service. But what exactly is this God that is worthy of service? The Koran never answers this question directly, partly because to ask about the "whatness" of God is already to misunderstand God's reality. If all things in the universe can properly be the object of the question "what?," God alone cannot, because He is outside the universe and different from all things within it.

Although the Koran does not say what God is, it does say what He is not—for example, that He is not like anything (42:11)—and it also speaks of Him in terms of names and attributes. It therefore tells us that God is merciful, compassionate, all-knowing, desiring, powerful, just, avenging, forgiving, and so on. None of these attributes defines God, however. Each of them announces a certain manner in which God interrelates with the universe. But what God is in Himself, as He Himself knows Himself, is humanly unknowable. Here one cannot help but be reminded of the first sentence of the *Tao Te Ching*.

The Koran and the first formula of the Shahadah establish a basic *furqān* or differentiation between God and the world. God is on one side, and the whole cosmos is on the other. If God is designated by the names and attributes that the Koran gives to Him, it follows that these names and attributes do not belong to the universe in any real sense. Thus, for example, God is one, but the universe along with everything within it is many. God is knowing, but the created things are ignorant. God is compassionate, but the created things have no compassion. God is the Real, but the universe is unreal. The first half of the Shahadah means that "There is nothing real but the Real." It establishes a separation between the Real and the unreal, the Absolute and the relative, the Permanent and the impermanent, the Living and the dead, the Knowing and the ignorant.

But the Koran and the first half of the Shahadah do not limit themselves to the perspective of *furqān*. They also establish *qur'ān*. They separate the Real and the unreal, but they also demonstrate how the Real and the unreal are interrelated. Thus the Koranic teachings explain that the unreal comes into existence from the Real, ultimately goes back to the Real, and, in the meantime, appears in function of the Real. The unreal, after all, is not absolute unreality, but relative unreality, which is to say that it is unreal in relation to God. But, since it is relatively unreal, it is also relatively real, which is to say that it is real in relation to absolute nothingness. It follows that everything in the universe displays certain traces of reality, certain signs of God, and hence the Koran repeatedly tells people to strive to comprehend and understand God's signs. These signs, the Koran says, are found in the natural world, in the human self, in the messages of the prophets, and in the very verses of the Koran itself.

These two ways of looking at reality—discernment or *furqān* and gathering together or *qur'ān*—are integral to the Koran and are found throughout the Islamic tradition, although frequently one side is stressed over the other, depending on who is speaking and which school of thought is being represented. For example, Kalam tends to stress *furqān*, because it wants to establish the utter difference between God and the world and the necessity for recognizing the rights of God over His creation. Kalam strives to show how human beings are servants of God who must accept His revelation and act accordingly. The juridical sciences also stress *furqān*, because they are rooted in the understanding that right and wrong activities must be differentiated and separated from each other. In contrast, many expressions of Sufism stress *qur'ān*, because the Sufis are concerned not so much with separating the servant from God, but rather with showing that God is present in the world and in the servant and that the servant should strive to find God here and now.

From about the seventh/thirteenth century onward, these two perspectives—one of which stresses *furqān* and the other *qur'ān*—are often described in terms of God's incomparability (*tanzīh*) and similarity (*tashbīh*). From the prespective of God's incomparability, ultimate reality lies infinitely beyond the world of phenomena. God cannot be compared to anything in the universe. God alone is truly real, and hence all things other than Him are like specks of dust in the face of infinity. The perspective of God's similarity recognizes the signs of God in everything that exists. It allows people to understand why the Koran says, *Wherever you turn, there is the face of God* (2:115), or *He is with you wherever you are* (57:4).

For many authorities, incomparability and similarity represent the two eyes with which people must look upon God in order to understand the full implications of *tawḥīd*. With these two eyes, people should understand that they are distant from God, but God is near to them. In effect, God is both far and near, absent and present, incomparable and similar. Incomparability asserts God's unique possession of the attribute of unity, whereas similarity asserts that the many are the creation and the manifestation of the One. The universe comes from God, and hence it is full of His signs, and it will return to God, because He is the unique reality that determines all relative reality.

In discussions of incomparability and similarity, Koranic divine names are employed to illustrate how the Koran asserts both God's distance and His nearness. Although every name of God can be understood as expressing both incomparability and similarity, some names express one side more clearly than the other. Thus, for example, the names of majesty (*jalāl*) are usually associated with incomparability. In contrast, the names of beauty (*jamāl*) are associated with similarity. The names of majesty—which are also called the names of wrath, severity, or justice—express God's utter reality in face of the unreality of the creatures. God is King, Majestic, Mighty, Tremendous, Great, Severe, Avenger, and, in face of these names, human beings are insignificant if not utterly nonexistent. In contrast, the names of beauty—also called the names of mercy, gentleness, or bounty—express God's concern for His creatures despite their insignificance. In respect of the names of majesty, God is infinitely distant from creation and simply expects to be obeyed. The only possible human response to God's majesty is to surrender and to be His servants. But, in respect of the names of beauty, God is infinitely close to His creatures, closer to them *than the jugular vein* (50:16), and He acts with much more compassion and gentleness than any mother ever acted toward her child. It is in respect of this nearness that human beings can be the vicegerents or representatives of God in the cosmos. Because of similarity, God *taught Adam the names, all of them* (2:31), and created him in His own image. Because of the attributes of beauty and gentleness, God sent the prophets with the message of guidance and compassion.

Human Ambiguity

Once we have established the fact that the relationship between the Absolutely Real and the relatively real, or God and creation, can be understood from two basic points of view, that is, incomparability and similarity, or *furqān* and *qur'ān*, we can usefully look at the human situation. Clearly, if human beings or other things are to be considered in relation to first principles, they must be considered from both points of view. But there is a mystery about human beings that sets them apart from other creatures. This mystery has detailed metaphysical and cosmological reasons that cannot be dealt with here. But the fact of this mystery is well-known. It is that human beings are not fixed in their nature, whereas other beings are what they are, and they cannot change in any radical way. But the very fact of human intelligence—of wisdom, sagehood, and prophecy—shows that a distinction, a *furqān*, needs to be drawn in the human case between what people *are* and what they *should be*. In other words, other things are what they are and cannot be otherwise. In contrast, human beings are what they are, but they can and should be otherwise. Other things are fully what they are without trying, but human beings have to learn to be fully human. Or, one can say that to be human is to have the possibility of being otherwise, to be more or less than what one is.

In terms of our previous discussion, we can say that the actual human situation is for people to be situated between *furqān* and *qur'ān*, between incomparability and similarity. Because of the disjunction established by the divine attributes associated with incomparability, people are utterly controlled by the Real, who is the Majestic, the Mighty, the Powerful. The Koran says, *To Him submits everything in the heavens and the earth* (3:83), and *There is nothing in the heavens and the earth but that it comes to the All-Merciful as a servant* (19:93). This is to say that everything in the universe is submitted to God and serves Him by its very nature. Nothing can act on its own. Whatever is done is done by the controlling power of the Real.

Human insignificance before the Real is understood through looking with the eye of incomparability. However, when we look at people with the eye of similarity, we find a different picture. In the actual human situation, people have a measure of knowledge and self-awareness and a sense of their own freedom. These attributes come from the Real. They allow people to understand that they are not yet complete, that their unfolding has not yet reached its end, and that their own activities and endeavors have an impact upon how they change and develop, or on what they become. Here, guidance, prophecy, and wisdom intervene. In other words, the Real addresses this freedom and self-awareness and establishes paths of guidance that allow these qualities to be fully developed and realized.

God, then, addresses human beings through their own innate intelligence and through the prophets and sages, telling them what the human situation *should* be. The basic message is that people live below themselves. They are dominated by ignorance, forgetfulness, and the lack of reality. In other words, their present situation in respect of the Real is predominantly that of *furqān* and incomparability, of distinction, difference, and otherness. They must attempt to change their situation by clinging to *qur'ān* and the divine attributes of similarity. They must seize on the signs of reality that fill the unreal domain of cosmic existence and follow these signs back to their Source, which is the Real.

The knowledge of *furqān* that the Koran brings establishes the separation of the Real from the unreal, the True from the false, the Absolute from the relative. From this perspective, human beings are utter slaves of the Real, since unreality possesses nothing in face of the Real. But in terms of similarity, people are given a certain understanding and self-awareness. The knowledge of *qur'ān* brought by the Koran asserts that people must surrender (*islām*) voluntarily to the Real. Although they are God's servants in actual fact, they must also surrender freely to Him through the trace of freedom and self-awareness that He has given them.

Having freely surrendered to the Real, people can live in harmony with the Real. It is this free submission to God that allows people to actualize the attributes of similarity that are latent in their nature, because God *taught Adam the names, all of them* (2:31). Having freely surrendered to God, people may eventually become His vicegerents in the universe. Only those whom God "brings near" (*muqarrab*) to Himself can be worthy of representing Him. In other words, by following the guidance of the prophets, people can move from a predominance of the attributes of incomparability and difference to a predominance of the attributes of similarity and sameness. The first message of the Koran is *furqān*, the separation of all things from God; but the second message is *qur'ān*, the togetherness of God with those who freely choose to serve Him.

The Precedence of Mercy

In the Islamic view, God's fundamental motivation for revealing the Koran does not lie in the establishment of *furqān*. On the contrary, God asks people to recognize *furqān*, their actual separation and distinction from what is truly real. Then, on the basis of that recognition, they are asked to follow the guidelines of the Real in order to bring about *qur'ān*, which is the togetherness and harmony of the servants and their Lord. The purpose of *furqān*, in other words, is to give people the discernment of their actual situation in order that they can overcome distinction, distance, and difference and establish togetherness, nearness, and sameness. *Furqān* gives way to *qur'ān*, and the attributes of incomparability are overcome by the attributes of similarity.

In theological terms, the primacy of *qur'ān* over *furqān* is understood as soon as we meditate on the divine names that are associated with the two sides. *Furqān* establishes distinction and difference. Hence, it is associated with knowledge and discernment, which separate the Real from the unreal and the Absolute from the relative. Knowledge discerns the levels, the differentiations, and the distinctions. Knowledge is a divine attribute, and God knows all things, as the Koran tells us repeatedly. Hence, God establishes all the distinctions and differences, not only cognitively, but also ontologically, by creating an infinitely diverse cosmos within which everything is put in its proper place on the basis of the divine knowledge. But there is something deeper in God than knowledge, and that is the very fact of being God. It is God who knows, and it is the fact that God actually *is* that allows Him to know. In philosophical language, Being is the precondition for knowledge. In terms of the Koranic names of God, God must first be alive before He can know. And God's life, God's reality, is a single reality, because He is one, as *tawḥīd* asserts. Therefore, the principle of the oneness of God's Being takes precedence over the principle of the manyness of the cosmos, even though that manyness is rooted in God's eternal knowledge.

Through knowledge, the Real establishes *furqān*—differentiation and distinction. Through Being, the Real establishes *qur'ān*—oneness and togetherness.

God creates the universe, but then He brings everything back to Himself. This bringing back to Himself is the third of Islam's first principles—the Return, the fact that everything goes back to God. In other words, the third principle asserts that *qur'ān* or gathering together is the ultimate end of *furqān* or distinction, just as *qur'ān* gave rise to *furqān* in the first place.[3]

Divine knowledge can be considered an attribute of incomparability inasmuch as it establishes *furqān*—difference and differentiation. Through the distinct identity of each thing in God's knowledge, all things are unique and thereby different. Hence, knowledge is allied with the attributes that assert difference, and these are the names of majesty, such as Mighty, Great, Transcendent, and High. In contrast, mercy and compassion are attributes of similarity, because these establish the existence of all things, and existence is a single attribute, shared by everything in the universe. Each thing is unique from the point of view of God's knowledge, but united and integrated with all things from the point of view of the existence that God gives to it.

The Prophet said that God has written on His Throne, "My mercy takes precedence over My wrath." The Throne of God is understood as the place where God sits while He governs the universe. Hence, the saying means that mercy embraces all things in the universe, and every appearance of wrath is in some way a manifestation of mercy. God's mercy has the first say, because through mercy He creates the universe. It also has the final say, because He brings everything back to Himself, and He is Being, that is, sheer reality, goodness, and mercy. And mercy also determines the present situation, because it takes precedence over every phenomenon that seems to manifest wrath, such as ignorance, suffering, death, and destruction.

The names of majesty and beauty, as already mentioned, are sometimes called the names of wrath and mercy. The statement that God's mercy takes precedence over His wrath can be understood to mean that the names of mercy and beauty are more fundamental to reality than the names of wrath and majesty. After all, the names of wrath depend upon difference and distinction. God is angry only with those who go against His command, and these can only be human beings (and jinn). But human freedom to act against God's command is exceedingly limited, because, by the nature of things, they are His creatures and hence His servants. They are submitted to Him along with everything else in the heavens and the earth. Divine names such as Mighty, Majestic, Avenger, and Transcendent depend on the independent existence of the creatures, but, in the last analysis, the creatures have no independent existence. All their reality is a reflection of the reality of the Real. Only the illusion of a real separation from the Real allows creatures to see themselves as different from the Real. But the relative cannot be separated from the Absolute, and the relatively unreal cannot be independent of the Absolutely Real.

If the attributes of majesty and wrath depend on distinction and *furqān*, the attributes of beauty and mercy speak to unity and *qur'ān*. Wrath depends on separation from reality, because reality is inherently merciful and compassionate, and to experience the divine wrath can only occur when one remains distant from the inherent reality of the Real. In contrast, the mercy that embraces all things is simply the nature of the Real. Through mercy, gentleness, compassion, kindness, benevolence, beneficence, and bounty, the Real shows Its own oneness and brings all things into harmony with Its own Self.

God is one, as *tawḥīd* assures us. In other words, unity, harmony, equilibrium, and balance pertain to the very nature of the Real. To the extent that the universe is unreal—the perspective of incomparability—it is multiple, dispersed, disharmonious, and imbalanced. However, these are attributes of the universe only when it is considered independently of its Principle and Source, which is the Real. In fact, it has no real independence, so the underlying attributes of the universe are unity, harmony, equilibrium, and balance. That is to say that oneness takes precedence over manyness, equilibrium over disequilibrium, similarity over incomparability, *qur'ān* over *furqān*, mercy over wrath, and Being over nonexistence.

The Priority of Inclusivism

I have just provided a roundabout survey of certain basic Islamic ways of looking at things. Let me repeat that not all Muslim thinkers have articulated the two basic standpoints of *qur'ān* and *furqān*, or similarity and incomparability, and many of them typically stress one side over the other. Those who stress incomparability and *furqān* will see difference as more important than sameness and the divine wrath as more basic than the divine mercy. In contrast, those who stress similarity and *qur'ān* will find that sameness is more significant than difference, mercy more fundamental than wrath.

I have already suggested that both Kalam and jurisprudence emphasize *furqān*, and therefore they stress difference and differentiation. Once differentiation is the primary issue, it is not too difficult to conclude that there is one correct way of seeing things, and all different ways are false. This one true way leads to salvation, and the other ways lead to damnation. Islamic history is full of polemics among various schools of thought, much of it motivated by the desire to prove the truth of one perspective to the exclusion of other perspectives. When Muslims who think in this way look at non-Islamic standpoints, they conclude with even more self-assurance that these viewpoints must be in error.

As suggested earlier, Islamic exclusivism is rooted in the second half of the Shahadah, the assertion that Muhammad is the messenger of God. This statement can be understood to abrogate the legitimacy of other prophets, that is, other messengers who have brought wisdom from the Real with the goal of eliminating ignorance. In contrast, Islamic inclusivism focuses on the first half of the Shahadah. *Tawḥīd* is taken as the universal message of the prophets, and is everywhere and always a path of salvation. To establish *tawḥīd* fully is to achieve *qur'ān,* which is the only goal of *furqān.* All prophets have come with messages of *furqān,* but, given the nature of *furqān,* each message must deal directly with the world of multiplicity and difference. Each must differentiate between right and wrong, true and false, absolute and relative, in specific and particular terms. The goal of all this is to overcome the error of seeing the many as completely separate from the One. In other words, the goal is to establish oneness, unity, harmony, equilibrium, balance, and wholeness. This is *tawḥīd,* the realization of the ultimate unity that underlies all multiplicity, and *tawḥīd* is the universal focus of all wisdom.

The full realization of *tawḥīd* establishes the precedence of similarity and eliminates the negative effects of incomparability, which are difference, multiplicity, dispersion, disintegration, ignorance, and suffering. All these negative effects grow up from the reality of God's otherness. However, God's otherness is established in relation to the relatively unreal, that is, the cosmos, and hence otherness is mixed with unreality, which is why it demands wrath—which is the repudiation of the false and the unreal. Reality in its very self is unity and oneness, so it knows no otherness and sees all things in terms of sameness. This is what similarity asserts—that God is present with all things, and, in respect of that presence, He embraces all things with mercy and compassion. Hence, all things are real through God's mercy and compassion, and mercy takes precedence over wrath, which is to say that the Real takes precedence over the unreal. The oneness established by *qur'ān* has the last word, and the difference that is established by *furqān* will be overcome by the oneness of mercy.

What I want to conclude from all this is that fruitful discussion of first principles demands a recognition of the precedence of the first half of the Shahadah over the second. In other words, in order to discuss first principles with followers of other traditions, Muslims need to recognize that the fundamental message of the Koran is God's universal truth and universal reality, and this means the precedence and predominance of mercy in all things. This precedence of oneness and mercy demands that God deliver the message of *furqān* and *qur'ān* to all peoples. *Every nation has a messenger* (10:47) because God's *mercy embraces all things* (7:156).

Hence, if Muslims understand the Koranic message of predominant mercy and predominant *qur'ān,* they should never doubt that the saving wisdom of mercy is found outside of Islam. This does not, of course, negate the possibility of error, ignorance, forgetfulness, and dispersion—whether outside of Islam or within. But it does assure us that mercy has the final say, not wrath. In a *ḥadīth qudsī* God says, "I am with My servant according to his opinion of Me." So God's servants should have a good opinion of Him, and certainly the idea that God is fundamentally merciful and compassionate to all creation is a good opinion. In the case of human beings, God's mercy and compassion demand sending the message of *furqān* and *qur'ān* to all peoples. The message is there, but the separation and multiplicity demanded by *furqān*—or the diverse forms that prophecy takes—may make it difficult to recognize wisdom for what it is. It is here that Muslims have a duty to know the diversity of the camels within the confines of their own community. If they are not aware of the diversity of their own wisdom, how will they be able to recognize wisdom when they see it in other pastures?

26

In Search of the Lost Heart

The Islamic tradition shares a great deal in common with Confucianism. This may not appear obvious to those who look at either of those traditions with respect to their historical situations, nor to those who are familiar with their respective sacred texts. Years ago, I would have thought that the two traditions must share some common metaphysical grounding and left it at that. However, since 1996 I have been collaborating with Sachiko Murata in investigating the ways in which Chinese-speaking Muslims, beginning in the seventeenth century, expressed their teachings by employing notions and concepts drawn from Confucianism. One of the most striking aspects of these authors' writings is the manner in which they are able to weave Islamic and Confucian teachings together to form an almost seamless garment that is at once authentically Muslim and authentically Confucian.[1] As an example of their approach, I offer a few remarks on their understanding of the significance of learning. I begin by quoting Mencius (d. 289 BCE), the second great sage after Confucius (d. 479 BCE): "The way of learning is nothing other than to seek for the lost heart" (6A:11).

The word here for "way" is *dao*, which everyone knows is the key concept in Taoism. It also plays an important role in Confucianism, as it does in Chinese Islam. One of its meanings is the road, path, or the process that people need to follow in order to reach their goal, which in this case is learning (*xue*). For the time being, we can take the word "learning" to mean in Chinese what it means in English: to gain understanding. I prefer not to say "to gain knowledge"—although the word also means that—because nowadays people tend to confuse "knowledge" with facts and information. You can know all sorts of things without understanding their immediate significance, not to mention their broad or ultimate significance.

Today, we have incredible access to knowledge—that is, to information. Yet, few people seem to have any sense of what it all means. This is one of the primary areas in which premodern scholars would have critiqued the modern educational enterprise. What we call "learning" today is focused on information, know-how, and technical expertise. It pushes us out into "the real world" with the idea that our purpose in life is to have successful careers and be well adjusted in terms of conventional notions of normalcy. But it cannot tell us why we should care about careers and normalcy. It does not have the means to ask the big questions—"Why do we exist?," and "What is the ultimate meaning of life?"

Instead of addressing such questions, modern learning directs us to acquire knowledge that has no relevance to our fundamental task in life, which, in Confucian terms, is to become truly human. In the Chinese language, gaining human status used to be called the "Great Learning" (*daxue*)—a word that, ironically enough, today designates the university.

In the traditional context, to learn something means to come to understand it, and to understand the big issues of life demands engaging in the quest for the Great Learning. The first goal of that learning is to fit all things into the overall picture and thereby make sense of them. But what exactly is the overall picture? What defines its limits? In order to gain real understanding of things, we need to know the big picture, and that in turn is determined by the worldview of the tradition in question. For those who are active and engaged members of a tradition, the worldview shapes and forms their tacit assumptions about life and living, their attitudes toward people and things, and the goals that they set for themselves. It is this "traditional context" that puts Confucian learning in a very different category from what we do nowadays at schools and universities.

Let me come back to the saying of Mencius, "The way of learning is nothing other than to seek for the lost heart." The key to grasping what he means here lies in the word "heart" (*xin*). In books on Chinese thought, this word is usually translated as "mind," or, more recently, "heart-and-mind" or "mind-and-heart." The Chinese character refers in the first place to the fleshly heart, the physical organ, but generally it designates the seat of our personhood. Classical Chinese thought speaks of the heart in the same way that it is spoken of in most other pre-modern civilizations: to designate the locus of consciousness and awareness, the deepest recesses of selfhood, the point of contact between the divine and the human. Islamic texts like to quote the *ḥadīth qudsī* in which God says, "Neither My heavens nor My earth embrace Me, but the heart of My believing servant does embrace Me."

In this traditional sense of the word, "heart" refers to a power of intuitive intelligence and spiritual awareness that transcends rational processes and unifies the knowing subject with the known object. When the word is translated as "mind," it is typically in order to follow modern usage, according to which the mind pertains to the rational, discursive, and analytical functions of the human self, whereas the heart refers to its emotions and feelings. In traditional contexts, however, such cognitive functions pertain only to the more external aspects of the heart's engagement with reality, those that support duality, difference, and otherness. In contrast, understanding that pertains to the core of the heart brings about unity and sameness.

Let me provide a typical example of a discussion concerning the heart from the Confucian tradition. The ancient classic called *The Book of Rites* tells us that "Man is the heart of heaven and earth" (7.3.7). In explaining what this means, the great sixteenth-century Confucian master Wang Yangming (d. 1529) says that the heart is "spiritual clarity" (*lingming*), or luminous, unitary intelligence, and it is the reality that lies behind all appearances. Among the myriad things, only human beings have access to it. He writes:

> We know, then, that in all that fills heaven and earth there is but this spiritual clarity. It is only because of people's forms and bodies that they are separate. My spiritual clarity is the lord-ruler of heaven and earth, of spirits and demons. . . . Separated from my spiritual clarity, there will be no heaven and earth, no spirits and demons, no myriad things. (3.57b–58a)[2]

But what does Mencius mean by the "lost" heart? If we say in modern English, with no explanation, that someone has lost his heart, we mean he has fallen in love, and if we say that he has lost his mind, we mean he has gone mad. But Mencius is not talking about love or madness. His point is that learning—which all of us do all the time, whether we want to or not—should be focused on recovering the most precious dimension of our own being, something of utmost importance to us. We had that precious something, but now we have lost it, so our human task is to find it again.

In short, Mencius is lamenting the situation of most people, who have lost touch with the innate luminosity and inherent goodness that the Chinese call *ren*—humanity, human-heartedness, humaneness, benevolence. *Ren* is in fact the key concept in the whole Confucian tradition, because it designates our true human nature, authentic goodness, and virtue. As Tu Weiming among others reminds us, the Confucian tradition is focused on achieving *ren* or, as he puts it, "on learning how to be human."[3] We are not born human, nor do we just grow up to be human—rather, *ren* is a luminous, spiritual clarity, an ultimate goodness that needs to be pursued and actualized. For Mencius, the lost heart is nothing other than this true human nature. This becomes clear when we quote his saying in context:

> *Ren* is man's heart, and righteousness [*yi*] his road. Sad indeed is it to neglect the road and not to follow it, to lose the heart and not to know enough to go after it. When someone loses his chickens and dogs, he knows enough to go after them, but when he loses his heart, he does not know enough to seek for it. The way of learning is nothing other than to seek for the lost heart.

The Muslim Worldview

Given that our understanding of the significance and role of learning depends on our worldview, I need to take a rather lengthy detour to clarify the Confucian and Muslim worldviews. In doing so, I am trying to look through the eyes of those Chinese Muslims who began writing about their religion in the

Chinese language in the eleventh/seventeenth century. They were happy to accept the general Confucian view of things and praised its focus on bringing personal and social life into conformity with the Dao of Heaven and earth, a goal that they understood to be exactly the same as the parallel teachings in Islam. Nonetheless, they thought that Confucian explanations of the human situation in the universe were inadequate, so they supplemented them with teachings drawn from Islam.[4]

One may be inclined to think that the Muslim critique of Confucianism was based on the fact that it does not talk about a personal God. However, the Muslim scholars—who were well-versed not only in Islamic thought but also in Confucianism, Taoism, and Buddhism—had no difficulty accepting basic Confucian notions about the Supreme Principle, the Real Substance, the Ultimate Truth. They had countless parallel discussions to draw from in their own Arabic and Persian texts, so they found nothing strange about this impersonal depiction of the Real.

It may be useful to recall here that the Islamic worldview is built on three basic principles. The first is *tawḥīd,* the assertion that God is one. The key to the meaning of God's oneness is found in the formula of witnessing, the Shahadah, which is the first pillar of Muslim practice and the foundation of faith. To be a Muslim, one begins by acknowledging that "There is no god but God," a formula called the "sentences of *tawḥīd*." For thoughtful Muslims over the centuries, this has never been a dogma, but rather the underlying truth of things, the fundamental theme of meditation, the guide to orienting oneself toward God, the world, and society. One does not simply recite it; rather, one strives to understand its implications for the big picture and for living out one's daily life with God in mind.

Tawḥīd has two basic implications, and these become clear when we insert any of the so-called "ninety-nine most beautiful names of God" into the formula. God is powerful, so "There is none powerful but God." God is merciful, so "There is none merciful but God." God is loving, so "There is none loving but God."

The first implication is that God alone is truly God, truly Real, truly One, truly Alive, truly Knowing, truly Powerful, truly Loving and so on down the list of the divine names. This means that anything other than God does not and cannot possess these qualities on its own. Reality, oneness, life, knowledge, power—all are exclusively divine attributes.

The second implication of the formula is that everything in the universe receives whatever qualities it may have from God. In other words, to say "There is none powerful but God" means that everything we call "power" can only be a sign or a trace of the divine power, bestowed on created things by the One Reality. Thus, the whole universe is, in Koranic terms, a vast collection of "signs" (*āyāt*) pointing to God as the Ultimate Reality and Supreme Principle.

It is perhaps worth stressing that this way of thinking about God does not allow for any real break between God and creation. People often say that Islam talks about God in terms of radical transcendence, which is true enough, but they forget that many of the same authors also talk about God in terms of radical immanence. Yes, God is infinitely transcendent, but He is also omnipresent.

One of the results of this way of looking at things is that Islam has no notion of Deism, which depends on severing the link between the divine and the human. Many if not most people today, whether they know it or not, think of God in Deist terms. For example, religious people who imagine that the "Big Bang" can mark the moment of creation, or that scientific notions of causality or evolution are sufficient to explain the nature of the world, are taking Deist positions. They think that God, having created the world, lets it run its course, standing off at a distance and rarely if ever interfering (the so-called "clockwork universe").

Such notions of God's aloofness are alien to the Islamic tradition. They fly in the face of *tawḥīd* by suggesting that the world has some sort of independent reality, such that it could bumble along on its own without God's constant support and sustenance. On the contrary, all things are utterly dependent on the Supreme Reality at every instant of their existence. There are no gaps in the divine omnipresence.

This brief explanation of *tawḥīd* follows in the line of numerous books written in Arabic and Persian over the past one thousand years. For those familiar with Neo-Confucianism—which has been the predominant form of Far Eastern religiosity for roughly the same period—explanations of *tawḥīd* in this manner can hardly seem strange. This is because the Neo-Confucian scholars constantly talk about the Supreme Principle as that which underlies "heaven, earth, and the ten thousand things," at every moment, always, and forever. The Muslim Chinese, reading Neo-Confucian texts, saw no contradiction between the basic Confucian views of reality and the standpoints found in their own Islamic sources. It was clear to them that Chinese thought is rooted in *tawḥīd*.

The second basic principle of Islam is "prophecy." Here one may be tempted to think that the Chinese Muslims would have had trouble expressing their teachings in Chinese terms. On the contrary, they had no difficulty at all, because they followed the basic teaching of the Koran that God sent a prophet to every people (10:47). They recognized that the Chinese had their own prophets, called "sages" (*sheng*) in the Chinese language. Hence, the Muslim Chinese spoke of Abraham, Moses, Jesus, Muhammad, and other Koranic prophets as "sages," and accepted that God sent sages to all peoples, including the Chinese. They found that the description of the characteristics of sages as found in Confucian classics like *The Doctrine of the Mean* were in keeping with their own understanding of prophets, and they often quoted from the Neo-Confucian scholars on the topic. One of their favorite passages belongs to the twelfth-century Neo-Confucian Lu Jiuyuan (d. 1192):

> Sages appeared tens of thousands of generations ago. They shared this heart, they shared this principle. Sages will appear tens of thousands of generations to come. They will share this heart, they will share this

> principle. Over the four seas sages appear. They share this heart, they share this principle. (22:5a)[5]

The third of the three principles of Islamic faith is the return to God, and it is this principle that Muslims thought was insufficiently explained in Chinese texts, so they paid special attention to clarifying what it means. In fact, the single most influential book translated from an Islamic language into Chinese before the fourteenth/twentieth century was not the Koran. Rather, it was Najm al-Dīn Rāzī's seventh/thirteenth-century Persian work, *Mirṣād al-ʿibād min al-mabdaʾ ilā'l-maʿād* ("The Path of the Servants from the Origin to the Return").[6] This book was extremely popular throughout the Persianate world, that is, from Turkey through Persia and Central Asia to the Indian Subcontinent. It is a long but poetic and extremely readable account of what it means to be human and how we may go about achieving the fullness of our humanity. As indicated by its title, this book focuses on the third principle of Islamic faith, the "return" to God. Moreover, it follows the Koran by discussing the Return to God in terms of the Origin, that is, our appearance from God in the first place.

The basic meaning of this third principle of faith is that people go back to where they came from, which is the Presence of God. If one were to ask, "Does Islam not teach that everyone will end up in either paradise or hell?," the answer would be "Yes," but with the caveat that we only get there by encountering God. That is, we meet Him in terms of His names and attributes, as discussed in Chapter 20. If we meet Him as merciful and forgiving, then certainly we end up in paradise. But, if we meet Him as just, wrathful, and vengeful, we will not be so fortunate. How we meet God after death depends on how we live our lives here and now.

One cannot overemphasize the fact that the "Origin and Return" is central to Islamic thinking. Without understanding it, people have no orientation. Moreover, we should not forget that it is simply an application of the first principle, *tawḥīd*, which tells us that everything comes from God, everything is sustained by God, and everything goes back to where it came from.

The Human Situation

For the Muslim Chinese, seeking for the lost heart meant trying to recover one's original situation with God. According to the Koran, after creating the universe with its myriad kinds, including not only plants and animals but also angels and demons, God created Adam—that is, the original human being, or human beings in general.[7] Moreover, He created Adam with a purpose, that is, to be His vicegerent (*khalīfa*) or representative on earth. The issue of human "vicegerency" is central to traditional Islamic thinking. If we can understand what a vicegerent is, then we can understand why God created us. "Vicegerency" is the answer to the aforementioned big questions: "Why do we exist?," and "What is the ultimate purpose of life?"

In the passage of the Koran where God says that He appointed Adam as His vicegerent, it also says that God taught him *the names, all of them* (2:31). These are the names of all things, including the names of God. We cannot live up to the proper human function of representing God if we do not know His creation and if we do not know Him. After all, "name" here does not mean simply "designation." God did not bestow on Adam encyclopedias of information. He gave him understanding. When Adam came to know all things, he was aware of their realities and the significance of their realities. He understood them in their big context. From the outset, he was given the Great Learning, which allowed him to know the exact significance of every form of small learning.

Adam was not only the first vicegerent, but also the first prophet, the first sage, the first complete and perfect human being. He played exactly the role that God created him for, and he did such a good job that he deserves to be imitated by all of us. He was also, of course, the first "sinner." His sin, however, was that he disobeyed God's command not to approach the tree (20:121), although God also provides his excuse: *He forgot* (20:115). After all, as the Koran tells us, *Man was created weak* (4:28). In the Koranic account, the moment God asked Adam and Eve why they ate the forbidden fruit, they recognized their mistake and asked for forgiveness, and God forgave both of them. That was the end of their forgetfulness. This is why Shams-i Tabrīzī can blame a seeker of God who keeps on slipping on the spiritual path by saying, "His father's tradition is once."[8]

To come back to the issue of the names that God taught to Adam, many commentators explain human vicegerency in terms of the hadith which states that God created Adam in His own form. The only way that human beings can "represent" God is by reflecting His total reality within themselves. Adam was taught *all* the names, not just some of them. And when God teaches something, it really sinks in, which is to say that it involves a transformation of the very being of the learner.

According to the Koran, God only has to say *"Be!"* (2:117) to a thing in order for it to come to be. When God said *"Be!"* to Adam, He gave him "being," and that being was a full and plenary manifestation of God's reality, which is designated by the ninety-nine most beautiful names. It is within Adam's being and awareness that God reveals and discloses His own reality, that is, all of His names. Only on this basis can Adam know God and represent Him.

So, God created Adam as His vicegerent. In the first place, this is an ontological vicegerency, by which I mean to say the very being of Adam—internally in his consciousness and externally in his body—shows forth and discloses the reality of God. Adam has no choice in the matter. In the language of Islamic theology, Adam is a "compulsory servant" of God, because he must obey the creative command to come into being. All things serve God in this respect.

What makes Adam different from all of the other servants of God is precisely that God taught him "all" the names. Bees know the names of flowers, and frogs know the names of bugs; but Adam knows the name of everything. That "everything" includes God—God as creator and destroyer, God as merciful and wrathful, God as just and forgiving. And this knowledge is woven into his very being.

It is this existential knowledge of all the names that bestows on Adam his freedom of choice. In terms of the formula of *tawḥīd*, "There is no one free but God." As the Koran puts it, God *does what He desires* (85:16), but human beings have limitations on doing what they want. Made in the image of that free God, they do have a certain freedom. No one denies this without living in contradiction, since we constantly make choices in our everyday lives. It is only because Adam recognized his own freedom that he felt responsible for disobeying God's command not to approach the tree, and it was his sense of responsibility that drove him to ask for forgiveness.

Notice that God's command not to approach the tree is quite different from the other command that Adam had received, that is, the command to come into being, which in the language of Islamic theology is called the creative or engendering command. In contrast, the command not to approach the tree was a prescriptive command. God's creative command brings us into existence, and His prescriptive command instructs us to observe good words, good deeds, and good thoughts—right speech, right activity, and right understanding.

Human beings, then, are faced with two commands. They can never disobey the first one, which tells them to come into being, because it makes them what they are wherever they may be—in this world, in the next world, in paradise, in hell. They can only disobey the second command, which comes by way of prophets and sages. Its pivotal importance for human destiny explains why "prophecy" is the second principle of Islamic thought. The prophets and sages explain the right way of being and doing, and they provide the instructions that people need in order to live up to the vicegerency that God has bestowed on them.

As for the third principle of Islam, it tells us, on the one hand, that we are compulsory servants of God. We serve His creative command whether we want to or not. He created us without our asking Him to do so, He sustains us as long as He chooses to do so, and He takes us back to Himself whenever He wants to. In none of this do we have any say. Where we have a say is in dealing with the prescriptive command. Do we follow it, ignore it, reject it, deny that it even exists? All these are options given to us by our freedom.

In any case, according to *tawḥīd*, everyone and everything will return to God so in this respect the return is "compulsory." Among human beings, however, many will choose to follow the instructions of God in order to live up to the requisites of servanthood and to try to make themselves worthy for vicegerency. They do this by engaging in the return "voluntarily," that is, by following God's instructions as issued to the prophets. This voluntary return is precisely the *dao* in the sense that we saw Mencius use the term—it is the way of learning how to be human and to act appropriately, and it leads to the recovery of the lost heart.

One very large issue in Islamic thought, much discussed and debated throughout Islamic history, is the degree to which human beings can in fact achieve harmony and conformity with the Ultimate Reality by engaging in the voluntary return. The Koran tells us that God is with us wherever we are (57:4), that He is closer to us than our jugular vein (50:16), and that we see His face wherever we look (2:115). If He is omnipresent and always with us, why can we not be with Him just as He is with us? Generally, Sufi teachers have answered that we can.

The Path of Love

Most Sufi teachers have held that the path of voluntary return is nothing other than the path of love. Love, as everyone knows, is the motive force that brings about nearness between lovers. Love for God is precisely what drives the worshiper to seek nearness to Him. The Koran recognizes love's importance in many verses, but it stresses the fact that if you want to love God as He should be loved, there are proper ways to do so.

After all, you cannot say to someone, "I love you," and then go about business as usual. There are procedures and protocols that need to be observed. You must show dedication and devotion if you want to achieve union with your beloved. What, then, is the proper way to show dedication when dealing with God? The Koran puts it this way: *Say [O Muhammad!]: "If you love God, follow me, and God will love you"* (3:31). Therefore, the procedures and protocols in love for God are rooted in following the Prophet.

This verse tells us that the end result of following in the footsteps of Muhammad is that God will love those who do so. Of course, no one denies that God loves us in any case, or else He would not have created us. However, we need to remember that He even loves those whom He puts in hell, so God's universal love does not necessarily yield the benefit that we might expect. To say that God loves everyone without exception is like saying, *He is with you wherever you are* (57:4)—this does not mean that we are with Him, nor does it mean that we participate in the blessings and peace of His unity.

Our problem is that forgetfulness and heedlessness prevent us from seeing God wherever we are and from entering into His Presence. We have lost our hearts, and until we find them, we will remain far from Him. If we want to find our lost hearts and be with God, then we need to follow what the Chinese Muslims call *li*, that is, "propriety" or "ritual."

In Confucian terms, *li* is the necessary foundation for a proper and worthy society, and it is determined by the norms set down by the ancient sages. Someone once asked Confucius how to become fully and properly human, in other words, how to achieve *ren*. He replied, "Discipline yourself by observing propriety" (*Analects*, 12:1). For the Chinese Muslims, "propriety" is precisely to follow the Sunnah of Muhammad and the Tariqah (which they often translated as *dao*).

The Koran says that when people follow Muhammad, God will love them. When God loves someone, as the *ḥadīth qudsī* says, He becomes his "hearing through which he hears, his sight through which he sees, his hand through which he grasps, and his foot upon which he walks."

In other words, when the servant follows Muhammad out of love for God, then, in loving him back, God somehow becomes indistinguishable from the servant. What exactly this presence of God in the hearing, sight, hands, and feet of the believer means has been the subject of endless discussion and debate over the centuries. Whatever it does mean, it certainly points to a mysterious conjunction between the divine and the human, a conjunction that is centered in the heart. This conjunction is possible only because people were created in the full and plenary image of God, so they can love Him as God, not simply as Provider, or Benefactor, or Forgiver, or some other specific name.

True love—and we all know this on the human level—is unqualified by any sort of desire for benefit or fear of loss. In matters of love, after all, the old dilemma is always there: "Does she love me for myself, or for my money?" In the case of love for God, He knows the secrets of our hearts, so He becomes the hearing and eyesight only of those who truly love Him for His sake alone. This is a rare situation indeed, so the only sure examples we have of those who have achieved it are the prophets and the sages—such as Muhammad and Confucius.

The Original Heart

Many Muslim thinkers refer to the lost heart by the Koranic term *fiṭra,* that is, the divine form that God bestowed on Adam when He created him, or the Divine Spirit that, according to the Koran, God blew into the clay of Adam in order to bring him to life.

Any discussion of "origins" in Islam has everything to do with explaining how God created the universe in stages, beginning with the invisible Divine Spirit. This Spirit is called by many names, such as the First Intellect, the Supreme Pen, and the Muhammadan Spirit. It is a single reality that is aware of all things and that gave Adam his knowledge of all the names. Or, we can say that the First Spirit is the creative command of God, his word *"Be!"* to all things. The Chinese Muslims have this last interpretation in mind when they call this Spirit, as they often do, the "Mandate of Heaven" (*tianming*).

What is perfectly obvious to all Muslim thinkers is that human beings, in coming into this world by the divine command, begin as invisible spirits. They descend through increasing darkness and density until they become embodied in clay. The movement goes from spirit to body, from life to death, from consciousness to unawareness. It is commonly called the "descending arc" (*al-qaws al-nuzūlī*) of existence. The Chinese Muslims called it "the Former Heaven" (*xiantian*), namely the heavenly realm where we existed before we descended onto earth.

Once we exist as embodied human beings, we begin to go back where we came from. The Chinese Muslims called the realm to which we go back "the Latter Heaven" (*houtian*), because we ascend up to it only after embodiment. We can all see the process of ascent occurring in the growth of children toward greater understanding and self-awareness. Infants are not at first able to distinguish themselves from their environment or their bodies. Only gradually do they come to realize that they are aware and that they are distinct individuals. All this is part of the natural flow of existence that follows the creative command, *"Be!"*

Thus, we have two movements in human existence. First there is emergence from nonmanifestation to manifestation, from invisibility to visibility, from inside to outside, from Heaven to earth, from spirit to body. Then there is a reversal of the flow of existence when things start moving from outside to inside, from immersion in the senses and bodily functions toward awareness and understanding, from constraint toward freedom, from forgetfulness and ignorance toward remembrance and awakening. This latter movement is often called *learning*.

According to Islamic law, observance of the prescriptive command becomes mandatory at puberty. This is the time when we are sufficiently self-aware to understand that we have responsibilities toward our Creator, toward other human beings, and toward our own immortal souls, which want to live in happiness, not only in this world, but also after death. At puberty, then, we can begin to move beyond elementary learning and to strive for the Great Learning. But what exactly does the Great Learning involve? To begin with, we have to understand who we are, where we have come from, and how to go back. But this is not the whole of it, because the Great Learning involves both understanding and practice. It demands not only grasping the big picture, but also putting all of our understanding to work in order to recover the lost heart.

The Prophet said, "Knowledge without practice is a tree without fruit." Knowledge here is understanding who we are and what we should be doing about it. Practice is actually doing what we should be doing, and that is based on observing propriety and following the Way, that is, the Shariah and the Tariqah. We never reach a point where we can relax and say that we have learned everything that we need to know. "Seek knowledge," the Prophet commanded, "from the cradle to the grave." The Koran tells the Prophet himself to pray with the words, *"My Lord, increase me in knowledge"* (20:114). If the greatest of the sages had to pray for increase in knowledge, what about the rest of us?

Stages of Learning

If Mencius were asked how to go about recovering the lost heart, he would certainly have pointed to Confucius himself, the model for those Chinese who would like to engage in the quest, just as Muhammad is the model for Muslims. In a famous passage of the *Analects*, Confucius sets down the stages that need to be traversed in order to achieve the goal. He speaks in the first person, but we do not need to assume that he is providing his own story. Sages and prophets voice their teachings in the language of their listeners. Confucius wants to explain the stages of the Great Learning in personal terms to which all of us can relate:

> From fifteen, I set my heart on learning. From thirty I stood firm. From forty I had no doubts. From fifty, I knew the Mandate of Heaven. From sixty, my ear was obedient. From seventy, I could follow my heart's desire without overstepping the right. (2:4)

The first step on the Confucian journey, then, is setting one's heart on learning. This is perhaps the most difficult stage of all. Yes, we are all engaged in a quest for more understanding of one thing or another, but what about understanding who we are? That is to say, how many of us have really put our whole selves into the task of becoming truly human?

By mentioning the age of fifteen, Confucius does not mean that people should start studying rather late. Far from it. As a round number, fifteen designates the time of puberty, approximately the age at which, in Islamic terms, it becomes incumbent upon Muslims to follow the guidance of the Koran and the Prophet. Puberty is the age when we are old enough to understand the difference between right and wrong, true and false, good and evil. It is the age at which the prescriptive command begins to play a role in determining the way we develop, rather than simply the creative command. In a traditional context, it is the ideal age for setting out on the quest for self-realization.

The next stage in the Confucian path is the age of thirty, when the seeker "stands firm" and is completely grounded in the quest for his lost heart. From forty, he has "no doubts" about the rightness of his quest. As is well-known, in the Islamic context, forty is the age when Muhammad became a prophet, and some Sufi teachers have said that it is the age of spiritual maturity, that is, when those who travel the path to perfection are opened up to the fullness of their own human nature.

At fifty, the seeker comes to know "the Mandate of Heaven," which, in Islamic terms, means that he knows not only God's prescriptive command—what people *should* do—but also His creative command—the destiny that God has doled out to His creatures.

Then at sixty, his "ear is obedient." Perhaps this means that at the previous stage, although he knew exactly what Heaven wanted from him, something of his own self-interest and self-centeredness still stood in the way of his submission to the heavenly command. Now, at sixty, whatever he does is in keeping with the Mandate of Heaven, for he follows the prescriptive command in all its details.

Only at seventy does the lost heart make its explicit appearance. It is then that the seeker can follow his "heart's desire without overstepping the right." There is no trace of self-centeredness left. He is firmly rooted in the prescriptive command: What his heart wants is nothing other than what Heaven wants, which is to say that there is no longer any distinction to be drawn between the prescriptive command and the creative command. Having found his lost heart, the finder "does as he desires" just like God, for his desire and God's desire are the same thing. God has become his hearing, eyesight, hands, and feet.

Let me end with one more quotation, this time from the book called by the term I have been using all along, *The Great Learning*. This is one of the four most important classics of Confucianism:

> The ancients who wished to clarify their clear virtue under Heaven would first govern their countries. Those who wished to govern their countries would first regulate their families. Those who wished to regulate their families would first cultivate their personal lives. Those who wished to cultivate their personal lives would first make their hearts true. Those who wished to make their hearts true would first make their intentions sincere. Those who wished to make their intentions sincere would first extend their knowledge. . . . From the Son of Heaven down to the common people, all must regard cultivation of the personal life as the root or foundation. There is never a case when the root is in disorder and yet the branches are in order. (4, 6–7)

This "cultivation of the personal life" that is the root of both the person and society is nothing other than the quest to recover the lost heart. As long as we do not recover it, our lives will remain disordered and incomplete, and we will not be able to live in peace and harmony with our own selfhoods, much less with the rest of humanity.

Appendix I

A Chronological List of Historical Figures Cited

With the exception of the Prophet, listed here are the names and death dates of those historical figures whose words have been quoted in this volume.

Confucius (d. 479 BCE)
Mencius (d. 289 BCE)
Plotinus (d. 270)
Abū Bakr (d. 13/634)
Ibn Masʿūd (d. 31/652)
ʿAlī b. Abī Ṭālib (d. 40/661)
ʿĀʾisha (d. 58/678)
Ibn ʿAbbās (d. ca. 68/688)
Jaʿfar al-Ṣādiq (d. 148/765)
Abū Ḥanīfa (d. 150/767)
Maʿrūf al-Karkhī (d. 200/815–816)
Abū Yazīd Basṭāmī (d. ca. 260/874)
Abū Saʿīd al-Kharrāz (d. 286/899)
Ḥusayn b. Manṣūr al-Ḥallāj (d. 309/922)
Abū'l-ʿAbbās Qaṣṣāb (fl. fourth/tenth century)
Abū'l-Ḥasan al-Būshanjī (d. 348/960)
al-Niffarī (d. 360/971)
Avicenna (Ibn Sīnā) (d. 428/1037)
Abū Saʿīd ibn Abī'l-Khayr (d. 440/1049)
Abū Rayḥān al-Bīrūnī (d. ca 442/1051)
Abū'l-Qāsim al-Qushayrī (d. 465/1072)
ʿAbd Allāh Anṣārī (d. 481/1089)
Abū Ḥāmid al-Ghazālī (d. 505/1111)
Bābā Ṭāhir (fl. fifth/eleventh century)
Rashīd al-Dīn Maybudī (d. ca. 520/1126)
Ḥakīm Sanāʾī (d. 525/1131)
ʿAyn al-Quḍāt Hamadānī (d. 525/1131)

Aḥmad Samʿānī (d. 534/1140)
Najm al-Dīn Nasafī (d. 537/1142)
Rūzbihān Baqlī (d. 606/1209)
Fakhr al-Dīn al-Rāzī (d. 606/1210)
Bābā Afḍal Kāshānī (d. 606/1210)
Farīd al-Dīn ʿAṭṭār (d. ca. 617/1220)
Bahāʾ al-Dīn Walad (d. 628/1230)
Ibn al-ʿArabī (d. 638/1240)
Shams-i Tabrīzī (d. 643/1246)
Ibn Sawdakīn (d. 646/1248)
Saʿd al-Dīn Ḥammūya (d. 649/1252)
Najm al-Dīn Rāzī (d. 654/1256)
Ibn Sabʿīn (d. 669/1270)
Jalāl al-Dīn Rūmī (d. 672/1273)
Naṣīr al-Dīn Ṭūsī (d. 672/1274)
Ṣadr al-Dīn Qūnawī (d. 673/1274)
Awḥad al-Dīn Balyānī (d. 686/1288)
ʿAfīf al-Dīn Tilimsānī (d. 690/1291)
Muʾayyid al-Dīn Jandī (d. 690/1291)
ʿAzīz al-Dīn Nasafī (d. before 699/1300)
Saʿīd al-Dīn Farghānī (d. 699/1300)
Shams al-Dīn Īkī (d. eighth/fourteenth century?)
Sulṭān Walad (d. 712/1312)
Ibn Taymiyya (d. 728/1328)
Dāwūd Qayṣarī (d. 751/1350)
Sayyid Ḥaydar Āmulī (d. after 787/1385)
ʿAbd al-Karīm Jīlī (d. ca. 832/1428)
ʿAbd al-Raḥmān Jāmī (d. 898/1492)
Wang Yangming (d. 1529)
Khwāja Khurd (b. 1010/1601)
Shaykh Maḥmūd Khwush-Dahān (d. 1026/1617)
ʿAbd al-Jalīl Ilāhābādī (d. 1043/1633–1634)
Mullā Ṣadrā (d. 1050/1640)
ʿAllāma Majlisī (d. ca. 1111/1699)
Hātif Iṣfahānī (d. 1198/1783)

Appendix II

Chapter Sources

1. "Islam in Three Dimensions." In W. C. Chittick, *Faith and Practice of Islam: Three Thirteenth Century Sufi Texts*. Albany: State University of New York Press, 1992, 1–23.

2. "The Bodily Positions of the Ritual Prayer." *Sufi* 12 (1991–1992), 16–18.

3. "Weeping in Classical Sufism." In *Holy Tears: Weeping in the Religious Imagination*. Edited by K. C. Patton and J. S. Hawley. Princeton: Princeton University Press, 2005, 132–144.

4. "A Shādhilī Presence in Shiʿite Islam." *Sophia Perennis* 1/1 (1975), 97–100.

5. "The Pluralistic Vision of Persian Sufi Poetry." *Islam and Christian-Muslim Relations* 14/4 (2003), 423–428.

6. "The Real Shams-i Tabrīzī." In *Beacon of Knowledge: Essays in Honor of Seyyed Hossein Nasr*. Edited by M. H. Faghfoory. Louisville: Fons Vitae, 2003, 99–110.

7. "The Koran as the Lover's Mirror." In *Universal Dimensions of Islam*. Edited by Patrick Laude. Bloomington: World Wisdom, 2011, 66–77.

8. "Rūmī and *Waḥdat al-wujūd*." In *Poetry and Mysticism in Islam: The Heritage of Rūmī*. Edited by Amin Banani et al. Cambridge: Cambridge University Press, 1994, 70–91, 104–110.

9. "Rūmī and *Waḥdat al-wujūd*." In *Poetry and Mysticism in Islam: The Heritage of Rūmī*. Edited by Amin Banani et al. Cambridge: Cambridge University Press, 1994, 92–104, 110–111.

10. "Ibn ʿArabī on the Benefit of Knowledge." *Sophia* 8/2 (2002), 27–48.

11. "The Circle of Spiritual Ascent According to al-Qūnawī." In *Neoplatonism and Islamic Thought*. Edited by Parviz Morewedge. Albany: State University of New York Press, 1992, 179–209.

12. "Spectrums of Islamic Thought: Saʿīd al-Dīn Farghānī on the Implications of Oneness and Manyness." In *The Heritage of Sufism*. Edited by Leonard Lewisohn (vols. 1–3) and David Morgan (vol. 3). Oxford: Oneworld, 1999, 2:203–217.

13. "The Perfect Man as the Prototype of the Self in the Sufism of Jāmī." *Studia Islamica* 49 (1979), 135–157.

14. "Khwâja Khord's Treatise on the Gnostic." *Sufi* 5 (1990), 11–12; "Khwāja Khurd's 'Light of Oneness.'" In *God is Beautiful and He Loves Beauty: Festschrift in Honour of Annemarie Schimmel*. Edited by Alma Giese and J. C. Bürgel. New York: Peter Lang, 1994, 131–151.

15. "On Sufi Psychology: A Debate Between the Soul and the Spirit." In *Consciousness and Reality: Studies in Memory of Toshihiko Izutsu*. Edited by S. J. Āshtiyānī et al. Leiden: Brill, 1998, 341–366.

16. "Traveling the Sufi Path: A Chishtī Handbook from Bijapur." In *The Heritage of Sufism*. Edited by Leonard Lewisohn (vols. 1–3) and David Morgan (vol. 3). Oxford: Oneworld, 1999, 3:247–265.

17. "Rumi's Doctrine of Evolution." *Iqbal Review* 43/2 (2002), 61–81.

18. "Bābā Afḍal on the Soul's Immortality." *Ishrāq: Islamic Philosophy Yearbook* 1 (2010), 132–140.

19. "On the Teleology of Perception." *Transcendent Philosophy* 1 (2000), 1–18.

20. "Eschatology." In *Islamic Spirituality: Foundations*. Edited by S. H. Nasr. New York: Crossroad, 1987, 378–409.

21. "The Circle of Life in Islamic Thought." In *Islamic Philosophy and Occidental Phenomenology on the Perennial Issue of Microcosm and Macrocosm*. Edited by Anna-Teresa Tymieniecka. Dordrecht: Springer, 2006, 205–213.

22. "The Goal of Islamic Philosophy: Reflections on the Works of Afdal al-Din Kashani." *Sacred Web* 5 (2000), 17–29.

23. "The Theological Roots of War and Peace in Islam." *Islamic Quarterly* 34 (1990), 145–163.

24. "'God Surrounds all Things': An Islamic Perspective on the Environment." *The World and I* 1/6 (June 1986), 671–678.

25. "Stray Camels in China." In *Islam and Confucianism: A Civilizational Dialogue*. Edited by Osman Bakar and Cheng Gek Nai. Kuala Lumpur: University of Malaya Press, 1997, 35–59.

26. "The Traditional Approach to Learning." *Sacred Web* 18 (2007), 29–47.

Appendix III

Books by William C. Chittick

Translations of Chittick's books are not listed here. All references provided (with the exception of entries 1.5, 2.1, 2.3, and 2.14) are to the original publication.

1. Monographs and Compositions

1. *In Search of the Lost Heart: Explorations in Islamic Thought*. Edited by Mohammed Rustom, Atif Khalil, and Kazuyo Murata. Albany: State University of New York Press, 2012.

2. With Sachiko Murata and Tu Weiming, *The Sage Learning of Liu Zhi: Islamic Thought in Confucian Terms*. Cambridge, MA: Harvard University Asia Center, 2009.

3. *Science of the Cosmos, Science of the Soul: The Pertinence of Islamic Cosmology in the Modern World*. Oxford: Oneworld, 2007.

4. *Ibn 'Arabi: Heir to the Prophets*. Oxford: Oneworld, 2005.

5. *The Sufi Doctrine of Rumi*. Bloomington: World Wisdom, 2005.

6. *Me & Rumi: The Autobiography of Shams-i Tabrizi*. Louisville: Fons Vitae, 2004.

7. *The Heart of Islamic Philosophy: The Quest for Self-Knowledge in the Teachings of Afḍal al-Dīn Kāshānī*. New York: Oxford University Press, 2001.

8. *Sufism: A Short Introduction*. Oxford: Oneworld, 2000.

9. *The Self-Disclosure of God: Principles of Ibn al-ʿArabī's Cosmology*. Albany: State University of New York Press, 1998.

10. *Varolmann Boyutlari* [*The Dimensions of Existence*]. Edited and translated by Turan Koç. Istanbul: Insan Yayınları, 1997.

11. With Sachiko Murata, *The Vision of Islam*. New York: Paragon House, 1994.

12. *Imaginal Worlds: Ibn al-ʿArabī and the Problem of Religious Diversity*. Albany: State University of New York Press, 1994.

13. *Faith and Practice of Islam: Three Thirteenth Century Sufi Texts*. Albany: State University of New York Press, 1992.

14. *The Sufi Path of Knowledge: Ibn al-ʿArabī's Metaphysics of Imagination.* Albany: State University of New York Press, 1989.

15. *The Sufi Path of Love: The Spiritual Teachings of Rumi.* Albany: State University of New York Press, 1983.

16. *A Shi'ite Anthology.* Albany: State University of New York Press, 1981. Available online at www.al-islam.org.

2. Major Translations

1. Khwāja Khurd, *The Treatise on the Gnostic* and *The Light of Oneness.* In *In Search of the Lost Heart: Explorations in Islamic Thought.* Edited by Mohammed Rustom, Atif Khalil, and Kazuyo Murata. Albany: State University of New York Press, 2012, Chapter 14.

2. Mullā Ṣadrā, *The Elixir of the Gnostics.* Provo: Brigham Young University Press, 2003.

3. Selections from Ibn al-ʿArabī's *Futūḥāt.* In *The Meccan Revelations.* Edited by Michel Chodkiewicz. New York: Pir Press, 2002, 1:27–64, 125–197.

4. Jāmī, *Gleams.* Published alongside Liu Chih, *Displaying the Concealment of the Real Realm,* translated by Sachiko Murata. In Murata, *Chinese Gleams of Sufi Light: Wang Tai-yü's Great Learning of the Pure and Real and Liu Chih's Displaying the Concealment of the Real Realm.* Albany: State University of New York Press, 2000, 128–210.

5. Ibn al-ʿArabī, Chapters 317 ("Concerning the true knowledge of the way station of trial and its blessings") and 339 ("Concerning the true knowledge of a waystation in which the *shari'a* kneels before the reality, seeking replenishment") of the *Futūḥāt.* In Chittick, "Two Chapters from the *Futūhāt al-makkiyya.*" In *Muhyiddin Ibn 'Arabi: A Commemorative Volume.* Edited by Stephen Hirtenstein and Michael Tiernan. Shaftesbury: Element, 1993, 90–123. Available online at www.ibnarabisociety.org

6. ʿAlī b. al-Ḥusayn, *The Psalms of Islam.* London: Muhammadi Trust, 1988. Available online at www.al-islam.org

7. Muḥsin Fayḍ Kāshānī, *The Kingly Mirror,* and extracts from Muḥammad Bāqir Majlisī, *The Fountainhead of Life.* In Chittick, "Two Seventeenth Century Persian Tracts on Kingship and Rulers." In *Authority and Political Culture in Shiʿism.* Edited by S. A. Arjomand. Albany: State University of New York Press, 1988, 267–304.

8. Javad Nurbakhsh (compiler), *Sufism [IV]: Repentance, Abstinence, Renunciation, Wariness, Humility, Humbleness, Sincerity, Steadfastness, Courtesy.* London: Khaniqahi-Nimatullahi, 1988.

9. ʿAlī b. al-Ḥusayn, *Supplication: Makārim al-akhlāq.* London: Muhammadi Trust, 1983. Available online at www.al-islam.org

10. With P. L. Wilson, Fakhr al-Dīn ʿIrāqī, *Divine Flashes.* New York: Paulist Press, 1982.

11. Javad Nurbakhsh (compiler), *Sufism [II]: Fear and Hope, Contraction and Expansion, Gathering and Dispersion, Intoxication and Sobriety, Annihilation and Subsistence*. New York: Khaniqahi-Nimatullahi, 1982.

12. ʿAlī b. Abī Ṭālib, *Supplication*. London: Muhammadi Trust, 1982.

13. Javad Nurbakhsh (compiler), *Sufism [I]: Meaning, Knowledge, and Unity*. New York: Khaniqahi-Nimatullahi, 1981.

14. Ibn al-ʿArabī, *The Imprint of the Bezels of Wisdom*. In Chittick, "Ibn 'Arabī's own Summary of the *Fusūs*: 'The Imprint of the Bezels of Wisdom'." *Journal of the Muhyiddin Ibn 'Arabi Society* 1 (1982), 30–93. Available online at www.ibnarabisociety.org

3. Edited Anthologies

1. *The Essential Seyyed Hossein Nasr*. Bloomington: World Wisdom, 2007.

2. *The Inner Journey: Views from the Islamic Tradition*. Sandpoint: Morning Light Press, 2007.

4. Bibliographies

1. With S. H. Nasr (vols. 1–3) and Peter Zirnis (vols. 2–3), *An Annotated Bibliography of Islamic Science*. Tehran: Imperial Iranian Academy of Philosophy, 1975–1978 (vols. 1–2); Tehran: Cultural Studies and Research Institute, 1991 (vol. 3).

2. *The Works of Seyyed Hossein Nasr Through His Fortieth Birthday*. Uppsala: University of Utah Press, 1977.

5. Major Editions and Indices

1. Edition of Mullā Ṣadrā, *Iksīr al-ʿārifīn*. In Ṣadrā, *The Elixir of the Gnostics*. Translated by W. C. Chittick. Provo: Brigham Young University Press, 2003.

2. Critical edition of ʿAbd al-Raḥmān Jāmī, *Naqd al-nuṣūṣ fī sharḥ Naqsh al-fuṣūṣ*. Tehran: Imperial Iranian Academy of Philosophy, 1977.

3. Indices to Saʿīd al-Dīn Farghānī, *Mashāriq al-darārī*. Edited by S. J. Āshtiyānī. Mashhad: Dānishgāh-i Firdawsī, 1978, 651–811.

Notes

Notes to Editors' Introduction

1. In 2002, one of North America's leading Muslim scholars, Hamza Yusuf, taught and commented on parts of Chittick and Murata's *The Vision of Islam* (1994) at the Zaytuna Institute (now Zaytuna College), an Islamic academy based in Berkeley, California. Also, in January 2008 in Santa Clara, California, Chittick's *Science of the Cosmos, Science of the Soul* (2007) served as the springboard text for the seventh annual winter meeting of The American Learning Institute for Muslims (ALIM). The selected theme for that year's meeting was, "Is Islamic Thought Dying?" The program was headed by several influential North American Muslim scholars: Umar Faruq Abd-Allah, Muneer Fareed, Sherman Jackson, and Zaid Shakir. For the complete bibliographical details to Chittick's works cited in this introduction, see the present volume's third appendix.

2. For the Festschrift, see *Zindigī-nāma wa-khadamāt-i ʿilmī wa-farhangī-yi Purūfisūr Wīliyām Chītīk* (Tehran: Anjuman-i Āthār wa-Mafākhir-i ʿIlmī, 2008).

3. See her book, *Chinese Gleams of Sufi Light: Wang Tai-yü's Great Learning of the Pure and Real and Liu Chih's Displaying the Concealment of the Real Realm* (Albany: State University of New York Press, 2000).

4. See, in particular, Chittick, *Imaginal Worlds* (1994); Vincent Cornell, "Practical Sufism: An Akbarian Foundation for a Liberal Theology of Difference," *Journal of the Muhyiddin Ibn 'Arabi Society* 36 (2004), 59–84; Reza Shah-Kazemi, *The Other in the Light of the One: The Universality of the Qur'ān and Interfaith Dialogue* (Cambridge: Islamic Texts Society, 2006). For a partial assessment of Chittick's "Akbarian approach" to the question of religious diversity, see Sajjad Rizvi, "A Primordial *e pluribus unum?*: Exegeses on Q. 2:213 and Contemporary Muslim Discourses on Religious Pluralism," *Journal of Qur'anic Studies* 6/1 (2004), 32–35. It should be noted that the diagram presented by Chittick in *Imaginal Worlds*, 157, is, as stated on the same page, Ibn al-ʿArabī's "schema" (cf. Rizvi, 33–34).

5. In more ways than one, this section complements Chittick's investigations in his *Science of the Cosmos, Science of the Soul*. For appraisals of Chittick's views on cosmology, anthropology, and modern science, see Salman Bashier, review of *Science of the Cosmos, Science of the Soul*, *Journal of the Muhyiddin Ibn 'Arabi Society* 43 (2008), 129–134; S. H. Nasr, "Reply to William Chittick" in Nasr, *The Philosophy of Seyyed Hossein Nasr*, eds. L. E. Hahn, R. E. Auxier, and Lucian Stone Jr. (LaSalle: Open Court, 2001), 710–715; Mohammed Rustom, "Equilibrium and Realization: William Chittick on Self and Cosmos," *American Journal of Islamic Social Sciences* 25/3 (2008), 52–60; Muhammad Suheyl Umar, "Response to the Anthropocosmic Vision in Islamic Thought," *Iqbal Review* 42/2 (2001), 71–74.

Notes to Chapter 1

1. The root meaning of *dīn* is to become obedient and submissive, to be obedient to God, to follow a way. For present purposes, it is sufficient to know that the term is differentiated from "Islam" by the fact that a person can follow any path as a religion, including a false belief or deviant way of doing things, whereas Islam denotes submission and obedience to God on the basis of the Koranic revelation.

2. In the hadith, which is found in several versions in the standard sources, Gabriel comes to the Prophet in the appearance of a Bedouin and asks him questions about the religion. For a translation of the text from Bukhārī and Muslim, see Tabrīzī, *Mishkāt*, 5. A number of modern scholars have used this hadith as a model for understanding Islam's concerns. One of the earliest was M. Lings, *A Moslem Saint of the Twentieth Century*, 44–45. For an exposition of the Islamic worldview based entirely on the Hadith of Gabriel, see Murata and Chittick, *The Vision of Islam*.

3. For a survey of the different responses in Islamic thought to the question of Pharaoh's salvation, see Ormsby, "The Faith of Pharaoh."

4. Ghazālī, *Iḥyā'*, 1:14 (Cairo). See also Faris' translation of the passage in its context in Ghazālī, *The Book of Knowledge*, 42.

5. The word *qadar* is commonly translated as "predestination" or "destiny," but these terms have too much theological baggage to suggest *qadar*'s Koranic meaning. In Sufi writings, such as the books of Ibn al-ʿArabī, the Koranic context is kept firmly in view.

6. See Chittick, "Mysticism vs. Philosophy in Earlier Islamic History."

7. One could interject a theological criticism here by saying that divine grace is being ignored. However, divine grace is implicit in all Islamic theology—when it is not explicit—because human activity is overshadowed by God's activity.

8. See Gardet, "Īmān."

9. For a detailed study of the heart, see Murata, *The Tao of Islam*, Chapter 10.

10. Ibn Māja, Muqaddima 9.

11. See Wensinck, *The Muslim Creed*, 125.

12. Gardet, "Īmān," 1171.

13. In sixteen verses, the Koran employs the root *ḥ.b.ṭ.* (to become null, to fail, to be fruitless) to explain the uselessness of activity without faith. For example, *Those who cry lies to Our signs and the encounter [with God] in the next world, their works are fruitless* (7:147); *They do not have faith, so God has rendered their works fruitless* (33:19).

14. Asad, *The Message of the Qur'ān*, 907.

15. For the stubborn willfulness implied by the Koranic term *kufr*, see Smith, *Faith and Belief*, 39–41. See also Asad, *The Message of the Qur'ān*, 4, n. 6; Izutsu, *Ethico-Religious Concepts in the Qur'ān*, Chapter 7.

16. Smith, "Faith as *Taṣdīq*," 107.

17. Ibid., 109.

18. Ghazālī, *Iḥyā'*, 1:191 (Cairo); *The Book of Knowledge*, 30. Rūmī (d. 672/1273) makes fun of the pretensions of the ulama in the story of the grammarian and the boatman (*Mathnawī*, 1:2835ff.). Having gotten in the boat, the grammarian asks the boatman:

> "Have you studied any grammar?" "No," he replied.
> "Well, half your life has gone to waste."

The boatman felt sorry for himself,
    but for the moment made no reply.
Then the wind threw the boat into a whirlpool
    and the boatman shouted out to the man,
"Do you know how to swim? Tell me!"
    "No," he said, "O you with good answers and fine face."
He said, "Then your whole life has gone to waste,
    since this boat will soon be going down."

Rūmī's conclusion is the same as that of Ghazālī. None of the sciences have any use unless they serve the fundamental science, which is that of practice. As Rūmī puts it, you do not need grammar (*naḥw*), but rather obliteration (*maḥw*), which is the dissolution of human limitations achieved by following the prophetic model. Then you will not be drowned when the boat goes down.

19. Ghazālī, *Iḥyā'*, 1:11 (Cairo); *The Book of Knowledge*, 31–32.

20. Among the many hadiths that connect God-wariness to perfected faith is the following, which refers to all three dimensions of Islam, but makes faith and God-wariness more or less identical: "The Prophet said, '*Islām* is public [*ʿalāniya*], while faith is in the heart.' Then he pointed to his breast three times, and said, 'God-wariness is here, God-wariness is here'" (Aḥmad, 3:153).

21. See Chittick, *The Sufi Path of Knowledge*, Chapter 19.

22. Ghazālī, *Bidāyat*, 14. Cf. Watt, *The Faith and Practice of al-Ghazālī*, 107.

23. Ghazālī, *Iḥyā'*, 1:14 (Cairo). Cf. Ghazālī, *The Book of Knowledge*, 43.

24. Qushayrī, *Risāla*, 607.

25. For a discussion of these eschatological terms, see Chapter 20.

26. Ghazālī, *Iḥyā'*, 1:15 (Cairo). Cf. Ghazālī, *The Book of Knowledge*, 46–48.

27. Many historians of Sufism have not had much sympathy with Ibn al-ʿArabī's theoretical orientation, preferring instead the apparent simplicity of earlier expressions. I say "apparent" because, as soon as one tries to analyze the early Sufi writings and sayings within their religious and cultural context, one finds them packed with nuances and allusions. To make them anything more than "nice sayings" for nonspecialists, one must take on Ibn al-ʿArabī's mantle oneself, explaining in detail all sorts of background information, ranging from theology and metaphysics to psychology, sociology, and grammar.

28. Ghazālī, *Iḥyā'*, 1:11–12 (Cairo); *The Book of Knowledge*, 34–35.

Notes to Chapter 2

1. Representative discussions can be found in Ghazālī, *Inner Dimensions of Islamic Worship*, 44–48; Rāzī, *The Path of God's Bondsmen from Origin to Return*, 183–185; Rūmī, *Mathnawī*, 3:2147–2175.

2. For the *barzakh* and its relation to Islamic eschatology, see Chapters 11 and 20.

3. For Ibn al-ʿArabī's treatment of the *ṣalāt*'s bodily gestures, see Chodkiewicz, *An Ocean Without Shore*, 109ff.

4. For the Day of Resurrection, see Chapter 20.

Notes to Chapter 3

1. Ibn Māja, Iqāma 176.

2. Muslim, Īmān 346.

3. Nasāʾī, Janāʾiz 101.

4. Bukhārī, Janāʾiz 43; Muslim, Faḍāʾil 62. Another hadith says, "We were with God's Messenger at a funeral. He sat at the edge of the grave and wept until the earth became wet. Then he said, 'My brothers, prepare for the likes of this!' " (Ibn Māja, Zuhd 19). The general tenor of the hadiths, however, is critical of ostentatious weeping and wailing as a sign of mourning, partly because this seems to have been the rule among women in the pre-Islamic period. The juridical literature strongly discourages it, and preachers criticize excessive grief as a sign of disbelief in the divine mercy. For a good selection of hadiths on weeping for the dead, see Tabrīzī, *Mishkāt*, 360–368.

5. Ibn Māja, Zuhd 35.

6. Bukhārī, Ṣalāt 86. For Abū Bakr's image in the Islamic tradition, see John Renard, "Abū Bakr in Tradition and Early Hagiography."

7. So says F. Meier in his article, "al-Bakkāʾ," which is an excellent survey of the literature that ascribes weeping to early Muslims.

8. Maybudī, *Kashf*, 1:239. Maybudī's major source of inspiration was ʿAbd Allāh Anṣārī (d. 481/1089), the famous author of a number of classic Sufi texts in both Arabic and Persian. For more on Maybudī and his work, see A. Keeler's groundbreaking study, *Sufi Hermeneutics*.

9. On the role that complementary attributes play throughout the tradition, see Murata, *The Tao of Islam*.

10. Bukhārī, Ṣalāt 1; Muslim, Īmān 263. See also Tabrīzī, *Mishkāt*, 1269.

11. This saying is frequently cited and is found in most of the standard hadith collections.

12. Ibn Māja, Zuhd 19.

13. Aḥmad, 4:11–12.

14. Muslim, Īmān 310. Cf. Bukhārī, Ṣalāt 129; Tawḥīd 24.

15. Muslim, Īmān 316.

16. The text is from the *Ḥaqāʾiq al-tafsīr* ("The Realities of Exegesis") by Abū ʿAbd al-Raḥmān al-Sulamī (d. 412/1021), cited in Nwyia, *Trois oeuvres inédites de mystiques musulmanes*, 48.

17. Sarrāj, *Lumaʿ*, 229.

18. Baqlī, *Mashrab*, 285. For the five passages on weeping, see pp. 110, 241, 265, 280, 285.

19. Ghazālī, *Iḥyāʾ*, 4:242 (Cairo).

20. Ibid., 4:243.

21. Bukhārī, Īmān 13. Cf. Muslim, Ṣiyām 74.

22. Ibn al-ʿArabī, *Futūḥāt*, 3:50–51 (Beirut).

23. Ibid., 1:511.

24. Ibid., 3:539.

25. Ibid., 1:356.

26. Ibid., 2:187.

27. There were diverse criteria by which theologians decided which divine names should be included in their discussions, and by no means did they necessarily adhere to the notion that God has "ninety-nine" names. If the three suggested names are not listed,

this is no doubt because they lack a certain majesty. In a similar way, the theologians exclude some divine names that are mentioned explicitly by the Koran, such as *the Best of Deceivers* (3:54).

28. To the objection that much of the universe is inert and lifeless, a Sufi like Ibn al-ʿArabī replies with metaphysical, theological, cosmological, and scriptural arguments to show that life and consciousness are the source of all things and are found everywhere. For more on this teaching, see Chapter 21.

29. Ibn al-ʿArabī, *Futūḥāt*, 2:211 (Beirut).

30. Ibid., 3:463. Ibn al-ʿArabī devotes a great deal of attention to the issue of the ultimate happiness of all creatures. For a survey of some of his arguments, see Chittick, "Ibn al-ʿArabī's Hermeneutics of Mercy."

31. Maybudī, *Kashf*, 5:637.

32. Ibid., 1:480–481.

33. Ibid., 1:653–654.

34. Ibid., 1:710–711.

Notes to Chapter 4

1. For its original Arabic text, see Qummī, *Mafātīḥ*, 531–560. For a complete translation, see Chittick, *A Shi'ite Anthology*, 93–113. Another important work belonging to this genre is *al-Ṣaḥīfat al-Sajjādiyya* by the fourth Imam, ʿAlī b. al-Ḥusayn (d. 95/712). For a complete translation of this collection, see *The Psalms of Islam*.

2. See Kāshānī, *Kalimāt-i maknūna*, 5, 29, 34, 88, 100.

3. See Sabziwārī, *Sharḥ al-asmāʾ*, 51, 190, 346; *Sharḥ duʿāʾ al-ṣabāḥ*, 13. One can also mention the Qajar prince Badīʿ al-Mulk Mīrzā ʿImād al-Dawla, who quotes from this part of the prayer in his translation of one of Mullā Ṣadrā's key works. See Ṣadrā, *Le livre des pénétrations métaphysiques*, 91 (Persian), 104 (French).

4. Majlisī, *Biḥār*, 98:227–228.

5. For a translation of the *Ḥikam* and the accompanying *munājāt*, see Ibn ʿAṭāʾ Allāh, *The Book of Wisdom*.

6. For which, see Nwyia, *Ibn ʿAṭāʾ Allāh et la naissance de la confrérie šāḏilite*, 209–229.

7. Majlisī's exact wording, occurring twice in the passage cited above, is *baʿḍ al-nusakh al-ʿatīqa*, "some of the old copies," which would leave the possibility open that this part of the prayer does exist in at least some early manuscripts. However, from the general context and the use of this fact to prove that this part of the prayer is most likely borrowed, it would rather seem that what Majlisī means is that it does not exist in the old copies he has seen.

Notes to Chapter 5

1. *Ka yakī hast u hīch nīst juz ū / waḥdahu lā ilāha illā hu*. An English translation of the whole poem can be found in E. G. Browne's classic study, *A Literary History of Persia*, 4:292–297.

2. It can be noted here that modern-day Iranians often hold the view that Sufism is an Iranian invention. This view, however, has much more to do with nationalism than with the actual situation. As many scholars have shown, the roots of Sufism can already

be seen in the Koran and the Sunnah of the Prophet, as is the case with the other branches of Islamic learning and practice. Like them, Sufism accompanied the religion wherever it spread, not only to Persia. Another common opinion is that Sufism has nothing to do with Islam. This idea first became prevalent in the late thirteenth/nineteenth century among reformers and modernists, who singled out Sufism as the cause of the backwardness of Islamic countries. These two opinions have produced a curious alliance between Islamist political activists and expatriate Iranians. The former claim that Sufism is a foreign borrowing or a decadence, and the latter agree that Sufism has nothing to do with Islam. However, in this all-too-common Iranian view, Islam is Arab fanaticism, and Sufism is a wonderful, gentle, universalistic, non-dogmatic way of life and thought that expresses the true spirit of Persian civilization.

3. Any discussion of bipolar concepts in Persian Islam invariably brings up the issue of the "influence" of pre-Islamic Iranian dualism on the Islamic period. Those Modern-day Iranians who are inclined to see Sufism as a Persian reaction to Islam are quick to seize on the prevalence of such ideas in Sufi poetry as proof of pre-Islamic influence. However, there is little historical evidence to support their opinion. First, to say that there was "influence" is really not to say anything. In the literal sense of the term, the fact of influence is self-evident, because everyone knows that pre-Islamic Persia gradually became Islamic Persia, and that the second/eighth century inexorably followed the first/seventh century. But what exactly does this tell us? "Influence" is a notoriously vague idea, and before it can function as a meaningful historical category, it needs careful definition and qualification. The word is typically employed not with evidence in mind, but rather with polemical intent. To say that Persian influence caused "dualistic" ideas to appear in Sufism is really to say that Sufi ideas are Persian, not Islamic, so Sufism has little to do with Islam. Second, "duality" in the sense of bipolarity or complementarity is practically universal in premodern cultures. It certainly was present not only in ancient Persia, but also in Greece, India, and, of course, China. And third, the Koran is full of verses that use bipolar language, a fact upon which Muslim thinkers of the past often remarked. The net result is that bipolarity is commonly found as a principle of Islamic theological thinking, without regard to geographical region. For more on this, see Murata, *The Tao of Islam*.

4. Rūmī, *Mathnawī*, 6:4303–4304. Cf. Chittick, *The Sufi Path of Love*, 208.

5. Rūmī, *Mathnawī*, 3:1258.

6. Hātif, *Dīwān*, 28–29.

Notes to Chapter 6

1. Nasr, *Jalāl al-Dīn Rūmī*, 23.

2. See, in particular, Lewis, *Rumi: Past and Present, East and West*, Chapter 4; Safi, *Rumi's Beloved*. For a translation of nearly two-thirds of Shams's *Maqālāt*, see Chittick, *Me & Rumi*.

3. Schimmel, *The Triumphal Sun*, 19.

4. Cited in Chittick, *Me & Rumi*, 194.

5. Cited in ibid., 189.

6. Cited in ibid.

7. Cited in ibid., 186.

8. Cited in ibid., 232.

9. Cited in ibid., 280.
10. Cited in ibid., 269.
11. Cited in ibid., 41.
12. Cited in ibid., 231–232.
13. Cited in ibid., 247.
14. Cited in ibid., 73.
15. Cited in ibid., 78.
16. Cited in ibid., 79.
17. Cited in ibid.
18. Cited in ibid., 156.
19. Cited in ibid.
20. Cited in ibid., 50–51.
21. Cited in ibid., 48.
22. Cited in ibid., 71.
23. Cited in ibid., 66.
24. Cited in ibid.
25. Cited in ibid., 154.
26. Cited in ibid., 263.
27. Cited in ibid., 255.
28. Cited in ibid., 97.
29. Cited in ibid., 90.
30. Cited in ibid.

Notes to Chapter 7

1. Theologically, this distinction is often drawn in terms of God's two commands: He issues the command *Be!* (*kun*) (2:117) to all things, and they can do nothing but obey; this is the creative or "engendering" command (*al-amr al-takwīnī*). To human beings (and jinn) He also issues the command, "Do this and don't do that," and they accept or reject it on the basis of their own free choice; this is the "prescriptive command" (*al-amr al-taklīfī*).

2. Rūmī, *Mathnawī*, 3:3287–3288. Cf. Chittick, *The Sufi Path of Love*, 114.

3. Bukhārī, Riqāq 38; Tabrīzī, *Mishkāt*, 91.

4. Cited in Chittick, *Me & Rumi*, 156.

5. Cited in ibid., 228.

6. Cited in ibid., 71.

7. Ghazālī, *Iḥyāʾ*, 3:96–97 (Beirut).

8. This is of course the Guarded Tablet (*al-lawḥ al-maḥfūẓ*), within which God writes with the Highest Pen (*al-qalam al-aʿlā*). The Pen and Tablet are also known as the First Intellect (*al-ʿaql al-awwal*) and the Universal Soul (*al-nafs al-kulliyya*), respectively.

9. Maybudī, *Kashf*, 1:54–55.

10. Ibid., 1:407.

11. Ibid., 1:412–413.

12. Ibid., 1:58.

13. For the Pond (*al-kawthar*) in Islamic eschatology, see Chapter 20.

14. Ibid., 1:59–60. I have taken a bit of help in reading this passage from parts of it that are also found in Anṣārī, *Majmūʿa-yi rasāʾil-i fārsī*, 367–377.

Notes to Chapter 8

1. On why *waḥdat al-wujūd* should be rendered as the "Oneness of Being" instead of the "Unity of Existence," see Chittick, "The Central Point," 27–28, n. 5.

2. See, for example, Pourjavady, *Sulṭān-i ṭarīqat,* 104ff. For the development of the school of Ibn al-ʿArabī, see Chittick, "The School of Ibn ʿArabī."

3. See Chittick, *A Shi'ite Anthology,* 37–38.

4. Abū Rayḥān al-Bīrūnī (d. ca 442/1051), the famous philosopher-scientist, summarizes a view that sounds very much like *waḥdat al-wujūd* while explaining the doctrines of the Greek philosophers; then he points out that this is also the position of the Sufis: "Some of them held that only the First Cause possesses true *wujūd,* since the First Cause is independent in its *wujūd* by its very Essence, while everything else has need of it. Moreover, the *wujūd* of that which is utterly in need of something else in order to possess *wujūd* is like imagination [*khayāl*]; it is not real [*ḥaqq*]. The Real is only the One, the First. This is also the opinion of the Sufis" (*Kitāb fī taḥqīq mā li-l-hind,* 24; cf. *Alberuni's India,* 33). For a few examples of relevant statements by Sufis in the context of *tawḥīd,* see the short but rich study by Gramlich, "Mystical Dimensions of Islamic Monotheism."

5. Quoted in ʿAyn al-Quḍāt, *Tamhīdāt,* 256; Nasafī, *Maqṣad-i aqṣā,* 272.

6. See ʿAyn al-Quḍāt, *Tamhīdāt,* 256–257.

7. Anṣārī, *Ṭabaqāt,* 180, 172, and 174, respectively; also quoted in Nurbakhsh, *Maʿārif-i ṣūfiyya,* 1:112, 113, 118.

8. Ghazālī, *Mishkāt,* 55. Cf. Ghazālī, *The Niche of Lights,* 16.

9. Ghazālī, *Iḥyāʾ,* 4:230 (Cairo).

10. Morris, "Ibn ʿArabī and His Interpreters," 540, n. 4 (Part I). Morris's article, especially Part I, is a fine study of the factors that make Ibn al-ʿArabī so difficult. For an inquiry into whether or not Ibn al-ʿArabī was a pantheist, see Rustom, "Is Ibn al-ʿArabī's Ontology Pantheistic?"

11. See Chodkiewicz, "Introduction" in Balyānī, *Epître sur l'unicité absolue,* 25–26; Ḥakīm, *Muʿjam,* 1145; Madkur, "Waḥdat al-wujūd bayna Ibn al-ʿArabī wa-Isbīnūzā," 369. It is of course possible that the term will one day turn up in some newly discovered manuscript of one of Ibn al-ʿArabī's works, but even if that happens, it will most likely not have a technical significance.

12. Ibn al-ʿArabī, *Futūḥāt,* 2:517 (Beirut).

13. Ibid., 2:519.

14. Ibid., 1:307.

15. Ibn al-ʿArabī, *Rasāʾil,* 9.

16. If one had to choose a single principle in Ibn al-ʿArabī's thought that synthesizes all his teachings, the best choice would probably be the Perfect Man (*al-insān al-kāmil*).

17. Cited in Chittick, *The Sufi Path of Love,* 279.

18. Izutsu, *Sufism and Taoism,* 81.

19. For a few examples of the term, see Chittick, *The Sufi Path of Knowledge,* index (under "unveiling").

20. See "Molé, *Les mystiques musulmans,* 59–61; Schimmel, *Mystical Dimensions of Islam,* 267.

21. See Austin, "Introduction" in Ibn al-ʿArabī, *The Bezels of Wisdom,* 25–26. Cf. Chittick, "Waḥdat al-Shuhūd."

22. Ibn al-ʿArabī also employs the term *wujūd* to refer to the "Breath of the All-Merciful" (*nafas al-raḥmān*), the supreme isthmus that is neither God nor creation, nor

different from the two. In order to keep the discussion as simple as possible, I will leave this "third thing" (*al-shay' al-thālith*) out of the picture, even though, ultimately, it is the integrating factor. See Chittick, *The Sufi Path of Knowledge*, Chapter 8.

23. See ibid., 83–88. Throughout *The Sufi Path of Knowledge* I rendered the expression as "immutable entities." For why "fixed entities" is a more accurate translation, see Chittick, *The Self Disclosure of God*, xxxviii. Cf. Dagli, "Translator's Introduction," xviii–xix.

24. For example, "There is nothing in *wujūd* but the One/Many" (Ibn al-ʿArabī, *Futūḥāt*, 3:420 [Beirut]). See Ḥakīm, *Muʿjam*, 1162–1164.

25. This formula is found already in Anṣārī. See his *Intimate Conversations*, 215. See also Schimmel, *Mystical Dimensions of Islam*, 147, 274, 283, 362, 376.

26. Ibn al-ʿArabī, *Futūḥāt*, 3:151 (Beirut). For the passage in its context, see Chittick, *The Sufi Path of Knowledge*, 368.

27. Aflākī, *The Feats of the Knowers of God*, 406. Aflākī also relates an incident that took place just before Qūnawī led Rūmī's funeral prayer. See ibid., 244.

28. See Chittick, "Mysticism versus Philosophy in Earlier Islamic History." For a critical edition of the Qūnawī-Ṭūsī correspondence, see Schubert (ed.), *Annäherungen*. Despite his sympathy for philosophy, Qūnawī considered it defective and perhaps even dangerous; this is undoubtedly why his will states that his own books on the subject should be sold, while the rest, mainly on religious topics, literature, and medicine, should be made into an endowment. See Chittick, "The Last Will and Testament of Ibn al-ʿArabī's Foremost Disciple and Some Notes on its Author," 53. Nevertheless, preserved in his own handwriting is a copy of the *Ḥikmat al-ishrāq* ("The Wisdom of Illumination") by Shihāb al-Dīn Suhrawardī (d. 587/1191), along with Rāzī's *Lubāb al-ishārāt* ("The Gist of the 'Remarks and Admonitions'"). See Chittick, "The Last Will and Testament of Ibn al-ʿArabī's Foremost Disciple and Some Notes on its Author," 51.

29. As Chodkiewicz remarks, Qūnawī "a donné à la doctrine de son maître une formulation philosophique sans doute nécessaire mais dont le systématisme a engendré bien des malentendus" (in Balyānī, *Epître sur l'unicité absolue*, 26).

30. Ibn Taymiyya, *Majmūʿa*, 1:176. Cf. Ibn Taymiyya's remarks on Qūnawī with the observations of ʿAbd al-Raḥmān Jāmī (d. 898/1492), where he says that Ibn al-ʿArabī's teachings cannot be understood in terms consistent both with Islamic principles and rational speculation without the aid of Qūnawī's writings. See Jāmī, *Nafaḥāt*, 556.

31. Qūnawī, *Miftāḥ*, 19–26. In his *Nuṣūṣ*, 69–74, Qūnawī quotes the same passage as one of the "greatest of the texts" he has ever written.

32. Qūnawī, *Nafaḥāt*, 239. The term "tasks" is derived from the verse, *Each day He is upon some task* (55:29). See Chittick, *The Sufi Path of Knowledge*, 98–99.

33. Qūnawī, *Nafaḥāt*, 246.

34. Qūnawī, *Miftāḥ*, 48.

35. The term is not mentioned in Jandī's 125-page explanation of Ibn al-ʿArabī's introduction to the *Fuṣūṣ*, nor in his Persian *Nafḥat*. Jandī's commentary was especially influential, even though it was preceded by at least two others, because it was the first to explain the whole text. The most important of the earlier commentaries are probably Qūnawī's *Fukūk*, which explains the meanings of the chapter headings, and one by ʿAfīf al-Dīn Tilimsānī, which, however, often ignores whole chapters and deals mainly with a few points on which the author disagrees with Ibn al-ʿArabī.

36. Jandī, *Sharḥ*, 388.

37. Jāmī, *Nafaḥāt*, 559.

38. For a translation of this work and the author's famous *Khamriyya,* see Ibn al-Fāriḍ, *Sufi Verse, Saintly Life.*

39. Farghānī, *Mashāriq,* 5–6. Jāmī quotes one Shams al-Dīn Īkī, a student of Qūnawī, concerning the circumstances of Farghānī's works: "In the sessions of our shaykh the possessors and seekers of knowledge used to attend. The shaykh would speak about different sciences. Then he would end the session with one verse from the *Naẓm al-sulūk,* on which he would comment in Persian. He expounded marvelous words and God-given meanings, but only the possessors of tasting could understand him. Sometimes on another day he would say that a different meaning of the verse had become manifest for him, and he would explain a meaning more wonderful and subtle than before. He often used to say, " 'One must be a Sufi to learn this poem and to be able to clarify its meanings for others.' " . . . Shaykh Saʿīd Farghānī would devote all his attention to understand what our shaykh said, and then he would record it. He wrote an explanation of the poem first in Persian and then in Arabic. This was all because of the blessing of our shaykh, Ṣadr al-Dīn" (*Nafaḥāt,* 542).

40. See the index to Farghānī's *Mashāriq.* Instances of its usage in the *Muntahā* include 1:101–102, 226; 2:202, 217.

41. Qūnawī makes the same point in many long passages and without contrasting these two specific terms, but sometimes he expresses the idea even more succinctly, as in the statement, "Know that distinction [*tamyīz*] pertains to knowledge, while *tawḥīd* pertains to *wujūd*" (*Iʿjāz,* 333/*Tafsīr,* 455). Why these two terms are singled out rather than any others is clear in the context of Islamic thought, especially as developed by Ibn al-ʿArabī and his followers. Knowledge is central because it is the necessary prerequisite for all activity. In Ibn al-ʿArabī's approach, the discussion has to do with the fact that certain of the divine attributes are broader in scope (*aʿamm*) than others, with Being (or mercy, or life) being the broadest. The argument runs something like this: The cosmos depends on the Creator (*khāliq*) or the Speaker (*qāʾil*) for its existence, while creativity and speech depend on the divine power (*qudra*). Power in turn is effectuated through desire (*irāda*), while desire depends on a knowledge of possibilities. Knowledge in turn presupposes *wujūd,* or the fact that there be a knower. Hence, Being and knowledge are the two primary attributes of Reality.

42. In this context Farghānī draws a horizontal distinction between *waḥdat al-wujūd* and *kathrat al-ʿilm.* In other words, these two principles lie on the same plane, and their duality is overcome only on a higher level, which is called *aḥadiyyat al-jamʿ,* the "Unity of All-Comprehensiveness." Farghānī writes, "*Waḥdat al-wujūd* and *kathrat al-ʿilm* are identical with each other at the level of the Unity of All-Comprehensiveness," while "these two realities must be actualized and differentiated at the level of Divinity" (*Mashāriq,* 344).

43. Ibid., 345.

44. See ibid., 359, 365, 395–396. See also Farghānī, *Muntahā,* 1:101–102, 226.

45. In the detailed notes that I took on manuscripts of Tilimsānī's *Sharḥ al-Fuṣūṣ* and *Sharḥ al-asmāʾ al-ḥusnā* in 1979, I found no mention of the term *waḥdat al-wujūd.*

46. For a thorough study, edition, and translation of this work, see Akasoy, *Philosophie und Mystik in der späten Almohadenzeit.*

47. However, Ibn al-ʿArabī figures in the *isnād* of Ibn Sabʿīn's *ṭarīqa* provided by his chief disciple, Abū'l-Ḥasan al-Shushtarī (d. 668/1270). See Chodkiewicz, "Introduction" in Balyānī, *Epître sur l'unicité absolue,* 36–37. Cf. Cornell, "The All-Comprehensive Circle," 34.

48. Ibn Sabʿīn, *Rasāʾil,* 194. For other instances of the term, cf. ibid., 38, 189, 264, 266. See also Cornell, "The All-Comprehensive Circle," 34ff.

49. See Chodkiewicz, "Introduction" in Balyānī, *Epître sur l'unicité absolue.*

50. Cited in Ibn al-ʿArabī [Balyānī], *"Whoso Knoweth Himself . . . ,"* 4.

51. For examples of his poetry, see Jāmī, *Nafaḥāt*, 262.

52. See the editors' introductions to Ḥammūya, *Misbāḥ*; Nasafī, *Le livre de l'homme parfait.*

53. Jāmī, *Nafaḥāt*, 429.

54. Nasafī, *Kashf*, 153. Immediately following this quotation, Nasafī begins discussing the "words of the people of oneness." Ibn al-ʿArabī sometimes employs the expression, "There is no existent but God," or states that "There is no existent other than He." See Ibn al-ʿArabī, *Futūḥāt*, 2:216, 563 (Beirut).

55. In his *Kashf*, Nasafī employs the term twice as part of headings (pp. 154, 159) and once in the text (p. 159). He also uses the term *waḥdat-i wājib al-wujūd* once (p. 152).

56. Ibn Khaldūn (d. 808/1406) employs the synonymous expression *aṣḥāb al-waḥda*, mentioning among others Ibn Sabʿīn and Shushtarī; he contrasts this group with the *aṣḥāb al-tajallī wa-l-maẓāhir wa-l-ḥaḍarāt*, and mentions Ibn al-Fāriḍ, Ibn al-ʿArabī, and others. See Ibn Khaldūn, *Shifāʾ*, 51–52. Cf. Ibn Khaldūn, *The Muqaddima*, 3:89.

57. See Landolt, "ʿAzīz-i Nasafī and the Essence-Existence Debate."

58. Nasafī, *Kashf*, 155; *Maqṣad-i aqṣā*, 252.

59. Ḥammūya, *Miṣbāḥ*, 66. That "everything other than God" is "imagination" constitutes one of Ibn al-ʿArabī's central ideas, although, as in his affirmation of *waḥdat al-wujūd*, this statement is not as simple and straightforward as it might appear. See Chittick, *The Sufi Path of Knowledge*, Chapter 7.

60. See, in particular, Knysh, *Ibn 'Arabi in the Later Islamic Tradition*, Chapter 4. See also Memon, *Ibn Taimīya's Struggle Against Popular Religion*, especially 29–46. Although Memon tries to be fair, he severely distorts Ibn al-ʿArabī's teachings by largely relying on Ibn Taymiyya's own accounts and outdated Western studies.

61. Ibn Taymiyya, *Majmūʿa*, 1:61–120; 4:2–101.

62. For example, ibid., 1:66, 68, 69, 76, 78.

63. Fakhr al-Dīn ʿIrāqī (d. 688/1289), one of Qūnawī's outstanding disciples, provides a succinct definition of unificationism in his *Lamaʿāt*. See ʿIrāqī, *Divine Flashes*, 93, 145–146. See also Farghānī, *Mashāriq*, 271–273; *Muntahā*, 1:292–293; Ibn al-ʿArabī, *Futūḥāt*, 2:130, 334; 3:37 (Beirut).

64. Ibn Taymiyya, *Majmūʿa*, 4:73.

65. Ibid., 1:66.

66. Ibid., 4:4; for a more detailed summary, see 4:53.

67. I was able to find one instance in Qayṣarī's long theoretical introduction to his commentary on the *Fuṣūṣ* (note the close connection between *wujūd* and *shuhūd*): "The truth of these words is only disclosed to that person to whom the reality of activity [*al-faʿʿāliyya*] becomes manifest and to whom *waḥdat al-wujūd* becomes manifest within the levels of witnessing [*shuhūd*]" (*Sharḥ*, 29; see also Āshtiyānī, *Sharḥ-i Muqaddima*, 291).

68. Qayṣarī, *Rasāʾil*, 50.

69. See Jāmī, *Naqd*, 18–19. See also Jāmī, *The Precious Pearl*, 36, 43, 65, 92.

70. Morris, remarking on Palacios's study of Ibn al-ʿArabī, *L'Islam christianise*, in "Ibn al-ʿArabī and His Interpreters," 544. For an eloquent appraisal of Ibn al-ʿArabī's importance and the dangers of various oversimplified interpretations, see Corbin, *Creative Imagination in the Ṣūfism of Ibn 'Arabī*. See also Burckhardt, *An Introduction to Sufi Doctrine*, passim; Nasr, *Three Muslim Sages*, 104–106.

71. On Sirhindī and *waḥdat al-shuhūd,* see Friedmann, *Shaykh Ahmad Sirhindi.* Friedmann's comparison of *waḥdat al-shuhūd* with *waḥdat al-wujūd* follows Sirhindī's own interpretation, so it has no validity in terms of what Ibn al-ʿArabī and his followers actually said. The debate between the supporters of *waḥdat al-wujūd* and *waḥdat al-shuhūd* is said to go back to ʿAlāʾ al-Dawla Simnānī (d. 736/1336), who exchanged well-known letters with Kāshānī, but Simnānī himself does not employ the terms, nor is it known who first contrasted them. See Landolt, "Der Briefwechsel zwischen Kāšānī und Simnānī über *Waḥdat al-Wuǧūd.*"

72. Molé, *Les mystiques musulmans,* 109.

73. This is not the place to attempt to show the error of this attribution, since to do so in the limited space available would force me to indulge in the same sort of oversimplifications that I am criticizing. Let me only remark that no one paints a more dynamic picture of creation and the human relationship to God than Ibn al-ʿArabī. For example, when he explains the similarity demanded by God's self-disclosure, Ibn al-ʿArabī constantly quotes the axiom, "Self-disclosure never repeats itself" (*lā takrār fī-l-tajallī*), which is the principle behind his well-known doctrine of the "renewal of creation at each instant" (*tajdīd al-khalq maʿa-l-ānāt*). One of the names that Ibn al-ʿArabī gives to the highest stage of spiritual realization, where the human receptacle becomes the full manifestation of the All-Comprehensive Name (*al-ism al-jāmiʿ*) "Allah," is "bewilderment," since within this station the Perfect Man constantly witnesses the infinite expanse of the divine *wujūd* through never-repeating and ever-changing revelations of light and awareness. Thus, he writes in the *Fuṣūṣ*: "Guidance is to be led to bewilderment. Then you will know that the whole affair is bewilderment, that bewilderment is agitation and movement, and that movement is life. There is no rest, no death, only existence—nothing of nonexistence" (*Fuṣūṣ,* 199–200).

74. Ghallāb, "al-Maʿrifa ʿinda Muḥyī al-Dīn Ibn al-ʿArabī," 202–206; Jahāngīrī, *Muḥyī al-Dīn Ibn-i ʿArabī,* 198.

Notes to Chapter 9

1. See below, where it is shown that in the specific instances where Nicholson claims that Rūmī draws inspiration from Ibn al-ʿArabī, there are more likely sources in Rūmī's immediate environment.

2. Rūmī, *Mathnawī,* 2:1022. Cf. Chittick, *The Sufi Path of Love,* 20.

3. Corbin, *Creative Imagination in the Ṣūfism of Ibn 'Arabī,* 70.

4. See, in this regard, Chittick, "Ibn 'Arabi and Rumi"; Chittick, *The Sufi Doctrine of Rumi,* xiii.

5. See Chittick, "Rūmī and the Mawlawiyyah."

6. For a translation of this work, see Pourjavady, *Sawāniḥ: Inspirations from the World of Pure Spirits.*

7. See Chittick, "The Myth of Adam's Fall in Aḥmad Samʿānī's *Rawḥ al-arwāḥ*"; also in Chittick, *Sufism,* Chapter 9.

8. In reading quickly through this work, I noted down the following instances that could have provided the inspiration for some of Rūmī's lines, without any attempt to be exhaustive: Iblīs and Adam (Samʿānī, *Rawḥ,* 90; cf. Chittick, *The Sufi Path of Love,* 82–84); alchemy (Samʿānī, *Rawḥ,* 162; cf. Chittick, *The Sufi Path of Love,* index under "alchemy"); Moses at Mount Sinai (Samʿānī, *Rawḥ,* 201; Chittick, *The Sufi Path of Love,* 296–297); the boasting of the planets and the rising of the sun (Samʿānī, *Rawḥ,* 253; Chittick, *The Sufi*

Path of Love, 203); Jesus and his ass (Samʿānī, *Rawḥ*, 330; Chittick, *The Sufi Path of Love*, index under "Jesus").

9. See the editors' introductions to Bahāʾ Walad, *Maʿārif*; Tabrīzī, *Maqālāt*.

10. For a translation of this work, see Hamadānī, *The Tamhīdāt of ʿAyn al-Quḍāt al-Hamadānī*.

11. See Chittick, "The Divine Roots of Human Love"; Chittick, "Ebno'l-'Arabi as Lover."

12. For further clarifications of these points, see Chittick, "Rūmī and the Mawlawiyyah."

13. See Bahāʾ Walad, *Maʿārif*, 73, 76, 77, 83, 128, 166, 169, 190, 281, 324; Tabrīzī, *Maqālāt*, 103, 203; ʿAyn al-Quḍāt, *Tamhīdāt*, 50, 265.

14. Samʿānī, *Rawḥ*, 32.

15. Ibid., 304.

16. Sanāʾī, *Ḥadīqat*, 295–298. See also Sanāʾī, *Sayr*, 212–213. For the role of *ʿaql* in Persian literature, see Chittick, "ʿAql (in Persian Literature)."

17. Bahāʾ Walad, *Maʿārif*, 281. Like Rūmī, Bahāʾ Walad frequently refers to the divine source of all things as "nonexistence," that is, nonexistent in relation to us but existent in reality; it is we who confuse the illusory existence of this world, which is truly nonexistent, with existence. In the same context, Rūmī likes to refer to nonexistence as "God's workshop." See Chittick, *The Sufi Path of Love*, 23–24, 175–178.

18. See ibid., 363, n. 49, l. 34.

19. Cited in ibid., 209. Cf. the other passages quoted in the same section.

20. See Chittick, *Me & Rumi*, 73, 187.

21. ʿAṭṭār, *Dīwān*, 817–820.

22. Ibn al-ʿArabī, *Futūḥāt*, 2:85 (Beirut).

23. Ibid., 2:654.

24. Ibid., 3:214.

25. Ibid., 2:313.

26. Ibid., 2:302.

27. Ibid., 4:357.

28. Ibid., 1:90.

29. Ibid., 2:10.

30. Ibid., 2:501.

31. Ibid., 2:466.

32. Ibid., 2:401.

33. Ibid., 2:114.

34. Ibid., 2:331.

35. Ibid., 4:279.

Notes to Chapter 10

1. Ibn al-ʿArabī's focus on knowledge is not unrelated to the fact that his writings are essentially commentaries on the Koran, which constantly stresses its importance. For the intimate relationship between his works and the Koran, see Chodkiewicz, *An Ocean Without Shore*.

2. On occasion, Ibn al-ʿArabī contrasts *ʿilm* and *maʿrifa*, but the distinction between the two terms plays no major role in his writings. See Chittick, *The Sufi Path of Knowledge*,

147–149. For a detailed discussion of some of Ibn al-ʿArabī's views on various aspects of knowledge, see ibid., Chapters 9–14.

3. Ibn al-ʿArabī, *Futūḥāt*, 3:448 (Beirut).

4. Ibid., 4:129.

5. Ibid., 2:620.

6. Ibid., 3:361.

7. Ibid., 2:117.

8. Ibid., 2:612.

9. Ibid., 4:315.

10. Ibid., 4:119.

11. Ibn al-ʿArabī, *Dhakhāʾir*, 191.

12. Ibn al-ʿArabī, *Futūḥāt*, 4:129 (Beirut).

13. Ibn al-ʿArabī, *Rasāʾil*, 6–7. Ibn al-ʿArabī is alluding here to a long hadith found in the *Ṣaḥīḥ* of Muslim that describes, among other things, how people will deny God when He appears to them on the day of resurrection. They will continue to deny Him until He appears to them in a form that they recognize as coinciding with their own beliefs. Ibn al-ʿArabī cites from this hadith in the continuation of the passage from his letter to Rāzī: "After all, he should be one of the folk of recognition [*ʿirfān*], not one of the folk of denial [*nukrān*]. Those homesteads [in the next world] are homesteads for making distinct, not homesteads of commingling that would give rise to error. When he gains this station of making distinct, he will be delivered from the party of that group who say, when their Lord discloses Himself to them, 'We seek refuge in God from you. You are not our Lord. We will wait until our Lord comes.' Then, when He comes to them in the form in which they recognize Him, they will acknowledge Him. So how great is their bewilderment!" For other examples of his explanation of this hadith's significance, see Chittick, *The Sufi Path of Knowledge*, hadith index under "He transmutes"; Chittick, *The Self-Disclosure of God*, hadith index under "Is there between you."

14. Ibn al-ʿArabī, *Futūḥāt*, 1:581 (Beirut).

15. Ibid., 2:473. On this point, see Chittick, *The Self-Disclosure of God*, Chapter 1.

16. Ibn al-ʿArabī, *Futūḥāt*, 3:275 (Beirut).

17. Ibid., 3:557.

18. Ibid., 3:282.

19. Ibid., 4:110. As Ibn al-ʿArabī often puts it, the God or gods that people worship—and everyone without exception is a worshiper of some god—is only the God that they understand, not God as He is in Himself. No one can truly understand God except God Himself. Hence everyone worships a God fabricated by his own belief, and from this standpoint—there are, of course, other standpoints—all human beings without exception are idol-worshipers. See Chittick, *The Sufi Path of Knowledge*, Chapter 19, and Chittick, *Imaginal Worlds*, Chapter 9.

20. Ibn al-ʿArabī, *Futūḥāt*, 2:298 (Beirut).

21. Ibid., 4:80.

22. Whether or not this question applies properly to God is an important theological and philosophical issue. According to Ibn al-ʿArabī, to ask it concerning God is to be ignorant of Him and should not be allowed. See Chittick, *The Self-Disclosure of God*, 213–214. That God has no "whatness" or quiddity other than *wujūd* itself, and that *wujūd* is not a proper answer to the question of whatness (which demands a definition), is a well-known theological and philosophical position, and it is referred to in Sufi works as early as Hujwīrī's *Kashf al-maḥjūb*. See Chittick, *Faith and Practice of Islam*, 202–203.

Notes to Chapter 11

1. For a recent study of this important text, see Adamson, *The Arabic Plotinus*.

2. For Qūnawī's personal library, see Ateş, "Konya kütüphanelerind bulunan bazi mühim yazmalar"; Konyalı, *Âbideleri ve kitabeleri ile Konya tarihi*, 501–503. See also Elmore, "Ṣadr al-Dīn al-Qūnawī's Personal Study-List of Books by Ibn al-ʿArabī."

3. My purpose here is only to represent the Sufis' own point of view, not to defend it. Especially because of a certain claim to "privileged" knowledge, the Sufis have been looked on at least with suspicion by most legalists or exotericists (*ahl al-ẓāhir*) since early times. Hence almost any Sufi text aimed at a wider audience than practicing adepts has emphasized the fundamentally Islamic nature of Sufism.

4. That Qūnawī directed a spiritual order is well-known. One of his treatises deals explicitly with the method of concentration that his disciples should employ. The two titles by which it is most commonly known indicate its nature: *al-Risāla al-hādiya al-murshidiyya* ("The Treatise Giving Guidance and Spiritual Direction"); *Ṭarīq al-tawajjuh al-atamm* ("The Way of the Most Complete Attentiveness"). This is the only one of Qūnawī's works that was translated into Persian at an early date, probably during his lifetime, a fact that may indicate that at least some of his followers were concerned only with practice.

5. Qūnawī discerns five broad categories of unveiling, depending on the ontological level where it takes place. See Qūnawī, *Ilmāʿ*, ms. Konya 1633, fol. 118b. Cf. the discussion of the five "faces" of the heart in Qūnawī, *Fukūk*, 246–247, partly translated in ʿIraqi, *Divine Flashes*, 162.

6. Badawī, *Aflūṭīn ʿinda al-ʿarab*, 22; Āshtiyānī (ed.), *Uthūlūjiyā*, 35. Cf. Plotinus's actual statement translated in Hadot, *Plotinus, or the Simplicity of Vision*, 25.

7. Qūnawī, *Nafaḥāt*, 18. As its title indicates, this work recounts many such visions and unveilings.

8. This reservation needs to be made, since according to Qūnawī one type of unveiling involves unification (*ittiḥād*) with the First Intellect. In his reply to Ṭūsī, Qūnawī discusses this point and remarks, *inter alia*, "Intellects are bounded to the extent that they are delimited [*muqayyad*] by their own thoughts. Thus they may judge that many things are impossible. But when a person's intellect roams freely without delimitation by such bounds, then he will know that those things are possible or even necessary, for nondelimited [*muṭlaqa*] intellects are not hemmed in by any boundary that might stop them. On the contrary, they ascend constantly and receive instruction from the high directions and the Divine Presences" (*al-Hādiya* in Schubert (ed.), *Annäherungen*, 162).

9. See Chittick, "Mysticism vs. Philosophy in Earlier Islamic History," 95.

10. It is certainly no accident that in alluding to the limitations of Peripatetic philosophy, Qūnawī employs the name of Avicenna's magnum opus. For a translation of its important section on metaphysics, see Avicenna, *The Metaphysics of the Healing*.

11. I.e., those who have verified and actualized the Truth. Qūnawī calls his own teachings the "way of realization" (*madhhab al-taḥqīq*).

12. Here Qūnawī alludes to a hadith, "Verily your Lord has breaths of His Mercy in the days of your time—so expose yourselves to them!" Qūnawī comments on the significance of this saying in his *Sharḥ al-arbaʿīn*, 171–173. The same passage occurs at the beginning of his *Nafaḥāt*, 3ff., whose title is based on the hadith.

13. Qūnawī, *Iʿjāz*, 12–14/*Tafsīr*, 110–113.

14. The inherent weaknesses of human language are discussed by Qūnawī in the introduction to *Iʿjāz*, 15/*Tafsīr*, 114ff. He quotes the same passage in his correspondence with Ṭūsī. See Chittick, "Mysticism vs. Philosophy in Earlier Islamic History."

15. See ʿIraqi, *Divine Flashes*, 11.

16. See ibid., 12ff.; Chittick, "The Five Divine Presences."

17. Qūnawī's most detailed discussion of how the four succeeding Presences come to be configured from the first occurs in *Miftāḥ*, 43ff., where he describes the four levels of "marriage" (*nikāḥ*): The four "Keys to the Unseen," divine names known only to God, interrelate and as a result produce the world of meanings (the world of knowledge). The meanings in turn "marry" and give birth to the world of the spirits, etc. See also Qūnawī, *Iʿjāz*, 78ff./*Tafsīr*, 185ff.; *Sharḥ al-arbaʿīn*, 132ff.

18. Because the command is in one respect identical with the divine Word *Be!* (2:117), its role in generating the universe is not unconnected with the fact that all creatures are words of God, a point that Qūnawī develops with great detail and refinement. See Qūnawī, *Nafaḥāt*, 64–65; *Miftāḥ*, 93–98; and especially, *Iʿjāz*, 85–106, 136ff./*Tafsīr*, 205–213, 246ff.

19. Qūnawī, *Miftāḥ*, 20–21, 56; *Fukūk*, 186; *Iʿjāz*, 197–198/*Tafsīr*, 310–311.

20. Other important synonyms are "things" and "quiddities."

21. Qūnawī, *Nafaḥāt*, 64.

22. Ibid., 67.

23. Ibid., 66–67.

24. Qūnawī, *Iʿjāz*, 43–44/*Tafsīr*, 145–146. Cf. Chittick, "The Central Point," 41–42.

25. Qūnawī, *Iʿjāz*, 298–299/*Tafsīr*, 417.

26. Qūnawī, *Iʿjāz*, 270–271/*Tafsīr*, 386–387.

27. Qūnawī, *Iʿjāz*, 300/*Tafsīr*, 418.

28. Qūnawī, *Miftāḥ*, 102.

29. Ibid., 99.

30. Ibid., 104–105. For the "universal" and "particular" preparednesses, see ʿIrāqī, *Divine Flashes*, 151.

31. Qūnawī, *Miftāḥ*, 105.

32. The "loving attachment" (*taʿashshuq*) of the soul to the body is discussed below.

33. According to the well-known Sufi saying, "None knows God but God." That which "enters into union" with God had never left God in the first place—that is, the divine mystery mentioned in the next sentence. Each of the manifestations of this mystery (for example, man's body, soul, and spirit) remains at the ontological level proper to it.

34. Qūnawī, *Miftāḥ*, 105–106. In this whole discussion Qūnawī derives a good deal of inspiration from Ibn al-ʿArabī, but, as in so many other instances (see, e.g., Chittick, "Ṣadr al-Dīn Qūnawī on the Oneness of Being"), he clarifies Ibn al-ʿArabī's underlying idea by bringing out its implications and giving it a coherent and logical structure. Although Ibn al-ʿArabī often alludes to the spiritual ascent of decomposition, his clearest explanation seems to be provided by the following passage: "When God desires to cause the spiritual ascent of those whom He wills amongst the inheritors of His messengers and amongst His saints . . . [He makes them ascend] such that their composition dissolves [*ḥalla tarkībuhum*]. Through this ascent He gives them cognizance of everything that corresponds to them in each world; this He does by making them pass over the various kinds of composite and simple worlds. The spirit of such a person discards in each world everything in his essence that corresponds to it. The form of his discarding is as follows: God lets down a veil between him and what he himself discards in that

sort of world so that he no longer sees [what he discarded], while he continues to contemplate what remains with him, until finally he subsists in the divine mystery, which is the specific face that God had turned toward him" (*Futūḥāt*, 3:343 [Beirut]; cf. *Futūḥāt*, 3:344ff. [Beirut]; Ḥakīm, *Mu ʿjam*, 571–579). Ibn al-ʿArabī employs the term *mi ʿraj al-taḥlīl* in *al-Anwār*, published in his *Rasā ʾil*, 9.

35. Qūnawī, *Miftāḥ*, 106. On the configuration of the next world from this world, see below. See also Qūnawī, *Nafaḥāt*, 91–93.

36. Qūnawī, *Miftāḥ*, 107.

37. Ibid., 107–109. A clear distinction is drawn here between the divine mystery and the specific face, even if, in essence, they are identical. The specific face is man's reality *in divinis*; the divine mystery is that same reality as it becomes manifest outwardly through God's self-disclosure. Hence, the divine mystery appears in different forms according to the ontological level at which it displays the specific face.

38. Qūnawī, *Miftāḥ*, 111–114.

39. Ibid., 115.

40. Qūnawī, *Nafaḥāt*, 87–88.

41. Chittick, "Ibn ʿArabī's own Summary of the *Fuṣūṣ*," 70.

42. See Farghānī's remarks in *Muntahā*, 71; *Mashāriq*, 47–49. Cf. Qūnawī, *I ʿjāz*, 270/ *Tafsīr*, 386; *Fukūk*, 195–196.

43. Cf. the fifth question Qūnawī poses to Ṭūsī, where he implies his own realization of such a station. He also says explicitly that he has experienced the "disengagement" of his soul from his body. In his reply to Qūnawī, Ṭūsī writes, "Cutting off [*inqiṭā ʿ*] the soul's connection to the body before death is impossible, since its governance of it is a connection. But it is possible for the soul to become independent [*istighnā ʾ*] of the connection while the connection still exists. This is actualized by the People of Perfection when they turn toward the next world and away from this; you yourself—God extend your days—have experienced this in yourself and witnessed it in others. The reason for it is that human souls reach perfection through intellectual perceptions. . . . So they have no need for the body. For such men death is the great victory and supreme felicity" (*al-Ajwiba* in Schubert (ed.), *Annäherungen*, 120–121).

44. Qūnawī, *Fukūk*, 285–286; quoted by Jāmī in *Naqd*, 242–243. The Perfect Man preserves the order of the universe and maintains the separation between the created and the uncreated. Cf. Qūnawī, *I ʿjāz*, 126ff./*Tafsīr*, 234ff.; Chittick, "Ibn ʿArabī's own Summary of the *Fuṣūṣ*," 38–40.

Notes to Chapter 12

1. M. Woodward has shown that the diverse positions of traditional Muslims in Java can be classified on the basis of the respective emphasis that they place on the outward and inward dimensions of the religion. Only in modern times have certain people considered one dimension valid to the exclusion of the other. Thus we have reformists who see the inward dimension as alien to Islam, and modern, universalizing mystics who see all the specifically Islamic dimensions as outward and extraneous. In both cases, the equilibrium between the two dimensions has been broken. As Woodward puts it, "The balance struck in traditional Javanese Islam is absent, as the complementary axioms are not subordinated but purged from the system" (*Islam in Java*, 250).

2. Farghānī, *Muntahā*, 1:15.

3. Ibid., 1:15.

4. Ibid., 1:22.

5. I have in mind the significance that is given in Sufi theoretical discussions in particular, and Islamic poetry and art in general, to such things as night and day, black and white, the veil, and so on.

6. Farghānī, *Muntahā*, 2:214; *Mashāriq*, 629.

7. Farghānī, *Muntahā*, 2:197; *Mashāriq*, 606.

8. These correlations are of course basic to Islamic thought. It is sufficient merely to look at the eight hundred and fifty instances in which the Koran employs the word *ʿilm* and its derivatives to see how these verses stress separation and distinction. In contrast, the word *ḥubb* and its derivatives is employed only about eighty times, but the idea of bringing together and nearness is always present.

9. Farghānī, *Muntahā*, 2:215.

10. As Ibn al-ʿArabī tells us, the divine name Wise "arranges affairs within their levels and places the things within their measures" (cited in Chittick, *The Sufi Path of Knowledge*, 174).

11. Farghānī, *Muntahā*, 2:215.

12. Ibid., 2:215–216.

13. Ibid., 2:216.

14. Farghānī's discussion parallels many of Ibn al-ʿArabī's formulations. As I have shown elsewhere, Ibn al-ʿArabī frequently talks about the perfected gnostic as one who sees clearly with both eyes. In contrast, other people see with difficulty and usually with only one eye. These two eyes correlate almost exactly with Farghānī's two faces. According to Ibn al-ʿArabī, one eye sees God's distance and incomparability, the other His nearness and similarity, one light and the other darkness, one permanence and the other transmutation, one manifestation and the other hiddenness, one unity and the other multiplicity. See Chittick, *The Sufi Path of Knowledge*, 361–363. These two eyes point to the vision that accompanies Farghānī's two faces: the face turned toward oneness and that turned toward manyness. A parallel discussion is found in Kāshānī, *Iṣṭilāḥāt*, 179–180, where he differentiates between the possessor of intellect (who sees multiplicity), the possessor of the eye (who sees oneness), and the possessor of the intellect and the eye, that is, the Perfect Man (who sees multiplicity and oneness at the same time).

15. Farghānī, *Muntahā*, 2:159.

16. This set of terms does not seem to help much in clarifying the issue, given the subtlety of the interrelationships between different levels of explanation in the Islamic context. Moreover, one frequently sees the two employed as if the Sufis themselves made the same distinctions in exactly the same way and with the same frequency and purpose, which is far from being true. The Sufis employ many sets of terms that allude to a similar or parallel relationship, but each set has its own nuances and needs to be investigated in its appropriate context.

Notes to Chapter 13

1. Although Jāmī's Arabic commentary on Ibn al-ʿArabī's *Fuṣūṣ* is longer than the *Naqd*, it follows the *Fuṣūṣ* closely and offers practically no detailed theoretical elaborations or digressions. One of Jāmī's most lucid expositions of theoretical Sufism—albeit much shorter than the *Naqd*—is his *Lawāʾiḥ* ("Gleams"), an influential prose work written

in Persian and rendered into Chinese by the important Muslim scholar, Liu Zhi (b. ca. 1081/1670). My translation of this text from its original Persian and S. Murata's translation of its Chinese version are published alongside one another in Murata, *Chinese Gleams of Sufi Light*, 128–210.

2. For the writings of several important Indian "members" of the school of Ibn al-ʿArabī, see Chapters 14–16.

3. Jāmī, *Naqd*, 199.

4. Ibid., 87. For other interpretations of the two hands, see ibid., 107–108; Murata, *The Tao of Islam*, Chapter 3.

5. Jāmī, *Naqd*, 94.

6. Ibid., 95.

7. Ibid., 34ff.

8. Ibid., 92.

9. Ibid., 84.

10. Ibid., 110.

11. Ibid., 40. Cf. Chapter 11, where the last two names are "Generous" and "Just." For variations in formulations of the Seven Leaders, see Chittick, *The Sufi Path of Knowledge*, 408, n. 14.

12. Jāmī, *Naqd*, 216.

13. Ibid., 61.

14. Ibid., 85.

15. Ibid., 60–61.

16. Ibid., 91.

17. Ibid., 106.

18. Ibid., 103.

19. Ibid., 89.

20. Ibid., 97.

21. Ibid., 90–91.

22. Ibid., 101.

Notes to Chapter 14

1. Among the many important Sufis writing in this period, probably the most careful student of Ibn al-ʿArabī's works and the most faithful representative of his school of thought was Shaykh Muḥibb Allāh Mubāriz Ilāhābādī, who died twenty-four years after Sirhindī in 1058/1648. He wrote many works in Persian and a few in Arabic. Several of these works are based squarely on the text of Ibn al-ʿArabī's *Futūḥāt*, which does not seem to have been much studied by Ilāhābādī's contemporaries; he also wrote two commentaries on the *Fuṣūṣ*, a short commentary in Arabic and a much longer commentary in Persian. For an edition and translation of one of Shaykh Muḥibb Allāh's works, see Lipton, *The "Equivalence" (Al-Taswiya) of Muhibb Allah Ilahabadi*. A survey of the unpublished writings of numerous Indian authors inspired by Ibn al-ʿArabī and his followers can be found in Chittick, "Notes on Ibn al-ʿArabī's Influence in India."

2. See Ernst, *Eternal Garden*, Chapter 2. See also Ernst, *The Shambhala Guide to Sufism*, Chapter 1, which contains an important discussion of how the term Sufism came to be formulated by Western scholars working in the Indian context. This formulation, along with the reactions to it by modern-day Muslims, helps explain the peculiar ways

in which various attempts continue to be made—both by Muslims and non-Muslims—to detach Sufism from the heart of the Islamic tradition.

3. Rizvi's *The History of Sufism in India* is unfortunately no exception to this rule. Although it is an invaluable work for those who want to gain a rough idea of the important Sufi authors in the Indian Subcontinent, the statements about content are invariably superficial, and the information about the Sufi learned tradition that the author offers is based on the Western secondary literature, not his own reading of the texts that he enumerates.

4. See below. See also ibid., 2:149–150; Schimmel, *Islam in the Indian Subcontinent*, 91.

5. Khwāja Khurd, *Fawāʾiḥ*, mss. AMU Subhanullah 297.7/34[3]; AMU Habibganj 21/83; KH 3997.

6. Rizvi, *A History of Sufism in India*, 2:195.

7. Khwāja Khurd, *Rasāʾil*, 79–91 (*Nūr*), 92–100 (*Partaw*).

8. Khwāja Khurd, *Nūr*, mss. IIIS 3175; AP 906; KU 2601.

9. For an edition of the text, see Khwāja Khurd, *Risāla-yi ʿārif*.

10. This introductory paragraph is only to be found in the printed edition.

11. "Traveling in the homeland" is one of the eight Naqshbandī principles, while wayfaring is a term employed universally.

12. Here, ms. KU 2601 adds the following sentence in explanation: "that is, Oneness is the same as manyness, and manyness is the same as Oneness."

13. Here the printed edition adds two sentences that seem to be interpolations: "Hence Oneness is the same as manyness, and manyness is the same as Oneness. In other words, in his essence and attributes the worshiper, who dwells in manyness, is identical with Oneness in acts and effects."

14. For this famous Sufi pun, see ʿAṭṭār, *Manṭiq al-ṭayr*, lines 4236ff.

15. This paragraph is only found in the printed edition.

16. An allusion to the famous *ḥadīth qudsī* cited in Chapter 7.

17. I.e., the shaykhs of the Naqshbandī Order.

18. Apparently, this term is the opposite of *luqma-parhīzī*, which the dictionaries define as taking care to be sure that one's food follows the rules of lawful (*ḥalāl*) and unlawful (*ḥarām*).

Notes to Chapter 15

1. See Rizvi, *A History of Sufism in India*, 2:97, 289–290.

2. Ilāhābādī, *Suʾāl wa-jawāb*, ms. IIIS 2139.

3. Ilāhābādī, *Rūḥ wa-nafs*/*ʿUbūdat al-tazyīn*, mss. LK Maj. 31/2.; AMU Subhanullah 297.7/46[4].

4. Jāmī quotes the passage at *Naqd*, 28 and 201. One passage in Ilāhābādī's *Rūḥ*/*ʿUbūdat* seems to be paraphrased from Jāmī's *Lawāʾiḥ*.

5. See Tirmidhī, *A Treatise on the Heart*.

6. See, for example, section one of Ghazālī, *The Marvels of the Heart*. Ghazālī rewrote this section in Persian at the beginning of his *Kīmiyā*, 9ff., an extremely influential work in the Indian Subcontinent.

7. See Kāshānī, *Miṣbāḥ*, 80ff.

8. For a detailed discussion of the finely nuanced terminology employed in Islamic psychology, see Murata, *The Tao of Islam*, Chapters 8–10.

9. See Awn, *Satan's Tragedy and Redemption,* 60–69.

10. For which, see ibid., part three.

11. On the various aspects of the heart in Ibn al-ʿArabī's thought, see Chittick, *The Sufi Path of Knowledge,* index (under "heart"); Chittick, *The Self-Disclosure of God,* index (under "heart"); Corbin, *Creative Imagination in the Ṣūfism of Ibn 'Arabī,* 221–245; Ḥakīm, *Muʿjam,* 916–920; Morris, *The Reflective Heart,* 53–99.

12. Cited in Qādirī, *Miftāḥ,* 57.

13. Ibn al-ʿArabī and his followers frequently quote this verse as asserting the point of view of the overwhelming authority of God's unity, which erases all difference and otherness. See Chittick, *The Sufi Path of Knowledge,* 314, n. 6.

Notes to Chapter 16

1. Eaton, *Sufis of Bijapur,* 146. I have chosen to present this work here not because I think it the most important or the most interesting of the period, but because I happen to have a copy of an adequate manuscript, the work is relatively short and clearly written, and its contents are especially instructive concerning the overall teachings of Sufism. The manuscript I am using is OU 1047. Other manuscripts that I have seen include OU 752, SJ Tas. 232/5, SJ Tas. 250, and AP 30682. The work is reported to have been lithographed in Lucknow in 1898, but I have not seen the edition.

2. See Schimmel, *The Mystery of Numbers,* 245–252.

3. The tables in the manuscript I have seen have thirteen levels. However, the twelfth level is the same in each case—*haft shughl* or "seven occupations." I do not think that this is meant to be a level of its own, but rather the designation for the significance of the seven letters that are mentioned in the thirteenth level, given that each letter designates a specific "occupation," that is, ritual form or duty, that the Sufi should employ.

4. I am not yet sure what he has in mind with the term "five treasures" (*panj ganj*). Perhaps he means those enumerated in a short treatise of this name (ms. AP 1905/11, its more complete title being *Yak ganj az panj ganj*) by Muḥammad Makhdūm Sāwī, a prolific Qādirī author (also from Bijapur) whose dated works were written between 1108/1696 and 1123/1711. Sāwī explains these five treasures as the treasure of Eternity and the Unseen; the treasure of the created, nondelimited light, which is the Prophet Muhammad; the name Allah; the knowledge of self; and the Koran.

Notes to Chapter 17

1. Rūmī, *Mathnawī,* 1:2128.

2. Rūmī, *Dīwān,* line 35277.

3. See Chittick, *The Sufi Path of Love,* 35–37.

4. Rūmī, *Mathnawī,* 3:125. Cf. Chittick, *The Sufi Path of Love,* 264.

5. Despite the necessity of visionary knowledge on the path to God, Rūmī holds that love conquers all. It is love that delivers the prophets and saints, not only from their rational and individual limitations, but also from the light of the Universal Intellect inasmuch as that light is anything other than God. The Universal Intellect may be the very radiance of God Himself, but it is not identical with Him. Only love can bring about utter oneness.

6. Rūmī, *Mathnawī,* 4:4138–4139.

7. Rūmī, *Fīhi mā fīhi*, 107.

8. Rūmī, *Mathnawī*, 1:1234–1235, 1246. Cf. Chittick, *The Sufi Path of Love*, 62–63.

9. Rūmī, *Fīhi mā fīhi*, 156. Cf. Chittick, *The Sufi Path of Love*, 25–26; Rūmī, *Signs of the Unseen*, 162.

10. Rūmī, *Mathnawī*, 2:1039–1045. Cf. Chittick, *The Sufi Path of Love*, 252.

Notes to Chapter 18

1. For a lengthy introduction to Bābā Afḍal's life and thought, along with translations of more than half of his writings, see Chittick, *The Heart of Islamic Philosophy*.

2. See Hadot, *Philosophy as a Way of Life*, especially part two.

3. This treatise is translated in Chittick, *The Heart of Islamic Philosophy*, 171–174.

4. Cited in ibid., 171.

5. Cited in ibid. (with modifications).

6. Cited in ibid., 235–236.

7. Cited in ibid., 172 (with modifications).

8. Cited in ibid., 173 (with modifications).

9. Cited in ibid.

10. Cited in ibid., 274 (with modifications).

11. Cited in ibid. (with modifications).

12. Cited in ibid., 281 (with modifications).

13. Cited in ibid., 229 (with modifications).

14. Cited in ibid., 176 (with modifications).

Notes to Chapter 19

1. Ṣadrā, *Asfār*, 3:507 (CD-Rom)/323 (Lithograph). Since the lithograph edition is only partially paginated, I follow the pagination as given in Āyatī, *Fihrist*.

2. Ṣadrā, *Asfār*, 3:508/323.

3. Ibid., 3:515/325.

4. Ibid., 3:360–361/290.

5. The basic problem with "abstraction" is that the word totally loses the sense of the intensification of existence and reality that takes place as the degree of disengagement increases. See my discussion of the word in *The Heart of Islamic Philosophy*, 14–18.

6. As Ṣadrā puts it: "As for sensory perceptions, they are contaminated by ignorance. Attaining them is mixed with failure to find, for sense perception attains only the outward side of things and the molds of the quiddities, without their realities and their inward sides" (*Asfār*, 3:367/292).

7. Ibid., 3:361–362/290–291.

8. Ibid., 3:362/291.

9. Ibid., 3:501/322.

10. In discussing these four domains of existence, Ṣadrā continues by explaining that they are four worlds, and each is one of the divisions of knowledge, because at each level the known forms pertain to a different domain of existence. Then he describes the sorts of "possible perceptibles" that pertain to each while also clarifying what he means by dividing the first three levels into complete, sufficient, and deficient: "The first sort

of perceptible is 'complete' in existence and knowability. These are the intellects and the intelligibles. Because of the intensity of their existence, luminosity, and limpidness, they are quit of bodies, apparitions, and numbers. Despite their manyness and their plentifulness, they exist through one, all-gathering existence. . . . The second is the world of celestial souls, disengaged apparitions, and quantitative images. These are 'sufficient' through their essence and their intellective origins because, by means of their conjunction with the world of divine forms that are complete in existence, their deficiencies are mended and they are affiliated with them. Third is the world of sensory souls, the lower spiritual realm [*al-malakūt al-asfal*], and all forms sensible in act and perceived by the tools of awareness and the organs, which also belong to the lower spiritual realm. These are deficient in existence as long as they pertain to this world. However, they may be elevated beyond this world and become disengaged from it—as far as the world of disengaged apparitions—by following along with the human soul's climb to it. Fourth is the world of bodily matters and their forms, which are transient, disappearing, transforming, and undergoing generation and corruption" (ibid., 3:502–503/322). For Ṣadrā's division of the worlds in terms of the soul's three "perceptual configurations" (*nashaʾāt idrākiyya*), see ibid., 9:21/826.

11. In one passage, Ṣadrā explains that the obscurations from which people need to disengage themselves in order to achieve the intellection of a thing are "alien accidents" (*aʿrāḍ gharība*). He writes, "The alien accidents from which the human needs to disengage himself in intellecting a thing are not the quiddities and meanings of the things, since there is no contradiction between intellecting a thing and intellecting another attribute along with it. In the same way, the [alien accidents] from which one must disengage oneself in imagining things are not their imagined forms, since there is no contradiction between imagining something and imagining another guise [*hayʾa*] along with it. Rather, the preventer of some perceptions is certain modalities of the existent things. This preventer is dark and accompanied by nonexistences that veil their own unseen affairs from the perceptual means. An example is being [*kawn*] in matter, because the situational matter necessitates the veiling of the form from perception unconditionally. So also is being in sensation and imagination; these too may prevent intellective perception because they also are a quantitative existence, even if the quantity [*miqdār*] is disengaged from matter. But, the intelligible's existence is not quantitative existence, because it is disengaged from the two realms of being and stands beyond the two worlds" (ibid., 3:363/291).

12. Ibid., 8:40/732. Cf. ibid., 8:165/764, 8:251/785.

13. For example, "Perception is the presence of the perceptible for the perceiver" (ibid., 4:137/377); "Perception consists of the existence of something for something else and its presence for it" (ibid., 6:146/635); "Perception consists of the existence of a form present at an existent thing whose existence belongs to itself" (ibid., 8:163/764); "Perception is nothing but the soul's regard [*iltifāt*] toward and its witnessing the perceptible" (ibid., 6:162/573).

14. The discussion of "presence" in the context of perception is directly related to the issue of two sorts of knowledge often discussed in later Islamic philosophy—"presential" (*ḥuḍūrī*) and "obtained" (*ḥuṣūlī*). The fact that "presence" is synonymous with "witnessing" is typically ignored in the secondary literature, and this helps obscure the connection with the whole issue of "witnessing" in the writings of Ibn al-ʿArabī and his followers, for whom witnessing is synonymous with "unveiling" (*kashf*) and "direct seeing" (*ʿiyān*). Moreover, it is also a synonym of *wujūd* when this term is used to designate the highest possibilities of human perception, as in the common expression *ahl al-kashf*

wa-l-wujūd, "the folk of unveiling and finding." On Ibn al-ʿArabī's use of these terms, see Chittick, *The Sufi Path of Knowledge,* index.

15. Ṣadrā goes on to point out that these two designations—the unseen and the witnessed—pertain to our limited, this-worldly point of view, in which the intellect has not been actualized in its full splendor. In actual fact, he says, the next world is more intense in its existence than is this world, and everything more intense in existence is also more intense in presence, witnessing, and manifestation: "Every stratum of the Gardens that is more intense in quittance from this cosmos and greater in disengagement from and elevation beyond matter is more intense in manifestation and greater in gathering" (*Asfār,* 6:152/571).

16. Ibid., 1:266/65.

17. Ibid., 8:221/777.

18. Ibid.

19. Ibid., 3:515–516/326. One might object that the human soul is not in fact a "pure potentiality," because it is born with instincts or innate knowledge. I think Ṣadrā would reply by reminding us that what we call by names such as "instincts" do not pertain to the *human* soul, but rather to the vegetal and animal souls. It is true that there can be no human soul without a vegetal and animal soul, but the discussion of unlimited potential pertains strictly to the human soul, not to other dimensions of human existence. The "humanness" of the human soul is precisely that point where human beings are indefinable and unfixed and, by that very fact, capable of becoming all things.

20. Ibid., 8:251/785.

21. Ibid., 1:287/70.

22. Ibid., 8:179–180/768.

23. Cf. ibid., 1:289–290/71: "When the soul perceives the universal intelligibles, it witnesses them as intellective, disengaged essences. But this is not by the soul's disengaging them and its extracting [*intizāʿ*] their intelligible form from their sensory form—as is held by the majority of the sages. Rather, it takes place through a transferal that belongs to the soul—from the sensory, to the imaginal, to the intelligible; and through a migration from this world to the next world, and then to what lies beyond it; and through a journey from the world of bodies to the world of images, then to the world of the intellects."

24. Ibid., 8:81/768. Cf. Rahman, *The Philosophy of Mullā Ṣadrā,* 224.

25. Ṣadrā, *Asfār,* 1:387/96; 8:160/763; 8:253/786; 8:301/798.

26. The reason that the soul is potentially all things is that it is an image of existence per se. This, in philosophical terms, is the meaning of the hadith, "God created Adam in His own form." Ṣadrā employs some of the standard theological language in this explanation of the soul's nature: "The Author [*al-bāriʾ*] is the creator of the existents, both the innovated and engendered [that is, the spiritual and corporeal]. He created the human soul as an image [*mithāl*] of His Essence, His attributes, and His acts—for He is incomparable with any likeness [*mithl*], but not with an image. Thus He created the soul as an image of Him in essence, attributes, and acts, so that knowledge of it would be a ladder to knowledge of Him. He made the soul's essence disengaged from engendered beings, spatial confinements, and directions. He made it become the possessor of power, knowledge, desire, life, hearing, and seeing. He made it the possessor of an empire similar to the empire of its Author. He *creates what He desires and chooses* [28:68] for the sake of what He desires. However, although the soul derives from the root of the spiritual realm, the world of power, and the mine of magnificence and ascendancy, it is weak in

existence and endurance because it has fallen into the levels of the descent, and it has intermediaries between it and its Author" (ibid., 1:265–266/65).

27. Ibid., 8:253/786.

28. Ibid., 3:373/293.

29. In criticizing the earlier philosophers on the issue of disengagement, Ṣadrā no doubt wanted to avoid the severe criticism leveled against the concept by Ibn al-ʿArabī. See, for example, Chittick, *The Self-Disclosure of God*, 346–347. Cf. Qūnawī's critique of the concept cited in Murata, *The Tao of Islam*, 221–222.

30. Ṣadrā, *Asfār*, 3:366/292.

31. Ibid., 9:98/846. Cf. ibid., 9:99–100/846: "In short, the state of the soul in the level of its disengagement is like the state of the external perceptible when it becomes a sensible thing, then an imaginalized thing, then an intelligible thing. It is said that every perception has a sort of disengagement, and that the levels of perception are disparate in respect of the levels of disengagement. The meaning of this is as we said: The disengagement of the perceptible does not consist of throwing off some of its attributes and leaving others. Rather, it consists of the alteration of the lower, more deficient existence into the higher, more eminent existence. In the same way, the human's disengagement and transferal from this world to the next is nothing but the alteration of the first configuration into a second configuration. So also, when the soul is perfected and it becomes an intellect in act, it is not that some of its potencies—like the sense-perceptual—are stripped from it and that others—like the intellective—remain. On the contrary, as the soul is perfected and its essence elevated, the other potencies are likewise perfected and elevated along with it."

Notes to Chapter 20

1. Cited in Taftāzānī, *Sharḥ*, 76–82. See also Elder's translation of the passage in Taftāzānī, *A Commentary on the Creed of Islam*, 99, 165.

2. Quḍāʿī, *Musnad*, 2:303. Cf. Ghazālī, *The Remembrance of Death and the Afterlife*, 10.

3. Majlisī, *Biḥār*, 6:234.

4. Tirmidhī, Qiyāma 26.

5. See Ghazālī, *Iḥyāʾ*, 4:370 (Cairo).

6. Majlisī, *Biḥār*, 7:250.

7. Ibid., 7:314–315.

8. Ibn Kathīr, *Tafsīr*, 6:494.

9. Majlisī, *Biḥār*, 5:60, 97, 101, 112.

10. Cited in Ghazālī, *The Remembrance of Death and the Afterlife*, 218, with a slight modification.

11. Majlisī, *Biḥār*, 8:34.

12. Ibid., 8:47, 64.

13. Ibid., 8:64.

14. Cf. ibid., 6:300.

15. Cf. ibid., 51:161. Cf. ibid., 51:66, 74.

16. Kāshānī, *Miṣbāḥ*, 49.

17. Ghazālī, *Kīmiyā*, 98.

18. Ghazālī, *Arbaʿīn*, 275.

19. Rāzī, *The Path of God's Bondsmen from Origin to Return*, 389–393.

20. Jāmī, *Haft awrang*, 109.

21. Ṣadrā, *Asfār*, 857 (Lithograph).

22. Rāzī, *The Path of God's Bondsmen from Origin to Return*, 363, with minor changes.

23. Nasafī, *Zubdat*, 325–327.

24. Avicenna, *Najāt*, 293. Cf. Arberry's translation of this passage in Avicenna, *Avicenna on Theology*, 67.

25. Cited in Meier, "The Problem of Nature in the Esoteric Monism of Islam," 195, n. 141.

26. Sanāʾī, *Ḥadīqat*, 382.

27. Rūmī, *Fīhi mā fīhi*, 77. Cf. Chittick, *The Sufi Path of Love*, 206–212.

28. Sulṭān Walad, *Walad-nāma*, 261.

29. Rūmī, *Dīwān*, line 6400. Cf. Chittick, *The Sufi Path of Love*, 212.

30. Ibn al-ʿArabī, *The "Tarjumān al-ashwāq,"* 67.

31. Ibn al-ʿArabī, *Fuṣūṣ*, 121. See also Chittick, *Imaginal Worlds*, Chapters 9 and 10.

32. Ṣadrā, *The Wisdom of the Throne*, 148–149, with minor changes.

33. Ṣadrā, cited in Āshtiyānī, *Sharḥ bar Zād al-musāfir*, 218, 244.

34. Rahman, *Major Themes of the Qurʾān*, 17, 112.

35. Ibn al-ʿArabī, *Futūḥāt*, 2:627 (Beirut).

36. Ibn al-ʿArabī, *Futūḥāt*, 3:187–188 (Beirut). Cf. Chittick, *The Sufi Path of Love*, 71–72.

37. Ṣadrā, *Asfār*, 853 (Lithograph).

38. See Ṣadrā, *The Wisdom of the Throne*, 161ff.

39. Ibn al-ʿArabī, *Futūḥāt*, 3:361 (Beirut).

40. See Jāmī, *Naqd*, 56–57.

41. For Ṣadrā's commentary on this hadith, see Rustom, "Psychology, Eschatology, and Imagination in Mullā Ṣadrā Shīrāzī's Commentary on the *Ḥadīth* of Awakening."

42. Ṣadrā, *The Wisdom of the Throne*, 163.

43. Ṣadrā, *Asfār*, 853 (Lithograph).

44. Ṭūsī, *The Nasirean Ethics*, 95, with minor changes. Cf. Avicenna, *Avicenna On Theology*, 72; Ghazālī, *Iḥyāʾ*, 3:39–40 (Cairo).

45. Ghazālī, *Maḍnūn*, 2:160.

46. Ghazālī, *Freedom and Fulfillment*, 377, with minor changes. Cf. Ṣadrā, *The Wisdom of the Throne*, 146.

47. Ghazālī, *Freedom and Fulfillment*, 349.

48. Farghānī, *Muntahā*, 2:82; *Mashāriq*, 467–468. Concerning the name the All-Compassionate, note the Koranic distinction pointed out by Ibn al-ʿArabī between the "mercy of gratuitous gift," given to all creatures, and the "mercy of prescription," given to the believers. See Chittick, "Ibn ʿArabī's own Summary of the *Fuṣūṣ*," 62.

49. Jīlī, *al-Insān al-kāmil*, 2:30.

50. See Wensinck, *The Muslim Creed* 126, 142ff.

51. Chittick, "Ibn ʿArabī's own Summary of the *Fuṣūṣ*," 61.

52. Niffarī, *Mukhāṭabāt*, 183. Cf. Niffarī, *Mawāqif*, 36, 120–121.

53. Schuon, *Understanding Islam*, 71, 73.

54. Niffarī, *Mawāqif*, 41.

55. Ibn al-ʿArabī, *Futūḥāt*, 4:389 (Cairo).

56. See Chittick, "Ibn al-ʿArabī's Hermeneutics of Mercy"; Ibn al-ʿArabī, *Fuṣūṣ*, Chapter 7; *Futūḥāt*, 3:67 (Cairo); *Futūḥāt*, 3:315, 328, 389 (Beirut); Smith and Haddad, *The Islamic Understanding of Death and Resurrection*, 95.

57. Smith, "The Understanding of Nafs and Ruh in Contemporary Muslim Considerations of the Nature of Sleep and Death," 153–154.

58. Bukhārī, Ta'bīr 2ff.; Muslim, Ru'yā 6ff.

59. Ghazālī, *Maḍnūn*, 166. Cf. Ghazālī, *Arba'īn*, 291; *Kīmiyā*, 93; Ibn al-'Arabī, *Futūḥāt*, 3:198 (Beirut).

60. Ghazālī, *Arab'īn*, 290. Cf. Ghazālī, *The Remembrance of Death and the Afterlife*, 153; *Kīmiyā*, 93–94.

61. Ibid., 94.

62. Ibid. Cf. Ghazālī, *Arba'īn*, 291.

63. Ibid., 282. Cf. Ghazālī, *Kīmiyā*, 85; *The Remembrance of Death and the Afterlife*, 138.

64. Ghazālī, *Maḍnūn*, 158.

65. Ṭūsī, *The Nasirean Ethics*, 138.

66. Rūmī, *Mathnawī*, 3:3441–3442.

67. Sanā'ī, *Dīwān*, 708.

68. Rūmī, *Dīwān*, lines 20435–20436. See also Chittick, *The Sufi Path of Love*, 101–107.

69. Rūmī, *Mathnawī*, 2:277–278. Cf. Chittick, *The Sufi Path of Love*, 56.

70. 'Ayn al-Quḍāt, *Tamhīdāt*, 287, 289. For a good summary of this whole discussion, see Lāhījī, *Sharḥ-i Gulshan-i rāz*, 521–527.

71. Ghazālī, *Iḥyā'*, 4:46–47 (Cairo). Cf. Ghazālī, *The Remembrance of Death and the Afterlife*, 184–185.

72. Maqṣūd, *Sharḥ-i aḥwāl*, 403.

73. Āmulī, *Asrār*, 104–136.

74. Jīlī, *al-Insān al-kāmil*, 2:49–52.

75. Ibn al-'Arabī, *Futūḥāt*, 3:250 (Beirut).

76. Ibn al-'Arabī, *Futūḥāt*, 4:456–457 (Cairo). See also Chittick, *Imaginal Worlds*, Chapter 7; Rustom, "Psychology, Eschatology, and Imagination in Mullā Ṣadrā Shīrāzī's Commentary on the *Ḥadīth* of Awakening."

77. Ibn al-'Arabī, *Futūḥāt*, 4:424 (Cairo).

78. Ghazālī, *Kīmiyā*, 80.

79. Rāzī, *The Path of God's Bondsmen from Origin to Return*, 391–392.

80. Qūnawī, *Nafaḥāt*, 115.

81. Sanā'ī, *Ḥadīqa*, 380.

82. Rūmī, *Mathnawī*, 2:1416–1419. Cf. Chittick, *The Sufi Path of Love*, 104.

83. Fārābī, *Alfarabi's Philosophy of Plato and Aristotle*, 64.

84. Aḥsā'ī, *Mujlī*, 506–507.

85. Ṣadrā, *The Wisdom of the Throne*, 145–147.

86. Qūnawī, *Nafaḥāt*, 116; Āshtiyānī, *Sharḥ bar Zād al-musāfir*, 56, 122–123, 128.

87. Avicenna, *Avicenna on Theology*, 69ff. Cf. Suhrawardī, *The Philosophy of Illumination*, 148ff.

88. Avicenna, *Risāla aḍḥawiyya*, 60–62. Cf. Averroës, *Tahāfut al-tahāfut*, 1:361.

89. Sulṭān Walad, *Walad-nāma*, 298.

90. Ghazālī, *Arba'īn*, 288–297; *Kīmiyā*, 91–96, 98.

91. See Tabrīzī, *Mishkāt*, 1197, 1200.

92. Ibn al-'Arabī, *Futūḥāt*, 5:77 (Cairo).

93. For hadiths on God's laughter, see Chapter 3.

94. Massignon, *The Passion of al-Ḥallāj*, 3:166–167.

95. Ibn 'Arabī, *Futuḥāt*, 2:628 (Beirut).

Notes to Chapter 21

1. Tymieniecka, "Differentiation and Unity," 9.
2. Ibid., 28.
3. Ibn al-ʿArabī, *Futūḥāt*, 4:85 (Beirut).
4. Ibid., 2:107.
5. Ibid., 3:324.
6. Ibid.
7. Ibn al-ʿArabī's arguments about the primacy of life among the divine attributes has striking analogies with the explications of the primacy of breath (*praña*) among the divinities in the *Brhadaranyaka Upanishad* (1.3.1–18, 6.1) and the *Chandogya Upanishad* (5.1–2).
8. Ibn al-ʿArabī, *Futūḥāt*, 2:107 (Beirut).
9. Cited in my introduction to Ṣadrā, *The Elixir of the Gnostics*, xxiv.
10. Cited, along with several other relevant passages, in Chittick, *Imaginal Worlds*, Chapter 7.
11. Ṣadrā, *ʿArshiyya*, 252. For this passage in context, see Ṣadrā, *The Wisdom of the Throne*, 165.

Notes to Chapter 22

1. Cited in Chittick, *The Heart of Islamic Philosophy*, 206.
2. Cited in ibid., 150–151.

Notes to Chapter 23

1. For the sense in which the word "unbeliever(s)" figures in this volume, see Chapter 1.
2. See Maybudī, *Kashf*, 6:405.
3. See Ghazālī, *Iḥyāʾ*, 3:42, 57 (Cairo).

Notes to Chapter 24

1. The most vocal exception to this rule is S. H. Nasr, one of the first to point to the importance of the environmental crisis and the spiritual malaise that lies behind it. For Nasr's most extensive treatment of the topic, see his *Religion and the Order of Nature*.
2. Though man is "active" in relation to nature in his role as vicegerent (whether or not he fulfills it), he is "passive" inasmuch as it manifests God's signs and thereby plays a revelatory role. Though man is nature's steward, he is also in need of the wisdom it imparts to reach the full perfection of the human state. It is in this doctrine of signs that close parallels are to be found between the Islamic view of nature and the Red Indian concept that man must learn from all living things.

Notes to Chapter 25

1. Neither of these hadiths is found in the most authoritative sources, but that is not the issue. The issue is rather that they represent a typically Islamic way of looking at things, which explains why they are well-known and often quoted.

2. There is, of course, the common Islamic belief that a later message abrogates (*naskh*) an earlier message, but this finds no strong support in the Koran. Quite the contrary, the Koran repeatedly stresses that the later messages confirm and strengthen (*taʾyīd*) the earlier messages. If we want to escape from exclusivist readings here, we need to let the Koran say what it says. When it affirms that *Every nation has a messenger* (10:47), this means that prophecy is a phenomenon that appears wherever there have been human beings. Moreover, the specific prophetic history that the Koran addresses is Abrahamic. Even if one can argue that the Koran abrogates earlier Abrahamic messages—and this is highly debatable—why should it abrogate messages addressed to religious worlds that stand outside the Abrahamic dispensation?

3. To put this somewhat differently, in the Koran, two divine attributes are said to "embrace" (*wasiʿa*) all things. One of these attributes is knowledge (6:80, 7:89, 20:98) and the other is mercy (7:156). In one verse, these two attributes are brought together. In it, the angels address God and say, *"Our Lord, You embrace everything in mercy and knowledge"* (40:7). Many commentators have thought that the order of the attributes here is no accident, because the divine mercy that embraces all things is precisely the divine reality in terms of which He knows all things. The existence of things is predicated on God's knowledge that they will be given existence, but God's knowledge of the things is predicated on His own Being and reality. Hence the manyness of the universe is predicated on the oneness of God's reality. The One gives rise to the many, which is to say that *qurʾān* gives birth to *furqān*. Then, in the cosmos, *furqān* prepares the way for the return to *qurʾān*.

Notes to Chapter 26

1. For the teachings of this school of thought, see Murata, *Chinese Gleams of Sufi Light*. For the history of the school, see Ben-Dor Benite, *The Dao of Muhammad*.

2. For a slightly different translation, see Chan, *Instructions for Practical Living and Other Neo-Confucian Writings by Wang Yang-Ming*, 257; Chan et al. (eds.), *A Source Book in Chinese Philosophy*, 690.

3. See Tu, *Confucian Thought*.

4. One of the foremost examples is provided by Liu Zhi, who in 1704 published a book called *Tianfang xingli* ("Nature and Principle in Islam"), which became the standard exposition of the Muslim worldview in Chinese for two hundred years. See Murata, Chittick, and Tu, *The Sage Learning of Liu Zhi*.

5. For another translation, see Chan et al. (eds.), *A Source Book in Chinese Philosophy*, 580. Ben-Dor Benite points to the popularity of this passage among Muslim scholars in *The Dao of Muhammad*, 166–167.

6. On the importance of Rāzī's book among the Chinese, see ibid., 86–88, 130–133; Murata, *Chinese Gleams of Sufi Light*, 32.

I say "human beings in general" not only because of the obvious symbolic significance of Adam as the father of the human race, and the repeated use of the word in

Arabic discussions to mean *insān* ("man," or human beings), but also because of Koranic passages that make the identification. For example, the Koran addresses human beings in general (with "you" in the plural) in these terms: *We established you in the earth and there appointed for you a livelihood; little thanks you show. We created you, then We shaped you, then We said to the angels, "Prostrate yourselves to Adam"* (7:10–11).

8. Cited in Chittick, *Me & Rumi*, 191.

Bibliography

Listed here are the works cited throughout this book, excluding the Editors' Introduction.

Adamson, Peter. *The Arabic Plotinus: A Philosophical Study of the 'Theology of Aristotle.'* London: Duckworth, 2002.

Aflākī, Shams al-Dīn. *The Feats of the Knowers of God*. Translated by John O'Kane. Leiden: Brill, 2002.

Aḥmad b. Ḥanbal. *al-Musnad*. Beirut: Dār Ṣādir, n.d.

Aḥsāʾī, Ibn Abī Jumhūr. *al-Mujlī*. Tehran: Aḥmad Shīrāzī, 1911.

Akasoy, A. A. *Philosophie und Mystik in der späten Almohadenzeit: Die Sizilianischen Fragen des Ibn Sabʿīn*. Leiden: Brill, 2006.

Āmulī, Ḥaydar. *Asrār al-sharīʿa wa-aṭwār al-ṭarīqa wa-anwār al-ḥaqīqa*. Edited by Muḥammad Khwājawī. Tehran: Muʾassasa-yi Muṭālaʿāt wa-Taḥqīqāt-i Farhangī, 1983.

Anṣārī, ʿAbd Allāh. *Intimate Conversations*. Translated by W. M. Thackston. Published along with Ibn ʿAṭāʾ Allāh, *The Book of Wisdom*. New York: Paulist Press, 1978.

———. *Majmūʿa-yi rasāʾil-i fārsī*. Edited by M. S. Mawlāʾī. Tehran: Tūs, 1998.

———. *Ṭabaqāt al-ṣūfiyya*. Edited by ʿA. Ḥ. Ḥabībī. Kabul: Maṭbaʿa-yi Dawlatī, 1962.

Asad, Muhammad. *The Message of the Qurʾān*. Gibraltar: Dar al-Andalus, 1980.

Āshtiyānī, S. J. *Sharḥ-i Muqaddima-yi Qayṣarī*. Mashhad: Kitābfurūshī-yi Bāstān, 1966.

———. *Sharḥ bar Zād al-musāfir-i Mullā Ṣadrā: Maʿād-i jismānī*. 2nd ed. Tehran: Imperial Iranian Academy of Philosophy, 1980.

——— (ed.). *Uthūlūjiyā*. Tehran: Imperial Iranian Academy of Philosophy, 1976.

Ateş, Ahmed. "Konya kütüphanelerind bulunan bazi mühim yazmalar." *Belleten* 16 (1952), 49–130.

ʿAṭṭār, Farīd al-Dīn. *Dīwān-i ʿAṭṭār*. Edited by Taqī Tafaḍḍulī. Tehran: Bungāh-i Tarjama wa-Nashr-i Kitāb, 1966.

———. *Manṭiq al-ṭayr: Maqāmāt al-ṭuyūr*. Edited by Sayyid Ṣādiq Gawharīn. Tehran: Shirkat-i Intishārāt-i ʿIlmī wa-Farhangī, 1968.

Avicenna. *Avicenna on Theology*. Translated by A. J. Arberry. London: John Murray, 1951.

———. *Kitāb al-najāt*. Cairo: Maṭbaʿat al-Saʿāda, 1938.

———. *The Metaphysics of the Healing*. Translated by Michael Marmura. Provo: Brigham Young University Press, 2005.

———. *Risāla aḍḥawiyya fī amr al-maʿād*. Edited by Sulaymān Dunyā. Cairo: Dār al-Fikr al-ʿArabī, 1949.

Averroës. *Tahāfut al-tahāfut*. Translated by Simon van den Bergh. London: Luzac, 1969.

Awn, Peter. *Satan's Tragedy and Redemption: Iblīs in Ṣūfī Psychology*. Leiden: Brill, 1983.

Āyatī, M. I. *Fihrist-i abwāb wa-fuṣūl-i kitāb-i Asfār*. Tehran: Chāpkhāna-yi Dānishgāh-i Tihrān, 1961. Also in *Yād-nāma-yi Mullā Ṣadrā*. Edited by S. H. Nasr. Tehran: Chāpkhāna-yi Dānishgāh-i Tihrān, 1961, 63–106.

Badawī, ʿA. R. *Aflūṭīn ʿinda al-ʿarab*. Cairo: Dār al-Nahḍa al-ʿArabiyya, 1966.

Bahāʾ Walad. *Maʿārif*. Edited by B. Furūzānfar. Tehran: Wizārat-i Farhang, 1954.

Balyānī, Awḥad al-Dīn. *Epître sur l'unicité absolue*. Translated by Michel Chodkiewicz. Paris: Deux océans, 1982.

Baqlī, Rūzbihān. *Mashrab al-arwāḥ*. Edited by N. M. Hoca. Istanbul: Edebiyat Fakültesi Matbaasi, 1974.

Ben-Dor Benite, Zvi. *The Dao of Muhammad: A Cultural History of Muslims in Late Imperial China*. Cambridge, MA: Harvard University Press, 2005.

Bīrūnī, Abū Rayḥān al-. *Kitāb fī taḥqīq mā li-l-hind*. Hyderabad-Deccan: Dāʾirat al-Maʿārif al-ʿUthmāniyya, 1958. Translated by E. C. Sachau as *Alberuni's India*. Delhi: S. Chand, 1964.

Browne, E. G. *A Literary History of Persia*. Cambridge: Cambridge University Press, 1964–1969.

Bukhārī, al-. *al-Ṣaḥīḥ*. N.p.: Maṭābiʿ al-Shuʿab, 1958–1959.

Burckhardt, Titus. *An Introduction to Sufi Doctrine*. Lahore: Sh. Muhammad Ashraf, 1959. Reprinted as *Introduction to Sufi Doctrine*. Bloomington: World Wisdom, 2008.

Chan, Wing-Tsit. *Instructions for Practical Living and Other Neo-Confucian Writings by Wang Yang-Ming*. New York: Columbia University Press, 1963.

Chan, Wing-Tsit et al. (eds.). *A Source Book in Chinese Philosophy*. Princeton: Princeton University Press, 1963.

Chittick, W. C. "ʿAql (in Persian Literature)." In *Encyclopaedia Iranica*, 2:195–198.

———. "The Central Point: Qūnawī's Role in the School of Ibn ʿArabī." *Journal of the Muhyiddin Ibn 'Arabi Society* 35 (2004), 25–45. Available online at www.ibnarabisociety.org

———. "The Divine Roots of Human Love." *Journal of the Muhyiddin Ibn 'Arabi Society* 17 (1995), 55–78. Available online at www.ibnarabisociety.org

———. "Ebno'l-'Arabi as Lover." *Sufi* 9 (1991), 6–9.

———. *Faith and Practice of Islam: Three Thirteenth Century Sufi Texts*. Albany: State University of New York Press, 1992.

———. "The Five Divine Presences: From al-Qūnawī to al-Qayṣarī." *Muslim World* 72/2 (1982), 107–128.

———. *The Heart of Islamic Philosophy: The Quest for Self-Knowledge in the Teachings of Afḍal al-Dīn Kāshānī*. New York: Oxford University Press, 2001.

———. "Ibn al-ʿArabī's Hermeneutics of Mercy." In *Mysticism and Sacred Scripture*. Edited by Stephen Katz. Oxford: Oxford University Press, 2000, 153–168. Also in Chittick, *Ibn 'Arabi: Heir to the Prophets*. Oxford: Oneworld, 2005, Chapter 9.

———. "Ibn ʿArabī's own Summary of the *Fuṣūṣ*: 'The Imprint of the Bezels of Wisdom'." *Sophia Perennis* 1/2 (1975), 88–128; 2/1 (1976), 67–106. Also in *Journal of the Muhyiddin Ibn 'Arabi Society* 1 (1982), 30–93. Available online at www.ibnarabisociety.org

———. "Ibn 'Arabi and Rumi." *Sacred Web* 13 (2004), 33–45.

———. *Imaginal Worlds: Ibn al-ʿArabī and the Problem of Religious Diversity*. Albany: State University of New York Press, 1994.

———. "The Last Will and Testament of Ibn al-ʿArabī's Foremost Disciple and Some Notes on its Author." *Sophia Perennis* 4/1 (1978), 43–58. Available online at www.ibnarabisociety.org

———. *Me & Rumi: The Autobiography of Shams-i Tabrizi*. Louisville: Fons Vitae, 2004.

———. "The Myth of Adam's Fall in Aḥmad Samʿānī's *Rawḥ al-arwāḥ*." In *The Heritage of Sufism*. Edited by Leonard Lewisohn (vol. 1–3) and David Morgan (vol. 3). Oxford: Oneworld, 1999, 1:337–359. Also in Chittick, *Sufism: A Short Introduction*. Oxford: Oneworld, 2000, Chapter 9.

———. "Mysticism vs. Philosophy in Earlier Islamic History: The Ṭūsī, al-Qūnawī Correspondence." *Religious Studies* 17 (1981), 43–58.

———. "Notes on Ibn al-ʿArabī's Influence in India." *Muslim World* 82/3–4 (1992), 218–241.

———. "Rūmī and the Mawlawiyyah." In *Islamic Spirituality: Manifestations*. Edited by S. H. Nasr. New York: Crossroad, 1991, 105–126.

———. "Ṣadr al-Dīn Qūnawī on the Oneness of Being." *International Philosophical Quarterly* 21 (1981), 171–184.

———. "The School of Ibn ʿArabī." In *History of Islamic Philosophy*. Edited by S. H. Nasr and Oliver Leaman. London: Routledge, 1996, 1:510–523.

———. *The Self-Disclosure of God: Principles of Ibn al-ʿArabī's Cosmology*. Albany: State University of New York Press, 1998.

———. *A Shi'ite Anthology*. Albany: State University of New York Press, 1981. Available online at www.al-islam.org

———. *The Sufi Doctrine of Rumi*. Bloomington: World Wisdom, 2005.

———. *The Sufi Path of Knowledge: Ibn al-ʿArabī's Metaphysics of Imagination*. Albany: State University of New York Press, 1989.

———. *The Sufi Path of Love: The Spiritual Teachings of Rumi*. Albany: State University of New York Press, 1983.

———. "Waḥdat al-Shuhūd." In *Encyclopaedia of Islam*², 10:37–39.

Chodkiewicz, Michel. *An Ocean Without Shore: Ibn 'Arabî, the Book, and the Law*. Translated by David Streight. Albany: State University of New York Press, 1993.

Corbin, Henry. *Creative Imagination in the Ṣūfism of Ibn 'Arabī*. Translated by Ralph Manheim. Princeton: Princeton University Press, 1969.

Cornell, Vincent. "The All-Comprehensive Circle (*al-iḥāṭa*): Soul, Intellect, and the Oneness of Existence in the Doctrine of Ibn Sabʿīn." In *Sufism and Theology*. Edited by Ayman Shihadeh. Edinburgh: Edinburgh University Press, 2007, 31–48.

Eaton, Richard. *Sufis of Bijapur, 1300–1700: Social Roles of Sufis in Medieval India*. Princeton: Princeton University Press, 1978.

Elmore, Gerald. "Ṣadr al-Dīn al-Qūnawī's Personal Study-List of Books by Ibn al-ʿArabī." *Journal of Near Eastern Studies* 56/3 (1997), 161–181.

Ernst, Carl. *Eternal Garden: Mysticism, History, and Politics at a South Asian Sufi Center*. Albany: State University of New York Press, 1992.

———. *The Shambhala Guide to Sufism*. Boston: Shambhala, 1997.

Fārābī, al-. *Alfarabi's Philosophy of Plato and Aristotle*. Translated by Muhsin Mahdi. New York: Free Press of Glencoe, 1962.

Farghānī, Saʿīd al-Dīn. *Mashāriq al-darārī*. Edited by S. J. Āshtiyānī. Mashhad: Chāpkhāna-yi Dānishgāh-i Mashhad, 1978.

———. *Muntahā'l-madārik*. Cairo: ʿA. R. al-Bukhārī, 1876.

Friedmann, Yohanan. *Shaykh Aḥmad Sirhindī: An Outline of His Thought and a Study of His Image in the Eyes of Posterity*. Montreal: McGill University, Institute of Islamic Studies, 1971.

Gardet, Louis. "Īmān." In *Encyclopaedia of Islam*², 3:1170–1174.

Ghallāb, Muḥammad. "al-Maʿrifa ʿinda Muḥyī al-Dīn Ibn al-ʿArabī." In *al-Kitāb al-tadhkārī: Muḥyī al-Dīn Ibn al-ʿArabī*. Edited by Ibrahim Madkur. Cairo: Dār al-Kitāb al-ʿArabī, 1969, 183–220.

Ghazālī, Abū Ḥāmid al-. *Kitāb al-arbaʿīn fī uṣūl al-dīn*. Edited by M. M. Abū'l-ʿIlā. Cairo: Maktabat al-Jundī, 1970.

———. *Bidāyat al-hidāya*. Cairo: ʿĪsā al-Bābī al-Ḥalabī, n.d. Translated in W. M. Watt, *The Faith and Practice of al-Ghazālī*. Lahore: Sh. Muhammad Ashraf, 1963, 86–152.

———. *The Book of Knowledge*. Translated by N. A. Faris. Lahore: Sh. Muhammad Ashraf, 1963.

———. *Freedom and Fulfillment: An Annotated Translation of al-Munqidh min al-Ḍalāl and Other Relevant Works of al-Ghazalī*. Translated by R. J. McCarthy. Boston: Twayne, 1980. Reprinted as *Deliverance from Error: An Annotated Translation of al-Munqidh min al-Ḍalāl and Other Relevant Works of al-Ghazalī*. Louisville: Fons Vitae, 1999.

———. *Iḥyāʾ ʿulūm al-dīn*. Beirut: Dār al-Hādī, 1992; Cairo: Maṭbaʿat al-ʿĀmira al-Sharafiyya, 1908–1909.

———. *Inner Dimensions of Islamic Worship*. Translated by Muhtar Holland. Leicester: The Islamic Foundation, 1983.

———. *Kīmiyā-yi saʿādat*. Edited by Aḥmad Ārām. Tehran: Chāpkhāna-yi Markazī, 1954.

———. *al-Maḍnūn bihi ʿalā ghayr ahlihi*. In *al-Quṣūr al-ʿawālī li-Abī Ḥāmid Muḥammad al-Ghazzālī*. Edited by M. M. Abū'l-ʿIlā. Cairo: Maktabat al-Jundī, 1970.

———. *The Marvels of the Heart*. Translated by W. J. Skellie. Louisville: Fons Vitae, 2010.

———. *Mishkāt al-anwār*. Edited by A. E. Afifi. Cairo: al-Dār al-Qawmiyya, 1964. Translated by David Buchman as *The Niche of Lights*. Provo: Brigham Young University Press, 1998.

———. *The Remembrance of Death and the Afterlife*. Translated by T. J. Winter. Cambridge: Islamic Texts Society, 1989.

Ghazālī, Aḥmad al-. *Sawāniḥ: Inspirations from the World of Pure Spirits*. Translated by Nasrollah Pourjavady. London: Kegan Paul International, 1986.

Gramlich, Richard. "Mystical Dimensions of Islamic Monotheism." In *We Believe in One God: The Experience of God in Christianity and Islam*. Edited by Annemarie Schimmel and Abdoldjavad Falaturi. Translated by Gerald Blacszak and Annemarie Schimmel. London: Burns and Oates, 1979, 136–148.

Hadot, Pierre. *Philosophy as a Way of Life: Spiritual Exercises from Socrates to Foucault*. Edited by A. I. Davidson. Translated by Michael Chase. Malden: Blackwell, 1995.

———. *Plotinus, or the Simplicity of Vision*. Translated by Michael Chase. Chicago: University of Chicago Press, 1993.

Ḥakīm, Suʿād. *al-Muʿjam al-ṣūfī*. Beirut: Dandara, 1981.

Hamadānī, ʿAyn al-Quḍāt. *Muṣannafāt-i ʿAyn al-Quḍāt Hamadānī*. Edited by ʿAfīf ʿUsayrān. Tehran: Chāpkhāna-yi Dānishgāh-i Tihrān, 1962.

———. *The Tamhīdāt of ʿAyn al-Quḍāt al-Hamadānī*. Translated by Omid Safi. New York: Paulist Press, forthcoming.

Ḥammūya, Saʿd al-Dīn. *al-Misbāḥ fī-l-taṣawwuf*. Edited by N. M. Hirawī. Tehran: Intishārāt-i Mawlā, 1983.

Hātif, Sayyid Aḥmad. *Dīwān-i Hātif Iṣfahānī*. Edited by Maḥmūd Shāhrukhī and Muḥammad ʿAlī-Dūst. Tehran: Intishārāt-i Mishkāt, 1992.

Ḥusayn, ʿAlī b. al-. *The Psalms of Islam*. Translated by W. C. Chittick. London: The Muhammadi Trust, 1988. Available online at www.al-islam.org

Ibn al-ʿArabī. *Dhakhāʾir al-aʿlāq*. Edited by M. R. al-Kurdī. Cairo, 1968.

———. *Fuṣūṣ al-ḥikam*. Edited by A. E. Afifi. Cairo: Dār Iḥyā᾽ al-Kutub al-ʿArabiyya, 1946. Translated by R. W. J. Austin as *The Bezels of Wisdom*. New York: Paulist Press, 1980. Translated by Caner Dagli as *The Ringstones of Wisdom*. Chicago: Kazi, 2004.

———. *al-Futūḥāt al-makkiyya*. Beirut: Dār Ṣādir, n.d. Partial critical edition by Osman Yahia. Cairo: al-Hay᾽a al-Miṣriyya al-ʿĀmma li-l-Kitāb, 1972–1991.

———. *Rasā᾽il Ibn al-ʿArabī*. Hyderabad-Deccan: Dā᾽irat al-Maʿārif al-ʿUthmāniyya, 1948.

———. *The "Tarjumān al-ashwāq": A Collection of Mystical Odes by Muḥyīu'ddīn ibn al-'Arabī*. Edited and translated by R. A. Nicholson. London: Oriental Translation Fund, 1911.

——— [Balyānī]. *"Whoso Knoweth Himself. . . ."* Translated by T. H. Weir. London: Beshara, 1976.

Ibn ʿAṭā᾽ Allāh. *The Book of Wisdom*. Translated by Victor Danner. Published along with Anṣārī, *Intimate Conversations*. New York: Paulist Press, 1978.

Ibn al-Fāriḍ. *Sufi Verse, Saintly Life*. Translated by Th. Emil Homerin. Mahwah: Paulist Press, 2001.

Ibn Kathīr. *Tafsīr al-Qur᾽ān al-ʿaẓīm*. Beirut: Dār al-Fikr, 1970.

Ibn Khaldūn. *The Muqaddima: An Introduction to History*. Translated by Franz Rosenthal. 2nd edition. Princeton: Princeton University Press, 1969.

———. *Shifā᾽ al-sā᾽il li-tahdhīb al-masā᾽il*. Edited by I. S. Khalīfa. Beirut: al-Maṭbaʿa al-Kāthūlīkiyya, 1959.

Ibn Māja. *al-Sunan*. Edited by M. F. ʿAbd al-Bāqī. Cairo: Dār Iḥyā᾽ al-Kutub al-ʿArabiyya, 1952.

Ibn Sabʿīn. *Rasā᾽il Ibn Sabʿīn*. Edited by ʿA. R. Badawī. Cairo: al-Dār al-Miṣriyya, 1965.

Ibn Taymiyya. *Majmūʿat al-rasā᾽il wa-l-masā᾽il*. Edited by M. R. Riḍā᾽. N.c.: n.p., n.d.

Ilāhābādī, ʿAbd al-Jalīl. *Rūḥ wa-nafs/ʿUbūdat al-tazyīn*. MSS. LK (Lucknow: Nadwat al-Ulama) Maj. 31/2 (10ff.).; AMU (Aligarh: The Maulana Azad Library of Aligarh Muslim University) Subhanullah 297.7/46[4].

———. *Su᾽āl wa-jawāb*. MS. IIIS (New Delhi: The Institute of Islamic Studies, Hamdard Nagar) 2139 (13ff.).

ʿIrāqī, Fakhr al-Dīn. *Divine Flashes*. Translated by W. C. Chittick and P. L. Wilson. New York: Paulist Press, 1982.

Izutsu, Toshihiko. *Ethico-Religious Concepts in the Qur᾽ān*. Montreal: McGill-Queen's University Press, 2002.

———. *Sufism and Taoism*. Berkeley: University of California Press, 1983.

Jahāngīrī, Muḥsin. *Muḥyī al-Dīn Ibn-i ʿArabī*. Tehran: Chāpkhāna-yi Dānishgāh-i Tihrān, 1980.

Jāmī, ʿAbd al-Raḥmān. *Ashiʿʿat al-lamaʿāt*. Edited by Ḥāmid Rabbānī. Tehran: Kitābkhāna-yi ʿIlmiyya-yi Ḥāmidī, 1973.

———. *Haft awrang*. Edited by Murtaḍā Mudarris Gīlānī. Tehran: Kitābfurūshī-yi Saʿdī, 1958.

———. *Gleams*. Translated by W. C. Chittick alongside Liu Chih, *Displaying the Concealment of the Real Realm*, translated by Sachiko Murata. In Murata, *Chinese Gleams of Sufi Light: Wang Tai-yü's Great Learning of the Pure and Real and Liu Chih's Displaying the Concealment of the Real Realm*. Albany: State University of New York Press, 2000, 128–210.

———. *Nafaḥāt al-uns*. Edited by Mahdī Tawḥīdīpūr. Tehran: Kitābfurūshī-yi Saʿdī, 1958.

———. *Naqd al-nuṣūṣ fī sharḥ Naqsh al-fuṣūṣ*. Edited by W. C. Chittick. Tehran: Imperial Iranian Academy of Philosophy, 1977.

———. *The Precious Pearl*. Translated by Nicholas Heer. Albany: State University of New York Press, 1979.

Jandī, Muʾayyid al-Dīn. *Nafḥat al-rūḥ wa-tuḥfat al-futūḥ*. Edited by N. M. Hirawī. Tehran: Intishārāt-i Mawlā, 1983.

———. *Sharḥ Fuṣūṣ al-ḥikam*. Edited by S. J. Āshtiyānī. Mashhad: Intishārāt-i Dānishgāh-i Mashhad, 1982.

Jīlī, ʿAbd al-Karīm. *al-Insān al-kāmil*. Cairo: Muḥammad ʿAlī Ṣabīḥ, 1963.

Kāshānī, ʿAbd al-Razzāq. *Iṣṭilāḥāt al-ṣūfiyya*. Published on the margin of Kāshānī, *Sharḥ Manāzil al-sāʾirīn*. Tehran, 1897–1898.

Kāshānī, ʿIzz al-Dīn. *Miṣbāḥ al-hidāya*. Edited by J. D. Humāʾī. Tehran: Majlis, 1946.

Kāshānī, Mullā Muḥsin Fayḍ. *Kalimāt-i maknūna*. Tehran: Farāhānī, 1963.

Knysh, Alexander. *Ibn 'Arabi in the Later Islamic Tradition: The Making of a Polemical Image in Medieval Islam*. Albany: State University of New York Press, 1999.

Khwāja Khurd. *al-Fawāʾiḥ*. MSS. AMU (Aligarh: The Maulana Azad Library of Aligrah Muslim University) Subhanullah 297.7/34[3]; AMU Habibganj 21/83; KH (Patna: The Khudabakhsh Library) 3997 (28ff.).

———. *Nūr-i waḥdat*. Edited by W. C. Chittick in "Khwāja Khurd wa-*Nūr-i waḥdat*-i way." *Iran Nameh* 11/1 (1993), 101–20. Also in Khwāja Khurd, *Rasāʾil-i sitta-yi ḍarūriyya*. Delhi: Maṭbaʿa-yi Mujtabāʾī, 1891, 79–91; MSS. IIIS (New Delhi: The Institute of Islamic Studies, Hamdard Nagar) 3175/2; AP (Hyderabad: The Andhra Pradesh State Oriental Manuscripts Library) 906; partial handwritten copy, KU (Srinagar: Kashmir University) 2601.

———. *Partaw-i ʿishq*. In Khwāja Khurd, *Rasāʾil-i sitta-yi ḍarūriyya*. Delhi: Maṭbaʿa-yi Mujtabāʾī, 1891, 92–100.

———. *Risāla-yi ʿārif*. Edited by W. C. Chittick in "*Risāla-yi ʿārif*-i Khwāja Khurd." *Ṣūfī* 4 (1989), 22–25.

Khwush-Dahān, Shaykh Maḥmūd. *Maʿrifat al-sulūk*. MSS. OU (Osmania University) 1047 (69ff.); OU 752; SJ (Salar Jung Museum) Tas. 232/5; SJ Tas. 250; AP (Andhra Pradesh State Oriental Manuscripts Library) 30682; Lucknow: Nawal Kishore, 1898 (Lithograph).

Konyalı, I. H. *Âbideleri ve kitabeleri ile Konya tarihi*. Konya: Yeni Kitap Basımevi, 1964.

Lāhījī, Muḥammad. *Sharḥ-i Gulshan-i rāz*. Edited by Kaywān Samīʿī. Tehran: Kitābfurūshi-yi Maḥmūdī, 1958.

Lane, E. W. *Arabic-English Lexicon*. Cambridge: Islamic Texts Society, 1984.

Landolt, Hermann. "ʿAzīz-i Nasafī and the Essence-Existence Debate." In *Consciousness and Reality: Studies in Memory of Toshihiko Izutsu*. Edited by S. J. Āshtiyānī et al. Leiden: Brill, 1998, 387–395. Also in Landolt, *Recherches en spiritualité iranienne*. Tehran: Insitut français de recherche en Iran, 2005, 119–125.

———. "Der Briefwechsel zwischen Kāšānī und Simnānī über *Waḥdat al-Wuǧūd*." *Der Islam* 50 (1973), 29–81. Also in Landolt, *Recherches en spiritualité iranienne*, 245–300.

Lewis, Franklin. *Rumi: Past and Present, East and West*. Oxford: Oneworld, 2000.

Lings, Martin. *A Moslem Saint of the Twentieth Century*. London: George Allen & Unwin, 1961. Reprinted as *A Sufi Saint of the Twentieth Century*. Cambridge: Islamic Texts Society, 1993.

Lipton, G. A. *"The Equivalence (Al-Taswiya) of Muhibb Allah Ilahabadi: Avicennan Neoplatonism and the School of Ibn 'Arabi in South Asia*. Saarbruecken: VDM, 2009.

Madkur, Ibrahim. "Waḥdat al-wujūd bayna Ibn al-ʿArabī wa-Isbīnūzā." In *al-Kitāb al-tadhkārī: Muḥyī al-Dīn Ibn al-ʿArabī*. Edited by Ibrahim Madkur. Cairo: Dār al-Kitāb al-ʿArabī, 1969, 367–380.

Majlisī, ʿAllāma Muḥammad Bāqir. *Biḥār al-anwār*. Qom, 1956–1972. Also on *Nūr* (CD-ROM). Qom: Computer Research Center of Islamic Sciences, 1999.

Maqṣūd, Jawād. *Sharḥ-i aḥwāl wa-āthār wa-dū-baytī-hā-yi Bābā Ṭāhir ʿUryān*. Tehran: Anjuman-i Āthār-i Millī, 1975.

Massignon, Louis. *The Passion of al-Ḥallāj: Mystic and Martyr of Islam*. Translated by Herbert Mason. Princeton: Princeton University Press, 1982.

Maybudī, Rashīd al-Dīn. *Kashf al-asrār wa-ʿuddat al-abrār*. Edited by ʿA. A. Ḥikmat. Tehran: Chāpkhāna-yi Dānishgāh-i Tihrān, 1952–1960.

Meier, Fritz. "al-Bakkāʾ." In *Encyclopaedia of Islam²*, 1:959–961.

———. "The Problem of Nature in the Esoteric Monism of Islam." In *Spirit and Nature: Papers from the Eranos Yearbooks*. Edited by Joseph Campbell. Translated by Ralph Manheim (other essays translated by R. F. C. Hull). New York: Pantheon Books, 1954, 149–203.

Memon, M. U. *Ibn Taimīya's Struggle Against Popular Religion*. The Hague: Mouton, 1976.

Molé, Marijan. *Les mystiques musulmans*. Paris: Presses universitaires de France, 1965.

Morris, James. "Ibn ʿArabī and His Interpreters." *Journal of the American Oriental Society*. Part I: "Recent French Translations," 106/3 (1986), 539–551; Part II, "Influences and Interpretations," 106/4 (1986), 733–756; Part II concluded, 107/1 (1987), 101–119.

———. *The Reflective Heart: Discovering Spiritual Intelligence in Ibn 'Arabi's Meccan Illuminations*. Louisville: Fons Vitae, 2005.

Murata, Sachiko. *Chinese Gleams of Sufi Light: Wang Tai-yü's Great Learning of the Pure and Real and Liu Chih's Displaying the Concealment of the Real Realm*. Albany: State University of New York Press, 2000.

———. *The Tao of Islam: A Sourcebook on Gender Relationships in Islamic Thought*. Albany: State University of New York Press, 1992.

Murata, Sachiko, W. C. Chittick, and Tu Weiming. *The Sage Learning of Liu Zhi: Islamic Thought in Confucian Terms*. Cambridge, MA: Harvard University Asia Center, 2009.

Murata, Sachiko and W. C. Chittick. *The Vision of Islam*. New York: Paragon House, 1994.

Muslim. *al-Ṣaḥīḥ*. Cairo: Maṭbaʿat Muḥammad ʿAlī Ṣabīḥ, 1915–1916.

Nasāʾī, al-. *al-Sunan*. Beirut: Dār Iḥyāʾ al-Turāth al-ʿArabī, 1929–1930.

Nasafī, ʿAzīz al-Dīn. *Kashf al-ḥaqāʾiq*. Edited by M. Mahdawī Dāmghānī. Tehran: Bungāh-i Tarjama wa-Nashr-i Kitāb, 1965.

———. *Le livre de l'homme parfait (Kitāb al-insān al-kāmil)*. Edited by Marijan Molé. Tehran: Institut Franco-Iranien, 1962.

———. *Maqṣad-i aqṣā*. Appended to Jāmī, *Ashiʿʿat al-lamaʿāt*. Edited by Ḥāmid Rabbānī. Tehran: Kitābkhāna-yi ʿIlmiyya-yi Ḥāmidī, 1973.

———. *Zubdat al-ḥaqāʾiq*. Appended to Jāmī, *Ashiʿʿat al-lamaʿāt*.

Nasr, S. H. *Jalāl al-Dīn Rūmī: Supreme Persian Poet and Sage*. Tehran: High Council of Culture and the Arts, 1974. Also in Nasr, *Islamic Art and Spirituality*. Albany: State University of New York Press, 1987, Chapters 7 and 8.

———. *Religion and the Order of Nature*. New York: Oxford University Press, 1996.

———. *Three Muslim Sages*. Cambridge, MA: Harvard University Press, 1964.

Niffarī, al-. *The Mawāqif and Mukhāṭabāt of Muḥammad b. ʿAbd al-Jabbār al-Niffarī*. Edited and translated by A. J. Arberry. London: Cambridge University Press, 1935.

Nurbakhsh, Javad. *Maʿārif-i ṣūfiyya*. London: Khaniqahi-Nimatullahi Publications, 1983.

Nwyia, Paul. *Ibn ʿAṭāʾ Allāh et la naissance de la confrérie šādilite*. Beirut: Dar el-Machreq, 1972.

———. *Trois oeuvres inédites de Mystiques musulmanes*. Beirut: Dar el-Machreq, 1973.

Ormsby, Eric. "The Faith of Pharaoh: A Disputed Question in Islamic Theology." In *Reason and Inspiration in Islam: Theology, Philosophy, and Mysticism in Muslim Thought*. Edited by Todd Lawson. London and New York: I. B. Tauris in association with The Institute of Ismaili Studies, 2005, 471–489.

Pourjavady, Nasrollah. *Sulṭān-i ṭarīqat*. Tehran: Intishārāt-i Āgāh, 1979.

Qādirī, Muḥyī al-Dīn Pādishāh. *Miftāḥ al-ḥaqā'iq fī kashf al-daqā'iq*. Hyderabad [?]: Maṭbaʿa-yi Sarkār-i Āṣafiyya, 1914.

Qayṣarī, Dāwūd. *Rasā'il-i Qayṣarī*. Edited by S. J. Āshtiyānī. Mashhad: Chāpkhāna-yi Dānishgāh-i Mashhad, 1978.

———. *Sharḥ Fuṣūṣ al-ḥikam*. Tehran: Dār-i Ṭibāʿa-yi ʿIlmiyya-yi Madrasa-yi Mubāraka-yi Dār al-Funūn, 1882.

Quḍāʿī, Muḥammad b. Salāma al-. *Musnad al-shihāb*. Edited by Ḥ. ʿA. M. al-Salafī. Beirut: Mu'assasat al-Risāla, 1985.

Qummī, ʿAbbās. *Mafātīḥ al-jinān*. Edited by M. H. ʿIlmī. Tehran: al-Maktaba al-Islāmiyya, 1961.

Qūnawī, Ṣadr al-Dīn. *al-Fukūk*. Edited by Muḥammad Khwājawī. Tehran: Mawlā, 1992.

———. *Iʿjāz al-bayān fī tafsīr umm al-Qur'ān*. Hyderabad-Deccan: Dā'irat al-Maʿārif al-ʿUthmāniyya, 1949; *al-Tafsīr al-ṣūfī li-l-Qur'ān*. Edited by ʿA. A. ʿAṭā'. Cairo: Dār al-Kutub al-Ḥadītha, 1969.

———. *al-Ilmāʿ bi-baʿḍ kulliyyat asrār al-samāʿ*. MS. Konya (Konya: Mevlana Müzesi) 1633.

———. *Miftāḥ al-ghayb*. Edited by Muḥammad Khwājawī. Tehran: Mawlā, 1997.

———. *al-Nafaḥāt al-ilāhiyya*. Edited by Muḥammad Khwājawī. Tehran: Mawlā, 1996.

———. *Risālat al-nuṣūṣ*. Edited by S. J. Āshtiyānī. Tehran: Markaz-i Nashr-i Dānishgāhī, 1983.

———. *Sharḥ al-arbaʿīn ḥadīthan*. Edited by H. K. Yılmaz. Istanbul: Marmara Üniversitesi Ilâhiyat Fakültesi Vakfı, 1990.

Qushayrī, Abū'l-Qāsim al-. *al-Risāla al-Qushayriyya*. Edited by ʿA. Ḥ. Maḥmūd and Maḥmūd b. al-Sharīf. Cairo: Dār al-Kutub al-Ḥadītha, 1972–1974.

Rahman, Fazlur. *Major Themes of the Qur'ān*. Minneapolis: Bibliotheca Islamica, 1980.

———. *The Philosophy of Mullā Ṣadrā*. Albany: State University of New York Press, 1975.

Rāzī, Najm al-Dīn. *The Path of God's Bondsmen from Origin to Return*. Translated by Hamid Algar. Delmar: Caravan Books, 1982.

Renard, John. "Abū Bakr in Tradition and Early Hagiography." In *Tales of God's Friends: Islamic Hagiography in Translation*. Edited by John Renard. Berkeley: University of California Press, 2009, 15–29.

Rizvi, S. A. A. *A History of Sufism in India*. Delhi: Munshiram Manoharlal, 1978–1983.

Rosenthal, Franz. *Knowledge Triumphant: The Concept of Knowledge in Medieval Islam*. Leiden: Brill, 1970.

Rūmī, Jalāl al-Dīn. *Kulliyyāt-i Shams yā Dīwān-i kabīr*. Edited by B. Furūzānfar. Tehran: Chāpkhāna-yi Dānishgāh-i Tihrān, 1957–1967.

———. *Fīhi mā fīhi*. Edited by B. Furūzānfar. Tehran: Amīr Kabīr, 1969. Translated by W. M. Thackston as *Signs of the Unseen: The Discourses of Jalaluddin Rumi*. Putney: Threshold Books, 1994.

———. *Mathnawī-yi Maʿnawī*. Edited, translated, and annotated by R. A. Nicholson as *The Mathnawí of Jalál'uddín Rúmí*. London: Luzac, 1925–1940.

Rustom, Mohammed. "Is Ibn al-ʿArabī's Ontology Pantheistic?" *Journal of Islamic Philosophy* 2 (2006), 53–67.

———. "Psychology, Eschatology, and Imagination in Mullā Ṣadrā Shīrāzī's Commentary on the *Ḥadīth* of Awakening." *Islam and Science* 5/1 (2007), 9–22.

Sabziwārī, Mullā Hādī. *Sharḥ al-asmā'*. Tehran, 1902.

———. *Sharḥ du'ā' al-ṣabāḥ*. Tehran, 1904.

Safi, Omid. *Rumi's Beloved: Shams of Tabriz*. Oxford: Oneworld, forthcoming.

Sam'ānī, Aḥmad. *Rawḥ al-arwāḥ fī sharḥ asmā' al-malik al-fattāḥ*. Edited by N. M. Hirawī. Tehran: Shirkat-i Intishārāt-i 'Ilmī wa-Farhangī, 1989.

Sanā'ī. *Dīwān*. Edited by Mudarris Raḍawī. Tehran: Ibn Sīnā, 1962.

———. *Ḥadīqat al-ḥaqīqa*. Edited by Mudarris Raḍawī. Tehran: Siphir, 1950.

———. *Mathnawī-hā-yi Ḥakīm Sanā'ī*. Edited by Mudarris Raḍawī. Tehran: Chāpkhāna-yi Dānishgāh-i Tihrān, 1969.

Sarrāj, Abū Naṣr al-. *Kitāb al-luma'*. Edited by R. A. Nicholson. Leiden: Brill, 1914.

Sāwī, Muḥammad Makhdūm. *Panj ganj [Yak ganj az panj ganj]*. MS. AP (Andhra Pradesh State Oriental Manuscripts Library) 1905/11 (incomplete).

Schimmel, Annemarie. *Islam in the Indian Subcontinent*. Leiden: Brill, 1980.

———. *The Mystery of Numbers*. Oxford: Oxford University Press, 1993.

———. *Mystical Dimensions of Islam*. Chapel Hill: University of North Carolina Press, 1975.

———. *The Triumphal Sun: A Study of the Works of Jalāloddin Rumi*. London: Fine Books, 1978.

Schubert, Gudrun (ed.). *Annäherungen: Der mystisch-philosophische Briefwechsel zwischen Ṣadr ud-Dīn-i Qōnawī und Naṣīr ud-Dīn-i Ṭūsī*. Beirut: Franz Steiner, 1995.

Schuon, Frithjof. *Understanding Islam*. Translated by D. M. Matheson. London: George Allen & Unwin, 1979.

Shīrāzī, Mullā Ṣadrā. *'Arshiyya*. Edited by G. H. Āhanī. Isfahan: Intishārāt-i Mahdawī, 1962. Translated by James Morris as *The Wisdom of the Throne*. Princeton: Princeton University Press, 1981.

———. *The Elixir of the Gnostics*. Edited and translated by W. C. Chittick. Provo: Brigham Young University Press, 2003.

———. *al-Ḥikma al-muta'āliya fi-l-asfār al-'aqliyya al-arba'a*. Tehran, 1865–1866 (Lithograph). Also on *Nūr al-Ḥikma 2* (CD-Rom). Qom: Computer Research Center of Islamic Sciences, 1998.

———. *Le livre des pénétrations métaphysiques*. Edited and translated by Henry Corbin. Tehran: Institut Franco-Iranien, 1964.

Smith, J. I. "The Understanding of Nafs and Ruh in Contemporary Muslim Considerations of the Nature of Sleep and Death." *The Muslim World* 69 (1979), 151–162.

Smith, J. I. and Y. Y. Haddad. *The Islamic Understanding of Death and Resurrection*. Albany: State University of New York Press, 1981.

Smith, W. C. *Faith and Belief*. Princeton: Princeton University Press, 1979.

———. "Faith as *Taṣdīq*." In *Islamic Philosophical Theology*. Edited by Parviz Morewedge. Albany: State University of New York Press, 1979, 96–119.

Suhrawardī, Shihāb al-Dīn. *The Philosophy of Illumination*. Edited and translated by John Walbridge and Hossein Ziai. Provo: Brigham Young University Press, 1999.

Sulṭān Walad. *Walad-nāma*. Edited by J. D. Humā'ī. Tehran: Iqbāl, 1937.

Tabrīzī. *Mishkāt al-maṣābīḥ*. Translated by James Robson. Lahore: Sh. Muhammad Ashraf, 1963–1965.

Tabrīzī, Shams al-Dīn. *Maqālāt*. Edited by M. 'A. Muwaḥḥid. Tehran: Khwārazmī, 1990.

Taftāzānī, Saʿd al-Dīn. *Sharḥ al-ʿAqāʾid al-Nasafiyya*. Delhi: Kutubkhāna-yi Rāshidiyya, n.d. Translated by E. E. Elder as *A Commentary on the Creed of Islam*. New York: Columbia University Press, 1950.

Tirmidhī, al-. *al-Jāmiʿ al-ṣaḥīḥ*. Edited by A. M. Shākir. Cairo: al-Maktaba al-Islāmiyya, 1938.

Tirmidhī, al-Ḥakīm al-. *A Treatise on the Heart*. Translated by Nicholas Heer. In Kenneth Honerkamp and Nicholas Heer, *Three Early Sufi Texts*. Louisville: Fons Vitae, 2003, 3–81.

Ṭūsī, Naṣīr al-Dīn. *The Nasirean Ethics*. Translated by G. M. Wickens. London: George Allen & Unwin, 1964.

Tu, Weiming. *Confucian Thought: Selfhood as Creative Transformation*. Albany: State University of New York Press, 1985.

Tymieniecka, Anna-Teresa. "Differentiation and Unity: The Self-Individuating Life Process." In *Life: Differentiation and Harmony . . . Vegetal, Animal, Human*. Edited by Marlies Kronegger and Anna-Teresa Tymieniecka. Dordrecht: Kluwer Academic Publishers, 1998, 3–36.

Wensinck, A. J. *The Muslim Creed: Its Genesis and Historical Development*. London: Frank Cass, 1932.

Wensinck, A. J. et al. (eds.). *Concordance et indices de la tradition musulmane*. Leiden: Brill, 1936–1969.

Woodward, Mark. *Islam in Java: Normative Piety and Mysticism in the Sultanate of Yogyakarta*. Tucson: University of Arizona Press, 1989.

Index of Koranic Passages

Index of Hadiths and Sayings

Index of Names and Technical Terms